Girding for Battle

Girding for Battle

THE ARMS TRADE IN A GLOBAL
PERSPECTIVE, 1815–1940

Edited by
Donald J. Stoker Jr. and Jonathan A. Grant

Westport, Connecticut
London

Library of Congress Cataloging-in-Publication Data

Girding for battle : the arms trade in a global perspective, 1815–1940 / edited by Donald J. Stoker, Jr., and Jonathan A. Grant
    p. cm.
Includes bibliographical references and index.
ISBN 0–275–97339–5 (alk. paper)
   1. Defense industries—History.   2. Arms transfers—History.   I. Stoker, Donald J. Jr., 1964–   II. Grant, Jonathan A., 1963–
  HD9743.A2G473 2003
  382′.453558—dc21   2002029899

British Library Cataloguing in Publication Data is available.

Library of Congress Catalog Card Number: 2002029899
ISBN: 0–275–97339–5

First published in 2003

Praeger Publishers, 88 Post Road West, Westport, CT 06881
An imprint of Greenwood Publishing Group, Inc.
www.praeger.com

Printed in the United States of America

The paper used in this book complies with the
Permanent Paper Standard issued by the National
Information Standards Organization (Z39.48–1984).

10 9 8 7 6 5 4 3 2 1

Copyright Acknowledgments

"The Art of the Deal" reprinted from *The Grand Illusion: The Prussianization of the Chilean Army* by William F. Sater and Holger H. Herwig by permission of the University of Nebraska Press. © 1999 by the University of Nebraska Press.

Excerpts from "Undermining the Cordon Sanitaire" by Donald J. Stoker, Jr. have been reprinted with permission of the Journal of Baltic Studies.

Excerpts from *Russia and Italy against Hitler: The Bolshevik Fascist Rapprochement of the 1930s* by J. Calvitt Clarke III. © 1991. Reproduced with permission of Greenwood Publishing Group.

Excerpts from *The Lord Stuart Rendel Papers* have been reprinted with permission of the Tyne and Wear Archive Service.

Dedicated to Kenneth J. Hagan, Ph.D., Capt. USNR (Ret.)
Professor Emeritus, United States Naval Academy
Sailor, Scholar, Mentor, Friend

Contents

Acknowledgments

As is always the case with such an effort, many people make it possible. The hard and timely work of the contributors was undoubtedly the most important, and the help of the coeditor, Jonathan Grant, was indispensable.

At Greenwood/Praeger, I would like to thank Jim Sabin and Marcia Goldstein.

The U.S. Naval War College was kind enough to give me the time to work on this project, and my thanks go out to Vice Admiral Arthur K. Cebrowski, Rear Admiral Rodney P. Rempt, Charlie Niemeyer, John Jackson, Tim Jackson, Doug Smith, Stan Carpenter, Fred Drake, Hal Blanton, and Harold Trinkunas.

Finally, I am grateful to Ken Hagan for his help, guidance, and encouragement. And to him this volume is dedicated.

Donald Stoker
Monterey, California

Abbreviations

AA-PA: Auswärtiges Amt, Politisches Archiv
ADM: Admiralty, Public Record Office
BA-AP: Bundesarchiv-Abteilung Potsdam
DGFP: *Documents on German Foreign Policy*
DVP: *Dokumenty vneshniaia politika SSSR*
FO: Foreign Office, Public Record Office
HAK-FA: Historisches Archiv Krupp, Familienarchiv, Essen
HAK-WA: Historisches Archiv Krupp, Werksarchiv, Essen
IAL: *US Records Relating to the Internal Affairs of Latvia, 1910–1944*
IWM: Imperial War Museum, London
MAE: Ministré des Affaires Etrangères, Paris
NARA: National Archives and Records Administration
NARG: National Archives Record Group
SHM: Service Historique de la Marine, Vincennes, Paris
WO: War Office, Public Record Office, London

Introduction: The Arms Trade in a Global Perspective

Jonathan A. Grant

This volume offers a collection of articles on the development of the global arms trade from its beginnings in the nineteenth century up to the eve of World War II. The purpose is to provide a wide variety of cases in order to appreciate the broader common trends within the developing global arms network and also to highlight specificities in different times and within particular countries. In accordance with that goal, the selections range across Africa, the Middle East, Europe, and the Americas. In place of overarching models or general theories of the arms trade we offer discrete and concrete empirical studies rooted in the available archival evidence. The arms trade participants can include leaders of state, government bureaucrats, sales representatives from private armaments firms, and armed forces personnel. The motives and methods of each set of players may vary over time and place. In quieter times, a receiver state might strive for self-sufficiency in military or naval production and officials might go about acquiring the means in a systematic fashion through a combination of imported technology and know-how. Khedival Egypt and the United States in the nineteenth century conform to this pattern, although with markedly different results. In times of heightened international tension and immediate threat, a receiver state lacks the time to lay the infrastructure. Under such conditions arms imports take on a greater urgency, and the choice of supplier carries correspondingly greater political importance as a public demonstration of outside support, alliance, or patronage. In this book, the studies of Ethiopia and the Soviet Union during the 1930s reveal the overtly political dimensions at work.

Perhaps the most marked difference exists between the pre-1914 era and the interwar years. The representatives of private armaments firms played a much more active role in the pre-1914 period than afterward. Indeed, one is struck by the high degree of laissez-faire in the international arms trade primarily conducted by private enterprise prior to the Great War. Whether selling their wares in the Balkans or Latin America, private European firms actively pushed their way to the front of the line and enlisted the diplomatic support of their home governments. In contrast, the interwar era characteristically witnessed much more governmental involvement and control. Overwhelmingly, the dealings had become state-to-state arrangements viewed as extensions of political alliances. As shown here, in the interwar period business interests usually came second to diplomatic interests in the sense that private armaments firms were not the initiators of most of the sales and contracts but rather they were brought into the loop by the governments. Also, the interwar articles reveal a great range of flexibility in the diplomatic constellations before 1939. The instances of German supplies to Ethiopia, Japanese talk of supplies to Ethiopia, and Italian sales to the Soviet Union each show how odd bedfellows could become enmeshed in armament deals and negotiations.

In the study of Egypt's nineteenth-century arms industry, John Dunn examines how Muhammad Ali Pasha and Khedive Ismail sought to establish an Egyptian military-industrial complex capable of supplying Egypt's military needs by internal means. The development of domestic military self-sufficiency appeared as a key element in order to enhance Egypt's position as a regional power. These efforts to embed a modern arms industry within a preindustrial society failed due to a lack of infrastructure, and thus could only be maintained through heavy outlays of scarce resources. The Egyptian case reveals an important connection to the private arms industry in the United States as the Remington Arms Company of Ilion, New York, played the key role as the bearer of technology transfer.

For private armaments producers in the nineteenth century, Jonathan A. Grant examines how Eastern Europe and the Balkan states served as the most important markets for rifles, artillery, and naval systems in the pre-1914 era. In both the timing and scale of the orders, Russia, the Ottoman Empire, Romania, Bulgaria, Serbia, and Greece were crucial customers for the private suppliers from west and central Europe, such as Mauser, Steyr, Krupp, and Schneider. Faced with insufficient domestic sales, these firms had to export in order to survive. On the receiving end, the east European states acquired the most up-to-date models. Because most of these countries completely lacked a domestic military-industrial base, their arms purchases laid the foundation for their defense capabilities.

The importance of imports even for a major industrial power comes through in Stephen K. Stein's article about the new navy of the United States and its reliance on European suppliers. In the 1880s, after a long atrophy in naval construction, pressure mounted to modernize the fleet as European-made ironclads entering service in several South American states outclassed the old wooden steamers of the United States. The new American navy looked to European expertise, technology, and material as the means to reinvigorate domestic production and gain self-sufficiency in warship construction. This program yielded as its fruit the navy's first new ships in more than a decade. The protected cruisers, known as the "ABCDs," proved to be modern steel vessels, equal to those produced by the world's leading naval powers.

William F. Sater and Holger H. Herwig explore the role of personal motives and not just official ones in fostering arms sales in their study of the German sales in Chile. As they demonstrate in detail, those who lobbied the hardest to sell German weapons to Chile had personal and business motives at heart, and they used the German government to achieve their ends. The world's largest weapons manufacturer, Friedrich Alfred Krupp of Essen, was the driving force behind expansion of armaments sales to Chile. Although he complained that German government officials never worked energetically enough to support his arms sales, Krupp fully expected diplomatic and military support from Berlin in urging foreign purchases of his goods. In particular, Krupp relied on German Army officers to spread the word to host countries about his newest models and he lavishly entertained foreign officers and local military attachés.

Donald Stoker takes up the problem of Great Powers and small states in his study of the interwar naval trade in Latvia. After World War I, Poland and the Baltic states of Latvia, Lithuania, and Estonia received small arms and other military equipment from Great Britain and France. However, the erstwhile allies quickly became rivals for naval sales and influence in the region as all of the nations of the eastern Baltic sought to strengthen their armed forces. The French hoped that they could use the newly independent states to contain a resurgence of German military power while at the same time holding British economic penetration of the region in check. The squabbling over the meager sales ultimately weakened any possible Anglo-French cooperation in the Baltic and ultimately undermined the position of both along with the small states.

Björn Forsén and Annette Forsén probe the semisecret dealings of German submarine exports during the interwar era. Although the Versailles treaty forbade Germany to construct or to acquire submarines, the German Navy refused to accept such limitations and immediately undertook plans to maintain German submarine know-how through the creation of a firm in Holland, IvS. Since Germany was itself prohibited from acquiring submarines, foreign markets in the South American and Scandinavian countries as well as in the Netherlands, Spain, and Japan offered prospects for exports. From its inception by the German submariner Karl Bartenbach and the *Marineleitung*, the dummy firm in Holland had primarily political motives and only secondarily economic ones. The main goal of the project was to circumvent the Versailles restrictions. As part of the general naval rearmament in the 1920s IvS's projects began to gain attention, and discussion about their activities took place at the Conference of Ambassadors of the League of Nations. Ultimately, IvS's activities proved more significant for German naval rearmament than for exports as few neutral powers actually agreed to cooperate with the suspect firm.

The political ramifications of potential arms sales are the focus of J. Calvitt Clarke III's piece covering Italy, Ethiopia, and Japan in the early 1930s. For Japan, the prospect of selling weapons to Ethiopia raised Ethio-Japanese relations to unprecedented levels and encouraged widespread public support for Ethiopia. On the Ethiopian side, hopes that Japan's support might counterbalance Italy's increasing pressure on their country and admiration for Japan as a model for modernization lay behind an Ethiopian request for arms and military supplies from Japan.

For their part the Italians had effectively used the rumors of Japanese military aid to Ethiopia as a means to neutralize potential opposition to Italian moves from Britain, France, or the Soviet Union. In the end, Japan's own army program made it unthinkable that military supplies would be diverted from East Asia to Ethiopia, and therefore Rome and Tokyo came to terms because Japan declined to send arms to Ethiopia.

Ed Westermann takes up another aspect of the Ethiopian war, this time from the German side. During the Italo-Ethiopian War of 1935–36, Nazi Germany provided Ethiopia with its greatest source of aid with which to resist Italian aggression. In spite of the German government's official stance of neutrality in the conflict and the lack of a long-standing relationship between Ethiopia and Germany, direct German government involvement in the supply of arms to Ethiopia continued as late as 1936. Using previously unpublished material, Westermann sheds new light on the roles played by the foreign ministry, members of the National Socialist Party chancellery, and ultimately Adolf Hitler himself in sustaining the Ethiopian resistance to Italian aggression. The Germans viewed Ethiopia as a potentially significant market for overseas exports, and secondarily they considered involvement in Ethiopia as an opportunity for Germany to increase her influence in the Horn of Africa at the expense of Great Britain and France.

Soviet efforts to acquire naval systems in the 1930s are the subject of the final two articles by Clarke and Thomas R. Maddux. Clarke analyzes Soviet naval acquisitions from the vantage point of relations with Fascist Italy. A series of military visits, consultations, technical collaborations, and constructions fostered a Soviet-Italian political rapprochement in 1933–34. The Kremlin always saw military exchanges as part of a larger international political policy, and the Soviets continued to work to draw Fascist Italy away from Nazi Germany. For Rome, these contacts were economically important. Desiring contracts for supplying naval systems, the Italians facilitated Soviet visits to major industrial establishments. Stalin sought foreign offers for naval machinery, armor plate, heavy guns, and even complete battleships. Moscow turned to Italy for needed foreign assistance, and one of the Italian firms most active in working on military contracts with the Soviet Union was Ansaldo of Genoa, which maintained a lively business relationship with the USSR.

Maddux cautions us not to ignore or to minimize the influence of the governmental bureaucracy on the implementation of policy in his study of the United States Department of the Navy's impact on Soviet efforts to purchase a battleship and two destroyers from American shipbuilding firms. Although President Roosevelt and the State Department approved the Soviet Union's efforts and American companies expressed interest in selling to the Soviets, senior line officers of the navy successfully blocked the sales. Navy officials obstructed the process even after the president intervened at different junctures to push for approval. The obstruction by bureau chiefs and middle-level officials led the State Department to endorse a final rejection to the Kremlin prior to World War II.

CHAPTER 1

Egypt's Nineteenth-Century Armaments Industry

John Dunn

> A sword and a strong arm are no longer sufficient for victory . . . only the
> most modern rifles will do.
>
> —Khedive Ismail

When Egyptian officials proudly displayed their first battalion of locally assembled M1 Abrams tanks in December 1994, they reaffirmed a long tradition
of importing military hardware. A significant adjunct to this is the use of
Egyptian-made, or assembled, weapons and equipment. While British and
American designs are still purchased, Egypt also produces her own armored
vehicles, helicopters, munitions, and many other types of martial equipment.[1]

Though today's powerful forces are based on reforms emanating from the
Nasser era, the program of importation, and home-based weapons construction, is a historic legacy of the nineteenth century. Two outstanding examples
of this are the policies of Muhammad Ali Pasha, and Khedive Ismail.[2] Both
leaders wanted an Egyptian military-industrial complex, and their goals included the establishment of large armed forces, exclusively supplied by internal means. While lower costs figured into such plans, more important was
the idea that military self-sufficiency freed Egypt from outside influence and
advanced her to the status of a regional power.

More than just an ambitious advance, this was a revolutionary scheme that
sought to graft a modern arms industry onto a preindustrial society. Like-
minded rulers from China and Japan followed similar strategies in the belief

An earlier version of this article appeared in *Journal of Military History* 61 (April 1997): 231–54.

that imported technology could create an adequate defense against European aggression. Except for the Japanese, these ventures failed to take root, mainly from a lack of infrastructure, and thus could only be maintained through heavy outlays of scarce resources.[3]

The Egyptian effort lasted sixty years, and, during the 1870s, featured an interesting connection to the budding arms industry of America. This was centered with the Remington Arms Company of Ilion, New York, which played a critical role in plans to develop Egypt's weapons-making capabilities. Although it ended in failure, the story of this first attempt to build a Middle East-based arms industry provides a blueprint regarding ends and means, one that plays well to this day.

The initial impetus for these programs came from Muhammad Ali, who ruled Egypt as *wali* (viceroy) from 1805 to 1848. Following mercantilist theory on the road to building an Egyptian war machine, his goal of curtailing the nation's dependency on foreign-made goods is nowhere more evident than in the field of arms production. Throughout his reign, he pushed for the establishment of native weapons-making facilities. Egypt's ruler had witnessed, firsthand, the value of modern weaponry, during the French invasion of 1798–1801. Results of battles fought by his own troops against Mamluk, British, and Wahhaby forces served only to increase this appreciation. Thus, in 1815, when Muhammad Ali decided to establish a Western-style army, he also wanted his troops equipped with top-notch weapons. Long-range plans called for the source of such armament to be Egyptian, thus avoiding Europe's higher prices and the danger of embargoes.

To pay for these goals, the *wali* instituted drastic changes. He once told an advisor that government was like a *hakeem* (doctor) and must "heal" economic problems.[4] One of these was the "Capitulations," a collection of treaties with European powers that gave their merchants significant advantages throughout the Middle East. Egyptians could not compete under these rules, which were, in a sense, a stacked deck.[5] Muhammad Ali's solution was to reshuffle the cards. He created a statist system through tax reform, increased agricultural production, and, above all, a system of government monopolies. Noted authority Dr. Helen Rivlin suggests that taken together, Muhammad Ali's fiscal policies allowed government revenues to increase 9.5 times in the period 1805–1847. Of these, anywhere from 33 to 60 percent were allocated for military spending.[6]

Taxation was the first means used to increase revenues. Faced with a pressing need for money in his battles with Arabia's Wahhaby dissidents, Muhammad Ali instituted sweeping changes in the old system. Previously, the Egyptian government was funded by a land tax called *al-miri*. While it provided significant revenues, collection was via *iltizam* tax farmers, who absorbed up to 60 percent of the gross. By eliminating these middlemen, the *wali* increased his resources and began an intense program to improve agricultural yields.[7]

Although deficient in coal, iron, and timber, Egypt made up for such economic handicaps with a climate and soil that allowed for three crops every two years. Cheap labor, combined with strong demand, allowed Muhammad Ali to sell grain at considerable profits. These increased geometrically with the introduction of long-staple cotton in 1819. Here was a product well suited both for Egyptian agriculture and European industry. The *wali* enhanced cotton's value through his public works program of pumps, canals, ginning stations, and weaving shops. Cotton soon supplanted grain as Egypt's main cash crop.[8]

Whatever the item, all such commodities were purchased from local farmers with credit, paper money, or debased silver coin and then resold at fixed rates, in gold, via government monopolies. Instituted between 1808 and 1816, these gave Muhammad Ali near total control over the national economy. In some cases, this was accomplished via cartels of European merchants, who advanced money to the *wali* in exchange for exclusive rights to purchase raw materials. As a bonus, Egypt used the same merchants to purchase western military supplies. It was expected that they would be more likely to provide good quality, as overpriced or shoddy goods were grounds for expulsion from the monopoly.[9]

Labor for all these projects came from Egypt's long-suffering fellahin. Vast armies of these serflike agriculturalists were drafted for work in the fields or on the canals. Artisans were conscripted just like soldiers and assigned to work in factories. Military industries were favored with the pick of these recruits, since weapons production was a major thrust of Muhammad Ali's economic strategies.[10]

Small arms represented the first of these ventures. While local gunmakers already had a long history, their individual efforts were not sufficient for a rapid expansion of military power. Initially, Muhammad Ali filled this gap by trading Egyptian agricultural products for armaments. During the Napoleonic wars, England maintained significant forces in Sicily and the Iberian Peninsula. Feeding these men with local supplies was not possible. The result was a trade of Egyptian grain for British muskets, ammunition, and artillery. After 1815, military downsizing allowed Muhammad Ali to purchase surplus firearms from several nations. His globe-trotting admiral, Ismail Gibraltar, bought Tower muskets for 18 francs each in 1817. Swedish, French, and Italian armaments sold for similar markdowns.[11]

Next, students were sent to study Western gun-making techniques. A small ordnance mission went to France in 1825, while individuals studied in that nation, and England, well into the 1830s. Finally, arsenals were established in Cairo and Alexandria to produce copies of English and French weapons. These represent Africa's first military-industrial complex, and by the 1820s, they began churning out a considerable array of armaments.[12]

Cairo and its suburbs, along with Alexandria and al-Raschid, obtained the most significant military factories. The capital had the largest, which was described by an eyewitness, Captain C. Rochfort Scott, as "the finest establishment in Egypt."[13] By 1833, these arsenals retained 15,000 employees, expended 1.75 million piastres for raw materials, and produced a wide array of firearms, artillery, ammunition, uniforms, and equipment. Output was significant, an example being the 3,000 muskets finished every month.[14]

Though impressive, what really counted was Egypt's newfound ability to produce large quantities of gunpowder and artillery. Howitzers, cannon, and mortars came from Cairo and Alexandria, while powder factories were strung between both locations. Equally impressive was the *wali*'s naval program, which by 1832 produced a fleet that included the first African-launched ship of the line. The ability to produce appreciable amounts of warships, guns, and munitions elevated Egypt to a major regional power. Only the sultan in Constantinople had such resources, and until the 1840s, they were inferior to those of Muhammad Ali.[15]

Even clothing was considered in this ambitious expansion. Textile mills began to produce white cotton uniforms that soon became the trademark of Egyptian soldiers. Tanning factories provided belts, cartridge boxes, shoes, and saddles. Finally there was the *tarboush* (fez) factory at Fouah, where imported Tunisian managers directed 2,000 employees in the completion of these distinctive red caps.[16]

While Muhammad Ali could proudly claim that his soldiers were armed and equipped, from head to toe, by Egyptian products, there was a certain lack of quality due to the rapid pace of expansion. General Charles Boyer inspected an 800-man battalion in 1824 and declared 200 of its muskets as "useless."[17] Other French observers used terms like *misérable état* and *mal* to describe the Cairo arsenal.[18] Of course these same officials were also advising the *wali* to purchase French-made armaments and supplies. Probably a more reasonable assessment is that Egyptian martial products were functional, albeit of rough design and finish.[19]

This is not to say that all Egyptian products were mediocre. If one had the cash, private gunmakers designed ornate pistols and rifles, which often featured significant amounts of artistic inlay. Most were of the rat-tail style so favored in the Balkans and Middle East. Their flint ignition employed the snap-lock *miquelet* system, which was uncomplicated and easy to repair. Egyptian-made pistols, carbines, and long-guns featured significant quantities of brass, silver, bone, or ivory inlay. Baron Frederick Henniker notes the addition of tongs to the end of pistol ramrods as a mark of local firearms. The purpose of such was to hold tinder for lighting up tobacco—a ubiquitous habit among the Egyptian military.[20]

Such expensive pistols functioned as weapons of war and also made excellent presents, especially when attempting to influence local officials. They were status symbols, and often, the higher the rank, the more fancy and costly the firearm. In addition, with strict gun control laws, owning weapons was considered a badge of office by the Turks, Circassians, and Albanians, who comprised Egypt's ruling elite. Yusef Hekekyan, a keen observer of the period, often referred to these men as the "pistol gentry."[21]

It thus seems fitting that the first American weapons sold on the Egyptian market were revolvers. Abbas Pasha, who ruled from 1848–55, equipped his 6,000 household troops with American revolvers. In 1865, the government purchased an additional 2,000 Colt M1851 Navy percussion revolvers. While the United States already enjoyed considerable status as a producer of handguns, this was not the only reason for these orders.[22] More important was the collapse of Muhammad Ali's empire. As Egypt expanded into Arabia, the Sudan, and Syria, the *wali*'s statist regulations advanced with the troops, creating instant friction with England and other proponents of free trade. One result was the Treaty of Balta Liman. Approved in 1838 by the Ottoman sultan, and thus technically applying to his then rebellious province of Egypt, it outlawed monopolies, cutting at the financial base of Muhammad Ali's military machine. By awarding large grants of land to trusted lieutenants, the *wali* managed to get around these provisions through informal understandings. Still, revenues decreased, and in addition, the continued defiance only encouraged British efforts to reduce his power. Events of 1840 concluded this struggle. Hemmed in by a powerful coalition of England, Austria, and the Ottoman Empire, Muhammad Ali pulled back into Egypt and reduced the size of his army. Now allowed only 18,000 men, he saw no purpose for a native weapons industry. Thus the intricate system of arsenals, powder magazines, and uniform shops quickly withered away. Egypt's first industrial revolution came to a halt; she reverted to her old position as an importer of finished products.[23]

Conservative by nature, Abbas was satisfied with this situation. It was far less expensive to purchase several thousand American revolvers than to establish a factory for their production. His brother, Said, who ruled Egypt from 1856 to 1863, followed a more erratic course. The new *wali* combined a collectorlike interest in militaria with profligate spending. He did have an eye for good products, one result of which was the first international order for Krupp artillery. Another example was his hire of French inventor and ballistics expert Colonel Claude-Etienne Minié, who established a Cairo factory for his rifled muskets.[24]

This new weapon represented a much needed addition. Before the Crimean War (1853–55), rifles were mainly the tools of specialists and little used by Egyptian troops. Russian doctrine maintained a similar stance, and as a result, the tsar's army suffered heavy casualties to the faster, more accurate, and, most important, longer-ranged fire of British and French soldiers. Under the old system, smooth-bore muskets, with their effective range limited to 100 yards, allowed only a few volleys against a well-timed charge by veteran opponents. Then, combat was decided by close quarter fighting and bayonet skills. Rifled muskets fired at far greater ranges, and good shots could inflict heavy casualties at 800 yards. It was impossible to overcome such fire unless equipped with similar weapons.[25]

As a former officer of Bashi Bazouks, Muhammad Ali was familiar with rifles, but when ruler of Egypt, he showed little interest in their employment.[26] Once he strayed from this course in a rather radical way, by approving the purchase in 1836 of some seven-shot repeating rifles. Although these novel weapons passed all tests, they were considered too sophisticated for the average Egyptian soldier and were not seen again. Thus the only significant pre-Crimean change was a slow conversion of flintlock to percussion ignition systems.[27]

In contrast, Said was very interested in weapons. He purchased rifles from Belgium and then supported Minié's Cairo-based factory. As a result, Egypt possessed 80,000 rifled muskets in 1860. Most of these were copies of the French standard issue and came with a sword bayonet. In keeping with Said's desire for variety, a small number, for use by elite guards, featured a barrel ten centimeters longer and a socket bayonet.[28] Even more exotic were the thousand Voltigeurs Corses purchased in 1863. A double-barreled rifle designed by Colonel Gustav Delvigne, these were also issued to chosen troops.[29]

Regular soldiers quickly obtained Minié's rifle, a state-of-the-art weapon for the mid-nineteenth century. Indeed, by 1861, arsenals were jammed with the new muskets, and Said's erratic financial policies caused yet another twist in the production of Egyptian firearms. In need of ready cash, he decided to enter the international arms market.

On November 19, 1861, William Seward, secretary of state for the United States, received eleven Egyptian .58-caliber Minié rifles with saber bayonets. These were samples of 47,000 muskets offered to federal authorities at eleven dollars each. Here was truly a bold step, for Said was attempting not only the home production of armaments but also to become a player in the international weapons trade. Sadly for Egypt, this was not to be, for European suppliers took up all the Union's ready cash. Seward informed United States Consul William Thayer that while the samples were of top quality, America could not purchase the lot. On the other hand, he was instructed to spare no effort in discouraging Said from selling these to the Confederacy.[30]

Although the resulting diplomacy was effective, America's Civil War continued to impact on Egypt. Ismail, *wali* from 1863–79, was a far better manager than his Uncle Said and able to mobilize considerable resources for his many ventures. Like Muhammad Ali, he envisioned an integrated strategy of military and imperial expansion. Funding such efforts seemed easy in the Egypt of the 1860s. Agricultural revenues were lucrative sources for quick cash during America's Civil War. Egyptian cotton fields, in the words of the American mercenary officer Samuel Lockett, "Produced a harvest of gold richer and vaster than ever came from Ophir or California. Everybody wanted to go to Egypt, just like the children of Israel, because there was much corn there."[31]

Demand, plus the elimination of American production, caused the price of Egyptian cotton to increase by 1,200 percent. While all Egyptians benefited,

Ismail's ruthless tax collectors assured the government a major share of this windfall.[32]

Cotton remains a major cash crop to this day, but its post-1864 price plummeted with the end of the American Civil War. Ismail, living in the shadow of Muhammad Ali, had big plans requiring large sums of cash. To make up for shortfalls, he plunged the nation into debt. Said's financial adventures saddled the nation with a significant but still manageable debt of about £4,000,000. New ventures soon converted this figure to small change. Loan after loan was negotiated with European banking firms, along with the sale of highly speculative government bonds, all with significant discounts and excessive interest rates. An eyewitness, Edward Dicey, noted that Ismail was "indifferent to such, so long as the advance was made."[33] By 1876, Egypt faced a staggering debt burden of £68,000,000 and a predatory collection of loan sharks who could call on London, Paris, or Berlin for help.[34]

Another problem was Ismail himself, who, in the words of Alexander Scholch, "distributed tens of thousands of pounds on all sides as if he were giving autographs."[35] Lavish spending attracted a class of parasites who first attached themselves to Egypt during Said's regime. This deluge of worthless European and Levantine adventurers enjoyed considerable support from consular officials, and thus were able to loot millions from the Egyptian treasury via the sale of shoddy goods, lawsuits, and outright fraud.[36]

All of these, however, represented a slow cancer, one not noticed in the heady 1860s. Short-term results from the cotton boom, bond sales, and loans were a steady cash flow and increased government spending, much of which went into public works programs and the military. Modern weaponry obtained for the latter represents part of the picture, for although Said's rifles never made it to the United States, American weapons would soon flood the Nile valley.

Several factors help to explain this. First, the United States Civil War marked a decisive transformation in the economic and industrial history of firearms. Heavy demands for both quality and quantity spurred the development of factories in both the North and South. These needs ended in 1865, leaving armaments companies with superior products, the capability of mass production, significant capital investment—and vastly diminished sales. Survival called for the capture of new markets overseas. One company superbly capable of such conquests was E. Remington & Sons of Ilion, New York. Samuel Remington, president and chief company salesman, clearly recognized the post-1865 challenge facing United States weapons makers. His leadership, plus innovative products, allowed the company to dominate a significant percentage of the international arms market.[37]

What was he selling? The rolling breech block system designed by Joseph Rider and Leonard Geiger, which became the mainstay of Remington sales well into the 1880s. Indeed, author George Layman claims that the design "saved the Remington Company from bankruptcy."[38] Immensely strong, accurate, and easy to operate and maintain, Remington's rolling block weapons were the most logical choice for the unsophisticated soldiery often found in conscript armies. No mere sales pitch, Remington's claims were backed up by prestigious authority. General George Armstrong Custer wrote the company to praise the rolling block's high degree of accuracy. General William T. Sherman thought highly of it, while United States government field testing graded this rifle as an "excellent infantry weapon."[39]

For a variety of reasons, foreign competition against Remington was nil. First, European gunmakers could match neither the output nor the efficiency of Remington. Second, most available breech-loading systems were inferior in design. England produced the Snider-Enfield, a musket conversion whose hinged breech did not have the rolling block's strength. While the Martini-Henry was better, poorly devised ammunition and fouling problems reduced its appeal. Prussia's *Zundnadelgewher* (needle rifle) was worse: clumsy, difficult to cock, and ineffective beyond 500 yards. The French Chassepot was better but used a silk-wrapped cartridge that caused much fouling and afforded a fragile gas seal. It should also be noted that the best of these weapons were entering military service for the first time, and as such, only small numbers were available for the export market. Finally, at the local level, Egyptian officials were less than pleased with quality and cost factors from their past dealings with French and British companies.[40]

The American connection begins in 1866, when Egyptian troops campaigned against Greek rebels on the island of Crete. Their commander, Shahine Pasha, made the acquaintance of Consul General William Stillman. After a discussion of the United States' industrial capabilities, he requested and received a collection of breech-loading small arms. While these passed on to Cairo, E. Remington and Sons won a silver medal at the Paris International Exposition of 1867. As this was the highest award for firearms, rolling blocks now had an international reputation. It was here that Samuel Remington met Ismail, and here also that dreams of an African empire meshed with those of lucrative contracts.[41]

Ismail realized the need for replacing his army's rifled muskets. While still functional, new breech-loading weapons, with their metallic cartridges, promised higher, more accurate, and safer levels of firepower. Conversion, whereby the muzzle-loading Minié metamorphosed into a breechloader, presented a possible solution. England's Snider system was suggested, and although a few "Snider-Miniés" resulted, the program was soon abandoned as a needless half measure. The remaining muskets were issued to irregular forces or kept as reserve weapons in Cairo's Citadel.[42]

The Egyptian military increased significantly during the 1860s and 1870s, and Ismail, with his new title of Khedive (prince), wanted a modern force. To accomplish such, he hired numerous foreign advisors, the majority of whom were Americans, and purchased first-rate equipment. As Egypt's army needed a top-of-the-line firearm, the main purpose of Ismail's Parisian visit was to make a suitable choice.

Shahine Pasha, now minister of war, headed an advance party of fourteen experts from every branch of the armed forces. Their job was to investigate weapons that might be useful to Egypt. As a new infantry rifle was top on the list, an important subgroup formed about Claude Minié Bey; Hassan Aflatun Bey, an ordnance expert; Muhammad Ratib Pasha, the commander in chief of the army; and Prince Hassan, the Khedive's third son. Working with the Commission Permanente du Tir des Armes Portatives, the Egyptians tested Martini, Remington, and Henry rifles, using their own Minié as a base for comparison. Graded for speed and accuracy out to 1,000 meters, their unanimous choice was the rolling block rifle—"A good practical military weapon."[43] Next, Ismail invited Samuel Remington to visit Cairo for a last round of testing.[44]

These trials took place in 1869 at the Toura Artillery School, where Remington displayed his flair both as a marksman and a salesman. Telling Ismail that United States troops were equipped with rolling blocks helped clinch the deal, even if far from the truth. The end result was a June 30, 1869, contract signed in London. It called on Remington to produce 60,000 rifles in what soon came to be called ".43-caliber Egyptian," and for production in Ilion to be supervised by a team of United States Army inspectors led by Minié Bey.[45]

As a bonus to an already lucrative agreement, Samuel Remington obtained a choice plot of Cairo real estate—a personal gift from Ismail. Here he built a mansion, which became his regional sales headquarters. The Khedive wanted Remington and Sons to become his agent for the purchase of more than just rifles. Artillery, machine guns, munitions, and armament factories all featured in his plans. As future deals loomed on a bright horizon, Remington's home became part of the winter social scene for Egypt's American colony. A former Confederate, Colonel Charles Graves, noted that everybody usually had a good time with Remington, "because there is no North or South here."[46]

This spirit of unity was not always part of the Remington success story, for Egypt, in the words of American Consul General George Butler, "was a fine field for American arms sales."[47] Butler and other American diplomats pushed for increased trade between the two nations. When one considers that Egypt's imports for 1872 were $29,500,00, and that the United States share was only $358,000, Remington's contract was not only considerable but viewed as a wedge to open the door for additional sales.[48]

Generals Thaddeus Mott and Charles P. Stone, Ismail's senior foreign mercenaries, now joined Remington and Butler in lobbying for the purchase of American weapons. Mott pushed for a contract with the Winchester Repeating Arms Company and was supported by Butler, whose uncle, Congressman Benjamin Butler, was to sell the ammunition for these weapons via his U.S. Cartridge Company. Stone backed Remington, arguing that Egyptian soldiers needed reliable and uniform firearms; in his opinion, the novel Winchester design and its smaller ammunition did not meet these criteria. Ismail sided with Stone, and thus Remington became Egypt's major supplier of military goods for the next decade.[49]

Sales of Rodman artillery, Gatling machine guns, a cartridge factory, and more small arms followed. As can be imagined, such rapid success caused suspicion and jealousy among the competition. Austrian, French, and British authorities were piqued at the influx of American advisors into the Egyptian armed forces and by the unprecedented weapons sales. The Franco-Prussian War (1870–71) temporarily ended such attention and also impacted on the Remington-Egypt connection.[50]

Ismail wanted to order an additional 100,000 rifles but was told by Butler that "with France in possession of the market, such was now impossible."[51] French ordnance needs were desperate, absorbing Remington's entire manufacturing capability. Ismail, always the consummate politician, saw this as a chance to gain influence with Paris. To do so, he delayed his own order and agreed to default on the remaining weapons already owed him, allowing France to purchase the lot.[52]

Such a delay also benefited Egypt in her relations with the Ottoman Empire. In the late 1860s, questions of status led to significant tensions between the Khedive and his nominal overlord, the sultan. Ismail's hiring of foreign mercenaries and the purchase of improved armament were viewed with great displeasure by Constantinople. Because of this, Egyptian officials made every effort to disguise their dealings with Remington.[53]

An official policy of disinformation started at the top, where Ismail ordered his foreign minister, Nubar Pasha, to leak several different stories about Egypt's purchase of modern rifles. By April 1870, confused diplomats reported that Russia was providing the weapons! Next, the Khedive moved in, telling England's Consul General Stanton that the contract was cancelled and there were no new orders for the future.[54]

At lower levels, information was withheld, account books closed, and every effort made to disguise the shipment of Remington firearms to Egypt. Liverpool was the transport nexus, the Americans being required to send their weapons to this port and then turn them over to Egyptian steamers. During these transactions, British observers noted Ismail's agents accepting large numbers of crates marked "Hardware" or "To Aden."[55]

While the English were not fooled, less adroit Turkish observers failed to report these shipments, so Ismail's charade continued into the winter of 1870. Then, he was almost undone by a blackmail scheme that involved stolen telegrams, in cipher, from him to Aflatun Bey. The Khedive lost these with the desertion of an aide during negotiations with the sultan. Unable to crack the code in Turkey, it was sent to London, where a certain R. Hassoun broke the cipher and determined that these detailed the purchase of weapons systems from America and Great Britain. Decoding, however, took so long that

Ismail was able to avoid payment, and unpleasantness, as the crisis with his Ottoman suzerain was over.[56]

While deliveries to Egypt resumed after 1871, it was not until 1875 that the majority of Egyptian soldiers obtained rolling blocks. Some retained their Minié rifles while a select few on the frontier were issued Snider-Minié rifles and carbines. Such weapons proved invaluable to Sir Samuel Baker's campaign to conquer the southern Sudan. Another of Ismail's many mercenaries, he credited his victory at Masindi (June 8, 1872) to his men's use of breechloaders. Indeed, it seemed "nothing could withstand Baker's impetuous daring backed by his Snider rifles."[57]

News of such triumphs only spurred the desire of most Egyptian commanders to obtain modern firearms. The years 1873 to 1875 were full of official requests for the new rifles. A Sudanese administrator, Emin Pasha, noted Remington rifles provided such a significant firepower advantage that in many cases small bodies of troops could travel through the Sudan's most dangerous regions without fear of resistance.[58]

James McCoan, writing in 1877, estimated a total of 200,000 rolling block weapons were stored in Egyptian arsenals. Adding another 20,000 for first-line active duty troops and considering attrition, one might guess that Remington sent slightly under 250,000 rifles and carbines to Egypt in the period 1869 to 1880.[59]

Remington was also involved in helping Ismail to recreate his grandfather's military industries. Trained technicians already existed from Minié's factory, and, in 1865, the Egyptian government purchased ex-Confederate small-arms machinery left over in England. Four years later, the acquisition of rolling block rifles terminated the value of such efforts.[60]

Producing the new weapons required a high level of workmanship and a completely different set of machines. Also, tools were needed to make and reload the brass cartridges used by this breechloader. Remington offered milling machines for the construction of its rolling blocks and ammunition factories. The new workshops would provide spare parts, repairs, and, most important, Egyptian-made ammunition.[61]

This was a significant improvement. Previously, locally made gunpowder was, in the words of Murray's *Handbook*, "scarce, bad and dear." In addition, Minié's paper cartridges could get wet and misfire or easily explode if placed close to a fire. Imported ammunition, from England and Germany, shared these handicaps and was expensive. Remington's cartridge machinery reduced these problems, as the powder was improved and the cases were metallic.[62]

Alexandria, Cairo, Suez, and Khartoum all obtained cartridge factories. The capital had the largest and most efficient of these plants. During the 1882 British invasion, it employed 2,000 people, with 24-hour shifts, and produced up to 60,000 rounds per day. Remington officials also helped in the establishment of a gunpowder factory near Toura, which at peak production could deliver 1,600 pounds per day. Work in these plants could be dangerous, as witnessed by a gun-cotton explosion of 1870 that killed over 200 people in Alexandria. Also, just like earlier efforts, the finished product was not always of the highest quality. Still, Ismail was very proud of these ventures, so much so that a locally designed Remington bullet mold was part of the Egyptian exhibit at 1873's Vienna International Exposition.[63]

Uniforms and individual gear were also of local manufacture, with the old tarboosh factory pumping out 50,000 caps per year. Artillery was another matter. Cairo's Citadel produced a four-pounder mountain gun, complete with carriage and caisson. An excellent design, it saw service throughout the Egyptian empire. More sophisticated weaponry, however, was beyond local capabilities, and larger weapons were imported.[64]

The main sources of supply were England and Germany. Consul Butler helped sell a few American-made Rodman guns, which were placed alongside the 200 British Armstrongs guarding Egypt's coastline.[65] Ismail saw the Rodmans as another chance to distance himself from European suppliers, but as United States makers could not compete price wise, Germany ended up with a lion's share of the market. This came after an 1873 inspection of major European designs by Soren Arrendrup, a former artillery officer and Ismail's only Danish mercenary. Krupp guns, mainly in 7.5 cm and 8.7 cm, soon became the most numerous artillery found in Egyptian service.[66] Almost 500 were available in 1882; of these 120 had field carriages, while the remaining tubes guarded coastal forts. England's Armstrong works provided larger coast-defense artillery, mainly eight- and nine-inch models.[67]

American firms, notably Colt's Fire Arms Company of Hartford, Connecticut, dominated the field in the sale of machine guns. Selling through Remington, Colt provided 120 of the M.1865 six-barrel Gatling battery guns. The most effective of these early rapid-fire weapons, Gatling guns were employed by both land and sea forces. It was considered especially effective in savage warfare, where dense bodies of tribal soldiers provided targets that could maximize the gun's lethality. In 1872, a few camel Gatling guns joined the Egyptian Army. These were smaller, more easily transportable models, which substituted a tripod for the M.1865's wheeled carriage.[68]

While artillery production was beyond Ismail's capabilities, the manufacture of native-made firearms was possible. Egyptian Minié rifles were proof that local talent had the technical skills needed for such a venture. A second contract with Remington & Sons called for the establishment of a factory to produce completed rolling block weapons. The cost, £E33,000, plus shipping, became a problem when the final third went past due in January 1877.[69] This, plus £E8,000 due for other material, presented an insolvable problem. Remington refused to ship any machinery. Prince Hassan, the minister of war, and his brother, Prince Hussein, the minister of finance, were "greatly agitated." They squeezed up £E10,000, but as this did not meet all debts, the plant was never established.[70]

Many individuals were "greatly agitated" due to Egyptian financial problems. James Shaw, a British contractor, complained that all he received in response to debts owed his firm was "the constant promise of *Bookrah! Bookrah!*."[71] Samuel Remington wrote a personal letter to Ismail stating that Egypt's failure to pay her debts "was creating a very present and dangerous situation for my company.""[72]

The Khedive received files full of such correspondence in the mid-1870s. His debts, piled on top of disastrous defeats in a war with Ethiopia, caused Egyptian stocks and bonds to plummet in value. Loans dried up, and Ismail began to default on contracted sales. In 1875, these impacted on military procurement when Ismail ordered the payment of a £E35,000 penalty fee, in lieu of accepting a new shipment of Remington rifles. Weapons piled up in the customs houses of Liverpool and Alexandria. By 1877, Remington refused to deliver 46,000 rifles prepared for Egypt and claimed her debt now amounted to $1,000,000.[73]

Military budgets next took a hit, being reduced by almost 20 percent in 1876. Although exact figures are not always reliable for the period 1877 to 1882, cash was short in all departments and often made up by late, or non-payment, of salaries and other commitments. Foreigners turned to their consuls for help. Without such, creditors could exchange a quit claim for about 26 percent of its full value.[74]

Remington requested aid from Secretary of State Hamilton Fish, who in turn ordered United States Consul General Elbert Farman to use "his unofficial good offices" to obtain redress.[75] Samuel Remington then sailed to Egypt, hoping his presence would hasten the process. Tired, hot, and distraught, he only exacerbated the situation, going so far as to draw a sword in the office of Aflatun Pasha. At this point, Stone suggested Remington return home "or there might be serious results."[76]

Despite the fact that bond holders obtained priority treatment, Farman convinced Ismail to pay off some of his debts to Remington. The diplomat noted that more was done for this one case "than for all the other Americans in Egypt combined."[77] His actions produced results. Remington was paid £E71,000 by 1877 and a final settlement of £E65,000 in 1880.[78]

Remington, having sold the Egyptians over $3,000,000 worth of war material, never returned to the valley of the Nile. As for Ismail's military-industrial complex, it lasted only a little longer than its creator. Deposed in 1879, the Khedive went into exile. His cartridge factories, Remington rifles, and Krupp guns began to disappear after the British conquest of Egypt in 1882.[79]

Ismail's system disappeared not from a lack of need, like the weapons factories of Muhammad Ali after 1840, but rather from a lack of means. He began his venture when weapons technology entered a period of change.[80] Unfortunately for Egypt, the pace was rapid and required significant investments in tools and trained personnel. Such were in short supply during the 1870s.[81]

While the basic idea of modern Egyptian-made rifles represented a sound investment for national defense, it, like many of the Khedive's projects, faced haphazard implementation and undercapitalization. Never able to command the financial scene like Muhammad Ali, Ismail's efforts floundered and became little more than an interesting chapter in the history of the arms trade.

On the other hand, nineteenth-century Egypt's sixty-year search for a weapons industry presents an intriguing response to the currents of imperialism. Its overall failure provides a cautionary tale on the limitations of imported technology. Both here and in other secondary powers, like the Ottoman Empire or China, an inability, or unwillingness, to incorporate significant political, cultural, and social changes doomed otherwise sound strategies. Thus dynamic policies converted into expensive ventures that could only produce weapons when rulers were willing, and able, to divert a significant percentage of the national wealth. In the case of Egypt, the well ran dry by 1879, and so ended the first effort to create a native-based armaments industry.

NOTES

1. A wide array of information is available on the armed forces of modern Egypt. Current editions of various Jane's publications are a good start, as is *Al-Defaa*, which features articles in Arabic and English. See also Jon D. Glassman, *Arms for the Arabs* (Baltimore: John S. Hopkins University Press, 1975); R. Hotz, "Egypt Plans Modernized Air Arm," *Aviation Week and Space Technology* 102, no. 26 (July 1975): 12–20; Samuel M. Katz, *Arab Armies of the Middle East Wars* (2) (London: Osprey, 1988); Edgar O'Balance, "Problems of the Egyptian Phoenix," *Army Quarterly and Defense Journal* 102 (July 1972): 451–57; J. Pergent, "L'Aide militaire de l'U.R.S.S. a l'Egypte," *Est & Ouest* 22 (1–15 July 1970): 16–18; R. Vayrynen and T. Ohlson, "Egypt: Arms Production in Transitional Context," in *Arms Production in the Third World*, ed. Michael Brzoska and Thomas Ohlson (Philadelphia: Taylor and Francis, 1986), 105–24.

2. Ottoman aristocratic titles of Bey, Pasha, and Khedive were granted by the sultan. The first two often came with promotion to colonel and general; the latter was created for Ismail. For biographies of these men, see Afaf Lufti al-Sayyid Marsot, *Egypt in the Reign of Muhammad Ali* (Cambridge: Cambridge University Press, 1984) and Pierre Crabites, *Ismail: The Maligned Khedive* (London: George Routledge and Sons, Ltd., 1933).

3. To examine this Western technology and how it was created, consult William H. McNeill, *The Pursuit of Power* (Chicago: University of Chicago Press, 1982), 185–307. For a comparative look at such efforts in Egypt, China, Japan, and the Ottoman Empire, see David Ralston, *Importing the European Army* (Chicago: University of Chicago Press, 1990).

4. Cattaui Bey, ed., "Une Lettre de Mohammed Aly le Grand," *Bulletin de l'Institut d'Égypte* 32 (1951): 22.

5. Etienne Combe, Jacques Bainville, and Eduard Driault, *Précis de l'Histoire d'Égypte*, vol. 3 (Cairo: L'Institut Français, 1935), provide insight on the origin of the "Capitulations." See also Osman Okyar, "Industrialization as an Aspect of Defensive Modernization (Egypt and Turkey Compared, 1800–1850)," in *Revue d'Histoire Maghrebine* 12, no. 37/38 (1985): 125.

6. John Bowring, "Report on Egypt and Candia," in House of Commons, *Sessional Papers, 1840, Reports from Commissioners* (London: HMSO, 1840), 6:44–45; A. E. Crouchley, *The Economic Development of Modern Egypt* (London: Longmans, Green & Co., 1938), 259; Helen Anne B. Rivlin, *The Agricultural Policy of Muhammad Ali in Egypt* (Cambridge, Mass.: Harvard University Press, 1961), 120; M. Russell, *View of Ancient and Modern Egypt* (Edinburgh: Oliver and Boyd, [1850?]), 334; James A. St. John, *Egypt and Mohammed Ali* (London: Longman, 1834), 2:470–71.

7. Peter Gran, *Islamic Roots of Capitalism: Egypt 1760–1840* (Austin: University of Texas Press, 1979), 14–21, gives a concise view of Egypt's economic woes in the decade preceding Muhammad Ali. See also Kenneth M. Cuno, *The Pasha's Peasants: Land Society and Economy in Lower Egypt, 1740–1858* (Cambridge: Cambridge University Press, 1992), 103–5; Roger Owen, *Cotton and the Egyptian Economy, 1820–1940: A Study in Trade and Development* (Oxford: Clarendon Press, 1969), 65; and Bayle St. John, *Village Life in Egypt* (1852; reprint, New York: Arno Press, 1973), 2:458.

8. Several excellent works on the Egyptian cotton industry include G. R. Glidden, *A Memoir on the Cotton of Egypt* (London: J. Madden, 1841); Francois Charles-Roux, *Le Coton en Égypte* (Paris: Armand Colin, 1908); and Owen, *Cotton and the Egyptian Economy*. See also G. A. Hoskins, *Travels in Ethiopia* (London: Longman, 1835), 96; Marsot, *Egypt in the Reign of Muhammad Ali*, 147–49; Patrick O'Brien, "Long Term Growth of Agricultural Production in Egypt: 1821–1962," in *Political and Social Change in Modern Egypt*, ed. P. M. Holt (London: Oxford University Press, 1968), 195; Owen, *Cotton and the Egyptian Economy*, 65; L. C. Wright, *United States Policy Towards Egypt, 1820–1914* (New York: Exposition Press, 1969), 19, 67–70.

9. Rivlin, *Agricultural Policy of Muhammad Ali*, provides tremendous detail on this subject. See also Crouchley, *Economic Development of Modern Egypt*, 86–87; Hoskins, *Travels in Ethiopia*, 178; John Marlowe, *Spoiling the Egyptians* (New York: St. Martin's Press, 1975), 18–19; Félix Mengin, *Histoire de l'Égypte* (Paris: Chez Arthus Bertrand, 1823), 2:437; J. R. Wellsted, *Travels in Arabia* (1838, reprint, Graz: Akademische Druck-u. Verlagsanstalt, 1978), 3:278.

10. Bowring, "Report on Egypt and Candia," 15; A. B. Clot-Bey, *Aperçu Général de l'Égypte* (Paris: Fotin Masson, 1840), 2:475; [Barthélémy Prosper Enfantin], *Oeuvres de Saint-Simon—d'Enfantin* (1865–78; reprint, Aalen: Otton Zeller, 1964), 192–93; Gran, *Islamic Roots of Capitalism*, 111; R. R. Madden, *Egypt and Mohammed Ali* (London: Hamilton & Co., 1841), 39; Rivlin, *Agricultural Policy of Muhammad Ali*, 117, 241–45; Victor M. Schoelcher, *L'Égypte en 1845* (Paris: Pagnerre, 1846), 55; J. St. John, *Egypt and Mohammad Ali*, 2:436–37.

11. Auriant, "Ismail Gibraltar, Amiral Egyptien (1810–1826)," in *Revue Politique et Littéraire: Revue bleu* 64 (1926): 627; Robert E. Brooker Jr., *British Military Pistols, 1603–1888* (Dallas: Taylor Publications, 1978), 128; Cook to Bathurst, 1 January 1813, Cadiz, WO 1/266; Henry Dodwell, *The Founder of Modern Egypt* (Cambridge: The University Press, 1967), 226; Edgar Garston, *Greece Revisited and Sketches in Lower Egypt* (London: Saunders and Otley, 1842), 2:276 n; Gabriel Guémard, *Les Réformes en Égypte d'Ali Bey el Kebir à Muhammad Ali, 1760–1848* (Cairo: Paul Barbey, 1936), 142; Misset to Bunbury, 26 December 1811, Alexandria, WO 1/349; David Nicole, "Nizam—Egypt's Army in the 19th Century, Part I," *Army Quarterly and Defense Journal* 108, no. 1 (January 1978): 70; General Weygand, *Histoire Militaire de Muhammed Aly et de Ses Fils* (Paris: Imprimerie Nationale, 1936), 1:190.

12. J. Heywood-Dunne, *A Introduction to the History of Modern Education in Egypt* (London: Luzac & Co., 1938), 172–74; Weygand, *Histoire Militaire*, 1:195.

13. C. Rochfort Scott, *Rambles in Egypt and Candia* (London: Henry Colburn, 1837), 1:164.

14. British Tower and French M1777 muskets were the main patterns copied by Egyptian arsenals. Scott, *Rambles in Egypt and Candia*, 1:165, notes that the resulting muskets were longer and had lightweight stocks, which combined to decrease accuracy and firepower. Models for pistols and edged weapons were mainly of French design. See also Bowring, "Report on Egypt and Candia," 24, 28, 43; Clot, *Aperçu Général de l'Égypte*, 2:210–11; Garston, *Greece Revisited*, 341–42; George Jones, *Excursions to Cairo, Jerusalem, Damascus and Balbek from the United States Ship Delaware During Her Recent Cruise* (New York: Van Nostrand & Dwight, 1836), 65–66; Marsot, *Egypt in the Reign of Muhammad Ali*, 161, 181; Félix Mengin, *Histoire Sommaire de l'Égypte de Mohammed Aly* (Paris: Firmin Didot Frères, 1839), 132–33; Owen, *Cotton and the Egyptian Economy*, 71; Jules Planat, *Histoire de la Regeneration de l'Égypte* (Paris: J. Barbezet, 1830), 350; B. St. John, *Village Life in Egypt*, 2:423–24; Weygand, *Histoire Militaire*, 1:218–19; W. R. Wilde, *Narrative of a Voyage to Madeira, Teneriffe and the Shores of the Mediterranean* (Dublin: William Curry, 1840), 1:297.

15. Bowring, "Report on Egypt and Candia," 28–29, 56; "Etat Comparatif des Forces de Terre et de Mer de la Turquie et de l'Égypte," *Le Spectateur Militaire* 21 (Avril 1835): 85; Moustafa Fahmy, *La Révolution de l'Industrie en Égypte et ses Consequences Sociales au 19e Siècle* (Leiden: Brill, 1954), 39; Garston, *Greece Revisted*, 341–42; Marsot, *Egypt in the Reign of Muhammad Ali*, 165; B. St. John, *Village Life in Egypt*, 2:423–24; Weygand, *Histoire Militaire*, 1:218–19. Egyptian naval development will be covered in a future article. Three excellent sources for the Muhammad Ali era are: Vice Admiral G. Durand-Viel, *Les Campagnes Navales de Mohammed Aly et d'Ibrahim*, 2 vols. (Paris: Imprimérie Nationale, 1937); Angelo Sammarco, *La Marina Egiziana sotto Mohammed Ali: Il Contributo Italiano* (Cairo: Institut Français, 1931); and Ismail Pasha Sarhank, *Haqaiq al-Akhbar an Duwal al-Bihar* (A precise history of maritime powers], vol. 2 (Bulaq: Matbaah al-Amiriyyah, 1314 a.h. [1896]).

16. Edward B. B. Barker, *Syria and Egypt under the Last Five Sultans of Turkey* (1876; reprint, New York: Arno Press, 1973), 2:157; Fahmy, *La Révolution de l'Industrie en Égypte*, 46; Owen, *Cotton and the Egyptian Economy*, 69; B. St. John, *Village Life in Egypt*, 1:84–85.

17. Georges Douin, ed., *Une Mission Militaire Francaise auprès de Mohamed Aly* (Cairo: Société Royale de Géographie d'Égypte, 1927), 21.

18. Georges Douin, ed., *L'Égypte de 1828 à 1830* (Roma: Nell'Istituto Poligrafico, 1935), 194.

19. Note that nineteenth-century European military institutions stressed function and appearance, sometimes the latter more than the former. Hence a perfectly sound musket might be declared defective if its stock was marred or the brass fittings blemished. Prince Pucklar-Muskau, *Egypt under Mehemet Ali* (London: Henry Colburn, 1865), 1:221, points out that Muhammad Ali was often cheated by such "experts" and had concluded that for all its problems, native industry was a better alternative to European imports. See also John Gadsby, *My Wanderings, Being Travels in the East in 1846–47, 1850–51, 1852–53* (London: n.p., 1862), 233; Planat, *Histoire de la Régéneration de l'Égypte*, 87–89, 350; Eliot Warburton, *Travels in Egypt and the Holy Land* (Philadelphia: H. C. Peck and Theo. Bliss, 1859), 2:234; Weygand, *Histoire Militaire*,

1:190; Sir Gardner Wilkinson, *Modern Egypt and Thebes* (1843; reprint, Weisbaden: Kraus, 1981), 1:89.

20. A very nice example of Cairene pistol making is to be found at the Metropolitan Museum, New York. Its catalogue number is 36.25.2245. Visitors at London's National Army Museum may also wish to see the "Turkish" carbine captured in Egypt and on display in the "Road to Waterloo" exhibit. William Arnold Bromfield, *Letters from Egypt and Syria* (London: William Pamplin, 1856), 74; Gadsby, *My Wanderings*, 206; Sir Frederick Henniker, *Notes During a Visit to Egypt* (London: John Murray, 1824), 305; Anthony North, *Islamic Arms* (London: HMSO, 1985), 9–14.

21. In an exchange of presents in 1811, Major Misset noted a "brace of silver mounted pistols" being worth £60. Misset to Bunbury, 26 December 1811, Alexandria, WO 1/349. Sale, import, and ownership of firearms were severely limited during the 1820s. Cairo's Dar al-Wathaiq has numerous examples of proclamations and hectographed forms on these restrictions. Examples are found in both the *Période Mehemet Aly a Said Pacha* and *Période Ismail* collections. On weapons as symbols of status, see Yusef Hekekyan, Papers (No. 37452), fol. 17–21, 2 March 1851, British Museum, London; B. St. John, *Village Life in Egypt*, 2:92.

22. Brooker, *British Military Pistols*, 128; Paul Merruau, *L'Égypte Contemporaine de Méhémet-Ali à Said Pacha* (Paris: Didier et Cie., 1864), 24.

23. On economic friction, see Ahmed Abdel-Rahim Mustafa, "The Breakdown of the Monopoly System in Egypt after 1840," in *Political and Social Change in Modern Egypt*, ed. P. M. Holt (London: Oxford University Press, 1968); Cuno, *Pasha's Peasants*, 105; F. Robert Hunter, *Egypt under the Khedives, 1805–1879* (Pittsburgh: University of Pittsburgh Press, 1984), 31–32; Marlowe, *Spoiling the Egyptians*, 81; Marsot, *Egypt in the Reign of Muhammad Ali*, 157–58; Owen, *Cotton and the Egyptian Economy*, 73–74, 123; Rivlin, *Agricultural Policy of Muhammad Ali*, 64, 133, 239; Wilkinson, *Modern Egypt and Thebes*, 1:96. For the Balta Liman text, see Jacob C. Hurewitz, *Diplomacy in the Near and Middle East* (Princeton, N.J.: Van Nostrand, 1956), 265–66.

24. Ian V. Hogg, *The Illustrated Encyclopedia of Artillery* (Secaucus, N.J.: Chartwell Books, 1988), 184; Merruau, *L'Égypte Contemporaine*, 38; Amédée Sacre and Louis Outueborn, *L'Égypte et Ismail Pacha* (Paris: J. Hetzel, 1865), 172.

25. Major F. Myatt, *The Illustrated Encyclopedia of Nineteenth-Century Firearms* (New York: Crescent Books, 1994), 66.

26. Bashi Bazouks were light infantry originally recruited in the Balkans. They employed long-barreled smoothbore and rifled muskets.

27. Journal de Mr. Piozin, Vice Consul de S. M. Britannique au Cairo, 19 November 1836, [p. 32]; and Khosrew to Moyne, Cairo, 11 Mars 1850, *Période Méhémet Aly à Said Pacha*, Dar al-Wathaiq, Cairo.

28. Said specifically ordered these weapons and probably desired the extra length so that his guards would have longer rifles than Napoleon III's Cent Gardes.

29. Aflatun Bey notes the cost of Egyptian Minié rifles at sixty French francs each. The longer version cost two more francs, weighed an extra half-pound, and was manufactured at the rate of 100 per month. Efflatoun Bey to Hassan Bey, 13 September 1862, Paris, Dossier "1862," *Période Méhémet Aly à Said Pacha*, Dar al-Wathaiq. Due to rapid changes in arms technology, similar rifles were offered to Egypt in 1870 for fifteen francs each. Frenkel to Ismail, 9 Fevrier 1870, Zurich, Carton 179, Dossier 50/7, *Période Ismail*, Dar al-Wathaiq. Another odd purchase, the *Shishkana*, featured a single hexagonal barrel. Georges Douin, *Histoire du Règne du Khédive Ismail, Tome III*,

L'Empire Africain. 1er Part (1863–1869) (Cairo: Institut Francais, 1936), 111, n. 4, mentions 4,000 of these being sent to the Sudan garrison. On double guns and Belgian sales, see Colquhoun to Russell, 27 August 1860, Alexandria, FO 142/25; Lemercier to Cherif Pacha, 28 September 1864, Paris, Carton 179, Dossier 50/7, *Période Ismail,* Dar al-Wathaiq.

30. Thayer to Seward, Alexandria, 19 November 1861, 26 November 1861, and 12 January 1862, in United States, Department of State, *Despatches from United States Consuls in Alexandria, 1835–1873;* and Seward to Thayer, Washington, D.C., 8 April 1862, in United States, Department of State, *Instructions to Barbary Powers.* Originals in National Archives, Washington, D.C. Also available on microfilm.

31. "Recent Military Events in Egyptian History," in Samuel Henry Lockett Papers, Southern Historical Collection, University of North Carolina, Chapel Hill.

32. Ismail was notorious for squeezing every last penny (para) out of Egypt's citizens. Lucie Duff-Gordon claims he even obtained a percent from the earnings of "dancing girls," thus earning the sobriquet of "Mawas [Pimp] Pasha." Lady Lucie Duff-Gordon, *Letters from Egypt,* ed. Gordon Waterfield (New York: Frederick A. Praeger, Pub., 1969), 293. On Egyptian cotton prices and production during the period 1860–1865, see Thayer to Seward, Alexandria, 21 July, 26 August, and 30 September 1861, in *Despatches . . . Alexandria;* David S. Landes, *Bankers and Pashas* (Cambridge, Mass.: Harvard University Press, 1979), 69, 329–40; Anouar Louca, ed., *Lettres d'Égypte, 1879–1882* (Paris: CNRS, 1979), 12; Marlowe, *Spoiling the Egyptians,* 120; Wright, *United States Policy Toward Egypt,* 67–68, 70.

33. Edward Dicey, *The Story of the Khedivate* (London: Rivingtons, 1902), 94.

34. Egyptian bond issues began in the 1860s. Never completely sold out, they were only completed through the sale of excess shares to brokers, hence the discount. As a result, it was not unusual for Ismail to obtain only 85 percent of the total. In addition, to attract creditors, bonds and loans had high interest rates. For more on these topics, see Thayer to Seward, Alexandria, 17 January 1863, in *Despatches . . . Alexandria;* Hoskins, *Travels in Ethiopia,* 13; Landes, *Bankers and Pashas,* 57, passim.

35. Alexander Scholch, *Egypt for the Egyptians* (London: Ithaca Press, 1981), 20.

36. Farman to Evarts, Cairo, 4 May 1878, in United States Department of State, *Despatches from United States Consuls in Cairo, 1864–1906;* Landes, *Bankers and Pashas,* 130; J. C. McCoan, *Egypt Under Ismail* (London: Chapman & Hall, 1889), 107, 118, 120.

37. For more details on post-Civil War problems in the United States arms industry, see Felicia Johnson Deyrup, *Arms Making in the Connecticut Valley* (New York: George Shumway Publisher, 1970), 202–4.

38. George T. Layman, *The Military Remington Rolling Block—50 Years of Faithful Service* (Prescott, Az.: Wolfe Pub. Co., 1992), xv.

39. David F. Butler, *United States Firearms: The First Century, 1776–1875* (New York: Winchester Press, 1971), 153; E. Remington & Sons to General Sherman, Ilion, 29 November 1869, in Sherman Papers, vol. 27, Microfilm Roll 15, Library of Congress, Washington, D.C.; Alden Hatch, *Remington Arms in American History* (New York: Rinehart & Co., Inc., 1956), 135–36; Layman, *Military Remington,* 19; Charles B. Norton, *American Breech-Loading Small Arms* (New York: F. W. Christern, 1872), 25–26, 36; Harold L. Peterson, *The Remington Historical Treasury of American Guns* (Edinburgh: Thomas Nelson, 1966), 71; Konrad F. Schreir, *Remington Rolling Block Firearms* (n.p., 1977), 4, 17.

40. Military experts considered multishot tubular feed weapons, like the M.1866 Winchester, too complicated for the average soldier. For an interesting examination of martial firearms of the period, see Léon Mares, *Les Armes de Guerre à l'Exposition Universelle* (Paris: Didot, 1867). See also Donald Featherstone, *Weapons and Equipment of the Victorian Soldier* (Poole, Dorset: Blanford Press, 1978), 25; and Myatt, *Illustrated Encyclopedia of Nineteenth Century Firearms*, 73–74, 88–89, 91, 95. Remington provided the Egyptian government with numerous testimonials from Italian, Danish, and Spanish officers who favored his system. Rapport du Armee d'Outre-mer a Cuba, 23 Mars 1869, and Rapport du Captain Poggio, Turin, 17 Mars 1869, Carton 179, Dossier 50/8, *Période Ismail*, Dar al-Wathaiq. See also Ronald Pearsall, "The Military Breech-loaders of 1871," *Army Quarterly and Defense Journal* 104, no. 1 (October 1973): 90–93; Reports to Commanding Officer by W. G. Chamberlain, 8 May 1871, Report of Observations at Remington's Armory, Ilion, N.Y., *Springfield Armory Records*, National Archives. For more on dissatisfaction with European salesmen, see McCoan, *Egypt Under Ismail*, 130 n and Landes, *Bankers and Pashas*, 225–26.

41. Layman, *Military Remington*, 3–4; Norton, *American Breech-Loading Small Arms*, 44–45; Seward to Morris, Washington, D.C., 18 October 1866, *Diplomatic Instructions of the United States, Turkey*, RG 84, NA.

42. Ismail gave over 42,000 of these Egyptian-made Minié rifles to the sultan during the Russo-Turkish War. Farman to Evarts, Cairo, 30 May 1877, *Despatches . . . Cairo*; Vivian to FO, Cairo, 23 June 1877, FO 78/2633. More were sold to surplus dealers in 1883, and today are rather rare from a collector's viewpoint. FO to Malet, London, 3 September 1883, FO 407/28. On Snider conversions, see Fedrigo Bey to Riaz Pacha, Alexandria, 11 October 1866, Carton 179, Dossier 50/7; and Minié Pacha to Ismail, Cairo, 15 Fevrier 1871, Carton 179, Dossier 50/8, *Période Ismail*, Dar al-Wathaiq; Stanton to FO, Alexandria, 3 June 1870, FO 78/2139.

43. Commission Permanente de Tir des Armes Portatives to Ratib Pacha, Vincennes, 18 Mars 1869, Carton 179, Dossier 50/8, *Période Ismail*, Dar al-Wathaiq.

44. Hassan Aflatun, Egypt's director of military workshops, was, next to Minié, the best equipped to advise Ismail. He rose to the ranks of Pasha, Ferik (major general), and chief of the Ordnance Bureau. For more on these topics, see James Heyworth-Dunne, *Introduction to the History of Modern Education in Egypt* (London: Luzac, 1938), 255, 349; Norton, *American Breech-Loading Small Arms*, 42–43; Commission Permanente du Tir des Armes Portatives to Ratib Pacha, Vincennes, 16 Avril 1869, Newley to Patib Pacha, Paris, 12 Avril 1869, and Procès-verbal des Résultats des Différents Tirs Executés à Vincennes les 15 et 16 Mars 1869, Box 179, Dossier 50/8, *Période Ismail*, Dar al-Wathaiq.

45. One of Ismail's American mercenaries, Frank Reynolds, later replaced Minié as the Egyptian inspector at Ilion. His death in 1875 saw Cairo's request for the appointment of a United States Army inspector. Beardsley to Fish, Cairo, 20 October 1875, *Despatches . . . Cairo*. The original contract can be found in Cairo's Dar al-Wathaiq, Contrat, London, 30 Juin 1869, Carton 179, Dossier 50/7, *Période Ismail*. Due to the destruction of their archives by fire in 1939, it is difficult to determine the exact prices charged by Remington. In the 1871 so-called "Persian Contract," which was probably a subterfuge to get weapons into France, 50,000 Egyptian rolling blocks were listed as having cost $13.76 each. Untitled Ledger, 1874, in Shepard and Richardson Papers, Herkimer Historical Society, Herkimer, N.Y. In 1877, 35,000 rifles were contracted for $500,000. Farman to Fish, Cairo, 3 April 1877, *Despatches . . . Cairo*. The Rem-

ington 1877 catalog featured them at $17.00, or $20.50 with bayonet, while the carbine version sold for $16.00. Butler to Fish, Alexandria, 30 December 1870, *Despatches . . . Alexandria*; Farman to Evarts, Cairo, 4 May 1878, *Despatches . . . Cairo*; Layman, *Military Remington*, 11, 98; Samuel Norris, "Facts About Small Arms," *New York Times*, 31 July 1898, 4–6; E. Remington & Sons to Col. J. G. Benton, Ilion, N.Y., 19 July 1869, *Springfield Armory Records*.

46. Farman to Evarts, Cairo, 4 May 1878, *Despatches . . . Cairo*; Graves to Wife, Cairo, 6 November 1875 and 4 January 1877, *Charles I. Graves Papers*, Southern Historical Collection; K. D. Kirkland, *America's Premier Gunmaker: Remington* (New York: Exeter Books, 1988), 36; *A New Chapter in an Old Story* (New York: Remington Arms, 1912), 21.

47. Butler to Fish, Alexandria, 30 December 1870, *Despatches . . . Alexandria*.

48. Other than weapons, the only significant American export to Egypt was petroleum. Beardsley to Fish, Cairo, 30 April 1873, *Despatches . . . Cairo*. On consular activities in support of Remington, see Beardsley to Fish, Cairo, 20 October 1875, and Farman to Fish, Cairo, 25 November 1876.

49. Along with plenty of ammunition, Mott's deal involved the purchase of 9,566 Colt revolvers for $14.50 each, 10,278 Winchester carbines at $28 each, 10,278 Winchester rifles with bayonet for $27.50 each, and the machinery for making 30,000 cartridges per day at $8,250. In all a total of $717,386, "plus shipping and handling." Contract Between Winchester Repeating Arms Company and Henry Mott; and Mott to Ismail, n.p., n.d., Carton 179, Dossier 50/7, *Période Ismail*, Dar al-Wathaiq.

50. Butler to Fish, 30 December 1870 and 29 April 1871, Alexandria, *Despatches . . . Alexandria*; photocopy of *New York Tribune* article of 5 May 1871, Ilion Free Public Library, Historical Room.

51. Butler to Fish, 30 December 1870, Alexandria, *Despatches . . . Alexandria*.

52. Warren E. Schulz, *Ilion—The Town Remington Made* (Hicksville, N.Y.: Exposition Press, 1977), 16, lists 154,120 rifles plus 19,777 carbines delivered by Remington to France. Nubar Pasha claimed that 20,000 rolling block rifles were delivered to Egypt by May 1870; the rest of the original 60,000 probably became French. Stanton to FO, Alexandria, 12 May 1870, FO 78/2139. See also Butler to Fish, Alexandria, 12 May 1870, FO 78/2139; Alfred J. Butler, *Court Life in Egypt* (London: Chapman & Hall, 1888), 168; Layman, *Military Remington*, 12, 35–36; Esquiros [to French Consul, Alexandria], Marseille, 19 Septembre 1870, Carton 97, Dossier 63/10, *Période Ismail*, Dar al-Wathaiq; Stanton to FO, Alexandria, 30 September 1870, FO 78/2140; telegrams, Tours to New York City, 20 August 1870 and 21 September 1870, *Shepard and Richardson Papers*.

53. For more on this, see Afaf Lufti al-Sayyid Marsot, "The Porte and Ismail Pasha's Quest for Autonomy," *Journal of the American Research Center in Egypt* 12 (1975): 89–96.

54. Ismail to Nubar Pacha, n.p., n.d., Carton 179, Dossier 50/7, *Période Ismail*, Dar al-Wathaiq; Stanton to FO, Alexandria, 28 April 1870, 14 June 1870, and 24 June 1870, FO 78/2139.

55. L'Armee du Khédive MSS, Carton 25, Dossier 50/1, *Période Ismail*, Dar al-Wathaiq, notes that by winter 1870, Egypt's possession of large numbers of Remington rifles was common knowledge in European military circles. See also Eumench to Barrot Bey, Alexandrie, 26 Septembre 1873, Carton 97, Dossier 63/24, *Période Ismail*;

Stanton to FO, Alexandria, 21 June 1870, FO 78/2139, 9 July 1870, and 14 July 1870, FO 78/2140.

56. Hassoun demanded 20,000 francs to keep quiet and threatened to publish copies of the telegrams in English and Arabic if refused. Hassoun to Federigo Pasha, Wandsworth, United Kingdom, 18 March 1873, Carton 179, Dossier 50/8, *Période Ismail*, Dar al-Wathaiq.

57. On Masindi, see Baker to Ismail, Khartoum, 5 Juli 1873, Carton 59, Dossier 72/1, *Période Ismail*, Dar al-Wathaiq; and Sir Samuel W. Baker, *Ismailia* (London: MacMillan & Co., 1907). Col. Charles Chaille-Long, sometimes noted for his tall tales, claimed to have defeated 400 local warriors with a Reilly No. 8 elephant gun and two privates armed with Sniders. Charles Chaille-Long, "Letter to the Editor," *Bulletin of the American Geographical Society of New York* 39 (1904): 349. For more on Egyptian Sniders, see Beardsley to Fish, Cairo, 3 September 1873, *Despatches . . . Cairo*; and Jerry Janzen, *Bayonets from Janzen's Notebook* (Tulsa: n.p., 1987), 39.

58. F. L. James, *The Wild Tribes of the Sudan* (London: John Murray, 1884), 56, notes that some Egyptian forces still used percussion muskets in 1881. Georges Douin, *Histoire du Règne du Khédive Ismail, Tome III, L'Empire Africain. 3e Partie (1874–1876)* (Cairo: L'Institute Français, 1941), 1154–55, 1202; Registre 31, Arrivé Maia Sanieh, No. 17, 31, Carton 20, Dossier 71/23[?], *Soudan et Afrique Oriental*, Dar al-Wathaiq; and G. Schweinfurth et. al., eds., *Emin Pasha in Central Africa* (London: Murray, 1888), 253.

59. J. C. McCoan, *Egypt* (New York: Peters Fenelon Collier, 1898), 97. See also Remington articles from *Herkimer Democrat*, 7 July 1869 and *Utica Press*, 21 July 1882, held by Ilion Free Public Library, Historical Room.

60. Hale to Seward, Alexandria, 14 June 1865, *Despatches . . . Alexandria*.

61. Remington offered a small "starter" factory to make rolling block rifles for $37,000. Minié Pacha to Ismail, Cairo, 1 Fevrier 1871, Carton 179, Dossier 50/9, *Période Ismail*, Dar al-Wathaiq. See also Charles Fitch, "Report on the Manufacture of Interchangeable Mechanisms," in United States Congress, *Miscellaneous Documents of the House of Representatives*, 4th Cong. 2d sess. (Washington, D.C.: GPO, 1882), 13 (pt. 2): 613–14; and McCoan, *Egypt*, 98, 292.

62. Dr. Moritz Busch, *Hand-Book for Travellers in Egypt*, trans. W. C. Wrankmore (Trieste: Austrian Lloyd, 1864), 19; Douin, *Histoire du Règne du Khédive Ismail*, 3:11, n. 1; Stanton to FO, Alexandria, 2 September 1870, in FO 78/2140; Paul Traub, "Voyage au pays des Bogos," *Bulletin de la société neuchateloise de Géographie* 4 (1888): 129; Sir Gardner Wilkinson, *A Handbook for Travellers in Egypt* (London: John Murray, 1867), 29.

63. Efforts to establish a Khartoum-based percussion cap factory failed in the 1860s. Douin, *Histoire du Règne du Khédive Ismail*, 3:100, n. 1. Butler to Fish, Alexandria, 22 October 1870, *Despatches . . . Alexandria*; Égypte, Commission à l'Expostion Universelle de Vienne, 1873, *Catalogue Raisonné de l'Exposition Egyptienne* (Vienne: Imprimérie Impériale et Royale, 1873), 173; Georges Guindi and Jacques Tagher, eds., *Ismail d'après les documents officiels* (Cairo, 1945), 141–42; Great Britain, Foreign Office, *British Documents on Foreign Affairs*, David Gillard, ed. (Frederick, Md.: University Publications of America, 1984), "B" 9:151, 241–42; Douglas Johnson, "The Myth of Ansar Firepower," *Savage and Soldier: Sudan Issue*, 22; Louca, *Lettres de l'Égypte*, 195; Mott to Riaz Pasha, Cairo, 7 Mai 1871, Carton 179, Dossier 50/9, *Période Ismail*, Dar al-Wathaiq; Norton, *American Breech-Loading Small Arms*, 285; Stone to Ministre du

Guerre, Cairo, 7 Mai 1873, Carton 179, Dossier 50/9, *Période Ismail,* Dar al-Wathaiq; Carlos [Charles P.] Stone, *Assuntos Militares en Egipto* (Habana: Tipografica de'El EcoMilitaire, 1884), 31; Charles P. Stone, "Military Affairs in Egypt," *Journal of the Military Service Institution* 5 (1884): 173.

64. Jacquier Bey, director of the arsenal, probably designed the mountain howitzer in 1865. "L'Armée de Khédive," ibid.

65. Although the Rodman was a smoothbore and the Armstrong rifled, placing such guns together was not unusual for the times. The former had great smashing power, while the latter fired at longer ranges. This combination was considered useful for engaging ironclad warships.

66. There was also a single eleven-inch Krupp gun, which supposedly became part of Alexandria's defenses. This may have been a purchase from Said's era. "L'Armée du Khédive," ibid; Stanton to FO, Alexandria, 3 June 1870, FO 78/2139.

67. Like small arms, artillery weapons of this period slowly converted to breech-loaders. These designs were difficult to produce and thus more expensive than the muzzle-loaders of Napoleonic and American Civil War fame. Some idea of the changes involved can be seen in Warren Ripley, *Artillery and Ammunition of the Civil War* (New York: Van Nostrand Reinhold, 1970).

A few samples of prices offered Egypt include 28.5-centimeter Finspong (Swedish) guns at £1,400, 10-inch Parrot rifles at £1,439, 15-inch Rodmans at £3,290, or a 20-inch monster for £6,185. Arrendrup Memorandum, Cairo, 19 Avril 1871; and Stone to Ministre du Guerre, Cairo, 8 Avril 1871, Carton 179, Dossier 50/7, *Période Ismail,* Dar al-Wathaiq. Carton 179, Dossier 50/8 from the Dar al-Wathaiq's *Période Ismail* collection contains numerous reports and advertisements for all kinds of artillery from the 1865–80 era, both standard and experimental. See also *British Documents on Foreign Policy,* "B" 9:151, 240–41; Butler to Fish, Alexandria, 29 April 1871, *Despatches . . . Alexandria;* McCoan, *Egypt,* 98; Stanton to FO, Alexandria, 18, 21, 24 June and 15 October 1870, FO 78/2139; Stone to Ministre du Guerre, Cairo, 7 Mai 1873, Carton 179, Dossier 50/10, *Période Ismail,* Dar al-Wathaiq; "Turkey and Egypt," *Times* (London), 16 June 1874, 14.

68. Gatling guns were expensive weapons. Those sold in 1870 cost $1,750 (£350) for a .58-caliber and $2,350 (£470) for a one-inch version. With 168,000 rounds of ammunition, limbers, and tack, the total cost was £40,192. Mott to Charif Pasha, Cairo, 1 Novembre 1870, Carton 179, Dossier 50/7, *Période Ismail,* Dar al-Wathaiq; and Myatt, *Illustrated Encyclopedia of Nineteenth-Century Firearms,* 182. See also Mott to Ismail, New York, 3 September 1872, and Mott to Riaz Pacha, Cairo, 7 Mai 1871, Carton 179, Dossier 50/7, *Période Ismail,* Dar al-Wathaiq; and Stanton to FO, Alexandria, 19 May 1870, 27 May 1870, and 3 June 1870, FO 78/2139.

69. The term "£E" is employed to differentiate Egyptian from slightly less valuable British pounds. The latter are designated by a "£" in front of the numerals.

70. *British Documents on Foreign Affairs,* "B" 9:151; Farman to Evarts, Cairo, 4 May 1878, *Despatches . . . Cairo.*

71. Although literally "tomorrow," *Bukra* can be very flexible, like the Spanish *mañana.* James Shaw to Barrot Bey, London, 15 September 1876, Carton 179, Dossier 50/13, *Période Ismail,* Dar al-Wathaiq.

72. Remington to Ismail, Cairo, 2 Juin 1876, Carton 179, Dossier 50/7, *Période Ismail,* Dar al-Wathaiq.

73. On the Remington contract, see Evarts to Farman, Washington, D.C., 28 March

1878, *Diplomatic Instructions;* Farman to Fish, Cairo, 25 November 1876, Farman to Evarts, Cairo, 3 April 1877, 15 June 1877, 26 July 1877, and 4 and 10 May 1878, *Despatches . . . Cairo.* On budgets, see *British Documents on Foreign Affairs,* "B" 9:216; Report on Revenue, 1 November 1876, *Despatches . . . Cairo;* McCoan, *Egypt Under Ismail,* 96.

74. Vivian to FO, Cairo, 16 March 1877, FO 78/2631.

75. Fish to Farman, Washington, D.C., 2 August 1876, in United States, Department of State, *Diplomatic Instructions, Egypt,* RG 84, NA.

76. Farman to Evarts, Cairo, 10 May 1878, *Despatches . . . Cairo.*

77. Farman to Evarts, Cairo, 4 May 1878, *Despatches . . . Cairo.*

78. Farman to Evarts, Cairo, 4, 10 May 1878, *Despatches . . . Cairo;* Farman to Fish, Cairo, 3 April 1877, *Despatches . . . Cairo;* Hay to Farman, Washington, D.C., 6, 15 July 1880, *Diplomatic Instructions, Egypt,* RG 84, NA.

79. Evarts to Farman, Washington, D.C., 28 March 1878, *Diplomatic Instructions, Egypt,* RG 84, NA. For details on the post-1882 disposal of Egypt's Remington rifles, see John Dunn, "Remington Rolling Blocks in the Horn of Africa," *Bulletin of the American Society of Arms Collectors* 71 (1994): 25–32.

80. This theme is covered by Myatt, *Illustrated Encyclopedia of Nineteenth-Century Firearms,* and Ian Hogg, *The Weapons that Changed the World* (New York: Arbor House, 1986).

81. The Military Workshop of Cairo's Industrial College never enrolled more than thirty students during the 1870s. Heyworth-Dunne, *Introduction to the History of Modern Education,* 358.

CHAPTER 2

The Arms Trade in Eastern Europe, 1870–1914

Jonathan A. Grant

For private armaments producers in the nineteenth century, tsarist Russia and the Balkan states served as vital markets for rifles, artillery, and naval systems. As an engine for growth, contracts from these east European customers proved crucial for the sustainability of the suppliers from west and central Europe, and the region became the most important defense market in the world in the period 1870–1914. The importance of purchases from states such as Russia, the Ottoman Empire, Romania, Bulgaria, Serbia, and Greece lay not just in the vast quantities of war materials ordered but also in the timing of those orders. Often private firms from Germany, Austria, and France found their salvation in orders from or business ventures with the east European customers at pivotal periods when insignificant domestic sales threatened the companies with financial loss or even collapse. At other times the firms, including British companies, looked eastward as part of a global export strategy for expansion. On the receiving end, the east European states acquired the latest models of military and naval systems at the same time or even slightly ahead of their deployment in the more advanced industrial powers. With the exception of Austria-Hungary and Russia, all these countries completely lacked a domestic military-industrial base, and therefore their procurement of state-of-the-art weapons proved integral to the defense postures of the buyers. Within the three-way relationship of private suppliers, state customers, and supplier governments, this article is devoted to the first two players. A consideration of the diplomatic interests of the Great Power supplier states lies outside the scope of discussion. Rather, the focus here centers on the business dimension of the arms trade: the sellers and buyers.

By and large, the existing literature on armaments and diplomacy focuses exclusively on the Great Powers in the decade before 1914. David Stevenson's book is the most comprehensive, but omits the small states in any detail, while David Herrmann's study concentrates on the technical aspects with less attention to the diplomatic connections.[1] The broadest study of armaments policy in eastern Europe is Peter Gatrell's monograph on tsarist rearmament in the period 1900–1914.[2] Gatrell considers the tsarist defense sector as a whole, and therefore is more concerned with the macroeconomic trends than in-depth analysis of any one firm. In terms of naval procurement in the region, Paul Halpern and Milan Vego have between them covered Austria-Hungary, Turkey, Greece, and Russia.[3] Once again, however, these works do not consider the longer term prior to 1900.

The scholarly literature pertaining to the armaments business has not delved into eastern Europe and the Balkans in any systematic fashion. Keith Krause offers a fine overview of the dynamics of military technology transfers, but the work is largely a synthesis of secondary works without any in-depth treatment of the period or the region.[4] Historical studies of individual European armaments firms do fit the period 1854–1914 but have not taken eastern Europe as their major area of interest.[5] Similarly, the major diplomatic works dealing with the Balkans do not take up the question of armaments and economic development, although Jehuda Wallach does examine the various German military missions to Turkey.[6] Among the few articles available that directly address the topic of foreign arms suppliers in Russia, Edward Goldstein has concentrated solely on the English firm Vickers, while Claude Beaud has examined the French firm Schneider. In addition, Dietrich Geyer summarizes the standard Soviet secondary works in his chapter on the arms trade in Russia.[7] Finally, Jacob Kipp has looked at foreign ties to Russian naval production during the 1860s and Gatrell has dealt with naval procurement after 1905.[8]

By and large, military considerations took precedence over naval concerns among eastern European states. Therefore, equipment sales for land forces, such as rifles and artillery, predominated over naval sales. As the technology changed rapidly in the second half of the nineteenth century, east European states kept abreast of the changes by importing the most current models. Overall, German and Austrian firms set the pace for exports beginning in the 1870s. Among rifle suppliers, Mauser and Steyr claimed the bulk of the market, while Krupp, the German giant, truly dominated the artillery business in the region. However, around the turn of the twentieth century Schneider-Creusot, France's leading armaments firm, made significant inroads in the Balkans.

THE RIFLE TRADE

The German rifle manufacturer Mauser turned into a world-class exporter, and the Balkan countries served as important clients. Mauser began as a supplier to the German Army and scored its first major contract with the Würt-temberg government for delivery of 100,000 rifles Model 1871. Mauser completed this order in 1878 while at the same time taking an order for 26,000 of the rifles for China. However, with those orders delivered, the Mauser factory at Oberndorf faced dim prospects for future work. Only a large order from the Serbian government saved the company from collapse. Having tried to sell rifles to Romania in 1879, Wilhelm Mauser left Bucharest for Belgrade. During the winter of 1879–80 the Serbian government conducted gun trials and determined that the Mauser rifle was the best. On June 19, 1880, the Serbian government officially accepted the Mauser rifle and the war ministry entered into negotiations over price and delivery. With the endorsement of the Serbian war ministry, the Serbian Skupshtina approved the money for the Mausers on February 14, 1881. Thus, Serbia purchased 120,000 of the Model 1871 rifles. Designated as Serbian Model 1878/80, but also known as the Mauser-Koka or the Mauser-Milanovic after the Serbian officer who modified it, Serbian Model 1878/80 was converted to use 7×57 mm rounds. The company delivered the final rifles on March 13, 1884. On July 5, 1884, the Serbian government invited Paul Mauser to Belgrade, and he returned to Oberndorf on August 2 with a contract for 5,000 repeater carbines and 3,000 repeater rifles for the artillery service. This order was completed in October 1885.[9]

If the large Serbian orders preserved Mauser, then the Turkish ones served to assure the firm's continued sustainability. In 1887 the Ottoman government placed an enormous contract with the firms of Mauser and Loewe for 500,000 rifles. In so doing the Turks became the first to acquire the Mauser magazine rifle in any significant number. The massive Turkish order was the result of a direct sales pitch from the firms of Mauser and Loewe. Paul Mauser and Isidor Loewe met on May 2, 1886, and decided to cooperate in securing the Turkish order. Subsequently, Paul Mauser personally traveled to Constanti-nople to persuade the Turks to buy a variation of their rifle Model 1871/84. On November 17, 1886, Paul Mauser held a meeting with Sultan Abdul Hamid II about adopting the rifle. Although the Russians sought to hinder Turkish rearmament, the German military adviser Colmar von der Goltz lob-bied the Turks forcefully in favor of the Mauser. On December 8 the Turks began field tests of two different Mauser models (11 mm and 9.5 mm) along with Belgian, Austrian, Martini, and Hotchkiss rifles. In February 1887 their efforts were rewarded when the sultan signed a contract that divided the order evenly between the firms of Mauser and Loewe. The unit price was 362 piasters (68.8 marks) per rifle. In addition to ordering 500,000 rifles, the Otto-man government also purchased 50,000 carbines. However, the Turks feared that they would be left behind by ongoing technological developments. Therefore, they stipulated in the contract that should a better rifle be pro-duced during the fulfillment of the order, any undelivered rifles would be upgraded to the latest model. The Turks actually invoked this clause when they learned of the Model 1890 rifle, which used smokeless powder instead of the black powder of the 1887 model and required a smaller caliber round. As a result, the Turks obtained a majority of the newer model (280,000).[10] Having committed to the Mauser system in such large numbers, the Ottoman government remained one of Mauser's best customers. In 1893 they ordered an additional 201,000 new rifles based on the Spanish model of that year (7.65 mm). Due to the financial weakness of the Ottoman Treasury, the Turks had to take a loan for the Mauser order. The nominal amount of the loan, arranged in Germany, was, in Turkish pounds, TL1,000,000 bearing 4 percent interest. The first installment of TL300,000 represented half of the total purchase price. A decade later they again placed a substantial order with the firm.[11]

In 1899 Serbia also looked to procure Mauser rifles. In October the Serbs signed a contract for 90,000 rifles (.275-inch bore) and 45,000,000 cartridges with Loewe. The total order cost 13,000,000 francs. After remitting 2,500,000 francs, the Serbs pulled 3,000,000 francs each from their Military Invalid Fund and the Prisons Fund. The government covered the remaining balance through loans from the Union Bank in Vienna, which arranged a promise of 3,000,000 francs from Germany, and from the National Bank of Serbia. By February 1900, Loewe was delivering rifles at a rate of 6,000 a month. However, late in 1900 problems occurred with delivery. By November Loewe had handed over 56,000 rifles from Berlin, but the Serbian Military Commission was complaining about the inferior quality. The Serbs found many of the rifles to be defective, and the commission refused to accept 64 percent. The Loewe firm compounded the dissatisfaction by rubbing down the markings and trying to present the defective rifles a second time. The German firm also caused difficulties for the Serbs by dumping large numbers of weapons for inspection at the last minute, thereby making thorough examination next to impossible. As a result of these practices, the Serbian government resolved to avoid granting any orders to Loewe in the future. Therefore, in 1901 Serbia ordered 100,000 Mausers from Oberndorf.[12]

The main Austrian rifle producer, Österreichische Waffenfabriks-Aktiengesellschaft in Steyr, emerged on the European scene as an exporter already in the 1870s. Josef Werndl, the general director at Steyr, understood the importance of exporting rifles not only according to patent but also through licensing agreements. Using licensing agreements Steyr sold the Prussian Army 500,000 Mauser rifles Model 1871, followed by the Spitalsky Werndl rifle Model 1873 for the Austrian Army and the Gras rifle Model 1874 for the French Army. For Steyr, the Balkan countries would soon become important customers. In 1876 Greece signed a major contract for 36,000 rifles based on the Gras model. Soon thereafter, beginning in 1879 Romania decided to replace its Peabody rifle system with the Henry-Martini system, and the Romanian government turned to Steyr to furnish 130,000 rifles into the early 1880s. Sales to the Balkans gained added importance in the years 1879–86 as domestic sales plummeted. Having peaked in 1877, Steyr dropped from

6,000 workers to 910 workers by 1884. During those lean years only Steyr's Balkan arms exports kept the company afloat. By 1914 Steyr had produced 6,000,000 rifles, of which foreign sales claimed 58.5 percent. Among those exports, 33 percent found their way to Balkan states. Romania was the largest Balkan customer, purchasing 594,944 weapons, followed by Greece (281,636), Bulgaria (235,940), Serbia (42,530), and Montenegro (20,000).[13] (See Tables 1 and 2.)

By the turn of the century the interests and dealings of a number of rifle and cartridge manufacturing firms had coalesced into a coherent entity, the Deutsches Waffen- und-Munitionsfabriken (DWM). In November 1896, DWM was founded through the merger of the following firms: Deutsche Metallpatronenfabrik (Karlsruhe), Loewe (Berlin), Rheinisch-Westfaelischen Powder Co. (Cologne), Rottweil-Hamburg Powder Co. (Rottweil), Fabrique Nationale d'Armes de Guerre (Herstal, Belgium), and Mauser (Oberndorf). Essentially, DWM functioned as a holding company that coordinated and

Table 1
Steyr's Rifle and Pistol Exports, 1876–86 (includes Mannlichers and Mausers)

YEAR	DOMESTIC	GREECE	ROMANIA	MONTENEGRO
1876/77	96,400	15,000	----	---
1877/78	85,077	42,600	---	---
1879/80	12,586	39,000	34,000	20,000
1880/81	16,490	5,000	30,000	---
1881/82	10,304	---	41,000	---
1882/83	7,867	---	25,000	---
1884/85	4,832	5,000	---	---
1885/86	3,154	26,500	---	---

Source: Martin Gutsjahr, "Rüstungsunternehmen Österreich-Ungarns vor und im Ersten Weltkrieg. Die Entwicklung dargestellt an die Firmen Skoda, Steyr, Austro-Daimler und Lohner" (Ph.D. diss., Universität Wien, 1995), 92–97.

Table 2
Steyr's Rifle and Pistol Exports, 1889–99

YEAR	DOMESTIC	BULGARIA	ROMANIA
1889/90	296,109	36,000	---
1890/91	223,842	54,000	---
1891/92	117,028	56,868	8,000
1892/93	8,055	350	111,904
1893/94	10,407	---	14,000
1896/97	29,986	3,000	22,000
1897/98	70,365	---	8,002
1898/99	145,897	20,000	29,000

Source: Gutsjahr, 92–97.

divided production among the participants. Later, Steyr also joined the arrangement.

By agreement, in 1904–5 DWM waved its exports to Greece and Serbia in favor of Steyr. Consequently, in 1907 Steyr contracted with the Serbs to provide 30,000 Mauser rifles. In addition, Steyr helped in the conversion of old 10.9 mm Koka-Mauser single-loaders to magazine-fed 7 mm rifles at the Serbian arsenal at Kragujevatz through the sale of 50,000 new barrels. Of the 30,000 7 mm Mauser magazine rifles and 10,000 7 mm magazine carbines ordered from Steyr in April 1907, about 20,000 rifles and no carbines had arrived by October 1908, when the remainder of the supply was interdicted by the Austrian government.[14]

In 1907, the German and Austrian firms extended their coordination so that Steyr would not compete for exports to Turkey or Spain, while DWM steered clear of Bulgaria and Romania. These arrangements lasted until 1914.[15] As a result of this cooperation, Steyr and Mauser effectively divided the Balkan firearms market between themselves. The distribution can be seen in Tables 3 and 4.

ARTILLERY

For Krupp already in the 1860s exports were becoming important. In the period 1860–71 the cannon for export were small guns under 10 cm, and domestic sales led exports 3,244 to 2,462. However, for large caliber pieces, exports almost doubled domestic sales, 1,165 as compared to 560 domestic. The trend toward growing exports continued in the years 1875–89, during which time Krupp sold approximately 84 percent of its war materials abroad in any given year, and peak years reached 92 percent. The following period 1889–1904 saw Krupp's arms exports fluctuate between a minimum of 51

Table 3
Steyr's Rifle and Pistol Exports, 1903–14

YEAR	DOMESTIC	BULGARIA	ROMANIA	GREECE	SERBIA
1903/04	17,234	65,208	70,948	---	---
1904/05	48,157	---	29,053	---	---
1906/07	1,291	300	---	69,280	---
1907/08	34,715	---	---	42,552	15,200
1908/09	44,861	150	---	3,004	24,800
1909/10	47,515	---	---	50	1,030
1910/11	11,046	---	15,424	1,000	---
1911/12	5,514	64	29,000	12,000	1,500
1912/13	35,016	---	3,813	8,600	---
1913/14	10,802	---	123,800	12,050	---

Source: Gutsjahr, 92–97.

Table 4
Mauser's Rifles and Carbines Exported, 1899–1911

YEAR	TURKEY	SERBIA	NON-BALKANS
1899/00	---	---	1,400
1900	---	---	44,100
1903/05	200,000	---	---
1904	406	---	1,000
1907	7,617	---	11,100
1908	15,000	---	6,750
1909	15,000	---	7,550
1910	---	32,000	29,800
1911	1,100	---	12,700

Source: Wolfgang Seel, *Mauser, von der Waffenschmiede zum Weltunternehmen* (Zürich: Verlag Stocker-Schmid AG, 1988), 63–64.

percent and a maximum of 87 percent of annual war material production. Finally, Krupp's arms exports as a percentage of the annual armaments production ranged between 54 percent and 65 percent in the period 1904–9.[16]

While arms exports turned into a major part of Krupp's business, the Balkans and eastern Europe proved to be the key export market. By 1873 Krupp had sold 1,148 cannon to Russia and another 1,384 to the Ottoman Empire, Russia's chief adversary in the Balkans. As armed conflicts heated up in the Balkans between 1874 and 1887, the main protagonists in the Balkan crises became Krupp's main customers. Russia purchased 1,948 Krupp guns, followed by the Ottomans with 1,389. Among the other states involved in the region Romania accounted for 298 guns, Greece 279, Bulgaria 128, and Austria-Hungary 62. Thus, these regional players imported 4,104 guns as compared to 4,191 for the remainder of Krupp's export sales, distributed among Latin America (426), East Asia (1,065), Scandinavia (454), Iberia (415), and Western Europe (1,831). Even as Krupp's artillery exports decreased from 650 pieces per year 1874–86 to 427 pieces per year 1887–99, Balkan states remained important customers. Between 1887 and 1899 Romania imported 312 Krupp guns, Bulgaria 303, Turkey 83, and Greece 61. Over the entire period 1854–1912, Krupp sales to the Balkan region amounted to 6,595 guns or 23.1 percent of total artillery exports, making the Balkans Krupp's largest market in Europe. Having imported 3,943 Krupp guns, Ottoman Turkey occupied first place as Krupp's biggest customer in the world, not just in Europe. At the other end of the spectrum, Serbia was the smallest Krupp customer with only six guns because it had been the first Balkan state to adopt the French system instead of the German.[17] (See Table 5).

The French firm Schneider et Cie in Le Creusot entered onto the Balkan stage in a significant way only beginning in 1897. In February of that year Bulgaria ordered twenty-four howitzers, twenty-four siege guns (12 cm), and three batteries of 75 mm field guns for 1,250,000 francs. The Serbian gov-

Table 5
Krupp Balkan Artillery Sales, 1854–1912

COUNTRY	QUANTITY
TURKEY	3,943
ROMANIA	1,450
BULGARIA	517
GREECE	356
AUSTRIA-HUNGARY	298
MONTENEGRO	25
SERBIA	6

Source: Zdenek Jindra, "Zur Entwicklung und Stellung der kanonenausfuhr der Firma Friedrich Krupp/Essen 1854–1912," *Vierteljahrschrift für Sozial- und Wirtschaftsgeschichte*, Beiheft 120 (Stuttgart: Franz Steiner Verlag, 1995), 974.

ernment soon followed suit and in June signed a contract with Schneider for twenty howitzers (12 cm) with 505 shells each, two howitzers (15 cm) without shells, six mortars with 505 shells each, and sixteen siege guns (12 cm) based on the Canet system with 505 shells each. Delivery took place over sixteen months with a price tag of approximately 3,000,000 francs. Also in 1897, Greece ordered four quick-fire cannon (47 mm) from the firm to rearm its ironclad *Pisara* in June. Prior to 1897, Schneider's only exports to the region had been some armor plate to the Greek government in 1887 and some steel fortification works for the Romanian government in 1890–91.[18]

Although a relative latecomer to the Balkan market, Schneider rapidly ensconced itself with a series of major artillery contracts in Bulgaria, Serbia, and Greece. In July 1903 the French had acquired one-third of Bulgarian artillery ammunition contracts at the expense of Krupp, which held onto the remaining two-thirds.[19] Then, in November 1904 Schneider scored a resounding victory by landing the huge Bulgarian order for quick-fire artillery. The Bulgarian contract amounted to 25,700,000 francs for eighty-one batteries of Schneider 75 mm field guns (total 324 pieces) with 1,000 rounds accompanying each gun. In contrast, Krupp only managed to sell the Bulgarians fifty-four mountain guns for 3,150,000 francs.[20] By the end of 1906, Schneider again emerged on top of Krupp, this time in Serbia, where the French received an order for forty-five batteries of quick-fire field guns, nine batteries of mountain guns, and two batteries of horse artillery to be delivered within eighteen months.[21] Following on the heels of its success in Serbia, Schneider won once more in the artillery competition in Greece. This time the order totaled thirty-eight field batteries and six mountain batteries.[22]

Schneider's gains in the Balkans did not rest simply on technical prowess. Financial considerations also contributed significantly to Schneider's rise. As Dr. Danev, president of the Bulgarian Parliament (Sobranye), explained to Lord Stuart Rendel of Armstrong's:

[U]p to date, Bulgaria had in ordering war material principally for the army almost invariably dealt with either Krupp or Schneider. The Government at present did not favor Krupp in any way . . . the reason that the orders were placed with Schneider was that the issue of Bulgarian loans had usually been effected through French houses, who made one of their conditions the ordering of war material through French firms. . . . Confidentially he said that French artillery for Bulgaria was thoroughly satisfactory but very expensive.[23]

From the very end of the nineteenth century to the eve of the Great War Schneider's arms exports rose sharply. In 1898–99 armaments exports yielded more than 35,000,000 francs, while in the period 1905–13 a high point of 85,000,000 francs in 1907 was surpassed during the Balkan wars in 1912–13 by a figure of 140,000,000 francs. Exports played the biggest part in Schneider's artillery sales. In 1898 about 60 percent of the firm's armaments production was exported, and these exports represented 80 percent of the company's total exports. In November 1912 Balkan orders altogether amounted to 127,000,000 francs. In 1913 out of Schneider's 170,000,000 francs in artillery and naval orders, Balkan countries claimed 60,000,000.[24]

Similar to the cooperative agreements regarding rifle sales, the artillery exporters also attempted to form arrangements to reduce competition. In this instance, however, the participants were British and French firms that hoped to break the German dominance in the Ottoman Empire. In March 1907 the British firms Vickers and Armstrong concluded an agreement with Schneider pertaining to business in Turkey. The aim of the arrangement was to avoid "unnecessary and useless competition" to improve chances for contracts. The three companies also agreed to share any orders equally between the French and British groups. The entente was in effect until January 1, 1910. The British foreign office subsequently instructed the embassy in Constantinople to work with the French ambassador as much as possible to promote the "united interests of their respective countries" in obtaining artillery orders. Meanwhile, Schneider officially informed the French government of the existence of the companies' agreement as well.[25]

Building on the 1907 agreement, Vickers and Armstrong considered a broader arena for coordination. In a meeting at the Carlton Hotel in London in December 1912, Frank Barker of Vickers sounded out Armstrong's representative Baxton Noble about the possibility of a business alliance for the Balkan states. Barker especially focused on Greece, "where he said finance could be arranged through certain Greek houses, the proposal being roughly that we should take over and maintain a small shipyard and that in return we should receive prior consideration for all orders placed abroad."[26]

The driving concern for the two British firms was their disadvantage vis-à-vis the French in financial resources. As Lord Stuart Rendel observed in his report to Armstrong's board:

The whole question of the value of an alliance with Vickers should, I think, be gone into very carefully. There appears to be little doubt that if orders are to be obtained from the Balkan states, the British firms concerned must be generally if not closely in touch with the financial houses who may be floating the loans necessary for the naval and military expansion and this presupposes that British financial groups will enter the market. If French groups remain in possession of the field, there is no hope whatever for orders to British manufacturers.[27]

Although no specific discussions came up regarding Turkey, Bulgaria, Romania, Serbia, or Montenegro in the meeting, Vickers did propose the establishment of a head office in Constantinople (under Vickers' management) to oversee a team of subagents for the Balkan states. In his report to the Armstrong Board Rendel acknowledged the merits of an alliance with Vickers but preferred that the head office be in London rather than Constantinople. Finally, he also suggested that an extension of the alliance with Schneider should also be considered.[28]

In the realm of artillery production, during the period 1890–1914 the Skoda works in Plzen followed Krupp and Schneider into export markets, although with less success. Like the Germans and the French, the Austrians looked for the key to export expansion in the Balkans after 1904. Skoda turned to foreign sales after proving unable to secure an order for its field gun from the Austrian government in August 1902. Thereafter, the company began to look toward the Balkan states for compensatory sales. In 1903 both Romania and Serbia expressed interest in Skoda guns, and the Serbs received a sample gun and 1,000 shells for trials. Skoda expected the Serbian order by February 2, 1904. However, the change of ruling dynasty in Serbia brought in a new government that decided to conduct a new series of trials. Ultimately, Skoda lost out to Schneider in 1906. Skoda did achieve a modicum of success with sales to the Ottoman Empire. In 1913 the Turks bought 36 field howitzers (10.4 cm) complete with ammunition for a price of 5,900,000 crowns. The Turkish order helped contribute to an economic upswing for the firm because the order accounted for roughly one-sixth of Skoda's 36,000,000 crowns' worth of foreign arms sales in 1913. Nevertheless, Skoda appeared distinctly in the second ranks for artillery exports behind Krupp and Schneider.[29]

THE NAVAL TRADE

For private naval producers, the era of increasingly intense international competition began in the late 1870s. Prior to that time British yards, especially Armstrong's of Elswick, had held uncontested dominance worldwide, including the eastern European markets. By the 1880s, however, French and German firms were giving serious chase to British ones, especially in eastern Europe. At the turn of the century the Krupp-Schneider rivalry had entered the naval arena as Krupp's own shipyard, Germania, competed against Creusot's. By the eve of the Great War, though, it was the British firm Vickers that had unquestionably emerged supreme.

Conflict in eastern Europe played a direct role in Armstrong's development as an armaments firm. Because of the Crimean War, Lord Armstrong had engineered the rifled, breech-loaded, wrought iron artillery piece. The new technology dramatically transformed the defense business not only on land but also for naval guns. After the war Armstrong guns had gained preeminence in the Ottoman Navy. During the 1860s all but two of the twenty-one iron-clads in the Turkish fleet possessed Armstrong guns, including the five built by French manufacturers. Later, as Armstrong increasingly gave preference to warship construction in the 1880s, the firm's first three vessels launched from Elswick in 1885 were destined for eastern Europe: the torpedo cruisers *Panther* and *Leopard* were built for Austria-Hungary and the cruiser *Salamina* was purchased by the Greek government. Then, in 1887 Romania bought the cruiser *Elizabeta*. Armstrong, having established itself as a warship builder, did not find good prospects for major contracts in the Balkans in the 1890s, and so the company diverted its attention to the more promising clients in Latin America and Japan. By 1914, Armstrong by itself only sold two more warships in the region, both to the Turks. In 1903 the Turks bought the cruiser *Abdul Hamid* launched at Elswick, and in 1914 they paid for the battleship *Sultan Osman I*, originally built for Brazil. Eventually, the British government seized the latter at the start of the war, and it never found its way to Turkey.[30]

As Armstrong's experience demonstrates, the Balkans prior to 1908 did not prove to be a primary market for larger warships. Nevertheless, firms that specialized in smaller craft, especially torpedo boats, found a better niche in the region. Between 1875 and 1885 the British producers Thornycroft and Yarrow each sold two third-class torpedo boats to Austria. The Austrian government also bought another two first-class boats from Yarrow. By the late 1880s, however, the Dual Monarchy had switched decisively toward its own domestic producers, acquiring thirty-eight torpedo boats from the Pola yard and six from Trieste.[31] Besides Austria, Yarrow managed to sell craft to Romania, where in fact Yarrow boats comprised the largest segment of the Romanian force in the 1880s (six river craft and two torpedo boats). Meanwhile, the German firm Vulcan, located in Stettin, accounted for the five first-class torpedo boats in the Greek Navy in 1885.[32]

The German company Schichau, located in Elbing, emerged as a major producer of torpedo boats beginning in the late 1870s. In 1877 the German and Russian navies expressed interest in Schichau boats at virtually the same time. The Russians conducted tests of the boat in St. Petersburg November 28, 1877. Subsequently, both governments made orders, but the Russian order proved larger. Whereas the German government only purchased two Schichau boats, the tsarist government ordered ten boats to be delivered in 1878. From this quick start Schichau would turn into the premier supplier of torpedo boats for Russia as part of the firm's expansion as an exporter. Based on the success of its torpedo boat the *Adler*, which at the time was the fastest ship in the world, in the period 1884–90 Schichau beat English and French competitors and sold seventy boats to foreign navies. Eastern Europe again provided the first customers for the new boat in 1884 when both Russia and the Ottoman Empire made purchases. They were followed by Austria-Hungary, Italy, and China (1885), Brazil (1888), and Japan (1890). In 1912, with the approval of the German government, Schichau actually established production facilities within the tsarist empire near Riga. In appreciation of this investment, Russia ordered two small cruisers of 4,350-tons displacement from the Schichau branch in Danzig. By the end of 1913 the Riga works entered production, and the tsarist government granted the plant contracts for nine more torpedo boats.[33]

As was the case with other armaments firms, Schichau found its largest market in eastern Europe. From a total of 167 Schichau boats sold abroad by 1914, Russia herself accounted for 49. The next highest customer was Italy with 36. If we include Austria-Hungary in the eastern European totals, then the region absorbed 77 ships, or 46 percent of Schichau's exports. Certainly, other regions saw some share of Schichau boats. East Asia received 40 boats (China 21, Japan 19), Latin America another 7 (Brazil 5, Argentina 2), and Scandinavia 6. The firm's prominence in Russia and the Balkans is evident in Table 6.

Torpedo boat exporters continued to find customers in the Balkans. In the 1880s the Ottomans started importing most of their vessels from non-British sources. While the French firms Des Vinges and Forges et Chantiers together provided five torpedo boats in the years 1885–87, German sales were more significant. Besides the five Schichau torpedo boats, the Turks also bought eight more from Germania along with two destroyers between 1888 and 1892. Later, during the naval program of 1903–7 the Turkish mix of suppliers

Table 6
Schichau's Warship Exports to Eastern Europe, 1877–1914

COUNTRY	QUANTITY	YEARS
RUSSIA	32 Torpedo boats	1877-1904
	3 Torpedo cruisers	1888-91
	4 Torpedo catchers	1899-1900
	1 Cruiser	1900
	9 Torpedo destroyers	1912
TURKEY	9 Torpedo boats	1884-1908
AUSTRIA-HUNGARY	9 Torpedo boats	1885-96
	4 Vedette ships	1886-87
	1 Depot ship	1891
	1 Torpedo cruiser	1896
ROMANIA	4 Gunboats	1893-94

Source: 100 Jahre Schichau, 1837–1937 (Berlin: VDI-Verlag, 1937), 186–87.

changed again. Armstrong-Ansaldo, the branch of the English firm in Genoa, claimed over half of the Turkish new orders with eleven of twenty-one torpedo boat destroyers. Among the remaining ten, Creusot supplied eight and Germania only two. In 1906 Yarrow supplied two Greek boats, and the Romanian Navy expanded with the purchase of eight new torpedo boats from the Thames Ironworks and four armored river monitors from Trieste (Tecnico Stabilimento).[34]

With its vast armed forces and its late-developing industrial base, tsarist Russia offered the major European armament firms tremendous prospects for sales and investments. These opportunities did not go unnoticed, and ultimately almost every major firm claimed some portion of the Russian defense market for its own. The tsarist government preferred as much as possible to procure warships from domestic sources, yet the demands of outfitting three fleets (Baltic, Black Sea, and Pacific) placed greater strains on production capacity than was possible to meet from exclusively native Russian sources. At the time of the Russo-Turkish War in 1877–78 the entire Russian Navy consisted of domestically manufactured ships. As mentioned previously, Russia began purchasing from abroad in 1878 with the acquisition of the Schichau boats. Soon the complement of foreign-made ships steadily increased. Among the forty-eight torpedo boats added to the Russian Navy in the period 1880–94, imported ships numbered eighteen. Schichau supplied half of the foreign boats, while six were French and the final three were British made.[35] In addition to vessels purchased abroad, many non-Russian firms supplied engines and boilers for Russian warships built in Russia. These foreign suppliers included Fairfield Co. (one), Cockerill (one), Napier and Sons (four), Mawdsley and Field (five), Humpreys and Tennart (four), Hawthorne and Leslie (two), Baird (four), Motola Co. in Sweden (six), Mannesman (one), and Belleville et Cie (three). [36] In the years 1895–1905, foreign yards produced two out of fifteen battleships (Cramps and La Seyne) and three out of six armored cruisers (two La Seyne and one Vickers).[37] By 1901 Germania had delivered the first-class cruiser *Aksold* while two French firms gained new orders for destroyers. The Forges et Chantiers de le Mediterranee (Havre) was building three destroyers and Normand another two.[38] Overall, foreign-built ships comprised about one quarter of the Russian Navy prior to the Russo-Japanese War of 1904–5.

Some French and German naval suppliers had come to count on the Russian state as a customer, and as a result the absence of Russian orders in the middle of the first decade of the twentieth century caused much anxiety. For example, in 1903 as the firm Forges et Chantiers de la Mediterranee was finishing up its work on the Russian battleship *Tsarevitch*, "In reply to a question as to whether any further orders were expected from Russia, M. Fournier, the manager of the works, stated that up to that date he had heard of no new orders either from Russia or from elsewhere. He appeared to be somewhat depressed in consequence."[39] Similarly, Germania had just finished Russian contracts for two destroyers and two submarines in 1906 when British naval officers reported that from a long interview with Admiral Barandon, the director of Germania shipyard, "He appeared to take a somewhat gloomy view of affairs, especially as just now they are not so near Russian contracts as they were this time last year when he returned from Russia with a signed contract for two battleships in his pocket, only dependent for its execution on 'money,' which has not been available."[40]

After 1908 prospects for extremely large naval orders to eastern Europe increased dramatically. First, the destruction of Russia's Pacific and Baltic fleets during the war with Japan meant that significant new orders for warships appeared on the horizon now that the tsarist government at last had the financial means to pay for the rebuilding programs. At the same time, the Young Turks had come to power in the Ottoman Empire, and they viewed naval expansion as a means of Turkish revitalization. In addition to purchasing ships outright, both the Russians and the Turks desired to have a domestic capability for building dreadnoughts.

In the end, Vickers won the lion's share of these major contracts. In terms of naval exports, Vickers' Russian sales amounted to £7,000,000 in 1911 with a further £1,000,000 worth of artillery orders annually starting in 1913. In obtaining these contracts, Vickers held off fierce French competition from Schneider. Similar victories followed in Turkey, where Vickers beat back the Germans to win Turkish contracts for £2,000,000 in 1911 and £5,000,000 in 1913. Moreover, Vickers' supremacy showed in the firm's success in capturing the huge docks concessions within Russia and Turkey. Thus, Vickers positioned itself as the preferred domestic supplier for the two Black Sea rivals.[41]

Taken together, military and naval imports played an enormous role in equipping the armed forces of the east European states. In turn, the armaments firms themselves came to rely on the exports to the region as part of their overall sales. During peacetime, the major private defense producers could not count on sufficient business from their home governments, and as a result exports proved vital to the firms' prosperity. Krupp, Schneider, Mauser, Steyr, Schichau, and Vickers all found huge stakes in eastern Europe. Given how eastern European states consistently served as big customers, it would be no exaggeration to conclude that for the global arms trade eastern Europe was the most important region in the period 1870–1914.

NOTES

1. David Stevenson, *Armaments and the Coming of War: Europe, 1904–1914* (Oxford: Clarendon Press, 1996); David G. Herrmann, *The Arming of Europe and the Making of the First World War* (Princeton: Princeton University Press, 1996).

2. Peter Gatrell, *Government, Industry and Rearmament in Russia, 1900–1914* (Cambridge: Cambridge University Press, 1994).

3. Paul G. Halpern, *The Mediterranean Naval Situation 1908–1914* (Cambridge, Mass.: Harvard University Press, 1971); Milan N. Vego, *Austro-Hungarian Naval Policy 1904–1914* (London: Frank Cass, 1996). For Russia, see also J. N. Westwood, *Russian Naval Construction 1905–1945* (London: Macmillan Press Ltd., 1994).

4. Keith Krause, *Arms and the State: Patterns of Military Production and Trade* (Cambridge: Cambridge University Press, 1992).

5. William Manchester, *The Arms of Krupp, 1587–1968* (Boston: Bantam Books, 1968); Willi Boelcke, *Krupp und Die Hohenzollern, aus der Korrespondenz der Familie Krupp 1850–1916* (Berlin: Rütten & Loening, 1956); Bernhard Menne, *Blood and Steel, The Rise of the House of Krupp* (New York: Lee Furman, Inc., 1938); Basil Collier, *Arms and the Men: The Arms Trade and Governments* (London: Hamish Hamilton, 1980); Zdenek Jindra, *Der Rüstungs-Konzern Fried. Krupp AG., 1914–1918* (Praha: Univerzita Karlova, 1986); Clive Trebilcock, *The Vickers Brothers, Armaments and Enterprise 1854–1914* (London: Europa Publications Ltd., 1977).

6. Barbara Jelavich, *Russia's Balkan Entanglements, 1806–1914* (Cambridge: Cambridge University Press, 1991); Hugh Ragsdale, *Imperial Russian Foreign Policy* (Cambridge: Cambridge University Press, 1993); Charles and Barbara Jelavich, *The Establishment of the Balkan National States, 1804–1920* (Seattle: University of Washington Press, 1977); Jehuda Wallach, *Anatomie einer Militärhilfe, Die preussich-deutchen Militärmissionen in der Türkei 1835–1914* (Dusseldorf, 1976).

7. Edward R. Goldstein, "Vickers Limited and the Tsarist Regime," *Slavonic and East European Review* 58, no. 4 (October 1980): 561–71. Claude Beaud, "De L'Expansion Internationale à La Multinationale Schneider En Russie (1896–1914)," *Histoire Économie et Société* 4 (1985): 575–602. See Dietrich Geyer, *Russian Imperialism: The Interaction of Domestic and Foreign Policy, 1860–1914* (New Haven: Yale University Press, 1977), 255–72.

8. Jacob W. Kipp, "The Russian Navy and Private Enterprise, A Peculiar MIC," in *War, Business and World Military-Industrial Complexes*, ed. Benjamin Franklin Cooling (Port Washington, N.Y.: Kennikat Press, 1981), 84–105; Peter Gatrell, "After Tsushima: Economic and Administrative Aspects of Russian Naval Rearmament, 1905–1913," *Economic History Review*, 2nd ser., XLIII, 2 (1990), 255–70.

9. Robert W. D. Ball, *Mauser Military Rifles of the World* (Iola, Wis.: Krause Publications, 1996), 8, 204; Wolfgang Seel, *Mauser, von der Waffenschmiede zum Weltunternehmen* (Zürich: Verlag Stocker-Schmid AG, 1988), 27–30.

10. Ball, *Mauser Military*, 236–39; Seel, *Mauser*, 33–34; *Geschichte der Mauser-Werke* (Berlin: VDI-Verlag, 1938), 89–94.

11. Ford to Earl of Rosebery, 24 April 1893, FO 78/4479.

12. Goschen to Salisbury, 22 October 1899, FO 105/127; WO 106/6177 "Reports on Changes in Various Foreign Armies During the year 1900," 71; Macdonald to Salisbury, 20 February 1900, FO 105/132; Macdonald to Salisbury, 7 September 1900, FO 105/133; Bonham to Lansdowne, 21 November 1900, ibid., "Report on Changes in Foreign Armies During 1907," 204, WO 106/6184.

13. Michaela Pfaffenwimmer, "Die wirtschaftliche und soziale Entwicklung der 'Österreichischen Waffenfabriks-Aktiengesellschaft' unter der Leitung des Generaldirektors Josef Werndl 1869–1889" (Ph.D. diss., Universität Wien, 1985), 165–66; Martin Gutsjahr, "Rüstungsunternehmen Österreich-Ungarns vor und im Ersten Weltkrieg. Die Entwicklung dargestellt an die Firmen Skoda, Steyr, Austro-Daimler und Lohner" (Ph.D. diss., Universität Wien, 1995), 5, 59–60, 90–97; Manfried Rein-

schedl, "Die Rüstung Österreich-Ungarns von 1880 bis zum Ausbruch des Ersten Weltkriegs" (master's thesis, Universität Wien, 1996), 101–5; *125 Jahre Waffen aus Steyr* (Steyr: Steyr Mannlicher Ges. M.B.H., 1989), 6, 9.

14. "Report on Changes in Foreign Armies During 1907," 204, WO 106/6184; ibid., 1908, 172.

15. Ball, *Mauser Military*, 8; Seel, *Mauser*, 64.

16. *Krupp 1812–1912. zum 100 jährigen Bestehen der Firma Krupp und der Gustahlfabrik zu Essen-Ruhr* (Essen: Friedrich Krupp A.G., 1912), 224.

17. Jindra Zdenek, "Zur Entwicklung und Stellung der kanonenausfuhr der Firma Friedrich Krupp/Essen 1854–1912," *Vierteljahrschrift für Sozial- und Wirtschaftsgeschichte*, Beiheft 120 (Stuttgart: Franz Steiner Verlag, 1995), 966–74.

18. Elliot to Salisbury, 22 February 1897, FO 78/4853; Fane to Salisbury, 9 June 1897, FO 105/117; Schnieder Archive-Le Creusot (SA), Repertoire General des Livres de Marches, Livre 69, f. 281, 20 Fevier 1897; SA, Repertoire General des Livres de Marches, Livre No. 70, ff. 219–227, 6 June 1897; SA, Repertoire General des Livres de Marches, Livre No. 70, ff. 335–343, 9 June 1897; SA, Blindages et Boulons a vis a blindages avec accessoires, Livre 38, f. 317, 28 December 1887; SA, Blindages et Boulons a vis a blindages avec accessoires, Livre 50, f. 127, 8 August 1891; SA, Blindages et Boulons a vis a blindages avec accessoires, Livre 45, f. 291, 8 August 1890.

19. Elliot to Lansdowne, 14 July 1903, FO 78/5294.

20. "Report on Changes in Foreign Armies During 1904," 24, WO 106/6181.

21. General Report on the Kingdom of Serbia for the Year 1906, FO 371/328, 298.

22. SA, SS 0426, Greek War Ministry to Schneider, 17 October 1907.

23. TWAS Rendel Papers 31/7616, Memorandum on Balkan States and Turkish Business (Lord Stuart Rendel), 31 December 1912.

24. Claude Beaud, "Les Schneider marchands de Canons 1870–1914," *Histoire, Économie et Société* 14, no. 1 (1995): 127–29.

25. Letter of Sir W. G. Armstrong, Chairman of Armstrong, Whitworth to Sir Charles Hardinge, Under Secretary of State for Foreign Affairs, 25 March 1907, FO 371/348.

26. TWAS Rendel Papers 31/7616, Memorandum on Balkan States and Turkish Business (Lord Stuart Rendel), 31 December 1912.

27. Ibid.

28. Ibid.

29. Protokoll uber die Verwaltungsrat-Sitzung, No. 14, 20 August 1902, Skoda Archive-Plzen; No. 17, 12 March 1903, Skoda Archive-Plzen; No. 18, 18 July 1903, Skoda Archive-Plzen; No. 21, 29 January 1904, Skoda Archive-Plzen; 2 August 1913, Skoda Archive-Plzen; Geschafts-Bericht, 1913.

30. Dick Keys and Ken Smith, *Down Elswick Shipways, Armstrong's Ships and People, 1884–1918* (Newcastle: Newcastle City Libraries, 1996), 7, 46–47.

31. Rept. 259, Austria. Guns, Torpedoes, Torpedo Boats, etc., 1890, ADM 231/19, 16.

32. Rept. 841, Turkey, Greece, and Roumania: War Vessels, 1908, ADM 231/49, 72–74.

33. *100 Jahre Schichau, 1837–1937* (Berlin: VDI-Verlag, 1937), 32–33, 38, 71–72; Eberhard Westpahl, *Ein Ostdeutscher Industriepionier, Ferdinand Schichau in sienem Leben und Schaffen* (Essen: West Verlag, 1957), 74–79.

34. Rept. 841, Turkey, Greece, and Roumania: War Vessels, 1908, ADM 231/49, 30–36, 72–74.

35. L. G. Beskrovnyi, *Russkaia armiia i flot v XIX veke* (Moskva: Nauka, 1973), 529.

36. Rept. 602, Lists Showing the Capabilities of France, Russia, Germany, Italy, United States for Building and Completing Vessels of War, 1900, ADM 231/33, 12.

37. Rept. 820, Shipbuilding Capabilities of the Principal Naval Powers, February 1907, ADM 231/48, 5, 10.

38. Rept. 624, Germany, Harbours and Dockyards, 1901, ADM 231/34, 21; Rept. 628, Reports on Foreign Naval Affairs, 1901, 55–56.

39. Rept. 689, Reports on Foreign Naval Affairs, 1903 (vol. II), ADM 231/37, 127.

40. Rept. 804, Reports on Foreign Naval Affairs, 1906 (vol. I), ADM 231/46, 46.

41. Trebilcock, *Vickers Brothers*, 120–21.

CHAPTER 3

The New Navy and the Old World: The United States Navy's Foreign Arms Purchasing in the Late Nineteenth Century

Stephen K. Stein

During the Civil War the United States Navy built a fleet totaling more than 700 warships, some of them the most modern examples of their type in the world. Yet in the dozen years after the war, the navy declined in size and effectiveness. As a result of budget cuts, corruption, and general neglect, the navy built only a few new ships, the last in 1874. By 1881 the navy possessed only 139 warships. Less than half of them were fit for service. These marvels of antique equipment and armament inspired laughter from naval officers around the world. Although adequate to the limited needs of the United States, the fleet did not inspire pride among American naval officers. In addition, its steadily contracting size slowed promotions to a crawl. Many ambitious officers, especially those with technical skills, left the navy to pursue other careers.[1] Others loudly demanded naval reform and modernization. The construction of what would later be called the new navy—a navy that would owe much to European expertise, technology, and material—was the result of their efforts.[2]

In the 1880s, as the United States increasingly focused its attention overseas, pressure mounted to rebuild the fleet. The assumption of virtually every naval officer, as well as a growing number of politicians, was that the nation's growing overseas commerce required the support of a strong navy. Several European nations had launched ambitious naval modernization programs while simultaneously launching new colonial enterprises to exclude commercial rivals including the United States. The purchase of modern European ironclads by several South American governments further highlighted the chasm that separated the United States' aging wooden steamers from the iron and steel ships of the rest of the world and fueled the increasingly successful lobbying efforts of reform-minded naval officers and their supporters. The reports of special Naval Advisory Boards in 1881 and 1882 laid bare the sad state of the fleet and presented plans for its reconstruction. In 1883 Congress authorized the construction of the navy's first new ships in more than a decade: the protected cruisers *Atlanta*, *Boston*, and *Chicago* and the dispatch ship *Dolphin*. Nicknamed the "ABCDs," all four were to be modern steel vessels, equal to those produced by the world's leading naval powers.[3]

Years of neglect had sapped the strength of the fleet and the navy's infrastructure on shore. Obsolete dockyards and ship construction facilities dedicated to the navy's antique wooden fleet found it difficult to retool to manufacture new steel hulls and assemble a truly modern fleet. Few naval architects, shipbuilders, or yard workers had experience with modern ships. Few factories existed to produce the specialized parts, armor, and armament for the new warships. Virtually no heavy ordnance had been manufactured in the United States since the 1860s.[4] While Congress and the Naval Advisory Boards both insisted that the United States needed to become self-sufficient in warship construction, the process would take some time. Throughout the 1880s, the navy remained dependent on European expertise to design its warships and on European suppliers to provide their armor, assorted critical parts, and even a portion of their armament. As late as the 1890s, the United States Navy remained dependent on Europe for some war materials, particularly during the Spanish-American War.

Despite the growing obsolescence of the United States fleet, its officers kept up with developments in Europe, and the Navy Department routinely sent officers to study naval architecture in Europe. The first of these was Assistant Naval Constructor Theodore D. Wilson, who later taught naval architecture at the United States Naval Academy. Wilson toured dockyards throughout Britain in 1872 and met with Sir Edward Reed, the famous ironclad designer. Wilson was followed by several other officers including Chief Engineer James W. King, who compiled a mammoth report on technical developments in Europe and the fleets of the major powers. Each year between 1879 and 1900 the navy sent the top two or three engineering graduates from the Naval Academy to study naval construction at the Royal Naval College at Greenwich or the Ecole d'Application du Genie Maritime in Paris. No comparable program existed in the United States until the Massachusetts Institute of Technology organized a course on naval architecture after the turn of the century. The intellectual and technical foundations of the new navy lay in Europe, and the officers who built the new navy were almost all trained in Europe or by European-trained officers.[5]

The United States Navy's Bureau of Construction and Repair designed the ABCDs. They were built by John Roach, a civilian shipbuilder notorious for his involvement in the corruptions of the Grant administration. Republican Secretary of the Navy William E. Chandler awarded the contracts for all four ships to Roach despite protests from other shipbuilders and Democrats in Congress. The construction of the ships proceeded slowly and met with constant delays and cost overruns, due in large part to the lack of experience of both the designers and the builders. The constant problems kept attention focused on the four ships and fueled the suspicions of many Democrats that Roach had won the contracts through fraud and corruption, and that he was once again defrauding the government.

The Democrats recaptured the White House in the 1884 elections, and Grover Cleveland became the first Democratic president since the Civil War. He appointed William C. Whitney his secretary of the navy. Whitney, a successful financier and corporate lawyer, had worked with Samuel Tilden to reform the Democratic Party in New York. By the mid-1880s, Whitney had become both popular and powerful in Democratic circles and had a solid reputation as a reformer. He entered office determined to clean up the corruption that pervaded the navy's administration. In his first year in office, he focused particular attention on Roach and the ABCDs. After the *Dolphin* snapped a propeller shaft in trials, Whitney refused to pay the balance due Roach, driving him into bankruptcy. Whitney seized the ships and ordered them completed in the navy's yards. Whitney was seriously interested in reforming and modernizing the navy, and there clearly were problems with the ABCDs, but his seizure of the ships was clearly motivated as much by politics and the hopes of discrediting his Republican predecessors as it was by his reforming zeal. The incident mars what was otherwise a very successful term in office during which he set the navy solidly on course for modernization and administrative reform.[6]

Congress, following bitter and partisan debates in 1884, authorized two new cruisers in 1885, the *Charleston* and the *Newark*, but the Construction Bureau dawdled in drawing up their plans. Frustrated, Whitney decided to look overseas for the design of the future *Charleston*. He left the design of the *Newark* in the hands of the Construction Bureau, which proved so slow to draft plans for the ship that construction did not begin until 1887.

As part of its reform and modernization, the navy developed an impressive, though chronically understaffed, intelligence agency. Created in 1883, the Office of Naval Intelligence (ONI) made obtaining information on the latest ship designs its highest priority. Many of the navy's most reform-minded officers served in the ONI during the 1880s and 1890s and gathered data on foreign navies. The ONI became the primary pipeline of information on naval architecture and technology from Europe to the United States. Whitney turned to the ONI in his search for modern warship designs.

Whitney's modernization plans faced material as well as technical and intellectual obstacles. The navy needed armor to finish the construction of several monitors languishing incomplete in the navy's yards since the Civil War, tying up limited dockyard space. While the Midvale Steel Company began producing forgings for six-inch guns, the eight-inch guns for all the new cruisers had to be purchased in Europe until the new gun factory at the Washington navy yard geared up for production. The navy also had to purchase a host of smaller parts in Europe. The ONI arranged many of these purchases.

The ONI's first (and for several years only) foreign attaché, Lieutenant Commander French Esnor Chadwick, operated out of London and sent back a regular stream of reports on European navies, occasionally dipping into his $100 expense allotment to purchase foreign blueprints. Chadwick arranged to purchase a variety of fittings for the navy's new warships including castings, guns, ammunition, and the armor plate. Chadwick developed contacts at the Woolwich Arsenal, the leading British shipbuilders, and even with British Admiralty officials, which quietly turned over specifications for Britain's new warships to him. Chadwick used these contacts to arrange the purchase of the plans for the navy's new cruiser, the *Charleston*, from the firm of Sir William Armstrong and Company. The *Charleston* was a substantial improvement over the ABCDs and would be the first American warship built without auxiliary sails.

Chadwick received some help in 1885 when Lieutenant Benjamin H. Buckingham became the navy's second attaché. Stationed in Paris, Buckingham observed French and German progress, allowing Chadwick to concentrate on British developments.[7] Both continued to facilitate American arms purchases, though Americans working for European arms firms, such as former United States Navy Lieutenant Edward Very at the Hotchkiss Company, arranged some arms purchases. Hotchkiss supplied some of the secondary armament for several of the navy's new cruisers.[8]

Chadwick and his successors proved a critical conduit between European navies and arms manufacturers and the United States Navy. While they normally only purchased plans, material, and subcomponents, in 1884 Chadwick purchased and leased ships for the Greely Relief Expedition. While exploring the arctic, Lieutenant Adolphus W. Greely, a United States Army officer, and his party had become trapped by foul weather and ice. Without supplies, they would soon succumb to hunger and exposure. Their supply ship, the *Proteus*, foundered on the ice while the crew of her escort, the USS *Yantic*, looked on helplessly from a ship too old and poorly built to risk breaking through the ice. Not a single ship in the United States Navy had enough engine power and hull strength to risk an Arctic voyage. Trapped, Greely's party faced a slow death from cold and starvation.

Faced with the collective concern of the American public, who closely followed newspaper stories of the courageous men, President Chester Arthur ordered the navy to attempt a rescue and pressured Congress to authorize the necessary funds. Chadwick arranged the speedy purchase of the *Thetis* and *Bear*, two Dundee whalers, and the British government, eager to improve relations with the United States, donated a third ship, the *Alert*, a veteran of previous Arctic expeditions. Chadwick also arranged to lease the collier *Loch Garry* and her crew from a British firm. Commander Winfield Scott Schley crewed the *Alert, Thetis,* and *Bear* with some of the best officers and men in the fleet. They successfully retrieved Greely and the handful of survivors from his party. This expedition highlighted the contrast between the dilapidated state of the navy's ships and the skill and bravery of its officers and sailors. Its success provided critical ammunition to the navy's supporters in their on-going budget battles and helped build support for naval expansion and modernization.[9]

The purchase of ships was the exception. The success of the *Charleston* encouraged Whitney to purchase more European designs, and Chadwick spent $2,500 on British plans in 1886. These designs and plans exposed American officers to the latest European techniques and technologies while they continued to hone their skills. Whitney hoped foreign designs would challenge his officers to improve upon them and eventually develop superior designs of their own, designs that would combine American ingenuity with the latest technology. By openly purchasing foreign plans and parts, he may also have been trying to pressure Congress into funding domestic arms plants.[10]

In 1886 Congress authorized construction of the nation's first battleships, the *Texas* and the *Maine*. Whitney wanted to procure the best designs possible so he sponsored a design contest and offered a $25,000 prize to the winning entries. Whitney received fifteen different submissions, most from European firms, though a few American naval officers entered designs. The American designs, though, all relied, at least in part, on British designs. For example, Washington Irving Chambers, who twenty-five years later would establish the navy's aviation program, submitted a well-received design. While most of it was his own work, James Howden, a Glasgow-based naval architect, designed the engines. The British Barrow Shipbuilding Company won the contest and prepared the plans for the *Texas*. The navy's Construction Bureau drew up the plans for the *Maine*, which were influenced by several of the contest entries.[11]

Congress became increasingly critical of the navy's reliance on Europe during its rearmament. Whitney's use of British plans for the *Texas* and yet another protected cruiser, the *Baltimore*, sparked bitter denunciations of his policies. Typical was one representative who demanded to know, "Why is it that we never hear of any but English-built ships as the original for our copies?" He was far from accurate when he claimed "other nations do not blindly follow in her [Britain's] wake in the construction of their vessels." Yet he clearly spoke for many in Congress when he concluded that "this abject pandering to English conceit . . . is repulsive to American feelings. The very thought of an emergency which makes us dependent upon England is humiliating."[12]

Congress placed greater and greater strictures on foreign purchases. It prohibited the foreign purchase of armor or gun steel after March 1885, forcing Whitney to let outstanding orders build to a quantity large enough to entice an American firm to bid on the combined contract, which Bethlehem Iron

Company won in 1887. In order to continue purchasing from Hotchkiss, Whitney convinced the company to build a plant in the United States managed by Edward Very. To sweeten the deal, Whitney gave Hotchkiss the rights to produce the American-designed Howell torpedo. Congress expanded restrictions against foreign purchases in succeeding years, eventually excluding virtually all foreign arms purchasing by the navy. Even plans were prohibited. The *Texas* would be the last American ship built to European plans. As American arms firms expanded, they increasingly competed on the international market, sometimes souring relations with European arms firms. While the navy occasionally relied on European expertise, as in 1887 when the ONI hired a European code expert, this became unusual.[13]

By 1889 the United States ranked twelfth among the world's naval powers, and new, modern warships entered the fleet regularly. As Bethlehem, Carnegie, several smaller firms, and the navy expanded and modernized their plants and yards, the United States built a series of ever-larger and more capable ships that rivaled those produced in Europe. Yet when war came with Spain almost a decade later, the navy once again turned to European suppliers to make up its deficiencies.

The United States Navy began preparing for war in earnest following the explosion of the *Maine* on February 15. The navy was particularly short of small vessels that would be vital to blockade Cuba. They resorted to purchasing and arming yachts, including one owned by J. P. Morgan. Several larger steamers were leased or purchased and converted to auxiliary cruisers, but the navy needed more. The United States had only recently begun building torpedo boats in quantity and was short of both torpedo boats and torpedoes. The navy was also short of such basic war materials as coal and ammunition. American facilities that were adequate for steady, peacetime expansion could not handle the rush of orders that poured in.

Assistant Secretary of the Navy Theodore Roosevelt ordered the navy's European attachés, Lieutenants John C. Colwell and William S. Sims, to determine what ships were available for sale, get bids for torpedo boats from the major builders, and to arrange the purchase of war materials. Colwell, operating in Britain, ran into obstacles as British shipbuilders raised prices and the Admiralty blocked his efforts to buy several warships that were under construction. In France, Sims managed to buy several small steamers along with torpedo tubes and some small ordnance, but it was not until the arrival of Commander Willard H. Brownson, the newly appointed special purchasing agent, that they received the funds to buy in earnest. Together Sims and Colwell purchased almost 300 tons of ammunition and other supplies. They continued their work after the United States declared war on Spain, shipping war materials to the United States using a variety of deceptions to avoid British neutrality laws.[14]

Aided by Sims and Colwell, Commander Brownson arranged the purchase of ships from a variety of nations. The United States purchased two 3,400-

ton cruisers being completed for Brazil by Armstrong, Whitworth, and Co. at Newcastle-on-Tyne in late March after negotiations with Brazil. One of these, the *Amazonas* (renamed the *New Orleans*) joined the United States squadron blockading Cuba; the other, the *Almirante Abreu* (renamed the *Albany*) failed to clear British customs before the American declaration of war and was held in Great Britain until 1900. The United States also purchased from Brazil the 6,888-ton Newport News-built liner *El Cid*, which Brazil had recently armed as an auxiliary cruiser. Colwell managed to purchase a gunboat in Great Britain and Sims bought two torpedo boats in Germany, though one of them, *Diogener*, was barely fit for service. Originally built for Portugal, she had been stripped of armament and sold to a private company from which Sims purchased her. Along with the German torpedo boats, Sims also bought fifty German torpedoes. Sims and Colwell continued to smuggle arms to the United States during the war and also coordinated the efforts of a small network of spies that passed them information on the Spanish fleet.

Defeated on sea and land, Spain agreed to the United States' peace terms following prolonged negotiations on December 10, 1898. One of the most contentious issues in the negotiations had been the status of the Philippines. Their purchase for twenty million dollars by the United States settled matters with Spain, but led the United States into a new, much longer war to secure its new colony. The prolonged struggle to suppress the Filipino independence movement led by Emilio Aguinaldo strained the United States Navy's resources more than the war against Spain had. Thousands of troops had to be transported across the Pacific Ocean and kept supplied. So Colwell and Sims continued their purchasing activities, which included a host of military goods, small craft, and the Australian refrigerator ship *Culoga*.[15]

Clearly the United States Navy could have completed its modernization without European expertise or material, but the process would have taken much longer and proved much more costly. Errors in plans, parts, or construction forced delay after delay in the construction of many warships authorized in the 1880s. While members of Congress decried the reliance of the navy on Europe, they likely would have protested the costs of going it alone even more. Congress's parsimony in funding support ships forced the navy to purchase or lease these when needed for either war or special assignment. Yet the United States' dependence on European expertise, armor, parts, and armament was short lived. The navy used European suppliers while it developed its own facilities and a network of domestic suppliers. While the Spanish-American War demonstrated that the navy had not achieved its goal of complete domestic arms production, it was close. With the exception of overseas coaling, none of the materials purchased by the navy during the war were critical to its victory.

The Spanish American War vindicated the navy and by extension its domestically designed and built warships. Wartime spending increases cleared the last obstacles in negotiations with steel and munitions manufacturers and new firms rushed to bid on wartime contracts. Following the war, the United States entered the worldwide naval arms race in earnest, designing and building a fleet of large, modern battleships and the infrastructure to support them. The era of foreign dependence was over.

NOTES

1. For example, Ensign Park Benjamin later became the editor of *Scientific American* and Lieutenant Edward Very joined the Hotchkiss Company.

2. The best short treatment of the navy in the 1870s and 1880s remains Lance C. Buhl, "Maintaining an American Navy, 1865–1889," in *In Peace and War: Interpretations of American Naval History 1775–1978*, ed. Kenneth J. Hagan (Westport, Conn.: Greenwood Press, 1978).

3. Secretary of the Navy, *Annual Reports*, 1882, 4–8 and 1883, 6–9.

4. *Report of the Gun Foundry Board, 20 February 1884*, 48th Cong., 1st sess., 1884, H. Doc. 97.

5. Jeffery M. Dorwart, *The Office of Naval Intelligence: The Birth of America's First Intelligence Agency, 1865–1918* (Annapolis, Md.: Naval Institute Press, 1979), 6–7; J. W. King, *Report of Chief Engineer J. W. King, United States Navy, on European Ships of War and their Armaments, Naval Administration and Economy, Marine Construction, Torpedo-Warfare, Dock-Yards, Etc.* (Washington, D.C: GPO, 1878); John D. Alden, *The American Steel Navy* (Annapolis, Md.: Naval Institute Press, 1972), 197.

6. Alden, *American Steel Navy*, 14; Leonard Swann, *John Roach, Maritime Entrepreneur* (Annapolis, Md.: Naval Institute Press, 1965), 85–208; Secretary of the Navy, *Annual Report*, 1885, "Report of the Dolphin Trial Board"; Harold and Margaret Sprout, *The Rise of American Naval Power* (1939; reprint, Annapolis, Md.: Naval Institute Press, 1990), 188; Walter R. Herrick, *The American Naval Revolution* (Baton Rouge: Louisiana State University Press, 1967), 34–36; and Mark D. Hirsch, *William C. Whitney: Modern Warwick* (New York: Dodd, Mead, 1948), 253–59. Whitney's decision to seize the ABCDs sparked considerable debate at the time and historians remain divided on his motives and justification. Swann remains the best treatment of the event, though he is partial toward Roach.

7. Dorwart, *Office of Naval Intelligence*, 33–34.

8. Dorwart, *Office of Naval Intelligence*, 19–32; Robert G. Angevine, "The Rise and Fall of the Office of Naval Intelligence," *Journal of Military History* 62 (April 1998), 291–312; A. G. Berry, "The Beginnings of the Office of Naval Intelligence," *U.S. Naval Institute Proceedings* 63 (January 1937), 102; Alden, *American Steel Navy*, 25.

9. Chandler to Chadwick, 29 March 1884, Chandler Papers, Library of Congress; John Edwards Caswell, *Arctic Frontiers: United States Explorations in the Far North* (Norman: University of Oklahoma Press, 1956), 106–8; David G. Colwell, "The Navy and Greely," *U.S. Naval Institute Proceedings* 84 (January 1958), 71–79.

10. B. F. Cooling, *Gray Steel and Blue Water Navy* (Hampden, Conn.: Archon Books, 1979), 63.

11. Alden, *American Steel Navy*, 31–32; Stephen Stein, "Washington Irving Chambers: Innovation, Professionalization, and the New Navy" (Ph.D. diss, Ohio State University, 1999), 131–35. For the extensive correspondence between Chambers and

Howden, see Chambers Papers, Library of Congress Manuscript Division, Box 5. Chambers's designs are in Boxes 33 and 34.

12. *Congressional Record*, 49th Cong., 1st sess., 24 July 1886, 7490.

13. Secretary of the Navy, *Annual Report*, 1889, iv; Cooling, *Gray Steel and Blue Water Navy*, 66–76; Hirsch, *William C. Whitney*, 265, 329; Dorwart, *Office of Naval Intelligence*, 26, 48–52.

14. Roosevelt to Colwell and Roosevelt to Sims, 3 March 1898, Spanish-American War Correspondence, NARG 38; Colwell to Assistant Secretary of the Navy, 2 March 1898; Colwell to Secretary of the Navy, 11, 14, 19, and 29 March 1898, all in Spanish-American War Correspondence, NARG 38; Dorwart, *Office of Naval Intelligence*, 58–61.

15. Alden, *American Steel Navy*, 111; David Trask, *The War With Spain in 1898* (New York: Free Press, 1981), 82–3, 88; Dorwart, *Office of Naval Intelligence*, 67.

CHAPTER 4

The Art of the Deal

William F. Sater and Holger H. Herwig

Chile may have triumphed over Peru and Bolivia in the War of the Pacific (1879–84) but it was a protracted struggle marked by errors which needlessly consumed the victor's blood and treasure. Surrounded by revanchist neighbors and a hostile Argentina, Chile realized it had to modernize its armed forces if it wished to escape future conflicts. Given its recent success in the Franco-Prussian War, the Moneda—Chile's equivalent to the White House—turned to the Prussian army for assistance. In the mid 1880s, and with the permission of Kaiser William I, the Chilean government hired a General Staff trained artillery officer, Captain Emil Körner, to reform and restructure Santiago's army.

Although a graduate of the Prussian War Academy, and a decorated veteran of the Franco-Prussian War, Körner was nearing the end of his military career. As the son of unaristocratic and middle class Saxon parents, he could not expect to rise to major and hence he would have to retire. The Moneda's offer to train the Chilean army, which included a promotion from captain to lieu-tenant colonel, a salary paid in gold that was twice what he would earn in Germany, and free transportation, seemed far more appealing than skimping by on a captain's pension. Don Emilio did not hesitate: in 1885 he sailed for Chile.

Initially Körner had difficulty overcoming the Chilean officer corps' reluc-tance to institute reforms. In 1891, however, a revolution erupted which changed Chile and Körner. Although the German minister to Chile specifi-cally prohibited Körner from becoming involved in the civil war, he none-theless did, throwing his lot in with the rebels. As a full colonel Körner helped lead the insurgents to victory and a grateful government promoted the Saxon officer to the rank of brigadier general.

Emboldened by his new power, and with many of his former opposition in exile, Körner completely revamped the Chilean army, increasing its size as well changing it into a conscript force, which, in war, could call upon trained reservists to flesh out its ranks. He instituted changes in educating Santiago's officer corps as well as restructuring the army along German lines. Indeed, under his aegis, the Chilean military carried the German Mauser, wore German style uniforms, and goose stepped to German martial airs played on German musical instruments. After viewing the Chilean units pass in review, more than one visiting German army officer declared that he felt as if he had never left Potsdam.

Unfortunately, the reforms proved illusory: the country simply did not have the manpower to staff such a large military; it lacked the funds to purchase the equipment and uniforms that the bigger army required; and the state did not have the infrastructure to support the military or even to manage its reserve components. These flaws became painfully clear in 1920 when a war scare forced the Moneda to mobilize. The results proved a disaster: most of the reservists failed to rally to the colors; those who did found themselves crammed into overcrowded transports, clothed in wretched uniforms, wearing shoes that tortured their feet, housed in squalid barracks, fed rotten food, and often without their weapons.

Not surprisingly, many Chileans wondered why Körner's vaunted reforms had failed. Logic would dictate that a man possessing such vast military knowledge and experience could not have committed so many errors. But he did. Worse, he continued to push for certain changes long after it became clear that they would not work.

Conscription is a prime example. Constructing a draftee-based military was the keystone of Körner's new model army. After 1900 inductees were supposed to provide the manpower to staff the reserves and the various units that don Emilio created. Within a few years, however, even Körner recognized that conscription had failed. Yet he still persisted: he instituted additional reforms, culminating in his omnibus 1906 reorganization, even after it became clear that the restructuring would fail because the army lacked the troops to man the new units and the officers to lead them.

Logically, don Emilio should have aborted his reorganization and instead perhaps concentrated on building a small—but well-armed and trained— purely professional army. But logic was not the only force at work. Körner desperately wished to demonstrate his devotion to Prussia, the same country that, in all likelihood, would not have permitted him to rise past the rank of captain. Denied the possibility of commanding large contingents of German troops, he served instead as the kaiser's auxiliary vanguard, driving the French army out of Chile just as he had driven it into the Paris garrison during the Franco-Prussian War. Those who opened the door to German weapons, technology, and consumer goods also served the fatherland, although clearly not in as exalted a post as the regular army officer. Körner also had a personal agenda: he would guarantee that his children would not have to suffer from the lack of resources that hampered his social and professional advancement. Hence, he would use his position to amass enough money so that he would finally enjoy the same high life as his more aristocratic former brother officers while simultaneously assuring his family's security.

THE KRUPP CONNECTION

Körner's victories from the 1891 Civil War opened Chile to an invasion of German military hardware. Within a few months of the Congressionalist triumph, the German house of Vorwerk & Co. became the official Chilean representative of Ludwig Loewe in Berlin, which in 1886 had acquired the rifle and pistol factory of Wilhelm and Peter Paul Mauser at Oberndorf. Through Vorwerk & Co., Loewe began to pressure Chile to buy Mauser rifles. Mauser was not the only company that would pester the Moneda. Germany's most prominent weapons manufacturer, Friedrich Alfred Krupp of Essen, recognized that it had to sell abroad if it were to overcome the dreadful effects of the "Great Depression" of 1878–90. Thus, Krupp would launch an expansion program that eventually targeted Chile.

Krupp, who became famous for running his business like a feudal lord, personally directed his Essen-based empire. Paradoxically, though he ferociously fought any government interference in his activities, Krupp nonetheless expected Berlin to help advance his economic interest. And he did not hesitate to request its assistance if, and when, it would enhance his profit margin. Krupp even used the Foreign Office's honors list to cultivate foreign dignitaries and told the Military Cabinet whom it should invite to the annual kaiser maneuvers. Krupp, however, was modest: the government was not to reveal that it was his company that had suggested the granting of the award or invitation.[1] The Wilhelmstrasse (that is, the German Foreign Office) could never do enough for the baron of Essen. Krupp routinely complained that the Reich's envoys, with the notable exception of the ambassador to Chile, Felix Baron von Gutschmid, were "too timid" in pushing his products. Berlin's formally clad diplomats, he lamented, refused to attend gunnery trials, which invariably took place on hot, dusty, and distant firing ranges. Nor did they enthusiastically encourage the government to which they were accredited to buy his weapons.

Krupp wisely turned to the army, with whom he shared mutual goals, to further his ends. He would invite to Essen any of those officers who were to be posted abroad to brief them about his company's relations with that nation. He also carefully educated them on the nature of his latest weapons. To facilitate their mission, Krupp provided the officers with formal letters of introduction to its agents. Krupp also developed a complex protocol to cultivate potential customers. The company wined and dined foreign officers and local military attachés. As a later Krupp executive, Arthur Beckmann, recalled, the visits to Essen became a critical part of the firm's sales pitch: "Important foreign delegations are to be picked up at the train station.[2] If need be, [taken] by personal train to Meppen" and housed at the Essener Hof, a first-class hotel. Everything was to be done to placate the visitor: "Gratify," Beckmann instructed, "even the smallest wishes. Much depends on this. Other firms do this as well."

Krupp literally rolled out the red carpet for those foreigners, such as Körner and Jorge Boonen Rivera, who came to Germany to pick up orders. These buyers received the best of treatment: tours of the Rhine, the Harz Mountains, and Berlin. Chilean officers visited Krupp's mansion, the Villa Hügel at Essen-Bredeney, where they dined on Chilean national dishes and consumed its wine. On such occasions, Chilean flags were flown on the grounds of the mansion and were placed at each setting in the dining hall. The national holiday or the president's birthday were formally recognized and the national anthem was played whenever appropriate. On one such occasion in 1910, a South American military commission traveled on Krupp's special train from Essen to Königswinter, near Bonn, where they were treated to a spectacular fireworks display and the surrounding hills were illuminated in their honor. The delegation was then sailed down the Rhine to Koblenz and back to dine in Königswinter.

The giving of gifts supplemented the trips. "Do not be cheap with gift items . . . Small presents maintain friendships!" Guns, clocks, china, lamps, swords, and even artillery pieces were frequently handed out. Krupp awarded monetary grants to the victims of natural disasters, such as the earthquake in Chile, as well as to the widows of foreign government officials who had purchased hardware in Essen. Books, albums, gun and shipmodels, and published manuals and regulations were frequently distributed to foreign academies and museums.[3] However, selling artillery, "the art of the deal" encompassed more than moonlit trips down the Rhine. Once in his velvet clutches, the foreigners were dragooned by Krupp into visiting the firing ranges at Essen, Meppen in Lower Saxony, and Tangerhütte near Magdeburg. The presence of external experts required the firm's approval. Pricing was done solely by Krupp.

The Essen giant naturally employed a large sales force. Krupp selected agents from among civilians of "good but not high status," decent but unobtrusive middlemen. Once abroad, an agent was to nurture contacts with German diplomats, military and naval attachés, and local government ministers; to host foreign dignitaries if they visited Essen; to cultivate the press so it could be used to Krupp's advantage; and to report all changes in government and military personnel. Furthermore, they were expected to act with calm and moderation at all times; to attend and report on the results of gunnery practices of Krupp's competitors; to help the Wilhelmstrasse rewrite attaché reports; and to "exploit political tensions" so as to stimulate weapons sales. The agent, moreover, had to become friendly with local military leaders and to use those contacts to ensure that only officers "sympathetic to Krupp" became involved in the purchasing of arms. The agent was also to engage in industrial espionage to discover what the competition planned to do so Krupp could meet the challenge by sending out "highly competitive equipment." As part of his program to ensure secrecy, an agent who quit Krupp's service immediately had to return all documents, price lists, plans, and materials.[4]

Krupp found one such ideal salesman early in 1889. Albert Schinzinger, the Freiburg-born Württemberg Army Lieutenant of Artillery, had attended the Prussian War School at Metz as well as the Artillery School in Berlin. Krupp had first heard of Schinzinger while traveling in Egypt. Following an exhaustive background check conducted by the Prussian army and the German Foreign Office, Krupp had signed Schinzinger to a personal services contract in May 1889. Henceforth, the officer agreed to work "exclusively and solely for the firm of Krupp and to act according to its directives." Reminiscent of the age of feudalism, the contract bound Schinzinger "to further [Krupp's] interests always with vigor and in good conscience and to the best of your abilities." The agent, moreover, had "to observe total silence" in all matters pertaining to Krupp practices, prices, and materials. The contract was to run for ten years at a salary of 6,000 marks per annum (equal to the pay of a major), and it could be renegotiated upward in case of service overseas.[5]

Schinzinger spent May and June 1889 in Essen, learning Krupp's "art of the deal." Armed with a special "diplomatic pass" procured by Krupp, Schinzinger was enjoined to display "tactful behavior" and to make a "confident impression." He had to familiarize himself with local customs, to learn Spanish, and to "avoid drunkenness." Once overseas, he was to meet military and political leaders as well as the indigenous and German-language press. Newspapers were to be "persuaded" to tout Krupp products and to suppress "unfriendly" reports. "Small gifts can be most helpful here," he was instructed. Additionally, "all wishes of the country in question, including even the smallest," were to be fulfilled. In case Krupp guns were to be displayed or tested, the agent was to make sure that the German ambassador or military attaché was present. Chilean war ministers and generals were to be "invited to a lavish breakfast." And if local soldiers were required for the test firing, they were to be "won over with small presents and promised monetary rewards in the event of a successful demonstration."[6]

Certain rules were to be followed strictly. "Simple, robust material" was never to be offered overseas because this would create the impression that the agent believed "that a complicated weapons system was beyond the capabilities of the limited intelligence of the people." Foreigners wanted only the most recent and the best; they would later have to learn how to operate it on their own. Single pieces were not to be sold because this would encourage foreigners to study and copy the design. Krupp personnel had to attend the testing of each gun. The firm would not repurchase old materiel or take it as trade-in on new guns. Sales were final and FOB Essen. Spare parts could be sent out "with the agent as personal baggage" so as to "avoid customs and import duties." Krupp guns cost more because they included "packaging, freight, insurance, and seasoning of the guns."

If need be, Krupp would help place loans with German banks. But if this proved difficult or impossible, the company would help finance the sale—against "securities" such as national treasury or customs bonds. Late or non-payment of such loans resulted in annual finance charges of 5.5 percent. Last but not least, Schinzinger learned that his sales commissions ranged between 1 and 3 percent. In the case of extremely large orders, they might fall by half. The thorny issue of offering bribes (*Bakschisch*) remained shrouded in secrecy. If Krupp did have to "buy off a potential buyer," Major Beckmann testified, "commissions could climb to 10%."[7]

Unbeknownst to Schinzinger, his main chance already was close at hand. In late 1888 then President José Manuel Balmaceda decided that Chile needed "100 thousand rifles, . . . 100 cannon, 8,000 sabers, and 5,000 carbines." The only outstanding issue was whether Santiago should buy French or German weapons.[8] In fact, Chile did neither: it ultimately purchased the Austrian-made Mannlicher rifle that proved so crucial to the rebel triumph. If the Germans lost out to the Austrians in small arms, they had a chance to recoup the loss by securing a contract to supply Balmaceda with artillery.

Krupp had an advantage in that area. In 1872 it sold Santiago twelve 6cm mountain L/21 artillery pieces and four 7.85cm L/25 field guns at a combined cost of 47,660 thaler.[9] Somewhat more promisingly, in 1879 the Essen firm had provided four 21cm L/22 coastal defense guns for Valparaíso as well as six 7.5cm mountain L/13 guns and eight L/27 field pieces of the same caliber. The following year, during the War of the Pacific, Krupp won another contract for thirty-two of the L /13 mountain guns. Obviously, the Essen company had its foot in the door for any postwar sales, not solely for artillery but also to provide the heavy guns to modernize Chile's coastal defense batteries. Ambassador Felix von Gutschmid at once sensed the magnitude of what was at stake. By April he had already apprised his government that while Balmaceda looked favorably upon Krupp and would welcome its envoy with open arms, the company needed to submit the lowest bid for the Chilean orders. The Foreign Office in Berlin immediately passed the information on to Essen. Gutschmid for all intents and purposes became Krupp's unofficial agent in Chile. In January 1889 the ambassador informed the Wilhelmstrasse that Krupp's main competitor was Col. Charles Ragon de Bange, the designer for Cail et Compagnie, near Paris. De Bange, heavily backed by the Comptoir d'Escompte in the French capital, had recently made a major sale to Serbia. His products were being praised to the heavens and compared favorably to Krupp's by the "Francophiles on the Chilean newspaper *El Ferrocarril*." It was most regrettable, the envoy cabled Berlin, that the Foreign Office did not take a more active role in the Chilean business since Krupp's old agent, Schuchard,

Grisar & Co., seemed unable (or unwilling) to push his interests sufficiently.[10] De Bange was at that very moment shipping two of his 8cm o/77 field guns as well as two mountain pieces to Chile.

Apprised at once of Gutschmid's reports, Krupp laid his plans well. He quickly invited Col. Diego Dublé Almeida to come to inspect his artillery at Essen. Next, Krupp put the Chileans off for months on end with petty excuses, such as the desirability of holding the tests in Essen, while using General Körner to feed Santiago literature that favorably compared his products to those of de Bange. In the meantime, Krupp readied both his newest guns and his special agent for service in Chile.

At the same time, Krupp turned his attention (and that of the Chileans) to the matter of coastal artillery for Valparaíso. Using to its advantage the good offices of General Körner and Maj. Gustav Betzhold, a Prussian officer and Krupp confidant in charge of harbor defenses, Krupp secured the contract for ten 28cm L/40 coastal guns.[11] Although the bids tendered by Schneider-Creuzot in France and Armstrong in Britain had come in under Krupp's price of 3.2 million marks, Krupp won the competition by arranging a loan of 30.6 million marks through the Deutsche Bank and Mendelssohn & Co.[12] In September 1889 Krupp and two or three fellow German producers landed another major contract, this one for 62,000 tons of steel rails for the new Chilean railway.[13] All the while, de Bange's guns languished in a Santiago warehouse.

When he was finally ready, Krupp directed Schinzinger to proceed to Chile with two each of the latest models of the 7.5cm field and mountain guns. Henceforth, the agent was accorded the munificent yearly salary of 15,000 marks (the pay of a Prussian major general) as well as expenses for travel, maintenance, and the cost of opening and operating an office in Valparaíso. Krupp instructed the Foreign Office to grant Schinzinger an audience en route to Chile.[14] Obviously, Krupp appreciated that what was at stake was not just the Chilean artillery order but a chance to extend its influence throughout South America. The *representante de la Casa F. Krupp* found Chile in turmoil upon his arrival. A scurrilous press campaign waged by Krupp's adversaries largely in the *Revista Militar*, the army's unofficial journal, praised the de Bange gun, thus threatening to frustrate Krupp's plans. On 13 February 1890 Ambassador von Gutschmid secured for Schinzinger an audience with President Balmaceda, who expressed his firm expectation (and that of his war minister, Gen. José Velasquez) that the contract would go to Krupp. After all, Balmaceda reminded Schinzinger, Chile had used its earlier purchase of Krupp guns to good advantage in its war against Peru and Bolivia.[15] Still, the president insisted on a competition. Thus, after much wrangling between the French and German embassies it was agreed that the Krupp and de Bange guns should be tested. Having traveled nine thousand kilometers, Schinzinger was determined to land the contract at all cost. On 16 February 1890 he cabled Krupp from Valparaíso, "I have good hopes for our business. I want to kill [*totmachen*] de Bange once and for all." Not even the last-minute threat of the

French ambassador, Henri de Bacourt, that the arms giant Canet might enter the picture deterred Schinzinger: "Have no fear, we will also deal with them."[16]

Two days later, the Chilean government announced that it would test fire the two 7.5cm Krupp guns, designed and produced in 1889, and the two 8cm de Bange cannons, designed in 1877 and produced in 1889. After yet another month of jockeying for advantage that was highlighted by charges of bribery by both sides, the contest was set to begin at dawn on 1 March 1890 under a "searing sun," raising temperatures "between 88° and 90°" Fahrenheit, on a "brown, bleak, and unattractive field" in an arid valley near Batuco, not far from Santiago.[17] It would last for two weeks and prove to be the event of the year. French and German diplomats as well as newspapermen, Chilean ministers and generals, representatives of both armaments firms, and a host of onlookers traveled to the Batuco test grounds. Oftentimes, spectators and roving animals had to be driven from the firing range by warning salvos. Dust and ground fog at times obscured the range.

The Krupp field gun began the contest, firing at a target that measured four by four meters first at a range of one thousand meters, then fifteen hundred, and finally four thousand meters. Suddenly realizing that the Krupp gun was a newer model, the French ambassador on behalf of de Bange inexplicably threatened to withdraw from the competition. Schinzinger protested to Balmaceda on 4 March; the president ordered de Bange either to compete or to withdraw. On 11 March the tests resumed with the mountain guns firing on "cavalry columns." Each weapon fired twenty shells each at three targets fifteen hundred meters away. Krupp's regular shells scored 357 hits to de Bange's 146; using shrapnel, 662 hits to 251. Two days later the tests began anew. Krupp's field artillery scored 1,639 hits to de Bange's 1,389 with regular shells, and 645 to 97 with shrapnel. On average, Krupp guns fired between three and ten times faster than de Bange's. Even worse, the French gun took sixty-two minutes to fire twenty shrapnels and the German only twenty-four. Disastrously, five of de Bange's first nine shrapnels burst in the tube, with the result that Krupp rested its case after firing only ten rounds. A formal inspection of the guns revealed that the French tubes had developed small tears, and the rough powder burned in the calico cartridge bags badly soiled the barrels and seared the packings and seals. Krupp's guns, which fired metal cartridges, passed a white-glove inspection by the Chilean Artillery Testing Commission. While Krupp supporters began openly to celebrate with *chicha*, Gen. José Francisco Gana, the head of the commission, chastised those Chilean officers who still openly sympathized with de Bange: "Those officers who refuse to recognize the superiority of the Krupp guns after this test firing display a lack of patriotism." On 17 March the Commission voted unanimously for Krupp.[18] William II, who assiduously read each of Gutschmid's communications and covered them with personal comments, was immediately apprised of the results. The kaiser later cabled his "heartiest congratulations" to Krupp.[19]

On 20 March 1890, when Schinzinger informed Krupp of the results, he could hardly contain his joy: "Today I am so happy to be able to report to you not only about a tough fight but also about a great victory. I have managed, thanks to your superb gun, to destroy de Bange once and for all." De Bange's "fate had been sealed from the moment that he agreed to the test." Both France's ambassador and its military had been "embarrassed." The crowds, composed mostly of "the mixed races of South America," had been wholly on the side of the French. "Our victories were received with resignation; the French defeats were glossed over." At times, the crowds and the press had become "ugly." "Thus, I became uglier and accosted them with great energy according to the motto *noli me tangere.*" Not without hubris, Schinzinger immodestly requested that Krupp have him promoted to the rank of captain to enhance his effectiveness as a salesman, a wish that William II readily granted.[20]

Within a month of the competition, Schinzinger signed a 1.6-million-marks contract to buy eighty-two 7.5cm Krupp pieces (six batteries of field guns and eight of mountain) as well as twenty-five thousand shells.[21] Though thanking the Wilhelmstrasse for its support, Krupp admonished Berlin to stand behind his agents elsewhere. In August 1890 Krupp granted Schinzinger a "gratuity" of 10,000 marks for his services. De Bange tried through the French embassy in Santiago to get "compensation" for having lost the contract, arguing that his guns had been two years older. But the new Chilean war minister, General Gana, who had presided over the Artillery Testing Commission, predictably refused even to answer the request.[22] Throughout this period Ambassador von Gutschmid had supplied Krupp with confidential Chilean telegrams via the German Foreign Office. He now basked in the radiance of his personal success. His only disappointment was that the Chilean navy continued to buy British, not German, warships.

The 1890 artillery contract opened the flood gates for Krupp. Saying "Körner is the hero of the day," Schinzinger used his ties to don Emilio to great advantage and spent 1891 cultivating relations with Chilean ministers and generals and visiting artillery garrisons. Commanders of the latter readily provided him with testimonials to the quality of the Krupp guns, which Schinzinger then had published in the Chilean press. Krupp's *representante* knew how to win friends and influence people: "I have discerned that we can engage these people with very little money." If Krupp would but spend 1,000 marks to buy "new uniforms and swords for 20 members of the officer corps," this would result in additional sales. General Körner thought the idea "delightful."[23]

Schinzinger was right on the mark. In January 1892, following a "splendid reception" first at the War Ministry and then at the presidential palace, he landed yet another contract to provide two 28cm coastal guns, two 28cm howitzers, four batteries of 8.7cm howitzers, and a large quantity of ammunition. Once again, the French firm of Canet had tried to challenge Krupp's monopoly. And once again, Schinzinger had been Johnny-on-the-spot. "I put an end to that!" he boasted.[24] Schinzinger never rested. First, he sold six batteries of Krupp field artillery to Buenos Aires. Then he encouraged Ambassador von Gutschmid to warn the Moneda that "Argentina's warlike preparations were directed against Chile."[25] Obviously, he wanted the Moneda to buy more weapons, which he would then use to encourage Buenos Aires to do the same. Schinzinger had clearly perfected the art of the deal.

Valparaíso fairly hummed with German deliveries throughout the decade of the 1890s. The port's customs receipts soared from $19.4 million in 1881 to $39.7 million in 1891 and then to $72 million by 1901.[26] The Hamburg steamship line Kosmos, partly owned by Vorwerk & Co., obtained an exclusive contract to deliver all arms shipments to Chile. German technicians arrived in droves to service the new weaponry and to instruct the Chileans in its use and care. Körner entrusted the inspection and acceptance of the Krupp guns to his closest associate, Col. Boonen Rivera. Ambassador von Gutschmid made sure that the Wilhelmstrasse on each occasion guaranteed the colonel a cordial reception in Essen. Indeed, in September 1892 Boonen Rivera, Gen. Estanislao del Canto, and Col. Florencio Baeza were wined and dined at the Villa Hügel, where the Chileans laid a wreath at the memorial to the firm's founder, Friedrich Krupp.[27]

The only snag in the arms trade was that the Chileans almost botched the unloading of the heavy coastal guns at Valparaíso. In July 1892, for example, the Kosmos steamer *Spartan* arrived with seven 28cm coastal guns as well as eight batteries of 7.5cm mountain cannons. Each coastal gun cost 297,000 marks and weighed forty-three tons. While the first cannon was unloading, the chain of the Chilean steam crane broke, and the gun fell down the ship's cargo hatch, failing to pierce its steel hull only because the *Spartan* carried a heavy layer of sand ballast. Gutschmid noted with malicious delight that Chilean authorities, who had been too proud to accept offers of assistance from both Krupp and Major Betzhold, could not even unload a ship.[28]

That notwithstanding, Chilean orders continued to rain down on Krupp. According to Krupp's records, Santiago paid 6.5 million marks for 48 guns in 1890, 36 in 1894, 102 in 1895, and 136 in 1898.[29] Schinzinger, who as first lieutenant would have earned 200 marks per month, continued to collect his annual salary of 15,000 as well as 60 marks per diem, travel costs, and "representation and other expenses"—and, of course, his sales commission ("gratification"). Krupp recorded the latter as 10,000 marks in 1890 and 12,500 in 1892. "Other expenses" in those two years came to 99,323 marks.

These vast amounts could only have been spent for one purpose: *Bakschisch*. Though Krupp records do not contain a category for bribes, they do include one for "travel," and it was beneath that rubric that the Essen company buried the *representante*'s "hidden expenses." During Schinzinger's first trip, these outlays had amounted to 6,186.29 marks from 19 June to 10 August and 12,322.37 from 11 August to 4 December 1889. For the following year, these outlays totaled 8,192.55 marks to 2 February, 14,520.78 in April, and 12,934.65 in July. To the penny, Krupp recorded a total "travel bill" of 54,138.64 marks.[30] Given that first-class passage from Europe to Valparaíso cost about 1,000 marks (£55), in one year Schinzinger would have to have undertaken fifty-four transatlantic passages to consume this amount of money! (It would also have required him to spend the entire time at sea.)

The 1889 "travel bill" was neither an isolated nor an abnormal expense. In a secret personal memorandum just before the turn of the century, Friedrich Alfred Krupp calculated Schinzinger's "other expenses," apart from salary, "travel," per diem, and representation, for his activity in Chile. Once again, this could only have been for additional *Bakschisch:*

1889–90 = 7,000 marks

1890–91 = 20,000

1891–92 = 140,000

1892–93 = 300

1893–94 = 2,300

1894–95 = 4,700

1895–96 = 64,000

1896–97 = 34,000

The "travel" expenses of 140,000 marks in 1891–92 alone would have required Schinzinger to undertake 140 trips to Chile in twelve months![31] By combining Schinzinger's "travel bill" of 54,000 marks for 1889–90 with his "other expenses" of 20,000 for 1890–91 and 140,000 for 1891–92, there is little question that Krupp spent roughly 214,000 marks in just over two years to land the Chilean artillery contract.

Krupp's lucrative business with Santiago prospered even after Schinzinger moved on to Montevideo and Buenos Aires late in 1892. Happily for the German arms manufacturer, don Emilio took up the slack. In accordance with standard Krupp business practice—"to exploit political tensions to propagandize for the procurement of war materials"—the general repeatedly spread rumors of war with Argentina, which invariably resulted in the purchase of new equipment by Santiago. For example, in September 1895, at the height of a particularly dangerous crisis in Argentine-Chilean relations, Körner personally negotiated for Santiago a 3.75-million-mark order with Krupp for forty-eight heavy and thirty light mountain cannons, twenty-four rapid-fire field guns, and fifty thousand shells. And though Krupp, as usual, submitted the highest bid, he received the contract largely because the Deutsche Bank assumed one-quarter (20 million marks) of a mammoth Chilean loan negotiated with Rothschild & Sons in London. Körner had become Krupp's agent at Santiago after the Essen giant had severed ties with Schuchard, Grisar & Co., in January 1894 because it suspected that firm of having "cooked the books" to the tune of 2.45 million marks.[32] If he received just the lowest sales commission of 1 percent, Körner would have realized the tidy sum of 37,500 marks in a single transaction, seven times his annual salary.

Again, in 1901, when an alleged Argentine violation of Chilean territory led to yet another international crisis, Krupp and Körner combined forces to convince Chile to purchase more artillery. At Körner's urging, Santiago rejected the bids from France's Canet, Sweden's Bofors, and Austria's Škoda for state-of-the-art guns that possessed a pneumatic recoil mechanism and were 25 to 50 percent cheaper than Krupp's less technologically advanced products. Instead, in December Chile bought seventy-three field and mountain guns plus ammunition from Krupp at a cost of 2.1 million marks. To sweeten the deal, Krupp had offered Chile a 3 percent discount in case additional orders surpassed 5.9 million marks. And abandoning for once its own rules, the firm had agreed to purchase some of its older guns, at, of course, bargain prices. The French embassy in Santiago caustically noted how Körner's personal fortune had grown.[33]

THE TRIUMPH OF MAUSER

Körner also used his power to ensure that, in addition to artillery, Chile also purchased its small arms from German manufacturers. Typical of this policy was his decision in the early 1890s to replace the army's approximately fifty thousand nearly new Austrian-made Mannlicher rifles.[34] Körner's desire to buy the Mausers seems inexplicable because it was the Austrian Mannlichers, captured from the Balmacedistas, that brought the Congressionalists their 1891 victory. Indeed, the Saxon officer had even praised the Austrian weapon to a *New York Herald* reporter in September 1891: "I consider the rifle the best made to date. . . . Its only fault—a weakness in the small springs of the breech—is easily remedied. . . . Its range and trajectory are unequaled." The Mannlicher was easy to operate, "there being but one motion in loading," and thus it could be "easily handled by inexperienced recruits." There was an additional advantage not apparent in peacetime: the Mannlicher was "a humane weapon owing to the absence of jagged and spreading wounds." The bullet, in other words, did not shatter on impact with bone but rather cut "a clean passage like a hole bored by a sharp tool." Surgeons found Mannlicher-inflicted wounds "easy to cure." Körner's Chilean protégé, Col. Boonen Rivera, also strongly endorsed the Austrian rifle.[35] Now, after less than five years, the Chilean army planned to discard the Mannlichers.

Körner's determination only makes sense when one sees it as part of a wider plan to manipulate international tensions for the benefit of German weapons procurers. In 1892 Peru placed an order for Mauser rifles. In the same year,

Buenos Aires announced that it too would purchase from Ludwig Loewe one hundred thousand rifles and twenty thousand carbines as well as twenty-five million bullets. Since the Argentine army numbered less than sixty-five hundred officers and men, the enormity of the acquisition indicated to Santiago that its neighbor's armed forces were planning on expanding.

Krupp's unseen but heavy hand soon made itself felt. Chile would never have learned of the Argentine order except that Schinzinger, Krupp's man on the spot, had "secretly" told Boonen Rivera, then Chile's military attaché in Berlin, what Buenos Aires planned to do. As if to confirm the story, Loewe generously took the colonel through its new plant at Martinickfelde, where he saw the Mausers, complete with the Argentine crest, awaiting delivery.[36] Körner, who as chief of the General Staff was also a department head in the War Ministry, quickly followed up. At a meeting of senior Chilean cabinet ministers and generals on 23 November 1894, he suggested to President Jorge Montt that Santiago immediately buy fifty thousand rifles and twenty thousand carbines from Ludwig Loewe. Moreover, Körner convinced Montt to send him to Europe as vice president of the Chilean Arms Purchases Commission, headquartered in Paris, and to create a special commission, headed by General del Canto and Colonels Boonen Rivera and Baeza, to supervise the weapons purchase.

But as much as Körner and Boonen Rivera might yearn for the Mausers, they ran into a roadblock. As a precondition for its order, Loewe had promised Buenos Aires that it would not sell its rifles to any other Latin American nation, "*especially Chile*" for a period of five years.[37] Hence, the Moneda was out of luck; its soldiers would have to do their killing with any weapon but the Mauser.

Fortunately for Santiago, Berlin-based Ludwig Loewe, which in 1896 reconstituted itself as the Deutsche Waffen- und Munitionsfabriken AG (DW & MF, or German Weapons and Munitions Factories), was not the only game in town. Desperate to compete with the Berlin giant, the Fabrique Nationale d'Armes de Guerre in Herstal, Belgium, tendered bids of 68 francs for each of its rifles and 135 francs per one thousand rounds. Not to be outdone, August Schriever, the agent for the Österreichische Waffenfabriks-Gesellschaft (ÖWG) at Steyr, promised to deliver its M90 Mannlichers in just five months and to spread the payments over two years.[38] When it came to purchasing rifles, it was clearly a buyer's market, and the Moneda held all the cards.

Then a strange thing occurred. An unexpected economic downturn prevented Buenos Aires from paying for the weapons in a timely manner. Schinzinger immediately leaked this news to the Moneda, urging it to quickly buy as many weapons as it could while Mauser's promise not to sell to Chile was no longer binding. Eventually, the Argentines managed to come up with enough money to buy 35,000 rifles, thereby reinstating the original prohibition against selling to Chile. By then, however, it was too late: since their ban took effect only as of 1 October 1892, Santiago had taken advantage of the small two- to three-month window of opportunity to acquire the Mausers.

General del Canto favored purchasing either a French or Belgian weapon, the Marga, or the 6.5mm Mannlicher, particularly because Steyr offered better terms and a shorter delivery time. He was therefore not so impressed with Schinzinger's warnings. Del Canto became so adamant that he even threatened to expose the procurement process, particularly the fact that there was no public bidding and the Mauser was a flawed weapon. In response to this charge, the DW & MF lowered the purchase price on its M/91 rifle with bayonet to a unit price of 77 francs and ammunition to 155 francs per one thousand rounds. It, moreover, guaranteed delivery in seven months. This price was still 7 francs higher than Herstal's. Two days later, Schriever countered with a unit price of 69 francs for the Steyr Mannlichers. For a brief moment the offices of the Chilean Commission in Paris became a Middle East bazaar.

Like Krupp, the DW & MF became so fixated on cornering the Chilean market that it began to use illegal practices to win the order. Director General Alexis Riese informed the Chileans that his firm was about to market a new, more modern rifle, the M/93, that made the M/91 and its competition obsolete. He added that his company would sue Herstal for patent violations if the Belgian firm tried to produce its own version of the M/93. Fearing that buying from Herstal might lead to a lawsuit over patent infringement and thus delay shipment, Augusto Matte Perez, head of the Military Committee, purchased the 7mm Mauser from the DW & MF in Berlin. Del Canto continued to argue that the Mauser had serious flaws, but it was too late. Pushed by Körner, Santiago awarded the DW & MF a 3.2-million-marks contract for 50,000 Mauser rifles and 10,000 carbines. The Austrians had to content themselves with an order for 54 million Mauser (7.65mm) and 8 million Mannlicher (8mm) bullets. It would be their last direct order from Chile.[39]

The Moneda, of course, had been gulled. A Chilean diplomat conceded that Schinzinger, without outright "lying," "might have exaggerated or manipulated somewhat the history of these events [so that] we would sign a contract with Lobel [sic] for a considerable amount of weapons before the deadline of 1 October."[40] Körner, of course, denied that he had allowed his close friendship with the manager of DW & MF, or his own German roots, to influence him when he successfully insisted that the Chileans exchange their Mannlichers for the Mausers.

The DW & MF had conquered the Chilean market. Isidor Loewe's factories ran around the clock to fill the vast orders from Argentina, Brazil, and Chile. While its competitors' profits declined, in 1894 Loewe returned a phenomenal 24 percent on its investment. In July 1895 the Berlin firm received a second Chilean order for twenty thousand Mauser rifles and ten thousand carbines and in September a third for ten thousand rifles. The two orders came to 2.04 million francs. In each case, Loewe had used the threat of a patent fight over the M/93 rifle to undermine Herstal. Using the Chilean profits, Loewe gained control over the Fabrique Nationale d'Armes de Guerre in 1896 after a lengthy and costly patent-violation suit concerning the Mauser M/91 and M/93 rifles.[41] As mentioned, that same year Isidor Loewe formally changed his company's name to the Deutsche Waffen- und Munitionsfabriken.

In 1897 the DW & MF secured a Chilean contract for sixty million Mauser bullets. The following year, it initiated design changes in its Mauser rifle and ammunition that led to additional orders both at home and abroad. After extensive experimentation by the DW & MF and the Prussian Rifle Testing Commission, the Reich's armed forces adopted the new "Rifle 98" in April 1898, which would become the German army's standard infantry weapon for the next fifty years.[42] Shortly thereafter, DW & MF also developed a new flat-trajectory S (Sharp) bullet, that allowed the infantry greater accuracy.

In 1901, to seduce the Chileans into purchasing the new Mauser M/98, the DW & MF invited both General Körner and Ramón Subercaseaux, the Chilean envoy to Berlin, to examine its supposedly secret order books, where, coincidentally, they quickly spied another mammoth Argentine order. Convinced of the immediate need for more and newer arms, Körner and Subercaseaux signed a contract for Mauser rifles valued at 3.8 million marks. The Chilean envoy balked at buying Maxim machine guns from the DW & MF, however, arguing that Škoda in Pilsen offered the rival French Hotchkiss weapon at half the price (4,500 francs). In fact, Santiago had already purchased sixty Hotchkiss guns during Körner's extended absence in Europe. Additionally, Subercaseaux advised his government to sidestep armaments agents (such as Schinzinger) because their services raised prices between 10 and 50 percent. But Körner would not be denied. In 1899 Körner heard rumors that the Swiss army had not been satisfied with the performance of the Hotchkiss. Through Director General Riese of the DW & MF Körner therefore mobilized the Foreign Office in Berlin, the German embassy in Bern, and the Prussian War Ministry to obtain these "negative results," which he then immediately delivered to Subercaseaux. Sufficiently intimidated, the diplomat agreed to give the DW & MF an initial order for one hundred Maxim machine guns.[43] Subercaseaux's role in subsequent negotiations was limited to signing the agreements that Körner personally negotiated with the DW & MF and with Krupp.

THE ARTILLERY DUELS

The Mauser deal was only the first phase in a massive Chilean rearmament program. Santiago would require additional weapons and equipment. Aware of the high economic potential, Germany's rivals also wanted a piece of the Chilean pie. Austria-Hungary, for example, became a player. In 1902 the Habsburg Monarchy had upgraded its legation at Santiago to the status of an embassy. Four years later, the dynamic Carl Baron von Giskra moved from Washington, D.C. to take up his post at Santiago. One of the ambassador's first acts in office in June 1906 was to approach President Pedro Montt and his cabinet with a list of potential arms merchants. It included the Imperial and Royal Shipyard at Pola and the Stabilimento Tecnico at Trieste for warships; the Whitehead Factory at Fiume for torpedoes; Škoda at Pilsen for artillery; and Bros. Böhler, Roth as well as the state Powder Monopoly Administration at Vienna for rifles, pistols, and ammunition.

Giskra deemed prospects for orders "unlikely" in the face of expected competition from France and Germany, "whose industries are incredibly well capitalized and use any and all means to reach their goals." Still, in a "confidential" note he encouraged his government to enter into the forthcoming competition by inviting the Chilean Military Mission to visit Vienna and Pilsen.[44] Giskra informed the Foreign Office at the Ballhausplatz that the best chances "for our industry to acquire a market for war materials" were in a new war between Chile and Peru. Throughout the fall of 1906, the envoy bombarded Vienna with requests to send Škoda guns for testing in Chile and train its officers in Bosnia and in the Tyrol.[45]

In one of his last communiqués from Santiago, Giskra explained why he had not managed to penetrate the Chilean market. First, the Austro-Hungarian companies would not cooperate: Škoda did not even have an illustrated catalog to send to Santiago. The second problem was less amenable to solution: "the omnipotent General" Körner, while denying the fact, had consistently "given his vote to German goods."[46] Indeed, Giskra had no love for Körner. According to Giskra, the general, "a national, albeit faithless, Chilean hero," was "no friend of our industry," given his "great sympathies for Germany." Vienna's envoy reminded the Ballhausplatz that Körner had conveniently forgotten that he never would have won the civil war "without the 30,000 [sic] Mannlicher rifles that we delivered to him speedily and absolutely without reliable credit" in 1891. (Giskra himself conveniently forgot that Vienna deserved no credit whatsoever. The Congressionalists had captured the weapons, which the Austrians had sold to Balmaceda). The ambassador warned Vienna "confidentially" to deal carefully with don Emilio, whose "flighty and erratic" way of "speaking in circles" should not be confused with kindness or joviality.[47]

The matter of arms sales became urgent in January 1907 when Giskra's successor, Johann Baron von Styrcea, discovered that through the Hamburg firm of Gleissner & Co. Chile had sold its stock of twenty-eight thousand Mannlicher M88 rifles and 11.2 million rounds for 1 million francs to Bulgaria and its 206 Krupp M95 and M98 mountain guns to Turkey. If Austria-Hungary believed that Chile would use the money generated by these sales to purchase new weapons it also had to recognize an unpleasant fact: German manufacturers enjoyed a "quasi-monopoly position" in Chile and would do everything in their power to maintain that position. Yet he discerned subtle signs that the Reich's once preeminent role in Chile "has for quite some time been in the process of eroding." In particular, War Minister Ramón Antonio Vergara was anxious "gradually to emancipate the Chilean army from the purely Prussian direction in which General Körner had taken it."[48] Hence, the ambassador pressed the Ballhausplatz to invite the Chilean Military Mission in Berlin to visit Pilsen and Steyr. In June 1907 Cols. José María Bari and Tobías Barros Merino toured the Škoda Works at Pilsen, where they tested the firm's mountain and field artillery. In August Gen. Vicente Palacios Baeze, the new head of the Chilean mission, inspected 28cm and 30.5cm coastal guns at Pilsen.[49] Other members of the mission followed in their path. At Vienna, the Chileans discovered that the Habsburg army's Technical-Military Committee knew neither the prices nor the delivery schedules for Škoda guns; in fact, they were utterly unaware of such basic technical information as their accuracy or rate of fire.[50]

Inexplicably, both the Ballhausplatz and Škoda blithely ignored the fact that the mission included a potential spy: Gen. Emil Körner. Don Emilio first carefully assessed Škoda's inventory and then coolly approached the Foreign Office and War Ministry in Vienna to obtain the firm's price lists and delivery schedules.[51] He then immediately passed on this confidential information to Krupp to use it as it would. As a final piece of cheek, Körner had the War Ministry in Vienna forward him Steyr's prices for Mauser rifles and Hotchkiss machine guns—which undoubtedly landed on the desk of the DW & MF in Berlin.[52] Körner, taking advantage of his position, served the interests of Germany more than those of Chile.

In fact, even before the Chileans had arrived at Pilsen, the DW & MF had received word of the Austrian interest in Chile "from a member of the Chilean Military Mission here in Berlin," by which the firm could only have meant Körner. Its new director general, Max Kosegarten, at once apprised the Wilhelmstrasse of the "pressure" that Habsburg diplomats in Chile were "mounting in favor of Austro-Hungarian industry." More, the DW & MF reminded the Foreign Office that it had to date supplied Chile with all its needs ("Mauser rifles, bullets for them, machine guns, materials for a powder factory"), demanded that Berlin preclude "a change of mind" in Santiago, and requested that it "respectfully instruct" its envoy in Santiago "to lobby on behalf of German industry." Within forty-eight hours, the Wilhelmstrasse admonished its new ambassador, Hans Baron von und zu Bodman, "to work on behalf of German industry." Bodman immediately raised the matter with the Chilean government, which instructed its mission "accordingly."[53]

Bodman was fully alert to the gravity of the situation. In January 1908 he dispatched Legation Secretary Hanno Count von Welczek to survey potential Chilean military needs. Welczek had married a daughter of the former president Balmaceda and thus had excellent contacts not only to Montt's government but to Chile's opposition parties. And Welczek, like Körner, was an investor in the German-South American Mining and Land Syndicate at Berlin. Welczek, like the Austrian ambassador von Styrcea before him, noted that don Emilio's "influence is more and more on the wane."[54] Still, Berlin had another ace in the hole: "the younger generation of Chilean officers trained in the German system" had become the Reich's apostles. Welczek honestly believed that "German military training had changed the [Chilean] national character" and that the subalterns, in conjunction with the German tailors, blacksmiths, mechanics, and artificers working in Chile, could be expected to toil ceaselessly on behalf of German industry.

In July 1908 Ambassador von und zu Bodman sent Chancellor Bernhard von Bülow a lengthy shopping list of the munitions Santiago could be expected to order in the next four or five years. Chile would require mountain and field guns amounting to between £1.2 and £1.4 million (25 million marks) in value. Although one could expect that "simply on the basis of gratitude, German industry would be given a monopoly over these orders," the intervention of Chilean officers from the "old school" once again forced the government to call for competitive bids and firing tests. The latter were to be held in the fall of that year at a new artillery range near Cartagena. The competition was expected to be fierce given the magnitude of the orders at stake. Apart from Krupp, the Chilean government had invited Škoda, Heinrich Ehrhardt's Rheinische Metallwaren- und Maschinenfabrik (Rheinmetall) at Düsseldorf, Bofors of Sweden, Vickers-Sheffield and Armstrong-Newcastle of Britain, and Schneider-Creuzot of France to compete. At the request of Škoda and Schneider, the tests were postponed until April 1909.[55] In the meantime, at the urging of its embassy attaché Johann Count Kolowrat-Krakowsky-Liebstensky, Austria dispatched a high-powered mission to Chile to lobby on behalf of its armaments firms. It was headed by Franz Prince Windisch-Graetz, the scion of an august Austrian noble clan, as well as Director Robert Hochstetter of the Škoda works at Pilsen.[56]

MAUSER VERSUS STEYR

Before the artillery tests took place, however, a titanic struggle erupted over Chile's decision to purchase parts to modernize its 1895 Mausers. Specifically, in 1910 Santiago decided to acquire some sights and new barrels to accommodate the newly designed S bullet. This seemingly unimportant and purely technical decision would replicate the German-Austrian competition of the early 1890s. This time, however, Germany could not act as aggressively as it had in the past: Berlin's precarious diplomatic position in Europe, where it had but one reliable ally, Vienna, forced the new ambassador, Friedrich Carl von Erckert, to acknowledge that an "attack through official channels would not be easy."[57] The Germans would have to stop the Austrians without confrontation.

Perhaps chastened by the Bohler and Škoda artillery debacle, Austria-Hungary was determined to lend full support to its arms merchants for future

Chilean orders. In the fall of 1910, Prince Windisch-Graetz arrived in Central and South America as a "special delegate" to drum up exports for Austrian industry during Chile's centenary celebrations. The prince sailed up and down the coast of Chile in the steamer *Sisak* in September and October 1910 and again in January and February 1911. His travel costs of well over 50,000 Kronen (or pesos) were split by the government and such interested firms as Hirtenberg, Škoda, and the ÖWG. Concurrently, the Vienna Board of Trade financed a special mission by Leo Königstein to Valparaíso.[58]

Prince Windisch-Graetz was not overly optimistic about Austria's chances of penetrating the Chilean market. He reported that German merchants (Folsch, Weber, Gyldemeister, Vorwerk) operating out of Valparaíso controlled almost three-quarters of the country's foreign trade. Austria-Hungary, moreover, lacked a shipping line connecting Trieste to Valparaíso, thereby impairing the development of Austro-Chilean trade. And finally, the German-owned banks, particularly the Banco aleman transatlántico, aggressively worked "against our modest attempts to expand" trade.[59]

Nevertheless, using his princely status to full effect, "Francisco" Windisch-Graetz managed to gain entrée to the Chilean president and his cabinet. We do not know how successful he was at managing to ingratiate himself and his nation. Certainly, he faced an implacable foe. Earlier, the prince had attended the annual spring parade of the cadet corps in Berlin. Among the various foreign military dignitaries on the reviewing stand next to Kaiser William II was none other than Gen. Emil Körner, "a man who draws a regular pension from Krupp, Essen."[60] Although aware of the difficulties facing them, the Austrians were willing to give it a try.

In 1909–10 Chile's Comisión Militar, now based in Berlin, opened bids on contracts to provide twenty thousand rifle stocks, twenty-six thousand rifle barrels, and thirty thousand rifle sights to modernize its Mauser rifles and carbines from the 1890s. The awards went to the ÖWG at Steyr—backed by the Wiener-Bank-Verein—and not, as expected, to the DW & MF in Berlin. This was a surprise, particularly to the Germans, who had expected that the DW & MF would, as usual, triumph. The German ambassador, Erckert, protested "even this relatively small order for army materials" to Chilean war minister Ramón Leon Luco.[61] He also cabled the Wilhelmstrasse to "agitate energetically" against the Austro-Hungarian orders and assured Berlin that they could be rescinded by Santiago if sufficient pressure were brought to bear: "Government inclined, if at all possible, to annul; thereby larger orders secured for deutsche Waffen Munitionsfabrik [sic] Berlin."[62]

Within twenty-four hours of Erckert's cable, Director Kosegarten of the DW & MF appeared at the Wilhelmstrasse, imploring the German diplomats to lobby on behalf of his company. The Foreign Office, while convincing Kosegarten that it could not simply "annul" a Chilean order, immediately secured an audience for him with Ambassador Matte and Gen. Arístides Pinto Concha. Both Chileans assured Kosegarten that the DW & MF "would be given full consideration in future deliveries." Germany's principal Chilean paladin, General Boonen Rivera, vociferously opposed this decision, arguing that the Austrian barrels could not be used interchangeably with the Mauser.[63] When his protests failed to stop the deal, the Germans would resort to other, less genteel methods.

In mid-1911, after examining the Austrian spare parts local Chilean ordnance officials concluded that 82 percent of the rifle barrels and 50 percent of the carbine barrels were "of such poor quality that they were considered totally useless."[64] Similar problems afflicted the bolts, firing pins, and locks. When Steyr protested the findings, the Dirección del Material convened a committee that conducted various tests and confirmed the barrel's flaws.

The Santiago authorities became livid. General Boonen Rivera attacked those officers stationed in Berlin for permitting an act that "defrauds the state [and] seriously endangers the Republic's security." *El Mercurio* demanded to know the party responsible for such egregious errors. Boonen Rivera carefully nurtured the feelings of outrage. Assisted by General Bari, he planted several articles in *El Mercurio* that argued that the government had squandered a million pesos on Steyr's defective rifle barrels, sights, and stocks. The ÖWG immediately responded: just as Erckert had furthered the interests of the DW & MF in Chile, it appealed to Foreign Minister Alois Lexa Count von Aehrenthal to encourage the Austrian ambassador von Styrcea to work in its behalf.[65] And it rushed a special gift of hunting rifles and pistols to President Barros Luco in hopes of pacifying the powers that be.

In early October the minister of war demanded that the chief of the Military Mission explain its actions while the pro-German General Boonen Rivera pressed his advantage, accusing the committee of failing to fulfill its responsibility. The press and the legislature quickly followed suit, clamoring to know how an error that cost 572,000 marks could occur. Gen. Roberto Silva Renard, the former head of the Military Commission, which had authorized purchasing the Steyr parts, responded to these charges by demanding a court of honor to clear his name.[66]

Perhaps the only one more upset was the house of Steyr, which joined with those legislators calling for more tests. Assisted by an Austrian arms agent at Valparaíso, Arturo Medina, Styrcea demanded that Santiago create a special military commission to investigate Boonen Rivera's charges. To keep them honest, two senior Steyr engineers, Maximilian Rechl and Hugo Lipowsky, who were then touring South America, rushed from Lima to Santiago, where on 11 November they began to test the Steyr barrels. In early December Rechl reported that having just safely fired four thousand rounds from numerous randomly selected rifles, the barrels were first-rate; the fault lay not in the barrels but in the tests' methodology. Lacking Nobel powder, the original committee had improvised and produced an explosive that exerted so much pressure on the barrels that they were twisted out of shape.

For Chilean army officials, the claims that the Steyr parts were unsuitable were the result of a "mistake" made by "incompetent technical personnel" using "unsuitable" powder, which had caused "unreal pressure" in the rifle barrels. Former Minister of War Alejandro Huneeus was more blunt. It was not a simple accident; the Comisión de Guerra and the Test Committee had deliberately sabotaged Steyr in order to give the parts contract to DW & MF. The journalist Joaquín Díaz Garcés went one step further, singling out two former Deutsche Waffen employees then employed by the Fábrica de Cartuchos for providing the defective powder.[67]

But while the barrels that Steyr fabricated were sound, the stocks could not accommodate the new Mauser housings. The army had to retool the rifles. This problem arose because the contract had not stipulated that Steyr produce barrels that could be used interchangeably with existing parts. Nor, apparently, did Santiago send the correct specifications or model. Thus, the minister of war had to contract with Steyr to supervise these modifications and then train Chilean technicians to perform these tasks at the Santiago arsenal.

The Steyr dispute both damaged some officers' reputations and called into question the army's technical services. Some of the press flayed General Boonen Rivera for failing to prevent the fiasco, for blaming his comrades when it occurred, and, finally, for not apologizing once it became clear that the Military Commission had acted appropriately. Boonen Rivera, who always claimed he acted out of the purest motives, initially refused to discuss matters of national security in the press. This excuse wore thin when the press revealed that while the good general refused to talk to them he happily repeated his libelous charges to anyone he meet in the Club de la Unión. Eventually, Boonen had to backtrack: he publicly stated that he had never meant to criticize his fellow officers who composed the Comisión Militar and he had intended to direct his hostile remarks to Steyr, whom he would also blame for the parts' lack of interchangeability. (This was not the first time that Boonen Rivera's mouth had caused him problems. Because of his public clash with the president in 1904 over the accelerated promotion of a major he was confined to barracks).[68]

Someone, besides General Boonen Rivera, of course, had to bear the onus for these failures. Rather than punish the pro-German elements who had tried to sabotage the purchase, the Comisión Militar became the scapegoat. Huneeus disbanded the organization, transferring the authority to make future arms purchases to the Chilean diplomatic envoy accredited to each European capital. The minister of war categorically denied that there was "any political motive as some newspaper has maliciously insinuated." Rather, good public administration had dictated the changes: the Comisión had become too independent and often acted without consulting the local diplomats.[69] Of course, it also meant that those with ties to the German-Chilean nexus would make sure that, in future, a trained professional officer would not apply technical standards to the purchase of weapons.

The Steyr debacle opened a debate on how Chile acquired weapons. To externalize the enemy, and thus perhaps exculpate if not exonerate the local oligarchy and the army, one journalist argued that a group of "skilled Hebrews" had deliberately fabricated a war scare with Peru in order to sell Chile military equipment. Critics may not have been referring to Chile's local Jewish community, which numbered but ninety souls out of a total population of 3.2 million, but to their foreign coreligionists. The fact that Steyr, Krupp, and Mauser were, in the term to be used by future purists, "Aryan" firms seemed immaterial. Chile had become the victim of an international conspiracy in which foreign salesmen, many with "Jewish noses," haunted government offices and suborned officials into signing contracts for shoddy but expensive war material. According to the press, these forces had bought the services of cabinet ministers, legislators, and even high-ranking army officers so they knew of the government's intentions even before Chile's diplomatic and military representatives. "The commercial houses that direct our government," one paper wrote, "have . . . demonstrated the power of their influence" by deliberately engineering the disbanding of the Military Commission because its members did their job so well that they threatened the arms manufacturers' profits. Thus, the lickspittles profited while those who did not cooperate suffered "destitution or dishonor."[70]

Conspiracy buffs soon had other reasons for concern. In 1910 the Chilean army, apparently in response to increased tensions with Peru, decided it needed thirty thousand rifles and four thousand carbines, plus some thirty million rounds of ammunition. Santiago agreed to leave this decision to General Pinto Concha, who headed the Comisión Militar in Berlin. Vienna's ambassador, Styrcea, was delighted. "Therein, I detect a good omen, since at the moment the mood in the Military Commission . . . is friendly toward our industry."[71]

To head off possible German intervention on behalf of the DW & MF, the Austrian government sent Prince Windisch-Graetz to Berlin. Between 22 and 31 August 1911, he met several times with General Pinto Concha and Col. Luis Altamirano and secured their agreement to visit both Hirtenberg and Steyr in October. The two Chilean officers confirmed their faith in Austrian industry. Though Altamirano conceded that Chile would always have to take the DW & MF into account in its dealings "due to the intimate contacts between the Chilean armed forces and the Prussian army," he nevertheless expressed his confidence that Santiago's "business connection with Steyr would remain long-term."[72] Indeed, while at Steyr Pinto Concha awarded the ÖWG a contract for thirty thousand Mauser rifles and carbines.

DW & MF's allies in Chile quickly went into action, arguing that the nation could ill afford to purchase weapons from a company that could not manufacture spare parts. El Mercurio, for example, reported that "powerful influences" had convinced the government to award the contract to Steyr, even though a majority of the army's technical experts "opposed giving the contract to the Austrians." Clearly, this combination worked: on 13 October 1911

President Barros Luco seized upon the "catastrophic" quality of the rifle and carbine parts purchased from the ÖWG to rescind the contract and insist that Chile purchase these weapons and ammunition from the DW & MF in Germany. Obviously delighted, Ambassador von Erckert cabled news of the "large army order" to Berlin. He apprised the Wilhelmstrasse that the Chilean War Ministry sought to finance the purchases through "German bank groups" and again warned that the Austrians remained the chief competitor: "If our banking industry lets Chile down now, our entire position here would be threatened."[73] The Diskontogesellschaft and the Deutsche Bank did not disappoint Erckert, granting Chile a loan of 100 million marks.

With the order and the financing in place, the Germans suddenly became coy. In November 1911 the DW & MF's director, Kosegarten, informed the Foreign Office that his company could not fill the order for the thirty thousand Mausers. Its plants' capacities were fully taxed for the next ten months by large orders from Argentina and Brazil—each for more than one hundred thousand Mausers—as well as a smaller purchase by Peru.[74] Minister of War Huneeus became desperate. First he tried to persuade the DW & MF to give Chile preference over its other customers. When that tactic failed, Huneeus offered to pay the DW & MF a bonus if it would undertake this commission. The German company churlishly refused.

Although still embroiled in the Steyr parts dispute, the Austrians tried to resurrect their earlier offer to sell Mausers to Chile. When this occurred, the DW & MF in Berlin changed tactics. The firm now assured the Chilean War Ministry that it could deliver the Mausers on schedule—provided that it received a written guarantee that Chile would not purchase them from Steyr! Körner also sprang into action. In a manner reminiscent of the extortionary tactics that the general had used against Ambassador Subercaseaux Vicuña in 1894 with regard to the Fabrique Nationale d'Armes de Guerre, Körner warned Ambassador Matte that Mauser-Oberndorf alone possessed the right to produce Mauser rifles.[75] The implication was obvious: an order placed with anyone but the DW & MF would result in endless litigation and hopeless delivery delays at a time when Peruvian politicians yet again threatened war over the unresolved Tacna-Arica dispute.

Finally, the DW & MF suggested a compromise. For a fee, it would supervise another armaments manufacturer that would produce the weapons. It is grotesque that the company that the DW & MF selected as its surrogate was the house of Steyr, the same firm that had underbid it and had been flayed for supposedly producing defective parts. It made no sense. In fact, the entire bidding war between the Austrians and Germans was a charade. Steyr's directors had become furious at having been cut out of the South American market in general and the Chilean in particular. Anxious to secure work for its employees, the Austrian firm had threatened to undercut DW & MF's prices globally. Kosegarten, the Mauser director, recognizing that Steyr's action "would render profitable conditions for the foreseeable future impossible," "sadly" saw no alternative but compromise. Better a mutually profitable agreement than reduce his firm's prices to meet Steyr's low bids; Mauser would split the Chilean contract with Steyr by hiring it as its subcontractor.

The behind-the-scenes maneuverings of DW & MF and Steyr should not have come as a surprise. As early as 1905, the DW & MF and its subsidiaries, Mauser at Oberndorf and the Fabrique National d'Armes de Guerre at Herstal, had concluded a cartel arrangement with the ÖWG at Steyr. In it, all four had agreed to avoid profit-cutting competition by submitting uniform bids on foreign orders and then dividing the work among themselves. In other words, all four firms would tender a minimum price of 75 francs per rifle, of which 15 would go into a common fund to be shared such that the ÖWG received 37.5 percent and the DW & MF group 62.5 percent (DW & MF 30, Mauser 21, and Herstal 11.5). Director Kosegarten, of course, requested that the cartel agreement remain secret and informed Erckert that two future bids—one for thirty Maxim machine guns at 285,000 marks and the other for an ammunition plant at 1.5 million marks—lay outside the cartel pact.[76] He was confident that all future orders would run through Berlin.

The 1911 compromise on the Mauser deal surprised the diplomats. Not knowing about the 1905 cartel agreement, Ambassador von Erckert felt betrayed. Styrcea, his Austrian colleague, took note of the cartel without comment. The DW & MF's agent, Vorwerk & Co., vented its frustrations at a banquet in Valparaíso: "Well, had we known that in Europe the Germans and the Austrians would have settled the matter so amicably between themselves, we here would not have had to conduct the entire battle against Steyr."[77] The Chileans could not be so philosophical. Painfully aware that the DW & MF was gouging Santiago, but unaware of the secret agreement, Minister of War Huneeus had no choice but to agree. Because the DW & MF's supervision would cost the government between 200,000 and 300,000 francs, Ambassador Matte denounced Huneeus' actions. The diplomat quite rightly grumbled about a conspiracy to steer the contract to Berlin and urged the Moneda to deal directly with Steyr, particularly after the tests demonstrated the quality of its spare parts.[78] Although his efforts failed, Matte did wring a discount from the DW & MF, but the company, knowing it faced no competition, proved distinctly ungenerous.

The Chileans became outraged. Joaquín Díaz Garcés denounced the actions of Silva Renard, Pinto Concha, and Altamirano. Steyr had lost to the DW & MF because it lacked friends at court. The result of these maneuverings demonstrated that the Germans regarded Chile as a "factory" that it could shamelessly exploit.[79]

At approximately the same time, another scandal developed that also involved the DW & MF. Recognizing the need to acquire new ammunition, the Comisión Militar in Germany tested various types of bullets. Citing quality, price, and delivery time, the Comisión selected the company of Hirtenberg as the supplier from a field of seven, including the DW & MF. On 30

June 1911 General Pinto Concha wired Santiago that he had purchased thirty million Mauser bullets at a cost of 150 francs per one thousand rounds. Ambassador von Erckert formally "complained" to the Chilean war minister and verbally berated his Austrian counterpart, Styrcea, for this "effrontery."[80]

In Santiago General Boonen Rivera tried to rescue DW & MF. As director of the National Arsenal and Steyr's former foe, he publicly informed the War Ministry that Chile's store of Hirtenberg ammunition—which had been manufactured in 1895—was "totally unusable" and needed to be sold off. Having once been cheated, Boonen Rivera warned, Chile should not trust Hirtenberg again. The new war minister, Carlos Larraín Claro, joined Boonen Rivera's crusade. He stated categorically that General Pinto Concha, having been authorized to order the ammunition "only under certain preconditions"—that is, formal testing—had "misused his authority" in awarding the order to Hirtenberg and threatened to cancel the order.

Ambassador von Styrcea at once sought out Foreign Minister Aníbal Rodríguez, who assured him that then war minister Luco had supplied Pinto Concha "with all the necessary powers" (he used the words *plenos poderes*) to place the order. Styrcea informed Foreign Minister von Aehrenthal that it was the first time in Chilean history that "a general who possessed full plenipotentiary powers to conclude a sale had been disavowed in this manner."[81] Hirtenberg demanded full compensation in case Santiago canceled the contract.

Meanwhile, Hirtenberg's agent at Valparaíso, Medina, intervened on behalf of his client, demanding that the fifteen-year-old ammunition be tested. Three days later, the minister of war ordered Pinto Concha to suspend the purchase of any ammunition: he did not wish to acquire any ammunition until he was sure that it would function in the Mausers using the Steyr barrel and sights. To ascertain this, he too demanded special tests. The Moneda's position seemed bizarre: the government only demanded to test the ammunition *after* having signed a 4-million-franc contract with Hirtenberg. General Pinto Concha remonstrated that Leon Luco's demands contradicted his earlier mandate, that Hirtenberg manufactured the best and least expensive bullet, and that it would guarantee early delivery. Besides, Pinto Concha noted, Chile could not act unilaterally. Hirtenberg expected to be paid for the quantities of raw materials it purchased upon signing of the arms contract. The minister of war went one step further, however. He not only insisted on performing special tests on the ammunition but called for the reopening of the bidding process, thus ensuring that the DW & MF could participate. The Germans agreed to match Hirtenberg in price and quality, doubtless delighted to have a second chance.

Obviously anxious to get paid, Hirtenberg agreed to allow the Dirección del Material de Guerra—the same organization whose sloppy testing had precipitated the Steyr fiasco—to retest its ammunition. It was, in the words of Yogi Berra, déjà vu all over again: the Dirección's tests supposedly demonstrated that the DW & MF ammunition was better than Hirtenberg's. As before, protesters demanded another round of tests, this time to be conducted by another laboratory.

The second round of tests were undertaken both at Hirtenberg and in Chile and confirmed that Hirtenberg's ammunition was first-rate. Ambassador von Styrcea, who gleefully reported to Foreign Minister von Aehrenthal that the material "met all expectations," observed that the news was "not gratifying for G[eneral] Boonen." Unfortunately, Leon Luco could not personally hand the tests to Boonen Rivera because the general "reported that he was ill." On 4 July Medina received confirmation of the Hirtenberg order for thirty million bullets.[82] The minister of war, however, refused to back off on his deal with Mauser: he insisted on purchasing ammunition from the DW & MF, even though its terms for delivery and quality control did not match Hirtenberg's.

The weapons procurement process had become utterly corrupt. Government officials, clearly in the thrall if not the pay of the DW & MF, first agreed to pay it a premium to supervise the manufacture of its Mausers. Then, after it had contracted to buy Hirtenberg ammunition for 4 million francs, the War Ministry spent another 4.488 million francs to purchase the same type of bullets from the DW & MF. This action made no sense and a legislative committee concluded that in order "to give business, regardless of the cost, to the factory of Deutsche Waffen . . . the request was duplicated, increasing thusly the amount of ammunition to amounts relatively unnecessary in an ordered and circumspect administration."[83]

Anxious to neutralize Matte's future influence, Erckert accused the Chilean ambassador of having worked consistently against German interests and of having been "bought" by the Austrians. Erckert also informed the Wilhelmstrasse that he suspected that Matte was under the influence of General Pinto Concha, the head of the Chilean Military Mission in Berlin. Both men had "cost" German industry orders estimated at 15 million marks in the past year or two.[84] Thanks to the campaign of Erckert, Vorwerk & Co. (Mauser's agent in Valparaíso), and Otto Eccius, a Krupp director, both Pinto Concha and Matte lost their positions. The Military Mission ceased to exist. (Erckert had the wisdom to keep a low profile in this case. Not so Eccius, whose foolish boasting that he had brought about the mission's dissolution and Matte's dismissal precipitated a raucous debate in the Reichstag).[85]

Over time, Ambassador von Styrcea came to realize that the Steyr contract for Mausers had been Austria's last hurrah. By 1914 he lamented that "German industrial goods nearly rule the local market." Since the Dual Monarchy's exports to Chile were transshipped via Hamburg they were considered to be "German."[86] For its part, the War Ministry in Vienna appeared perplexed that the government failed to fund a shipping subvention for a direct line from Trieste to Valparaíso to expedite Austrian saltpeter imports and colonization projects. It omitted any mention of weapons exports from its brief.[87] Clearly, Vienna had dropped out of the arms race. The ambassador reported less and less on armaments sales and more and more on what he termed the alarming radicalism of Austrian Slavs residing in Chile.[88]

THE KRUPP-EHRHARDT ARTILLERY DUEL

Another and more expensive scandal would further demonstrate the power of the German arms merchants. In 1910 the tension between Chile and Peru over the border issue became so acute that Lima broke diplomatic relations with Santiago. War became a possibility. Times had changed: Peru had rebuilt its military, which numbered some ten thousand, and had recently acquired a large store of excellent French 75mm artillery. Chilean legislators became increasingly frightened by Lima's rearmament program, one that the Chileans had not matched. "While Peru has armed itself to the teeth," remarked one deputy, "we have only the naked chest of our *rotos* to oppose them." Such remarks were not hyperbole. Of the Chilean army's 590 field and mountain guns, 400 were either the 1896 or 1898 model; the remainder dated back to 1886 or 1887. In 1910 the same war scare that forced Chile to purchase more small arms and ammunition made it authorize the expenditure of £500 million to modernize its field artillery.[89]

Artillery had undergone a virtual revolution since Krupp had last tested his guns in Chile, and the Essen giant had failed to keep pace. In fact, as early as the mid-1890s one of Krupp's designers, Konrad Haussner, had submitted drawings for a novel gun that recoiled on its carriage, only to be rebuffed by his employer. After several more attempts to get his ideas tested at Krupp, Haussner abandoned the firm and joined Ehrhardt's Rheinmetall at Düsseldorf. Using Ehrhardt's breakthrough technology, a lightweight, seamless-tube technology, Haussner invented a hydraulic buffer brake that absorbed a gun's recoil and thereby allowed almost continuous firing. In 1897 Ehrhardt offered this revolutionary design to the Prussian army's Ordnance Research Board—only to be turned down in favor of Krupp's rigid pattern 96 gun.[90]

Norway and the United States, on the other hand, recognized Ehrhardt's superior product and purchased Rheinmetall's artillery. That same year, Schneider-Creuzot in France also introduced a gun that was superior to Krupp's pattern 96 piece, and in 1900 it put two advanced artillery guns with hydraulic recoil brakes on the market. Mexico, Greece, China, Peru, Portugal, and Spain at once bought Schneider-Creuzot guns. The anonymous "1" wrote a letter to Valparaíso's *El Mercurio* that concluded that "The superiority of the French equipment is irrefutable" because it had the better recoil device, demonstrated greater stability, and possessed better ballistic qualities and rate of fire.[91] Thus, in the first decade of the twentieth century Chile possessed an opportunity to surpass its model, the Prussian army, in both mountain and field artillery.

In January 1909 Ambassador von und zu Bodman informed Berlin that President Montt had set 1 April as a firm date for competitive trials. He was less than enthusiastic. Artillery tests in Argentina in July 1908 had brought great success for Schneider-Creuzot, but the Paris bourse's refusal to underwrite a large loan had soured the deal. Having arranged financing, Krupp won the Argentinean contract in December.[92] In February 1909 Bodman informed Berlin that a new military commission would leave for Europe. Headed by General Körner, it included Generals Boonen Rivera and Silva Renard, Colonels Altamirano and Bari, Majs. Juan Bennett and Ernesto Medina, and 1st Lt. Guillermo Novoa—all artillery specialists. It was an open secret in Santiago, Bodman stated, that "one had decided in principle to award the contracts to German industry and that accordingly the commission would look at non-German suppliers only pro forma."

Therewith, agreement ended. Within the commission, Boonen Rivera and Silva Renard favored Ehrhardt. Among "influential military circles" in Santiago, Bodman reported, there existed a deep-seated "antagonism" against Körner, who was seen (quite rightly) as little more than "Krupp's agent." Senior Chilean officers held Körner responsible for "outfitting Chilean artillery with guns of diverse calibers." And they argued that Krupp's prices continued to be "1/3 higher than those of Schneider-Creuzot and 1/2 higher than those of Ehrhardt." Finally, Bodman warned that the new Chilean war minister, Darío Zañartu, was a former business "ally" of the German house of Gleissner & Co., which represented Ehrhardt in Chile. Only President Pedro Montt remained solidly in Krupp's camp. In the face of these facts, Bodman suggested a compromise: Chile could split its orders between Krupp and Ehrhardt and thereby cut the chief competitor, Schneider-Creuzot, out of the market. But the initiative had to come from Essen.[93]

Unlike the DW & MF, Krupp would never compromise with its competition. In May 1909 Essen instructed Vorwerk & Co., its Valparaíso agent, to mount a scurrilous press attack against Ehrhardt. It backfired. General Zañartu complained to Bodman that he had been offended by what he termed "the arrogant behavior" of Krupp's agent. Next, the war minister lectured the envoy concerning a recent case that highlighted the differences between Krupp and Ehrhardt. When Chile invited bids to modernize the antiquated Krupp guns it had bought from Schinzinger, Krupp demanded that Santiago cover all transportation costs. Ehrhardt, on the other hand, offered to pay them. When Vorwerk & Co. discovered that three Krupp guns had, indeed, been sent to Düsseldorf where they were modernized and tested successfully, the agent protested "this aggravated incident," arguing that only Krupp could alter its guns. Vorwerk conveniently overlooked the fact that Ehrhardt had already modernized Krupp guns for the Prussian army. Zañartu refused to accept Vorwerk's protest because of "its unacceptable tone," whereupon the agent attacked the war minister personally in the Chilean press. And when Vorwerk & Co. discovered that one of the German instructors, Maj. Viktor von Hartrott, "as well as numerous Prussian officers," had purchased Rheinmetall stock it curtly demanded that Hartrott be excluded from any future firing tests.[94]

In the meantime, the Chilean Military Commission studied European gun designs. Its secret instructions left no doubt about President Montt's intentions: "It is to study and to test exclusively the prototypes shown it by Krupp and Rheinische Metallwaren- und Maschinenfabrik, without accepting invitations to inspect or to test the prototypes of other firms." As a Chilean legislator subsequently stated, thanks to "certain unspecified incidents," Škoda, Armstrong, Vickers, and Schneider-Creuzot were in effect cut out of the competition for the two hundred Chilean mountain and field guns before it ever took place. This should come as no surprise. As Senator Carlos Walker Martínez had earlier observed, the committee that was to select the new guns included General Körner who, despite his supposed love for Chile, was fundamentally a German who wished to spend his remaining days in the nation of his birth.[95] When it came to a choice, he would side with the German product.

The Chilean artillery tests proceeded as planned in April 1909 near Cartagena, using only Krupp guns and without Major von Hartrott present. In June Ambassador von und zu Bodman reported the results in a confidential report to Berlin that was based on an equally confidential report by Capt. Hans von Mohs, the Württemberg artillery specialist in Chile. It was a disaster for Krupp's rigid pattern 96 gun. The locking action in the breech had failed as early as the pretest trials. And when the Chileans tested fifty-six of the remaining Krupp pieces bought between 1898 and 1902, similar defects were discovered in two-thirds of the guns. "During the very first shot, the inner tube slid with a loud bang as much as 2/10 mm out of the cotter slot, so that the breech could no longer be locked." The problem was with the guns rather than the ammunition, which had been brought out fresh from Essen. According to Mohs, Krupp engineers had underestimated the pressure on the gun's jacket. And while the defects could be repaired, this proved to be time-consuming ("several hours" per tube) and expensive. In Bodman's view, the disastrous tests damaged not only Krupp but German industry itself. The official Chilean report, leaked to Bodman, concluded that its army would have been placed "in a highly compromising position had it moved into the field in case of war, blindly trusting the reliability of its Krupp material." If the defect had not been noticed before battle the results could have been "devastating." Bodman suggested that Krupp provide a formal apology and repairs.[96]

Far from doing either, Gustav Krupp von Bohlen und Halbach instead trained his guns on Bodman. In August 1909 Krupp interrupted his Bavarian vacation and in a blistering epistle protested to Foreign Secretary Wilhelm Baron von Schoen Bodman's "pessimistic interpretations." The problems with the inner tubes, Krupp declared, were not only well known but "in no way call into question the quality and usefulness of Krupp-delivered material."

Indeed, quite the opposite! That a minuscule shifting of the inner tubes by 0.2mm could cause the breech to fail to lock "could rather be interpreted as evidence of the incredibly precise work that goes into all materials delivered by Essen." Moreover, Krupp averred, had the Chileans routinely exercised their guns instead of storing them in hot arsenals they would have detected this slight imperfection, "which can be remedied without difficulty by any locksmith in a quarter of an hour." Krupp deemed the entire matter to be "not unusual" and in any case "irrelevant in peacetime." It had been blown up into a cause célèbre "through ignorance or malevolence on the part of those involved."

The last comment was aimed squarely at Bodman. Bohlen und Halbach, a colorless bureaucrat handpicked by William II to marry the Krupp heiress Bertha, suggested that the real problem lay with the ineptitude of German diplomatic representation in Chile: "I can only regret deeply that the German ambassador, despite [my] stated remarks, has chosen to view the matter in the darkest light possible." Had Bodman but noticed the "despicable manner" in which Ehrhardt had attacked Krupp in both Argentina and Chile he would have taken a less offensive stance. Krupp closed his brief by demanding that "the prestige of the firm of Krupp" be energetically defended in Chile.[97]

The Austrians seized on the poor test results in an eleventh-hour attempt to displace Krupp from the Chilean market. Bros. Böhler lectured the War Ministry on the "great economic importance" of gun orders "for Austrian industry" in that 240 tubes and 120,000 shells were at stake. But it was critical, Böhler instructed the War Ministry, that Austrian firms tender joint bids for guns as well as ammunition. The War Ministry and Foreign Office thought the Chilean business sufficiently important to approach Francis Joseph II for formal approval, which the kaiser readily gave "to further our industry." Obviously worried about the abysmal Krupp test results, President Montt and War Minister Zañartu instructed the Chilean Commission to inspect Böhler's 8cm M5 guns at Felixdorf and Kapferberg.[98] At the urging of Friedrich Johann Baron von Seidler, Vienna's new attaché at Santiago, Foreign Minister von Aehrenthal instructed the boards of trade at Vienna, Eger, Prague, Graz, Troppau, Olmütz, Klagenfurt, Pilsen, and Rechenberg to mobilize Austrian firms for the Chilean orders. Friedrich Carl von Erckert, the new German ambassador at Santiago, got wind of the Austrian initiative. As a board member on the Berlin Council on Africa, Erckert had already come to appreciate the value of overseas markets for German industry. At Santiago, he later defined his chief mission as "exploiting our relations with the Chilean army in the interests of our industry. . . . I use every opportunity to impress upon leading [Chilean] circles that with regard to military deliveries we have a certain moral right to be considered first and foremost."[99] Erckert admonished senior German instructors—Hartrott, Mohs, and Hans von Kiesling—to lobby Chilean officers on behalf of German industry.

In the meantime, the Chilean Military Commission gathered at Ambassador Matte's residence in Berlin and agreed to first test fire Krupp's guns at Essen in July and then, in September, Rheinmetall's at Düsseldorf-Derendorf. The results were inconclusive. In October General Körner informed the Chilean War Ministry that both prototypes were acceptable. Although Rheinmetall's gun was superior in ease of handling, stability, and rapidity of fire, Krupp's was the more accurate. Paul Desprez, the French ambassador to Santiago, claimed that five members of the commission, including Boonen Rivera, favored the Ehrhardt; three wanted the Krupp.[100]

As the head of the Chilean commission, Körner insisted on a new series of trials at Krupp's Meppen firing range in November to test the durability of the Krupp and Ehrhardt guns. It too produced no clear winner. The tailspade, traversing lever, and handle of Rheinmetall's gun broke after 50 kilometers in the field; the same fate befell the Krupp gun after 212 kilometers. Ambassador Matte thereupon recalled the commission to Berlin and pieced together a compromise: the best parts of each gun were to be combined into a single, new model, to be built by Krupp. But, true to form, Krupp refused to accept any compromise, especially one that could lead to possible patent infringements. The Chilean commission was so narrowly divided that it submitted separate briefs to Santiago on behalf of both German competitors.[101]

The final decision rested with Pedro Montt. Early in January 1910, the president opted, against the advice of Foreign Minister Rodríguez, to purchase all guns and ammunition from Krupp at a cost of 21.3 million marks. The Austrian attaché at Santiago, Baron von Seidler, informed Vienna that President Montt had "categorically explained" that he had reached his "*vis major* in the interest of the uniformity of armaments" in Chilean artillery. To Ambassador Matte in Berlin, Montt confided that he had reached his decision mainly on the basis of "the reputation of Krupp material" and because Chile dared not "blaze new trails" in this matter. "Körner," he wrote, "has resolved all doubts" about the wisdom of buying from Krupp. The general's actions should come as no surprise. Though Senator Walker Martínez conceded that Körner was "as adoring of Chile as the best of the Chileans," he nevertheless instructed the War Ministry that don Emilio would never "go against the wishes or preoccupations of his emperor . . . or alienate the goodwill of his fellow citizens, among whom no doubt he will wish to spend his last days."[102]

Other Chileans believed that merit had not inspired Montt's decision. Santiago's *La Lei* claimed that, thanks to bribery, "the house of Krupp has, in the last days, been able to win a public bid, at a cost of 8,000,000 marks to the Chilean treasury." Blaming not just Körner and the Comisión Militar, the paper even intimated that the president had been paid off.[103] A Chilean congressman, Ricardo Cox Méndez, carried the fight to the legislature. He demanded that the government explain its actions, noting that a pamphlet that had appeared in Santiago indicated that the Krupp gun was antiquated and inadequate compared to its competition. We do not know what argument the minister of war offered, but the legislature, meeting in secret session, ratified the deal, which called for Chile to spend approximately 40 million marks on 144 field guns, howitzers, and ammunition.[104]

Krupp's victory, like that of the DW & MF, had been a foregone conclusion. A U.S. envoy claimed that if Santiago had not bought from Krupp, the kaiser would have repatriated the German officers serving as instructors in the Chilean army as well as Chileans serving in German regiments. In a "highly confidential" report, Austria's attaché at Santiago, Baron von Seidler, also reported that the Prussian War Ministry had used "high-pressure" tactics to influence the decision by warning that Chilean officers then serving in Germany would be denied all military information if Santiago preferred "foreign firms in gun deliveries."[105] Seidler's report prompted the Austro-Hungarian navy to inform Santiago that because of "state security interests" it would no longer train Chilean officers.[106]

President Montt's decision to embrace Krupp cost his nation dearly. He had signed a contract without even knowing its unit prices, delivery schedules, or terms of payment. Krupp's eventual price of 172,250 francs for each battery of four tubes and six munitions wagons turned out to be higher than those of Schneider-Creuzot and Ehrhardt. To guarantee payment of the roughly 40 million marks, Krupp took possession of 5 percent Chilean Treasury bonds for three years. Once more, the Essen giant had landed the deal in part by persuading one of its partners, the Diskontogesellschaft, to join Rothschild-London in granting Chile a loan of 53 million marks. In 1911 Diskonto and another Krupp ally, the Deutsche Bank, underwrote a further Chilean loan of 100 million marks (Rothschild assumed an equal amount). Both loans were at 5 percent interest. In both cases, Chile received but 90 percent of the face value of the loans.[107] Thus, once again, Chile paid dearly for Krupp purchases—and then financed them just as dearly through long-term, high-interest German loans.

Not surprisingly, Heinrich Ehrhardt was irate. On 18 January 1910 he angrily reminded the Wilhelmstrasse that the Chilean Military Commission had "*unanimously*" voted to purchase its ammunition from him and that "the majority of its members" had "preferred our material" to that of Krupp, even though the Essen firm "had used our hydraulic recoil-barrel buffer brake." "Despite our lower prices," all orders had gone to Krupp. Ehrhardt detected a pattern in these overseas deals: "Strings are being pulled behind the scenes by forces that, despite the fact that their origin is not unknown, are still hard to pin down. [They] press the financially weaker up against the wall and deprive him of the success due him for his accomplishments." Ehrhardt lectured the Wilhelmstrasse that it was his "duty" to combat such nefarious "forces" by asking Chile to reconsider its peremptory decision. Within forty-eight hours, Baron von Schoen coldly replied that the Foreign Office, though neutral in business matters, was obviously delighted that a German firm had won the order.[108]

Predictably, the Chilean decision did not thrill Krupp's foreign competitors.

Schneider-Creuzot of France, which had leased 197,600 acres of forest at Corral Bay to get a leg up on Krupp, formally protested the award of the artillery order to the Essen firm. Schneider-Creuzot argued that it had spent approximately 221,000 francs building three models of the 75mm gun—a field piece, a howitzer, and a mortar—and had provided one thousand rounds of shells per piece. Since the Moneda had requested a bid from Schneider and then never held the shoot-off it demanded payment for its expenses.[109] When Santiago refused, the company's owners became livid.

This issue involved more than Schneider's wounded amour propre; money was at stake. According to Antonio Huneeus, French industrialists knew about the Chilean government's unconventional behavior and threatened to retaliate. Predictably, they appealed to their own government. Noting Chile's hostility to French economic interests, the specialist on American affairs in the Ministry of Foreign Relations, Abel Chevalley, had indicated that Paris would not permit Santiago to sell its bonds on the Paris bourse. Chile, he noted, "cannot be under any illusions: a small country because of the single fact of contracting with the subjects of a great power loses in a certain way a portion of its sovereignty." Santiago, he suggested, should try to salve Schneider's anger. The Moneda ignored Schneider's champions. Desprez, the French ambassador at Santiago, poured his "lamentations" out concerning what he termed "Krupp's monopoly position" in Chile to his Austrian colleague Styrcea. Styrcea could only commiserate by agreeing that it was "incredibly difficult to contest the deep German influence in all matters pertaining to the Chilean army."[110]

Privately, Gustav Krupp appreciated that he had almost lost the Chilean deal. In an internal memorandum of 30 April 1910, he drew the lessons from the near loss of the Chilean orders to Rheinmetall. In the future, the company would use all its influence both in Berlin and Santiago to prevent competitors from being allowed even to ship test guns to Chile. Not only were trials "too problematical" for the security of future orders, they also encouraged "polemics" against Krupp in local newspapers. When in the summer the Foreign Office refused a request by two members of the permanent Military Mission in Berlin (General Pinto Concha and Colonel Altamirano) to attend German maneuvers, Krupp quickly overturned the decision by appealing directly to William II.[111]

Krupp would soon have to do battle to protect his interests. Ehrhardt would get a second bite at the apple because the Chilean army had decided to purchase twelve batteries of mountain guns at a cost of £233,000. And since Krupp, unlike Ehrhardt, did not specialize in mountain artillery, it appeared quite possible that Krupp would lose in an open, fair competition. To prevent precisely that possibility, Krupp promised to build a special model mountain gun for Chile, provided that Santiago committed itself to the Essen firm. The mountain gun functioned well enough on the Krupp test ranges, but the Chilean Artillery Commission sent to supervise the construction discovered some flaws that required correction. It also insisted that Krupp ship the weapon to Chile, where it could be tested under field conditions less antiseptic than those of the German firing range. Krupp had little alternative but to comply; it dispatched the weapon with a team of gunners to Chile. Still, the agreement with the Moneda seemed ironclad: Santiago had to purchase the Krupp guns if the latter met the technical specifications.

To ensure its triumph, Krupp employed its usual tricks. First, it pulled strings to prevent Ehrhardt from ever testing its weapon in Chile. Initially it enjoyed some success; various ministers of war would not permit Ehrhardt to bring its wares to Chile. But eventually public pressure forced War Minister Leon Luco to allow Ehrhardt's participation in a proposed shoot-off with Krupp. Essen fought the good fight: it called upon its Chilean allies for additional help and they responded. The head of customs, for example, refused to allow Ehrhardt to remove its weapons from a Los Andes customs shed, supposedly because it could not decide what import duty the artillery manufacturer should pay. It took some legislative efforts to end the months of haggling before a customs official allowed the weapons to enter the country for the firing trials.[112]

Meanwhile, the hour of truth for Krupp's mountain gun had come. After the conclusion of the portability trials in Aconcagua the artillery piece arrived at the Batuco range for a test firing. These trials would be supervised by Krupp's representative, a retired army captain named Grünveller and his mechanic, a Herr Flache; an all-German gun crew would do the actual firing. The Chileans showed up in force. The government provided support personnel from the telegraph battalion as well as some artillerymen and a special train to transport the new minister of war, Claudio Vicuña, four of his predecessors, seven generals, a gaggle of politicians, and numerous senior artillery officers from Santiago to Batuco.

After the opening ceremonies, which included some lectures extolling the virtues of Krupp, the Germans fired the gun over distances of one thousand to four thousand meters. These results must have humiliated Krupp: in the three sets of tests the mountain gun generally missed the five-by-four-meter target. Worse, the recoil device apparently failed, which sometimes allowed the barrel to slam into the ground. Eventually, the gunners had to dig a roughly twenty-centimeter hole to permit the barrel to recoil freely. An anonymous high-ranking Chilean officer watching the exercises blamed the gun's lackluster results on faulty ammunition or an unskilled gun crew. (Refreshingly, he, at least, did not blame the Jews.)[113] Given that the tests had caused some "indecision," the officer suggested that it might not be a bad idea for the army to test fire the Ehrhardt weapon.

Logically, Krupp, which had already missed one deadline, should have been out of luck: customers rarely rush to buy an artillery piece that cannot hit a twenty-square-meter target. But logic did not seem to be the minister of war's long suit. Rather than disqualify the Essen company, Vicuña ordered another round of trials, claiming that the tests had occurred under "unusual circumstances" rather than "regular conditions"—whatever that meant. The second series of tests proved only slightly more felicitous. Although the German gun crew managed to hit the target with more regularity, the recoil device, despite Krupp's promises to remedy the problem, still failed to function properly.[114]

The combination of the gun's faulty recoil device and less-than-sterling accuracy naturally caused some dismay. *El Mercurio* wondered how long Chile would have to wait before Krupp learned how to manufacture a mountain gun. Senator Gonzalo Bulnes appeared intolerant: Chile should regard any agreement with Krupp as provisional; if the company did not meet its specifications Santiago should go elsewhere.[115] But the government, unlike Bulnes, had the patience of Job. Minister of War Vicuña called for the gun's recoil device to be tested yet again, this time at the Fábrica de Cartuchos. (It must be remembered that German personnel supervised this factory, which during the Steyr affair had apparently sabotaged the inspection of the spare parts.) Not surprisingly, he also reconstituted the test committee. Vicuña then rescheduled additional trials for Batuco.

The final round of tests proved disappointing. When fired at its highest elevation, the weapon's barrel still occasionally struck the ground. Worse, an officer argued that the act of readjusting the piece after each round had been fired called into question the test's results. Clearly, the mountain gun needed additional modifications. Rather than continue, the committee's members suspended the trials when Krupp promised to improve the gun's recoil device. The committee stipulated, however, that it would not accept any modifications if the Essen firm altered the weapon's stability or precision. Of course, any final decision required that the cannon be "tested again before the artillery officers in Europe, who would be selected by the government."[116]

As the Krupp equipment suffered one mishap after another, the company's advocates became shrilly defensive. Luis Barceló, Krupp's local attorney, demeaned his competition. The Ehrhardt mountain gun, he noted, was fit only for fighting "the Hottentots"; anyone seriously interested in killing white people, like the warring sides in the then raging Balkan War, invariably opted for Krupp's field piece. (Barceló's observations, like many of his charges, were about as accurate as the Krupp mountain gun. As one anonymous letter writer to *El Mercurio* noted, most of those fighting in the Balkans used the Schneider-Canet. Only the Turks, who like their Chilean cohorts had employed a German Military Mission, relied on Krupp. This fact brought little comfort: the Ottoman army's poor performance made many question the value of the German weapon and methods.) Barceló became almost absurd in his defense of Krupp. Ehrhardt not only produced a bad gun, he claimed, but its financial condition was weak. Those Chileans who favored sound finances over technical considerations might have had second thoughts, however, had they heard an Argentine artillery officer's recent warning that a reliance on Essen's mountain gun "would cost much Chilean blood" in any future war.[117]

Ehrhardt finally got its chance to test fire its weapon in December 1912, when it conducted a series of trials at El Culenar. It is difficult to assess this contest's results because the members of the test committee themselves could not agree, although most (including General Silva Renard and Majs. Alfredo Gacitua and Carlos Harms) seemed to favor the weapon over the Krupp version. One has the distinct feeling that the authorities stacked the deck against Ehrhardt. The government, for example, chose to test fire the Ehrhardt not at Batuco but at El Culenar, which was not really a proper firing range; it had been purchased the year before and lacked facilities. Moreover, various prominent artillery officers admitted that the conditions were not the same. For example, Ehrhardt had to perform the tests under certain unusual time constraints and without the proper ammunition. Since the test conditions differed, the test results could hardly be equated. Of course, this distinction did not deter Generals Boonen Rivera and Bari from flaying their colleague, General Silva Renard, or indeed anyone, for daring to support the purchase of the Ehrhardt gun.[118]

Everyone could have saved their energy. Once the "imperial eagle [had] extended its protective wings" over the house of Krupp it was a done deal; the contest *was* rigged before it began. As the British military attaché tartly noted, "Some of the influential advocates of the Krupp guns, however, are . . . directly interested in the acquisition of the guns of that firm and it is hardly to be expected an impartial verdict as regards the Ehrhardt pattern can be looked for."[119] The anti-Krupp forces were right. Someone had orchestrated a campaign to ensure that the Moneda purchased the Krupp gun. Even before the tests, Leon Luco had specifically ordered Matte to "Buy from Krupp. Contract with Krupp; we will not contract in any way with Ehrhardt." It was an order the minister obeyed, albeit with "deep disgust [and] indignation." Matte subsequently revealed that Krupp had used its clout to force the removal of unsympathetic bureaucrats "to ensure that its interests prevail even when these conflict with those of the state." Krupp had also employed its tradition of offering bribes. An American officer reported that the German firm owned at least two legislators. Indeed, the local Krupp representative, a Herr Schumacher, even admitted that Krupp had suborned various officers serving on Chile's European Comisión Militar, which willingly compromised the nation's security "for commercial interests or the love of a certain firm." The minister of the interior, Ismael Tocornal, denied this allegation as well as the charge that he had received a letter from Matte stating that he believed the Ehrhardt gun was better than Krupp's. The time had come, a legislative budget committee argued, to end the "habitual abuses and the chronic corruption that has penetrated public administration and threatens to end all order in the state's finances."[120]

These charges did not go unchallenged. *La Razón*, paladin of the Radical Party, defended the procurement procedures and by implication the reputation of Alejandro Rosselot, the Radical minister of war. It did not see corruption "because it does not exist." Another journal called for an end to the debate, which not only damaged Chile's reputation but threatened to jeopardize Santiago's relations with Krupp, "whose services we will need one hundred times in the future."[121]

Krupp's defenders may have bought its tales, but the Wilhelmstrasse did not. The German ambassador conceded privately, very privately, that Krupp had triumphed over Ehrhardt by conducting a campaign "skillfully and emphatically behind the scenes."[122] But this scheming did not seem to bother him as much as the spectacle of one German firm fighting another in "malicious battle." Such public displays of pique might have damaged Germany's image in Chile. Thus, Erckert admonished the Foreign Office to censure Rheinmetall for its "actions, which had damaged the national interest." The Wilhelmstrasse complied at once. Finally, Erckert suggested that Foreign Secretary von Schoen instruct Krupp to act more prudently in the future.[123] Berlin's recriminations, however, were uttered sotto voce.

Regardless of its methods, Krupp's smashing triumph reaffirmed what Ambassador von Erckert called Germany's "monopoly position" in supplying the Chilean army. "Contracts are not tendered internationally," the envoy boasted, "but mainly given out directly by the Military Mission in Germany." Essen would subsequently win a supplementary contract for 48 mountain, 24 field, and 16 coastal guns as well as 8 howitzers and 304 munitions wagons. The DW & MF meanwhile filled an order for 37,000 rifles and knapsacks, 30 million bullets, and 30 machine guns. Other German firms sold Chile

37,000 Prussian-issue knapsacks at 90,000 Marks; 30,000 Parabellum semiautomatic pistols with 15 million rounds at 2.5 million Marks; 30,000 (perhaps 50,000) rifles along with 30 million bullets being negotiated with Mauser at 8 million Marks; 6,000 harnesses for mules, 1,500 waist belts, 15,000 bandoleers, 15,000 Prussian-issue billhooks, equipment for two medical companies and 12 field hospitals at 2 million Marks; 60 (possibly 140) field kitchens, 35,000 saddles, new equipment for the munitions factory at 1.5 million Marks.[124]

Even horseshoes and musical instruments had come from Germany. Precise totals for the German deliveries are hard to ascertain, although Erckert estimated that the Reich had sold over 80 percent of the 60 million marks' worth of goods Chile imported.[125]

The artillery orders brought a flood of Chileans to Essen. Earlier, in July 1909, General Körner had been feted at the Villa Hügel and given a tour of the Tangerhütte firing range. In January 1910 Krupp hosted a delegation of Chilean and German naval engineers from Valparaíso, who were sent to inspect the company's latest 25cm coastal artillery pieces. In October Körner arrived again, this time with a party of five Chilean officers in tow, to take possession of the first field guns. Krupp rolled out the red carpet. The group was wined and dined at Villa Hügel; shown workers' quarters in the Alfredshof, Altenhof, and Friedrichshof; taken through the firm's museum; and given formal tours (denied to almost all foreign visitors) of Krupp's plate mill, rolling mill, forges, Bessemer converter, smelting house, open-hearth steel plant, and press works. Krupp recorded for posterity that they were handed precisely seven postcards as souvenirs. Körner and the Chileans proudly posed for Krupp photographers. Overall, no fewer than sixty-nine Chilean visitors toured the firm's facilities at Essen, Meppen, and Tangerhütte in these years.[126]

Throughout the Krupp-Ehrhardt and DW & MF-ÖWG confrontations, General Körner had been the silent "force" guiding affairs from Germany. Don Emilio had taken advantage of the 1910 centenary celebrations to retire—with his full salary as a pension—and to guide Santiago's military purchases from Berlin and Essen as honorary head of Chile's Ordnance Acceptance Commission. Krupp records attest to Körner's vigor. The general visited Essen, Magdeburg, Meppen, Rheinhausen, and Tangerhütte in October 1910; in April 1911; in May, June, August, and September (twice) 1912; and in August 1913. Ambassador von Erckert happily informed Berlin that an earlier order for fifty-six mountain guns had gone directly through General Körner. When Chilean orders exceeded what Congress had funded, as in 1913, for example, don Emilio enthusiastically offered his services, in this case, arranging a 5.5 percent penalty on the excess orders in return for a "gift" of four field howitzers. Upon learning that by 1913 Chile had purchased French aviation materials, the indefatigable Körner, at the urging of several German aircraft manufacturers, personally arranged for Capt. Roberto Ahumada to be trained and certified in Fokker's newest monoplane at Johannisthal.[127]

General Körner had abetted and profited from the activities of Krupp and DW & MF. Even his supposed retirement did not end his manipulations of the Chilean army. Obviously, the German industrialists and to a lesser extent the German government had derived substantial benefits from the general's activities as well as those of Schinzinger and the people whom he suborned. Predictably, Erckert looked forward to the arrival of new military instructors. As in the past, their direct "influence over the Chilean army" would "further secure our economic and political position in South America."[128]

Ambassador von Erckert's dreams did not materialize. In August 1914 Germany's officers returned home to put into practice the lessons in mayhem they had tried to impart to the Chileans. Germany had received good value from its instructors, from Krupp, and from his colleagues: millions of Chilean pesos, excluding the few that clung to the hands of the middlemen, including Schinzinger and the ubiquitous Körner, had flowed to Essen and thus into the German economy. The First World War and the Treaty of Versailles finished Germany as an arms exporter. During the bleak 1920s, Krupp, Mauser, and the countless others no doubt fondly remembered don Emilio's magic touch during the golden years. The Chilean army, however, had ample cause to regret the Germans: "the art of the deal" had cost it, and the nation, dearly.

NOTES

1. Historisches Archiv Krupp, Werksarchiv, Essen (hereafter HAK-WA), 7f14448, "Erfahrungen im Kriegsmaterialgeschäft mit dem Auslande," 10501 NIK 9.9.1937, 9–18.

2. Beckmann joined Krupp's Gunnery Division II in February 1901, became director of all firing ranges in 1912, and from 1917 to 1926 worked in various Krupp bureaus (information courtesy of the HAK-WA). For an age in which there existed no regulatory agencies, no Internal Revenue Service, no income taxes, and no public audit of private financial records, this document, submitted to the International Military Tribunal at Nuremberg for the case against Krupp, is of critical importance. In an internal memorandum, "The Significance of the Friedr. Krupp Co. for German Industry," the armaments tycoon crowed that as a private firm, it did not have to publish annual reports. Krupp instructed his directors "to keep the purchases of war materials strictly secret."

3. HAK-WA 7f1148, 61–66.

4. HAK-WA 7f1148, 1–7.

5. Historisches Archiv Krupp, Familienarchiv, Essen (herafter HAK-FA), 3 870, Briefwechsel Krupp . . . und Verschiedenen Personalia, 1887–1901.

6. HAK-WA 7f1148, 28–31.

7. HAK-WA 7f1148, 2, 20–26, 33–34, 42–52, 60.

8. José Manuel Balmaceda to Carlos Antúnez, Santiago, 9 October 1888; in the possession of William F. Sater.

9. HAK-WA 4/1051, "Kontrakte zwischen Friedr. Krupp, Essen, und der Republik Chile vom 9. Oktober und 8. Nov. 1872 über Lieferung von 4 Feld-u. 12 Gebirgs-geschützen nebst Zubehör."

10. Gutschmid to Bismarck, 23 April 1888, 11 and 16 January 1889, Bundesarchiv-Abteilung Potsdam (hereafter BA-AP), Lieferungen der Firma Krupp für die Chilenische Regierung, vol. I, Nr. 344.

11. Betzhold to Krupp, 27 December 1889, HAK-WA 4/2036, Briefwechsel F.A. Krupp—Major Betzhold 1889–1900.

12. See Jürgen Schaefer, *Deutsche Militärhilfe an Südamerika. Militär- und Rüstungsinteressen in Argentinien, Bolivien und Chile vor 1914* (Düsseldorf, 1974), 34; and Jürgen Hell, "Deutschland und Chile von 1871–1918," *Wissenschaftliche Zeitschrift der Universität Rostock*, 14 (1965): 87.

13. Foreign Office note of 12 September 1889, BA-AP, Lieferungen der Firma Krupp . . . , vol. I, no. 344.

14. HAK-FA 3870, Briefwechsel Krupp . . . 1887–1901; BA-AP, Lieferungen der Firma Krupp . . . , vol. 2, no. 344.

15. Gutschmid to Bismarck, 14 February 1890, BA-AP, Lieferungen der Firma Krupp . . . , vol. 2, no. 344.

16. HAK-WA 4/2284, Briefwechsel F.A. Krupp—A. Schinzinger 8.3.1883—1.8.1911.

17. The technical results of the contest are detailed in Schinzinger to Gutschmid, 27 March 1890, BA-AP, Lieferungen der Firma Krupp . . . , vol. I, no. 344. They were published in "Das Vergleichsschiessen zwischen Krupp und de Bange bei Batuco in Chile," *Militär-Wochenblatt* (1890): 1579–94.

18. Schinzinger to Gutschmid, 27 March 1890, BA-AP, Lieferungen der Firma

Krupp . . . , vol. I, no. 344; also, HAK-FA 4CI93, Privatbureau Dr. Gustav Krupp v. B. u. H. Chile. Allgemein; Gutschmid to Bismarck, March 1890, BA-AP, Lieferungen der Firma Krupp . . . , vol. I, no. 344. Two months later, the Francophiles on the commission submitted a minority report in favor of Canet, which had not taken part in the test!

19. Foreign Office to Krupp, 6 May 1890, BA-AP, Lieferungen der Firma Krupp . . . , vol. I, no. 344.

20. Schinzinger (Santiago) to Krupp, 20 March 1890, HAK-WA 4/2284. "You may fly to touch me."

21. Gutschmid to Caprivi, 15 April 1890, BA-AP, Lieferungen der Firma Krupp . . . , vol. I, no. 344.

22. HAK-FA 3870; Gutschmid to Caprivi, 4 January 1891, BA-AP, Die Lieferungen der Firma Krupp . . . , vol. l, no. 344.

23. Schinzinger to Krupp, 20 January 1892, HAK-WA 4/2284, Briefwechsel Krupp—Schinzinger.

24. HAK-WA 4/2284, Briefwechsel Krupp—Schinzinger.

25. Gutschmid to Foreign Office, 15 January 1892, Auswärtiges Amt-Politisches Archiv (hereafter AA-PA), Bonn, R 16630, Chile I, vol. 17.

26. A. Wilckens, *Hundert Jahre Deutscher Handel und Deutsche Kolonie in Valparaiso 1822–1922* (Hamburg, 1922), 127.

27. Gutschmid to Foreign Office, 19 September 1891, BA-AP, Lieferungen der Firma Krupp . . . , vol. I, no. 344; Lauter to Frau Krupp, 10 September 1892, HAK-FA 3CI I, Briefe Adolf Lauter an F.A. Krupp.

28. Voigts-Rhetz to Caprivi, 28 July 1892, BA-AP, Lieferungen der Firma Krupp . . . , vol. I, no. 344.

29. HAK, Geheim. 5.a. VII f.862 Chile.

30. Internal memorandum, Krupp Rechnungs-Revisions-Bureau, "Schinzingers Reise-rechnung," HAK-FA 3B70, Briefwechsel Krupp . . . , 1887–1901.

31. HAK-FA 3B70, Briefwechsel Krupp . . . , 1887–1901, Chile "Auslagen," Krupp's notes are undated, in pencil, from his private notes.

32. Krupp to Ernst Hengstenberg (Valparaíso), 2 January 1894, HAK-FA 3C225, Privat-bureau F.A. Krupp. Chile. Vertretung 1892–1894.

33. Schaefer, *Deutsche Militärhilfe an Südamerika*, 72–73, 236–37.

34. Carlos Rivera Jofre, Santiago, 7 January 1895, in Archivo Nacional (hereafter cited as AN), Legación de Chile en Francia, vol. 2306.

35. Hollmann (Washington) to Caprivi, 20 September 1891, AA-PA, R 17182, Ver. Staat. v. Amerika No 5. Militär und Marineangelegenheiten, interview dated 19 September 1891; Gutschmid to Caprivi, 13 October 1891, AA-PA, R 16628, Chile I, vol. 15.

36. Schaefer, *Deutsche Militärhilfe an Südamerika*, 40–43. Given that the Mauser and Loewe archives were destroyed during the Second World War, this story has been reconstructed on the basis of the records of the German Foreign Office as well as those of the Chilean Commission in Paris (as researched by Schaefer).

37. Galo Irarrazaval, minister of foreign relations, Berlin, 24 July 1892 (secret), AN, Legación de Chile en Francia, vol. 317 (italics in original).

38. Schaefer, *Deutsche Militärhilfe an Südamerika*, 45.

39. Carlos Rivera Jofre, 7 January 1895 in AN, Legación de Chile en Francia, vol. 2306; Armando Donoso, *Recuerdos de cincuenta años* (Santiago, 1947), 393–94; and his

"El Jeneral del Canto," *Pacifico Magazine*, 9 (1917), 54; Schaefer, *Deutsche Militärhilfe an Südamerika*, 45–46; Waltraud Winkelbauer, *Die Österreichisch-Chilenischen Beziehungen vom Vormärz bis zum Ende der Habsburger-monarchie* (Cologne, 1988), 184–85. The material was delivered by the Patronen-, Zundhütchen- und Metallwarenfabrik in Hirtenberg, formerly Keller & Co.

40. Galo Irarrazaval-Errázuriz, Berlin, 24 and 29 July 1892, AN, Legación de Chile en Francia, vol. 317.

41. *El Mercurio* (Valparaíso), 8 February 1904 (hereafter cited as MERV); *Ludw. Loewe & Co. Actiengesellschaft Berlin 1869–1929* (Berlin, 1930), 32–34.

42. See Robert W. D. Ball, *Mauser Military Rifles of the World* (Iola WI, 1996), 80.

43. DW & MF Berlin to Foreign Office, 2 November 1900, AA-PA, R16640, Chile I, vol. 27; Schaefer, *Deutsche Militärhilfe an Südamerika*, 72–73.

44. Giskra to Foreign Office, 24 June 1906, Haus-, Hof- und Staatsarchiv (hereafter HHSA), Vienna, Gesandschaftsberichte Santiago I, 1903–1907.

45. Giskra to Goluchowski, 12 July 1906, HHSA, Vienna, Gesandschaftsberichte Santiago I, 1903–1907, PA XXXXVII 3, Chile: Berichte, Weisungen 1905–1908; Giskra to Foreign Office, 6 and 7 August, and 24 October 1906, HHSA, Gesandschaftsberichte I.

46. Giskra to Ballhausplatz, 15 November 1906, HHSA, Gesandschaftsberichte 2.

47. Giskra to Foreign Office, 24 October 1906, Österreichisches Staatsarchiv-Kriegsarchiv (hereafter ÖSA-KA), Vienna, Kriegsministerium, 7A10–4/42.

48. Styrcea to Aehrenthal, 27 January 1907 and 26 June 1907, HHSA, Gesandschaftsberichte I.

49. Foreign Office to Styrcea, 4 July and 21 August 1907, HHSA, Gesandschaftsberichte I.

50. Technical-Military Comité to War Ministry, 1 July 1907, ÖSA-KA, Kriegsministerium, 7.A104–28/3.

51. Foreign Office to War Ministry, 4 June 1907, and War Ministry memorandum of 16 July 1907, ÖSA-KA, Kriegsministerium, 7.A104–28/3.

52. Steyr to War Ministry, 25 July 1907, ÖSA-KA, Kriegsministerium, 7A104–28/3–2.

53. Kosegarten to Foreign Office, 1 and 5 June 1907, AA-PA, R 16650, Chile I, vol. 37; Bodman to Bülow, 29 September 1907, AA-PA, R 16650, Chile I, vol. 37; Kosegarten to Foreign Office.

54. Bodman to Bülow, 30 January 1908, AA-PA, R 16651, Chile I, vol. 38.

55. Bodman to Bülow, 22 July 1908, AA-PA, R 16651, Chile I, vol. 38.

56. Kolowrat-Krakowsky-Liebstensky to Aehrenthal, 14 November 1908, HHSA, Gesandschaftsberichte I.

57. Erckert to Bethmann Hollweg, 31 October 1911, AA-PA, R 16651, Chile I, vol. 44.

58. Windisch-Graetz's reports of 3 and 4 May 1911, ÖSA-KA, Vienna, De 25, Nr. 1180, Berichte des Prinzen Windisch-Graetz. The prince filed the formal reports after his return to Austria.

59. Windisch-Graetz's reports of 6 May and 1 July 1911, ÖSA-KA, Vienna, De 25, Nr. 1180, Berichte des Prinzen Windisch-Graetz.

60. ÖSA-KA, Vienna, De 25, Nr. 1180, Berichte des Prinzen Windisch-Graetz. The Berlin parade had taken place on 6 June.

61. Embassy to Foreign Office, 23 June 1910 and 9 July 1911, HHSA, F 94, Karton

16; and Styrcea to Aehrenthal, 19 July 1911, HHSA, F 94, Karton 16, Gesandschaftsberichte 2.

62. Erckert to Foreign Office, 24 August 1911, AA-PA, R 16657, Chile I, vol. 44.

63. Foreign Office memoranda of 25 and 31 August and 20 September 1911, AA-PA, R 16657, Chile I, vol. 44; report signed 6 October 1911, in MERV, 10 April 1912.

64. Report signed 6 October 1911, in MERV, 10 April 1912.

65. *El Mercurio* (Santiago), 19 October 1911 (hereafter cited as MERS); Steyr to Aehrenthal, and Aehrenthal to Styrcea, 31 October 1911, HHSA, F 94, Karton 16.

66. Steyr to Aehrenthal, and Aehrenthal to Styrcea, 31 October 1911, HHSA, F 94, Karton 16; MERV, 14 April 1912.

67. MERV, 7 January 1912; Engineer Rechl to Styrcea, 8 December 1911, and Styrcea to Aehrenthal, 21 January 1912, HHSA, F 94, Karton 16; Camara de Diputados, Sesiones Ordinarias (hereafter cited as CDSO), 18 April 1912, quoted in MERV, 19 April 1912; MERS, 28 March 1912.

68. MERS, I, 2, 9, and 10 April 1912, *El Diario Ilustrado* (Santiago), 14 April 1912 (hereafter cited as DILUS); Camara de Senado, Sesiones Ordinarias, 24 October 1904, 103–5 (hereafter cited as CSSO).

69. MERS, 9 November 1911.

70. Mario Matus Gonzalez, *Tradición y Adaptación. Vivencia de los Sefaradíes en Chile* (Santiago, 1993), 55; MERS, 31 March and 24 April 1912; DILUS, 7, 15, and 24 April 1912.

71. Styrcea to Aehrenthal, 19 July 1911, HHSA, Gesandschaftsberichte 2.

72. Windisch-Graetz's diary, 22 to 31 August 1911, ÖSA-KA, De 25 Nr. 1180, Export 1911.

73. MERS, 11 October 1911; Schaefer, *Deutsche Militärhilfe an Südamerika*, 168–69 (the order was for thirty thousand rifles, four thousand carbines, and thirty million bullets); Erckert to Foreign Office, 29 October 1911, AA-PA, R 16657, Chile I, vol. 44.

74. Foreign Office memorandum, 4 November 1911, AA-PA, R 16657, Chile I, vol. 44.

75. Schaefer, *Deutsche Militärhilfe an Südamerika*, 169–70.

76. DW & MF to Erckert, 11 April 1912, AA-PA, R 16658, Chile I, vol. 45.

77. Erckert to Bethmann Hollweg, 12 February 1912, AA-PA, R 16658, Chile I, vol. 45; Styrcea to Aehrenthal, 21 January 1912, HHSA, F 94, Karton 16.

78. MERV, 24 April 1912.

79. *La Mañana* (Santiago), 2 April 1912.

80. Styrcea to Aehrenthal, 19 July 1911, HHSA, F 94, Karton 16.

81. Styrcea to Aehrenthal, 19 July 1911, HHSA, Gesandschaftsberichte 2.

82. Ibid.

83. Report of the Comisión Permanente de Presupuesto, in Camara de Senado, Sesiones Estraordinarias (herafter cited as CSSE), *Documentos Parlamentarios*, 2 January 1914, 423.

84. Erckert cables to Foreign Office, 4 May and 5 July 1912, AA-PA, R 16658, Chile I, Vol. 45.

85. Krupp somewhat lamely denied that Eccius had ever made the remark; Krupp to Foreign Office, 1 August 1912, and Foreign Office to Santiago, 2 August 1912, AA-PA, R 16658, Chile I, vol. 45.

86. Styrcea to Berchtold, 6 May 1914, commenting on Prince Henry's goodwill mission to Chile, HHSA, Gesandschaftsberichte 2.

87. War Ministry memorandum, 10 December 1913, ÖSA-KA, 2A/W43–77/15–4, 1913.

88. See, for example, his report to the Foreign Office of 31 January 1912, ÖSA-KA, 2A/W43–77/15–4, 1913.

89. Estado Mayor Jeneral, *Breve informacion sobre el ejército del Perú* (Santiago, 1911), 16–17; CDSO, 27 July 1909,1430; Lt. Francis A. Ruggles, "War Material. Chilian," Santiago, 9 June 1910, U.S. MIC, No. 1982–12, Registers of Communications Received from Military Attaches and Other Intelligence Officers "Dispatch Lists," 1889–1941; Ricardo Anguita, *Leyes Promulgadas en Chile desde 1810 hasta el 1 de Junio de 1913* (5 vols., Santiago, 1913), 4:313.

90. Bernhard Menne, *Krupp or The Lords of Essen* (London, 1937), 176–77.

91. MERV, 9 April 1909.

92. Bodman to Bülow, 20 January 1909, AA-PA, R 16652, Chile I, vol. 39.

93. Bodman to Bülow, 14 February 1909, AA-PA, R 16652, Chile I, vol. 39.

94. Bodman to Bülow, 24 May 1909, AA-PA, R 16652, Chile I, vol. 39.

95. Cited in Schaefer, *Deutsche Militärhilfe an Südamerika*, 160; CSSO, 28 October 1912, 195. It did not help Schneider-Creuzot's cause when its new "Powder B" proved to be unstable and caused an accidental explosion that destroyed the battleship *Iéna* in 1907; CSSO, II August 1909, 789–90.

96. Bodman to Bülow, 15 June 1909, AA-PA, R 16652, Chile I, vol. 39.

97. Krupp to Schoen, 20 August 1909, AA-PA, R 16653, Chile I, vol. 40.

98. Böhler to War Ministry, 12 May 1909, HHSA, F 94, Karton 16; and ÖSA-KA, Kriegsministerium 1909, 7A104–24; Seidler to Aehrenthal, 8 and 14 June 1909, HHSA, F 94, Karton 16.

99. Erckert to Foreign Office, 31 October 1911, AA-PA, R 16657, Chile I, vol. 44.

100. Schaefer, *Deutsche Militärhilfe an Südamerika*, 162.

101. Schaefer, *Deutsche Militärhilfe an Südamerika*, 163. Ambassador Desprez informed Paris that five of the eight commission members now favored Krupp.

102. Seidler to Aehrenthal, 10 January 1910, HHSA, F 94, Karton 16; Schaefer, *Deutsche Militärhilfe an Südamerika*, 163; Pedro Montt to Augusto Matte, Santiago, 17 January 1910, AN, Fondos Varios, vol. 204; CSSO, 17 August 1909, 818.

103. *La Lei* (Santiago), 8 January 1910.

104. Cámara de Diputados, sesiones estraordinarias (herafter cited as CDSE), 27 January 1911, 1719–23; CDSE, 11 and 12 February 1911; "Aufstellung Krupp über seine Waffenlieferungen an Chile," AA-PA, R 3877, Preussen I Nr 3 Prinz Heinrich von Preussen, vol. 13.

105. Seth L. Purrepont to Secretary of State, Santiago, 4 August 1910, United States of America, Report of Department of State Relative to the Internal Affairs of Chile, 1910–1929, 825.24 (hereafter cited as RDS); Seidler to Aehrenthal, 12 November 1909, HHSA, F 94, Karton 16.

106. War Ministry to Foreign Office, 23 March 1910, HHSA, F 94, Karton 16.

107. Schaefer, *Deutsche Militärhilfe an Südamerika*, 266, n. 46; internal memorandum, Foreign Office, 12 December 1911, AA-AP, Regierungen Waffenlieferungen dt. Firmen an fremde (Amerika), vol. I. See also Hell, "Deutschland und Chile von 1871–1918," 90–91.

108. Rheinische Metallwaren- und Maschinenfabrik to Foreign Office, 18 and 21 January 1910, AA-PA, R 16653, Chile I, vol. 40.

109. Telegram from Chilean Minister to Santiago, Paris, 2 December 1909, in AN, Ministerio de Relaciones Esteriores (hereafter cited as MRE), vol. 1376; Menne, *Krupp or The Lords of Essen*, 239.

110. Renato Sanchez to Minister of War, Viña del Mar, 24 February 1912; Antonio to Huneeus-Minister of War, Santiago, 12 December 1912, in AN, MRE, Oficios dirigidos al M. de Guerray de Marina, vol. 1601; Styrcea to Aehrenthal, 23 June 1910, HHSA, Gesandschaftsberichte I.

111. Krupp memorandum, 30 April 1910, Allgemein. Krupp memorandum, 22 August 1911 HAK-FA4, C193, Privatbureau Dr. Krupp v. B. u. H. Chile.

112. CSSO, 19 August 1912, 656–57; CSSO 21 October 1912, 113–14; MERS, 22 August 1912.

113. MERS, 15 and 17 October 1912.

114. MERS, 20 and 21 October 1912.

115. MERS, 23 October 1912.

116. MERS, 1 and 3 November 1912.

117. MERS, 30 October 1912 and 4, 6, and 23 November 1912.

118. MERS, 25, 27, 29, and 30 December 1912.

119. MERS, 5 April 1912; CDSO, 3 January 1913, 1374–76; CSSO, 21 October 1912, 117; Public Records Office, Kew, FO 371/1588/217; Annual Report of 1912," 7 FO 371/1588/325.

120. CSSO, 21 and 28 October 1912, 117–18, 198; MERV, 22 July 1912; C., "Contracts for War Material in Chile," 17 August 1912, RDS, 825.25; Schaefer, *Deutsche Militärhilfe an Südamerika*, 73; William Manchester, *The Arms of Krupp, 1587–1968* (Boston, 1964), 166; "Summary of Recent Events for the Month of April, 1913," FO 371/1589/822, 3; MERV, 17 February 1910; CSSO, 28 October 1912, 202, 204; MERS, 17 February 1910; MERV, 6 January 1914. In fairness, the Germans were not the only ones to play that game; Armstrong apparently paid some £50,000 to ensure that it won a contract to build two battleships for the Chilean fleet. See C., "Contracts for War Material in Chile," 17 August 1912, RDS, 825.25.

121. *La Razón* (Santiago), 29 October 1912; *La Unión* (Valparaíso), 9 July 1912.

122. Erckert to Foreign Office, 13 July 1912, BA-AP, Waffenlieferungen . . . (Amerika), vol. I.

123. Erckert to Foreign Office, 23 January 1913, AA-PA, R 16659, Chile I, vol. 46.

124. Erckert to Bethmann Hollweg, 31 October 1911, AA-PA, R 16657, Chile I, vol. 44.

125. Erckert to Bethmann Hollweg, 12 February 1912, AA-PA, R 16658, Chile I, vol. 45.

126. HAK, 48/51, 48/94 Besuche; HAK-WA48 Besuchwesen.

127. HAK-WA 6Y Besuche; and HAK-WA 48/94 Besuche; Erckert to Foreign Office, 7 April 1911, M-PA, R 16657, Chile I, vol. 44; HAK-WA 7.f.1448; Beckmann, "Erfahrungen im Kriegsmaterial-Geschäft," NIK 1051, 9.9.1937, 60; Fokker Aeroplanbau to Embassy Santiago, 28 November 1913, AA-AP, Waffenlieferungen . . . (Amerika), vol. 2.

128. Erckert to Foreign Office, 1 January and 18 December 1912, BA-AP, Militärwesen Chile, Nr. 122, vol. 8.

CHAPTER 5

Undermining the *Cordon Sanitaire:* Naval Arms Sales and Anglo-French Competition in Latvia, 1924–25

Donald J. Stoker Jr.

In the aftermath of World War I, Britain, France, and the other Allied powers assisted the independence struggles of the new nations of Central and eastern Europe. In some respects, Britain and France pursued this policy out of sympathy for the former subject peoples of the disintegrating Romanov, Hohenzollern, and Habsburg Empires. Self-interest, though, soon proved a stronger driving force than any esoteric emotional attachment. Great Britain, but more particularly France, hoped to create among these new and reborn nations a group of states that would help France to offset any future resurgence of German military power. The French also hoped to forestall what they saw as growing British economic penetration in the region.[1]

This policy continued to evolve in the period of instability immediately following World War I and merged with a desire in both Britain and France to also establish a barrier against Bolshevism and keep it contained in Russia.[2] The combined fears of Germany and Lenin's Russia led both Britain and France to begin arming in at least some small fashion the region's new nations.

This is an expanded version of an article that appeared in *Journal of Baltic Studies* 28, no. 2 (1997): 171–80. Some of the material is from the author's doctoral dissertation, "Undermining the Cordon Sanitaire: Naval Arms Sales, Naval Building, and Anglo-French Competition in the Baltic, 1918 1940 Poland—Finland—The Baltic States" (Florida State University, 1997). A revised and expanded version, *Britain, France, and the Naval Arms in the Baltic 1919–39: Grand Strategy and Failure*, is forthcoming from Frank Cass Publishers, 2003.

During the initial period of instability after World War I, Poland, Finland, and the Baltic States of Latvia, Lithuania, and Estonia received small arms and other military equipment from Great Britain and France, sometimes without charge. When the immediate threat of Lenin's Russia and adventurers such as Colonel P. M. Bermondt-Avalov and Count Rudiger von der Göltz passed, all of the nations of the eastern Baltic began to reorganize their military forces and embark upon efforts to strengthen them. To do this these states needed modern military equipment, most of which could only come from foreign nations. Part of the armament programs of all of the nations of the eastern Baltic included some expenditure for the creation of naval forces. When it became known in Great Britain and France, as well as in other industrial powers, that Latvia intended to create a small but modern naval force, the news did not provoke Anglo-French cooperation in an effort to strengthen the nations that Britain and France had helped create, but instead provoked intense competition between the powers for the prospective contracts. The rivalry between Britain and France for what was a small number of contracts provides insight into the manner in which the two powers conducted policy in the eastern Baltic in the 1920s and 1930s. It also depicts the continuity in the economic concerns that strongly influenced the initial British and French involvement in the Baltic region after World War I,[3] presenting a clear picture of each state's true goal: regional economic dominance.

After the establishment of regional stability came the development of the private and public institutions necessary for the creation and maintenance of naval forces. Elements within each of these states lobbied for naval growth and debates on various naval bills raged in many of the respective parliaments. All of these states eventually voted funding for the acquisition of warships, naval aircraft, and other equipment. Their quests for builders and suppliers provided fertile ground for often-intense competition among the various European arms producers and shipbuilders. British and French firms, as well as a few from other nations, waged particularly bitter struggles for the orders. The governments of Britain and France also became involved in the fights, often on an intimate level. The French and British businessmen, as well as many of the respective government officials involved in brokering the treaties, frequently proved willing to go to extremes to claim the often very limited contracts offered by the states of the eastern Baltic. The foreign salesmen and government officials usually labored in the belief that an initial success would reap long-term rewards.

A hallmark of the competition between the two powers is the constant effort by both parties to undermine the influence of the other and to discredit their opponent in the eyes of the various small states. This served not to strengthen but to undermine the very security system that Britain and France had constructed—the *Cordon Sanitaire*.

LATVIAN NAVAL DEVELOPMENT AND THE GREAT POWERS

The Latvian impetus to purchase naval armaments began in 1921 when the Latvian parliament, or Saeima, began examining the nation's coastal defense needs as a means of improving the nation's security and contributing to the maintenance of the fledgling state's independence.[4] Extensive discussion of the nation's naval defense requirements followed until April 10, 1924, when after much partisan debate, the Saeima passed the Latvian Naval Defense Law. It provided for the expenditure over a four-year period of 9,989,200 lats, or about £440,000, and approved the purchase of two submarines, two mine-sweepers, and 500 mines. The Latvians did not issue a public call for the submission of bids for the contracts but solicited prices from three British and one French firm.[5]

As early as July 1921, long before the Latvians voted any funding for the warships, they asked France about the terms that French builders might offer. The French representative in Riga, de Martel, quickly decided that winning the contracts would allow the placement of French advisors in France and increase French influence in Latvia. The French Navy had a similar view and eagerly foresaw the possibility of a French naval mission in the event of a French firm winning the contract.[6]

The proceeding statements give a clear indication of the earnestness with which the French approached winning the contracts related to the naval program. Long before the allocation of any funds the French embarked upon a number of attempts to corral the sales. De Martel, an eager and industrious representative of French governmental and industrial interests, recommended the cession to Latvia of a certain number of smaller, obsolete vessels, such as destroyers and submarines, but with a catch: any future Latvian naval orders would have to go to French industry. The French Navy liked the idea and offered the destroyer *Hussard*, which could be put into a navigable state for 300,000 francs. The Latvians also liked the arrangement and apparently gave the nod on the deal, but an unforeseen event intervened: the Great Powers concluded the Washington Naval Treaties, a clause of which prevented the sale of existing warships for military use to third parties. De Martel had to be satisfied with 3,000 francs for entertaining the officers of the visiting French Baltic naval squadron and sundry local dignitaries.[7]

In the competition for the contracts, French officials and firms began maneuvering for position shortly after the Latvian minister of defense revealed his nation's intention to purchase a number of seaplanes. Capitaine de frégate Vennin, the French naval attaché for the Baltic States and Scandinavia, was one of the major figures involved in the contract battle. To Vennin, bringing the Latvian naval orders to a French firm was one of his primary tasks. Many of the parties involved in the deals, both British and French, used various and often-questionable measures in their attempts to sway the Latvian's decisions, a point subsequently addressed in more detail. Vennin was certainly not alone in hoping that such efforts would provide him with an advantage over his competitors.[8]

Despite the often-strenuous efforts of Vennin, de Martel, and others, the French were thwarted in their attempt to obtain the initial contracts for seaplanes and sea mines, which went to the British firm Vickers. But they proved successful in the battle for the more substantial portions of the Latvian naval program. The official Latvian decision regarding who would receive the contracts eventually came to rest on one point more than any other: training; but other, less publicly discussed elements also played a part. The Latvian government asked both the British and the French about the possibility of Latvian officers and men attending their respective naval training schools. They approached the British in April 1924 and inquired about sending three officers to the Royal Navy submarine school to gain practical experience, as well as another to the torpedo school. The British naval attaché and other British representatives in the region warned that if the Admiralty did not agree to the request, the contract would go to the French because of France's willingness to accede to Latvia's wishes. The Admiralty replied that it would favorably consider any application for the torpedo school, but that it was against Admiralty policy to train foreign officers on British submarines. The Admiralty did agree to give the Latvians instruction on their own boats—if they purchased the vessels in Great Britain.[9]

General Radzin, the commander of the Latvian Army, brought the question of training Latvian naval personnel to the attention of Capitaine de frégate Vennin. Vennin assured him that the French government would agree to the Latvian request, especially considering the past relations between the two states. Vennin encouraged his superiors to take positive action on this matter because he felt sure that it would aid French "political and moral" influence in Latvia. He also wrote that France had arrived at "an important point in the struggle against English influence in Latvia. Hopefully it will end to our advantage." The French agreed to open all of their naval schools to Latvian officers and also consented to their completing their training with a period of duty on ships in service with the French fleet. The French did not make the offer without attaching strings. The deal could only be struck if the orders for the items anticipated by the naval law found their way to French industrial concerns. The instructions for this came from Contre-Amiral Brisson, now undersecretary of the French Admiralty Staff. To the Latvians, Brisson was a hero, having commanded the French naval squadron that intervened on the side of the Latvians in the battle for Riga during the young nation's struggle for independence.[10]

The primary British competitor for the warships was Vickers. Another British firm, Beardmores, had recently won a Latvian contract for a pair of icebreakers. De Martel postulated bribery as the reason for the British success but could prove nothing. The strong interest of Vickers in the Latvian deal prompted de Martel to ask the French foreign ministry to put pressure on the Latvian minister to Paris. De Martel believed it necessary to use any influence he might possess to bring the contracts to France and urged French intervention on behalf of Normand, Chantiers de la Loire, and Sautter-Harle.[11]

SALES FOR SECURITY?

In December 1923, while the Latvian parliament still debated funding the naval bill, Prime Minister S. Meierovics embarked upon an ambitious attempt to use the awarding of the contracts to garner a security guarantee for Latvia. On December 10, 1923, Meierovics told Sir Tudor Vaughan, the British representative in Riga, that political considerations had a strong bearing on Latvia's decision regarding the awarding of the contracts. The Latvian prime minister intimated to Vaughan a supposed French promise that if the order for the ships went to France, the French would send warships to Latvia's coastline if the nation came under attack. Meierovics confessed that he did not put much faith in such a promise, but Vaughan feared that any remarks along this line might be enough to sway Latvia into the French industrial camp. Foreign Office officials inquired if the statement made by the French had included the term "weather permitting" and advised Vaughan to ask the Latvians to make a comparison between French and British naval presence in the Baltic and to point out that "French men-of-war depend more on 'weather' (political and meteorological) than British."[12]

This was only the first part of Meierovics's gambit. He told de Martel, the French consul, in "strictest confidence," that Vaughan, the British representative, had said that in the event of a conflict he had no doubt that a British fleet would come to the Baltic and that the British would intervene with Moscow on Latvia's behalf.[13]

Meierovics obviously wanted to extract some type of promise of support in the event of a Soviet attack and seized upon an opportunity. And, at least in regard to getting local French officials to fall into his trap, he had some success. De Martel urged his superiors to grant the French consul permission to give the Latvians some type of imprecise declaration of French support on a par with the "rather vague assurances" de Martel believed Britain had offered. Moreover, he thought the position of France vis-à-vis the awarding of the contracts a very weak one because France had not yet signed a commercial accord with Latvia. To help the French position he urged the visit of a large, French naval force to the Baltic.[14]

At least one of the French industrial representatives eager to get the contracts also succumbed to Meierovics's plan. Capitaine de Corvette René Jouen, a former French naval officer and at the time the representative of Ateliers et Chantiers de la Loire, met with Meierovics and discussed the meeting with his superior, Marcel Haas. The Latvian prime minister said that the Latvians would award the contracts based upon three considerations: financial, technical, and political. Meierovics said that financially, the French and British were in line with one another, and that technically the French vessels were seen as superior. But on the political point, Haas insisted that France stood on less solid ground because of the supposed British promise of support against the Soviets—an assurance not matched by the French government. Commandant Jouen believed that Meierovics wanted to give the French the contracts if they would grant the same "assurances" as the British or at least similar ones. If he received these, then Meierovics would award the bid based upon the technical superiority of the French vessels. Haas, on behalf of the French builders, wanted de Martel instructed to give just such "assurances" so that Atelier et Chantiers de la Loire got the orders, and he wanted this information passed on to Grosvald, the Latvian minister in Paris.[15]

Haas also believed that a second naval program would follow and that the Latvians, in order to preserve the homogeneity of their forces, would certainly pass the second order on to the same party that built the first ships. Moreover, he believed that the Latvian-Estonian military alliance opened up the possibility of contracts with the Estonians if the French could emerge victorious in the Latvian conflict.[16] The salesmen habitually assumed that the winning of one order would result in follow-on sales. They were usually disappointed.

According to Haas, the enormous French desire to gain the contracts was not confined to the diplomats and businessmen who dealt with the Latvians. Some in the French Navy also hoped that the vessels of the Latvian Navy would be built in French yards. Having under construction in France warships of a French type for a foreign power would, in the event of mobilization, provide a ready reserve of compatible material that the navy could requisition. Because of the then reduced state of the French naval forces, in the eyes of the French admirals this new construction provided potentially important additions. Above everything, Haas insisted that the decision on who got the contracts hinged above all on the "benevolent support" of the head of the French foreign ministry and the efforts of French diplomats to put French political influence in Latvia on the same par as that of Great Britain.[17]

The French foreign ministry proved not so eager to take Meierovics's bait. The French made inquiries in London and found that the British had made no such declarations of the "tenor" that French reports from Latvia had intimated. The British committed to following the provisions of the League of Nations (which also bound France) regarding the defense of a state under attack but certainly had no intention of unilaterally intervening with a naval force on Latvia's behalf. The French found it "particularly unbecoming" to link any eventual French political and military intervention to the granting of an order to private industry. De Martel was authorized to tell the Latvians that possible French assistance would have a more "concrete character" if Meierovics extended the Latvian-Estonian alliance to Poland.[18]

THE WARSHIP SALES

As the political maneuvering continued, the Latvians considered the plans and bids submitted by the various British and French firms such as Vickers, Hawthorne Leslie & Co., Chantiers de la Loire, and Chantiers Augustin Normand. Captain (later Admiral) Archibald von Keyserling, the head of the Latvian Navy, proved his devotion to the French cause by delivering to Vennin the plans for submarines submitted by the British firms. Vennin made critical remarks about the validity of the British designs and particularly doubted the stated speed and battery capacity. He believed the plans to be a "bluff," the submarines impossible to produce, and that the British had simply found a way "to beat" the Latvians. Vennin also remarked that he had information from an unnamed "good source" on the inferiority of the British subs. Finally, he recorded his belief that the plans submitted by the British applied only to a vessel designed for export and it would be interesting to compare the designs submitted to the Latvians with those for a submarine constructed for the British Navy. Vennin believed that if he could prove these allegations he would have a powerful weapon in the fight for the contracts for the naval program.[19] His charges were mere suspicion and probably an example of the rabid Anglophobia affecting the officer corps of the French Navy. The Royal Navy commonly supported its shipbuilders by allowing them to sell based upon Admiralty designs. This kept British yards busy and reduced the cost of the Royal Navy's own vessels.[20]

The British did not remain inactive and Vaughan believed that he could influence the Latvian decision if a British squadron, which included a submarine flotilla, visited Latvia. Such visits are not uncommon and not a few of the government and military officials involved in the competition, Vennin for example, believed, correctly, that navies serve a valuable role as tools of foreign policy. Vaughan requested from his superiors a definite date for the visit and suggested that if the contract went to the French the visit could be canceled as a protest. The Foreign Office did not appreciate his last suggestion. One official commented that it "savours too much of French methods."[21]

Eventually, the order for the Latvian submarines went to the French firm Chantiers de la Loire, while Chantiers Augustin Normand of Hâvre received the contract for the two minesweepers. But this did not occur until July 4, 1924, after the resolution of a Latvian ministerial crisis and much pleading for intervention on their behalf by the French industrial concerns. Keyserling went to France to supervise the building of the vessels purchased by his government. The French probably won the contracts because the British Admiralty would only provide theoretical instruction to Latvian officers, while the French promised theoretical training combined with shipboard service. Price apparently played a minor role. The French submitted a bid of 6,432,800 lats for the submarines and 1,556,900 lats for the minesweepers. The French offered the lowest price for the latter vessels, the bid being 58 percent less than that offered by the association of Vickers and Hawthorne Leslie & Company. J. Samuel White, another British firm, submitted a lower bid for the submarines, 6,356,116 lats, but did not receive the order. A British diplomat in Riga commented that the "French appear to have held out many other inducements which we were precluded from doing," a point addressed momentarily.[22]

After striking the deal for the vessels, members of Prime Minister Meierovics's government informed British officials that the order for the two minesweepers and the two submarines remained open and still might be awarded to a British firm. The British speculated that this was an attempt by the Latvians to play the French corporations off the British in order to get some concessions from the French. Another Foreign Office official expressed his belief that Meierovics's statement came from the prime minister's "desire to say pleasant things to English M.P.'s" then visiting Latvia. The Latvian minister for foreign affairs remarked that the government had hesitated only about spending the money and not on where to spend it. The minister of finance had proved difficult because he insisted that Latvia's financial position could not tolerate the amounts projected for defense. Despite the opposition, the purchases went through, the French built the ships, and the *Virsaitis* left for France on August 9, 1926, to escort the new vessels to Latvia. On board were the officers and men of the two new Latvian minesweepers, *Vesturs* and *Imanta*, as well as some of the crewmen for the new submarines, *Ronis* and *Spidola*. The minesweepers were scheduled to arrive in Riga in the middle of September, the submarines sometime later.[23]

BEHIND THE SCENES

As previously demonstrated, the contracts for the minesweepers and submarines apparently went to the French because of their willingness to train Latvian officers. But other factors, some of which did not come to light until several years later, also had a part. Corruption played a significant role. Major H. W. C. Lloyd, the British military attaché for the Baltic States and Finland, observed that in Latvia and the other Baltic States the old Russian tradition of bribery and corruption still existed in government circles. American officials noted that Latvians involved in the arrangement of government contracts expected "an indirect compensation usually in the neighborhood of 10% of the transaction." The Latvians made an attempt to correct this by establishing a State Control Commission. Minor officials sat on the commission and had the power to examine all questions of expenditure. As a result, when the ministry of defense compiled their military estimates these figures passed through the State Control Commission. If the measure managed to emerge from this process it was usually in an altered form. Purchases of war materials abroad went through a similar procedure and the expert advice of the military once again suffered from interference. In the end, the system failed to deal with the bribery issue because those who wished to ensure that a proposal survived the commission merely bribed its members.[24]

Both the French and the British made use of the tradition of corruption then in place in Latvia. In 1928, after the delivery of the submarines purchased in France, General Janis Baladois, the Latvian minister for foreign affairs, expressed to Joseph Addison, the British representative in Riga, his regrets that the order had not gone to a British firm. Baladois also appended his hope that any future orders for submarines would go to Britain and commented that Britain failed to receive the contract because they would not provide training for Latvian naval officers. Some British officials believed that other factors contributed to deciding the fate of the contracts for the naval program. Addison wrote in his report to the Foreign Office on his conversation with the Latvian minister that Baladois

Naturally did not supplement this simple explanation by stating the other, and more cogent reason for our failure to secure this contract, namely that the Latvian Admiral [Keyserling] had become convinced of the superiority of the French submarines only after he had received the Legion of Honour, as well as the certainty of a reward of a more substantial nature.[25]

Addison went on to express his belief that as long as Keyserling remained head of the "Latvian 'Navy'" the scales would remain "heavily weighted in the favour of France" and because of this any British bids would have little chance of succeeding. Addison divulged other reports of collusion between the French and Keyserling:

Acting on the French proverb that "les petits cadeaux entretiennent l'amitié" Count Keyserling continues to enjoy little favours destined to keep alive his sentiments of gratitude. I have it for instance, on the best of authorities, that he is able periodically to renew his cellar from the French Legation on most-favoured-nation terms, instead of having to pay the blackmailing charges of one of the local bootleggers. In the words of Figaro "qui diable y resisterait?"[26]

It is hardly surprising that Keyserling proved much more pliable in the hands of the French representatives, because it would be quite difficult to bribe a gentleman with English wine.

Addison was not the only British official to report such irregularities. Vaughan also mentions the offer of "high French decorations" to Latvian officials if the orders for the naval program went to France. But it seems that this accusation could be, at least in some respects, a case of sour grapes. Count Keyserling received his Legion of Honor on November 19, 1924, and the French recommended that a number of other officials also receive decorations, six in all. These six were not recommended for their awards until 1926, more than two years after the signing of the contracts. The French foreign ministry wanted to give the awards to demonstrate the importance they placed upon the planned launch of the Latvian submarine *Spidola*. Those recommended for the award were in some way connected to the submarine launch and included the commanders of the two submarines and General Radzin, the commander in chief of the Latvian forces. Only five of these six received the proposed honor. The French government refused the urging of Monsieur Augustin Normand to decorate Feldmans, the Latvian chargé d'affaires in Paris, who Monsieur Normand said had been "actively" involved in the sale of the submarines. The foreign ministry followed its professed protocol of not giving such awards to diplomats unless they were leaving France after serving there for at least two years.[27]

Addison believed that another factor also contributed to the British failure to obtain the orders for the Latvian submarines. Vickers had been competing for the orders and Addison contended that the loss of the contract resulted partially from the actions of Vickers's special agent in Latvia, "an idiot of the name of Savitsky." This is a marked contrast with French views regarding their personnel involved with the bidding. One French official applauded de Martel's role and considered the "patient intelligence" of Chantiers de la Loire's representative Commandant Jouen instrumental to French success.[28]

Addison was also critical of another Vickers agent, Sakovsky, and remarked that the Latvians liked neither of the men and refused to deal with them. He gathered that the Latvians disliked Sakovsky because he "chatters too much and does not keep such promises as he may have made to distribute certain sums of money to the persons interested." Addison also wrote that:

Sakovsky is such an ass in his own business that he actually went to somebody I know here and asked him whether he could introduce him to Admiral Keyserling and fix up the proper bribe. Anything more idioted [*sic*] I cannot imagine."[29]

Addison went on to recommend that Vickers send a special agent "who should be an intelligent person and not, as usual, a silly ass." Addison also commented that Vickers should not have expected to obtain a contract for submarines unless they expected to "pay a certain sum for services rendered," an obvious allusion to the necessity of bribing the proper people.[30] It is likely that much of official Latvian hostility toward Sakovsky arose because he was Russian. The intensely nationalistic Latvians disliked doing business with Russians and British firms that employed Russians as their local representatives in Latvia, as well as Estonia, often did great damage to their chances of winning orders. Latvian governmental and business personnel treated Jewish representatives in the same manner.[31]

Keyserling's apparent collusion with the French seems to have brought him no immediate ill effects. On November 18, 1927, on the ninth anniversary of Latvia's independence, he received a promotion to rear admiral. Five years later, though, Admiral Keyserling was forced to resign by the Latvian government, an event that some British observers must have considered just and that others clearly regarded as a boon for the future of British naval sales to Latvia. Their hopes did not bear fruit, as the Latvian Navy remained "clearly Francophile" under the leadership of Captain Theodor Spade, Keyserling's replacement and a graduate of the French Naval War College.[32]

Before his resignation, Keyserling had involved himself in several incidents that had helped discredit him in the eyes of his superiors. The immediate cause of his dismissal resulted from an incident at sea. During a return trip of the fleet from Estonia, members of the Social Democratic Party serving in the navy observed the transfer of large quantities of liquor from another vessel to *Virsaitis*, the Latvian flagship. Exactly what the admiral intended to do with the smuggled goods remains unclear, but it is possible that he had a problem with alcohol as the mention of it often appears in the documents when he does. For example, during one visit of the Latvian fleet to Estonia, Keyserling immobilized himself by getting drunk and falling down a stairwell on his own gunboat.[33]

A customs officer visited the ship and confirmed the allegation. On September 17, 1931, the minister of war reported to the president that there existed irregularities in the Latvian Navy and recommended a change in the high command. The president consented and the minister of war ordered Admiral Keyserling to tender his resignation. Keyserling agreed to go without a fight and the government withdrew an order that it had issued for his compulsory retirement.[34]

Politics played a role in the entire matter. After the admiral's impropriety came to light, the Democratic Center Party approached the minister of war and demanded Keyserling's immediate dismissal. Reportedly, the minister informed them that a decision had already been reached on the issue. Because Keyserling was a German Balt, the leaders of the Baltic-German faction attempted to intervene, albeit unsuccessfully, on his behalf. The admiral insisted that his demise was the result of a plot hatched by the Social Democrats and that the campaign against him began during the temporary absence of President Kviesis. During this time, Dr. P. Kalnins, the president of the Saeima and a member of the Social Democratic Party, served as president. The Social Democrats had been demanding the admiral's resignation for some time and Keyserling considered this an election stunt engineered in order to get the anti-German vote.[35]

The British military attaché at the time believed that the real reason for Keyserling's resignation lay in the fact that he was a Baltic German. The attaché expressed doubts that an ethnic Latvian officer would have been forced to retire if the same irregularities had occurred under his tenure. The attaché also reported that the local gossips maintained that the Latvian military authorities wanted to replace Keyserling and were only waiting until they had a Lettish officer sufficiently trained to take over the admiral's tasks. The government now possessed such an officer, Captain Spade, and supposedly used the smuggling incident as an excuse to remove Keyserling. The attaché, though, did agree with the statements made by the minister of war regarding past improper behavior by Keyserling. Keyserling "strenuously" supporting a recent French bid for submarine batteries had brought the admiral into direct conflict with the director of the Armament Department and the chief of staff. The attaché closed his discussion of this part of the scandal with, "but it is more than probable that he would have remained at the post had his origin not been German-Baltic." Others commented that the feelings that helped produce the downfall of Admiral Keyserling might not have erupted but for the impending national elections.[36]

CONCLUSION

In the end, the effort exerted by the French and British governments to establish influence in Latvia through winning naval arms sales netted both parties very little. The French secured the orders for a few vessels and the British scored some minor successes, but one wonders if the effort exerted by these powers and the friction that competition between rivals inevitably produces was worth the price of a few contracts. Each party's fear of the other gaining the upper hand, as well as their contempt for the methods of their rivals, which often differed very little, was exacerbated by their competition, and this at a time when the balance of power in Europe was slowly shifting back to Germany's favor. It is obvious that cooperation would have served all parties involved, France, Britain, and especially Latvia. Additionally, the constant conflict could do little to encourage Latvian faith in Britain or France, and especially not in the possibility of future Anglo-French cooperation in the event of a crisis in the region. French and British rivalry only made the position of the former Entente partners in eastern Europe more untenable, undermined the *Cordon Sanitaire*, and by this, injured the strategic position of Latvia much more than any supply of arms could aid it.

Clearly, Anglo-French competition in Latvia arose from the efforts of British and French diplomats to increase the political and economic influence of their respective nations. Arms sales were seen as a means of furthering both of these nonmilitary goals.

NOTES

1. Kalervo Hovi, *Cordon Sanitaire or Barriere de l'Est? The Emergence of the New French Eastern European Alliance Policy 1917–1919*, Annales Universitatis Turkuensis, Ser. B, Tom. 135 (Turku, 1975), 12; id., *Alliance de Revers. Stabilization of France's Alliance Policies in East Central Europe 1919–1921*, Annales Universitatis Turkuensis, Ser. B, Tom. 163 (Turku, 1984), 68–69.

2. Hovi, *Cordon Sanitaire*, 217.

3. Hovi, *Alliance de Revers*, 67–69.

4. "Lettland wird seine Kriegsflottille haben," *Latvijas Kareivis*, 28 October 1924, cited in Po 14, Lettland, Auswärtiges Amt, Berlin.

5. Goodden to WO, "Reports and Letters to Director for Military Operations & Intelligence," 15 April 1924, Imperial War Museum (hereafter cited as IWM), Colonel R. B. Goodden Papers, PP/73/137/7; Lowdon to Dept. of Overseas Trade, 11 April 1924, FO 371/10369; Vennin to Ministre de la Marine, 3 July 1923, Service Historique de la Marine, Vincennes, Paris (hereafter cited as SHM), carton 1BB⁷ 128 Lettonie; *Rigasche Rundschau*, February 1924, cited in Vennin report, 1 April 1924, SHM, carton 1BB⁷ 129 Lettonie. For the text of the Latvian Coast Defense Law, see enclosure in 24 April 1924, FO 371/10369. *Latvijas Kareivis* was a daily newspaper published with the assistance of the Latvian government. Its readers were primarily members of the military. Swett report, 15 October 1922, United States, Military Intelligence Division, *Correspondence of the Military Intelligence Division Relating to General Political, Economic, and Military Conditions in Poland and the Baltic States, 1918–1941* (Washington, D.C., 1981), microfilm, roll 10, file MID 2621–58.

6. De Martel to Briand, 28 July 1921, Ministré des Affaires Etrangères (hereafter cited as MAE), Paris, Lettonie 22; de Martel to Briand, 28 September 1921, MAE, Paris, Lettonie 22; sig. ill., Ministre de la Marine to Chef de la Division Navale en Baltique, 28 October 1921, MAE, Paris, Lettonie 22.

7. Ministre de la Marine to MAE, 6 March 1922, Lettonie 22, MAE; MAE to de Martel, 18 March 1922, Lettonie 22, MAE; MAE note, 25 April 1922, Lettonie 22, MAE. For the regional impact of the Washington Naval Treaties on the Baltic successor states, see Donald J. Stoker Jr., "Unintended Consequences: The Effects of the Washington Naval Treaties on the Baltic," *Journal of Baltic Studies*, 21, no. 1 (spring 2000): 80–94.

8. Vennin report, 3 July 1923, SHM, carton 1BB⁷ 128 Lettonie; Vennin to Ministre de la Marine, 26 December 1923, SHM, carton 1BB⁷ 128 Lettonie.

9. Naval attaché to Admiralty, 16 April 1924, FO 371/10369; Vaughan, 18 April 1924, FO 371/10369; Admiralty to naval attaché, 16 April 1924, FO 371/10369; Jürg Meister, "Den Lettiska flottan 1918–1941," *Tidskrift i sjöväsendet* 136 (June 1974), 300–301. I would like to thank Hege Carlson for translating this article.

10. Vennin to Ministre de la Marine, 8 April 1924, SHM, carton 1BB⁷ 129 Lettonie; French legation to Keyserling, 23 April 1924, SHM, carton 1BB⁷ 129 Lettonie; Vennin to Keyserling, 23 April 1924, SHM, carton 1BB⁷ 129 Lettonie; Vennin to Ministre de la Marine, 12 September 1924, SHM, carton 1BB⁷ 129 Lettonie.

11. De Martel to Poincaré, 27 July 1923, Lettonie 22, MAE; de Martel to Poincaré, 17 October 1923, Lettonie 22, MAE; de Martel to MAE, 22 November 1923, Lettonie 22, MAE; de Martel to Poincaré, 27 July 1923, Lettonie 22, MAE.

12. Vaughan to FO, 18 December 1923, FO 371/9267; Mascre, FO minute, 1 January 1924, FO 371/9267. A Foreign Office official made the following comment: "French naval support is a very flimsy safeguard beyond perhaps the mouth of the Seine," Ovey, FO minute, 1 January 1924, FO 371/9267. The British made yearly cruises to the Baltic. After the dissolution of the French Baltic Division, the French did not.

13. De Martel to Poincaré, 21 December 1923, MAE, Lettonie 22; Haas report, 29 December 1923, MAE, Lettonie 22.

14. De Martel to Poincaré, 21 December 1923, MAE, Lettonie 22.

15. MAE report, 4 March 1924, MAE, Lettonie 22; Haas report, 29 December 1923, MAE, Lettonie 22.

16. Haas report, 29 December 1923, MAE, Lettonie 22.

17. Ibid.

18. MAE to de Martel, 11 January 1924, MAE, Lettonie 22.

19. Phipps to MacDonald, 15 July 1924, FO 371/10380; Vaughan to FO, 15 July 1924, FO 371/10380; Vennin to Vice Amiral, sous-chef de l'Etat Major de la Marine, 19 May 1924, SHM, carton 1BB⁷ 129 Lettonie; Vennin to Ministre de la Marine, 12 Feb. 1924, SHM, carton 1BB⁷ 129 Lettonie.

20. Christopher Bell, *The Royal Navy, Seapower, and Strategy Between the Wars* (Stanford: Stanford University Press, 2000), 158–59.

21. Vaughan to FO, 23 April 1924, FO 371/10369; Carr, FO minute, 23 April 1924, FO 371/10369; Vennin to Chef de 2ème Bureau, EMG, 9 April 1924, SHM, carton 1BB⁷ 129 Lettonie; Mounsey to Admiralty, 23 April 1924, FO 371/10369; Merja Liisa Hinkkanen-Lievonen, *British Trade and Enterprise in the Baltic States, 1919–1925* (Helsinki, 1984), 211. The British Admiralty planned to send HMS *Curacoa*, HMS *Conquest*, and the 1st Submarine Flotilla to the Baltic. The ships visited the area from 13–18 June 1924, Admiralty to FO, 30 April 1924, FO 371/10369. A squadron of French torpedo boats visited Latvia in May 1924.

22. Vennin to Ministre de la Marine, 23 July 1924, SHM, carton 1BB⁷ 127 Finlande; Lescuyer to Herriot, 5 July 1924, MAE, Lettonie 22; "Count Keyserling," *Riga Times*, 4 April 1925, 5; Lt. Colonel F. P. Nosworthy report, "Visit to the Baltic States. 9th May, 1924/2nd June, 1924," n.d., WO 106/1573; Vaughan to FO, 30 July 1924, FO 371/10380; Phipps to MacDonald, 15 July 1924, FO 371/10380; Vaughan to FO, 15 July 1924, FO 371/10380; Lowdon to FO, 11 July 1924, FO 371/10380; Lowdon to Dept. of Overseas Trade, 29 October 1924, FO 371/10380.

23. Leigh-Smith to MacDonald, 18 September 1924, FO 371/10380; Carr, FO minute, 6 October 1924, FO 371/10380; Leigh-Smith to MacDonald, 2 November 1924, FO 371/10380; Vaughan to MacDonald, 23 August 1924, FO 371/10380; "Naval Officers," *Riga Times*, 14 August 1926, 3. When the submarine *Ronis* was launched at Nantes on 1 July 1926, the ceremony marking the event was hailed as "one of the most stirring manifestations of Franco-Latvian amity." Keyserling and other Latvian officials as well as important members of the French government and military attended the event. See "Franco-Latvian Amity," *Riga Times*, 10 July 1926, 1.

24. Lloyd to Vaughan, "Report of H. W. Lloyd, Military Attaché, Baltic States and Finland," 26 April 1926, FO 371/11735; Harrison to Secretary of State, 10 June 1929, United States, Department of State, *Records Relating to the Internal Affairs of Latvia, 1910–1944* (Washington, D.C., 1981), roll 5, file 868p.248/1, no. 374.

25. Addison to Chamberlain, 5 December 1928, FO 371/13271.

26. Ibid. Addison's reports are always interesting to read and include comments ranging from allusions to classical history to multipage diatribes leveled at incompetent British industrial representatives. A foreign office official commented that the report was "interesting and typical both of Latvia and Mr. Addison." Collier, FO minute, 14 December [1928], FO 371/13271.

27. Nosworthy, 1924, WO 106/1573; *Annuaire Officiel de la Légion D'Honneur* (Paris, 1929), 2376; MAE to EMG, 24 September 1926, MAE, Lettonie 23; Ministère de la Marine to MAE, 2 October 1926, MAE, Lettonie 23; "Note pour le service du protocole," 5 October 1926, MAE, Lettonie 23. G. Zemgals, a member of the Latvian

parliament and an ex-minister of defense received the Legion of Honor in March 1925. See "French Recognition of Latvian Soldier," *Riga Times*, 28 March 1925, 2.

28. Addison to Villiers, 4 March 1929, FO 371/13982; Lescuyer to Herriot, 5 July 1924, MAE, Lettonie 22. It is possible that Savitsky and Sakovsy were the same individual. Mistakes regarding the names of eastern Europeans are common in the documents.

29. Addison to Villiers, 4 March 1929, FO 371/13982.

30. Ibid. Addison, in another dispatch written in an attempt to "correct the impression which I may have conveyed, in my despatch above-mentioned," wrote "that the failure of Messrs. Vickers to supply submarines was almost entirely due to their failure to make such arrangements," meaning bribery. He went on to reiterate that he still believed that the main reason that a British company did not receive the contracts was the refusal of the British Admiralty to provide training for Latvian officers and that other events were only contributing factors. He also remarked that the Vickers agent "gave to the proper person the usual 2 1/2% commission" that was expected for the awarding of contracts. Addison does not reveal the identity of the "proper person." Addison to Chamberlain, 2 January 1929, FO 371/13982.

31. Hinkkanen-Lievonen, *British Trade and Enterprise in the Baltic States*, 220–21.

32. Vaughan to Chamberlain, 7 December 1927, FO 371/12551; Addison to Chamberlain, 5 December 1928, FO 371/13271; report, "La Baltique en 1937," SHM, carton 1BB[7] 132 Pologne; MAE to Neyrac, ? June 1927, MAE, Lettonie 23.

33. MA (military attaché) to Knatchbull-Hugessen, 2 October 1931, FO 371/15538; French minister to Estonia to Briand, 22 August 1927, MAE, Lettonie 23.

34. MA to Knatchbull-Hugessen, 2 October 1931, FO 371/15538.

35. Ibid.; Knatchbull-Hugessen to Marquis of Reading, 5 October 1931, FO 371/15538.

36. Ibid. Knatchbull-Hugessen also wrote the following: "As to the alleged offence, I find it difficult to believe that if equal retribution had been meted out to all concerned the result would not have produced a very wholesale measure of naval disarmament in Latvia. But the authorities knew where to draw the line." Collier's FO minute in the same file bears another related comment that shows British feelings on the matter: "As usual, the right thing seems to have been done for the wrong reason."

CHAPTER 6

German Secret Submarine Exports, 1919–35

Björn Forsén and Annette Forsén

At the end of the First World War Germany was the leading nation in submarine development. It had not only the largest submarine flotilla in the world but in technical terms its submarines were also unqualifiedly the best. With the signing of the Versailles treaty Germany was forbidden to construct or acquire submarines, even for commercial purposes. All existing submarines had to be broken up, and no submarine parts could be exported. All existing submarine documentation and drawings had to be given to the Inter-Allied Control Commission. The purpose of these restrictions was to put an end to any future German submarine arm.

The German Navy, however, could not accept the idea of a future without submarines, and the Treaty of Versailles had hardly been ratified before the first plans were made for the future preservation, secretly, of German submarine know-how. Leading this work was the chief of the submarine department of the German Navy, Korvettenkapitän Karl Bartenbach. In 1907–9, Bartenbach had served as one of the commanders of the first submarine of the German Navy, *U1*, with Ulrich Blum as second officer and Heinrich

This paper is the result of cooperation between the two authors. The sections "From the First Export Projects to the Founding of IvS," "The German Navy enters IvS," and "The Finnish Projects" are the work of Annette Forsén, the rest, in turn, of Björn Forsén. In the footnotes we have tried to confine ourselves to referring to printed sources or secondary literature that gives more exact references to archival documents. We wish to express our thanks to Donald Stoker, not only for inviting us to write this article but also for helping to correct our English. It is dedicated to the memory of Gisela Bartenbach, the niece of Karl Bartenbach, who passed away early in 2000.

Papenberg as chief engineer.[1] The *Kameradenschaft* thus born between these three officers was later strengthened by continuing parallel careers in the German submarine arm, and would, after the end of the First World War, be of great importance for the secret development and export of German submarines.

After two years as commander of *U1* Bartenbach served as the first chief of the new German U-Boots-Abnahmekommission, then as the officer responsible for the navy's dockyard department for the coordination of the construction of submarines, as head of the German submarine school, and from 1915 to the end of the First World War as commander of the submarine flotilla Flandern.[2] The Flandern flotilla was an independent submarine flotilla belonging to the Marinekorps and competed with the submarine flotilla of the Hochseestreitkräfte (High Seas Fleet) to become the most successful unit in the war. Bartenbach also took a strong interest in submarine warfare strategy and tried in 1915, together with the Naval Minister, Grand-Admiral von Tirpitz, to convince Wilhelm II to declare unrestricted submarine war, something that Germany did not do until 1917.[3] Thus, at the end of the First World War, when Bartenbach was appointed commander of the submarine department, he was without a doubt the leading German submarine expert.[4]

FROM THE FIRST EXPORT PROJECTS TO THE FOUNDING OF IVS

Only one month after the Treaty of Versailles was ratified in June 1919, Ulrich Blum wrote a letter to the management of the Krupp steel and coal corporation and suggested a submarine construction office be founded at the Krupp Germaniawerft shipyard in Kiel. Blum's idea was that this office would collect and develop German submarine knowledge, and that retired submarine officers could sell drawings prepared by the office to neutral countries. He believed a market for German submarines existed in the South American and Scandinavian countries as well as in the Netherlands, Spain, and Japan.[5] It should be noted that when Blum wrote this letter he was still on active duty in the German Navy, presumably working under the command of Bartenbach. When all German submarines had been dismantled or given to the Allied powers, the submarine department and all the other groups working with submarine questions in the German Navy were closed down, and Blum and Bartenbach retired from active duty in November 1919 and January 1920, respectively.[6]

Blum's July 1919 suggestion brought Germaniawerft and its former director of submarine construction, Dr. Hans Techel, into the picture. We do not know exactly which form the secret work took at this early stage, but it is clear that in 1920 work was in progress on two possible projects, the first one aimed at Russia and the second one at Japan.[7] The Russian project never materialized, but the Japanese contact proved more promising. The Germans tried to convince the Japanese to employ Bartenbach as a naval advisor in order to be able to directly influence the Japanese decisions.[8] The Japanese declined the offer, but on the other hand declared themselves interested in buying designs for a U-cruiser and for a mine-laying submarine and asked whether Germaniawerft could place key supervisory personnel at the disposal of the Japanese shipyards. Techel led the project and at least three German engineers were sent to Japan in order to supervise the construction work. Later, the former German submarine officer Robert Bräutigam headed Japanese testing.[9]

From 1920, Bartenbach was based in Costa Rica,[10] from where he either led the negotiations with the Japanese or where he already was planning for the next large project, one aimed at Argentina. Argentina was interested in acquiring submarines and in 1921 employed Bartenbach as naval advisor. Bartenbach managed to persuade the Argentine Navy to employ two German naval designers. One of them was Friedrich Schürer, who had played an important role in the construction department of the German Navy at the end of the war and who also would play an important role in the development of a new German submarine arm in the 1920s and 1930s.[11]

Argentina wanted to order submarines, torpedoes, and mines from Europe, and more specifically from Germany. Therefore Bartenbach, in December 1921, traveled together with two Argentine naval officers to Europe in order to organize the project.[12] One of the first persons Bartenbach contacted was his old colleague Blum. Blum immediately traveled to Holland to discuss the question with Techel, who after having returned from Japan was working as a supervisor for a Dutch naval construction project.[13] As the Germans were not allowed to build any submarines nor export any war material whatever its nature, they had to open a submarine design office in a neutral country.

During the winter and spring of 1922, intensive discussions between Bartenbach, the German Navy, the large Krupp conglomerate, and various German shipyards were conducted. The idea of founding a dummy design office in a neutral country was supported by the chief of the Marineleitung, Admiral Behncke, as long as several German shipyards took part in the project.[14] The German Navy's interest in the project was founded on the belief that this effort would "keep together an efficient German submarine design office and by practical work for foreign nations keep it in continuous practice and on top of technical development."[15] The prospects for finding customers for the planned design office were considered good; in a document from March 1922 possible projects in Argentina, Italy, and Sweden are mentioned. One month later Argentina, Spain, and Finland were considered to be the most promising customers.[16]

As base for the new submarine design office, Holland, a country in which several other German armament companies already had founded subsidiaries,[17] was chosen. The design office was named Ingenieurskantoor voor Scheepsbouw (IvS) and Blum was selected as its commercial director, Techel as its technical director. However, German optimism regarding the prospects of the success of the office proved very exaggerated, and IvS carried on a languid existence at Germaniawerft in Kiel until 1925, when the operations were finally moved to Holland.[18] The Argentine project never materialized and in May 1924, Bartenbach left his position as naval advisor in Argentina and moved on to a similar position in Finland, which apparently at this stage, when Argentina was lost and the negotiations with Spain dragged on, was considered the most promising customer.[19]

THE GERMAN NAVY ENTERS IVS

Early in 1925 Germany managed to convince Turkey to enroll Vice Admiral Ernst von Gagern as naval advisor, and only shortly later Blum completed negotiations in Istanbul for IvS's first major project, two 500-ton submarines for the Turkish Navy.[20] Because Turkey did not have any shipyard industry of its own, this project, just like the Argentine one, involved not only designing the submarines but their construction as well. IvS was only a design office and did not own any shipyards, and German shipyards were not allowed to build submarines. Another problem was caused by IvS's poor financial situation. The Turks were not willing to make any down payment and even had to be bribed to place the order at IvS. After the British involvement in the Greek-Turkish War of 1921–22, IvS's major competitor to the Turkish order became the American Electric Boat Company because the United States had stayed out of the conflict. The Electric Boat Company had the means to supply the submarines and fought fiercely for the order by trying to bribe the Turkish minister of war.[21] Obviously, IvS would never have managed to get the contract without help from Germany.

In order to alleviate IvS's financial problems the German Navy contributed 1,000,000 reichsmarks as a single payment and promised, if needed, to support IvS with a further 120,000 reichsmarks on a yearly basis. The money was supplied from a secret fund, the Sonderfond, which the navy had created with the help of money received from illegal scrapping sales of arms directly after the end of the war, and which between 1920 and 1927 was run by Kapitän zur See Walter Lohmann. As a favor in return for its financial support the German Navy received 28 percent of IvS's shares as well as the chairmanship of the design office.[22] In order to keep the navy's participation in IvS secret, all contacts between the navy and IvS had to go through another dummy firm, Mentor Bilanz GmbH, in Berlin, the costs of which were also covered by the secret Sonderfond.[23] IvS now had the financial underwriting needed to begin the project but still needed a shipyard where the submarines could be built. In order to solve this problem Krupp bought into the Dutch Fijenoord shipyard in Rotterdam, where several former Germaniawerft submarine designers and engineers were employed.[24]

Receiving the Turkish order was of decisive importance for IvS. Without this project it is questionable if the design office could have managed to stay alive. Now the financial position of the office was sound, giving IvS a totally different starting point from which to bid for other projects. Additionally, from now on the design office was also connected to the German Navy, which would soon secretly commission IvS to make submarine designs for its own purposes. It is obvious that the Marineleitung, by entering IvS, had started to plan for a new German submarine arm. A new submarine department, Au, was founded in the Marinekommandoamt, with the official purpose of handling antisubmarine questions. In reality, the newly appointed chief of Au, Konteradmiral a.D. Arno Spindler, was preparing mobilization plans for the submarine arm. One of his first tasks was to decide which submarine type or types the navy was interested in, in order for IvS to be commissioned to prepare the needed designs.[25]

THE FINNISH PROJECTS

Bartenbach had, since his arrival in Finland in 1924, tried to persuade the Finns to order their planned submarines from IvS. Finally, in 1926 the Finnish ministry of defense asked for competitive bidding on a 400-ton and a 99-ton submarine. In September of the same year, it was decided to order the larger submarine from the Finnish shipyard Crichton-Vulcan, which was cooperating with IvS. The designs were, however, continually changed until April 1927, when the keel of the boat was laid. At the same time, two additional similar boats were ordered from Crichton-Vulcan. The submarines finally weighed 493 tons and corresponded closely to the German First World War submarine type C III, one of the types that in 1926 the Marineleitung had decided to develop for its mobilization plans.[26] Additionally, the Finns had decided that all parts of the submarines had to follow German standards from the First World War. By closely monitoring the design and construction—partly through Bartenbach but also through the large number of German designers, engineers, and workmen that Crichton-Vulcan had employed with the help of IvS[27]—the German Navy had full access to all information about the project.

Crichton-Vulcan's and IvS's main competitors in 1926 for the large Finnish submarine were the French firm Chantiers & Ateliers Augustin Normand and the Swedish Kockums Mekaniska Verkstad. Both Sweden and France had experience in building submarines for the Baltic Sea, Sweden had a submarine flotilla of its own, and the French had constructed submarines for the Polish and Latvian navies.[28] As was the case with Turkey, the order would probably not have gone to IvS and their German backers had it not been for the presence in Finland, just as in Turkey, of a German naval advisor. However, Bartenbach's position in Finland was more important than von Gagern's in Turkey and clearly a source of irritation for the former Entente states. Thus, the French and Italian legations in Finland filed a complaint with the Finnish ministry of foreign affairs over the role Bartenbach was playing in the process of choosing among the proposals. The Finnish ministry of foreign affairs answered the French and Italian notes kindly, saying that a committee consisting of only Finnish citizens would make the decision as to which submarines were chosen.[29]

France was obviously not pleased with this answer, as it in September 1926 tried to stop the project by appealing to the Conference of Ambassadors of the League of Nations. France wrote its appeal to the Conference of Ambassadors together with Great Britain, asking whether the Finnish submarine project, based on cooperation with the German dummy firm IvS in Holland, was a violation of the Treaty of Versailles. Great Britain did not want, however, to press the question too far in the Conference of Ambassadors, as it was at the same time involved in negotiating trade quotas with Germany, which had just become a member of the League of Nations. This may also have been one of the reasons why the Conference of Ambassadors in March 1927, perhaps slightly surprisingly, ruled that the events did not infringe upon the Treaty of Versailles.[30] Another reason mentioned in the conference discussions was the fact that there existed no legal way in which to proceed against IvS.[31]

British armament corporations had also turned to the British ministry of foreign affairs with complaints regarding the German experts who had convinced Finland to place the order with IvS, which they suspected was a German firm. British research into the question in the autumn of 1926 reached the conclusion that IvS belonged to Deutsche Werft shipyard (sic) in Kiel, which also controlled the Dutch shipyard Fijenoord, where IvS constructed submarines for Turkey.[32] At roughly the same time Great Britain took part in the French appeal to the Conference of Ambassadors of the League of Nations. This appeal was, however, directed toward Germany, and Great Britain chose never to file any complaint with Finland. Instead, Great Britain obviously decided to undermine Bartenbach's position by convincing Finland to employ a British naval advisor, something the Finns managed to postpone until 1929, when they finally felt they had to accept Commander Maximilian Despard. The Finns, though, managed to include as a stipulation for his appointment the provision that the British advisor would have nothing to do with the construction of the Finnish Navy.[33]

The USSR was also unhappy with the idea of Finland acquiring submarines designed by the Germans and made several attempts to stop the project. Early in 1926, when the awarding of the contract for the Finnish submarines was still undecided, the USSR contacted IvS and the German Navy, declaring an interest in constructing submarines with German help.[34] A rumor was spread in Helsinki, which stated that the USSR was cooperating with IvS and contemplating the purchase of the same designs as the Finns. Only the fact that IvS and Crichton-Vulcan intervened and strongly denied the accusations saved the project. When the order still went to Crichton-Vulcan and IvS, the USSR withdrew its own proposal of collaboration with Germany on submarines.[35] Instead, the USSR through the Red International of Trade Unions, the *Profintern*, instigated and financially supported a metalworkers strike at the Crichton-Vulcan shipyard that began in March 1927 and continued for nine months, effectively delaying the largest part of the construction work at the shipyard.[36]

The Finnish project was of great importance for IvS because it paid well financially. Contrary to the Turkish project, IvS had won this one without the input of financial support from the German Navy. This was without a doubt to a large degree the result of Bartenbach's influence. Bartenbach also managed to delay the decision regarding in which shipyard the small 99-ton submarine should be constructed. Originally, it had looked as if the order would be given to the Finnish shipyard Hietalahden Laivatelakka (Sandvikens Skeppsdocka), which worked in cooperation with the Electric Boat Company. This cooperation was, however, interrupted when another Finnish shipyard, Kone ja Siltarakennus Oy (Maskin och Brobyggnads Ab), in December 1926, bought into Hietalahden Laivatelakka. The fact that Kone ja Siltarakennus Oy, just as Crichton-Vulcan, cooperated with IvS secured this project for the Germans, although the final contract was not signed until April 1928.[37] Likewise of financial importance for IvS was the fact that Bartenbach, in 1929, managed to convince the Finnish ministry of defense to order two coast defense armored ships from Crichton-Vulcan and IvS.[38]

THE GERMAN NAVY ORDERS THE SUBMARINES *E1* AND *LILIPUT*

The Spanish project to build five submarines, which had been on the agenda at the time of the founding of IvS in 1922, was lost to the Spanish state shipyard Constructura Naval that worked in conjunction with the Electric Boat Company.[39] However, in 1924 the Spanish government drew up new plans for building another forty submarines. Constructura Naval immediately got an option on twenty-eight of these in cooperation with the British firm Vickers Armstrong, but the Spanish authorities opened up the contract for the remaining twelve boats to competitive bidding. IvS, which cooperated with the Spanish shipyard conglomerate Sozieda Anonima Espanola Union de Levante, or UNL, was not the only German design office to take part in the competition. Somewhat astonishingly IvS's strongest competitor proved to be the German shipyard Blohm & Voss, which earlier had taken part in the Japanese project. Although the German prospects looked good, the project never materialized as the Spanish authorities in 1925 decided to cut down on the submarine construction program.[40]

Apart from the Finnish projects IvS had not managed to convince a single other customer to buy its products, but starting in 1926 IvS had a new customer that seemed unafraid of violating the strictures of the Treaty of Versailles. This new customer, which since 1925 also owned the majority of the shares in IvS, was the German Navy itself. By April 1926, the new submarine department, Au, had made its decision as to which First World War submarines it wanted to develop for mobilization purposes. Apart from the C III mine-laying submarine that could be tested through the Finnish project, Au was also interested in a small B II submarine of 270 tons and a large B III submarine of 520 tons. Work began immediately on the B III submarine, which soon grew to 650 tons.[41] The only question was where the German Navy could find a shipyard or a country interested in building and testing a prototype of the planned boat.

In 1926, a possible road along which to proceed unexpectedly opened up through the Spanish industrial tycoon Echevarrieta, who wanted to build up a war materials industry of his own in Spain. He turned to Germany asking for financial support. The question was discussed in the Reich's cabinet, which after some hesitation accepted the project.[42] From 1922 onward Korvettenkapitän Wilhelm Canaris, who later became the chief of Hitler's intelligence service, had been responsible for all contacts with Spain, but as a possible contract seemed more plausible, Germany sent a naval advisor, Oberleutnant zur See a.D. Messerschmidt, to the Spanish Navy.[43] In July 1927 the Marineleitung decided to support the planning and construction of a 655-ton submarine in Spain with 4,000,000 reichsmarks.[44] The details of the contract signed in November 1927 itself are not known, but it seems as if it was the German Navy and not the Spanish Navy that finally ordered the submarine.

Officially, the boat, called *E1*, was built and sponsored by Echevarrieta in collaboration with IvS speculatively, the Spanish Navy having the first option. Therefore the Spanish Navy also had the right to influence the designs to a certain point, whereby the boat finally grew to 755 tons.[45] Until the Spanish Navy bought the boat, it officially belonged to Echevarrieta, but in reality it was owned by IvS, which had paid four-fifths of the costs of its planning and construction.[46] As IvS did not have the financial means to enter such a risky project, its share of the costs was covered by the German Navy, which thereby probably took over the ownership of the boat from IvS. That the submarine was considered the property of the German Navy is also obvious by the fact that it sent its own submarine engineers and workmen to Cadiz, and not only the ones of IvS, to supervise and finalize the construction of the submarine.[47]

The contract drawn up for *Liliput*, a 250-ton submarine, was very similar to that for *E1*. In this case more details of the contract are known. Bartenbach had for a long time tried to convince the Finnish ministry of defense to build a 250-ton submarine, in which the Marineleitung also had its own interest as a possible type for its mobilization plans.[48] Although the Finns showed a certain interest in the project, the Great Depression had come to Finland. After finishing their recent naval construction program they had no financial means to start building yet another submarine. With the approval of the German and Finnish governments a gentlemen's agreement was reached.[49] In March 1930, the Finnish ministry of defense and Crichton-Vulcan signed a contract, according to which Crichton-Vulcan was allowed to start constructing a 250-

ton submarine after IvS's designs. The Finnish ministry of defense had the first option on the boat and could also to a certain degree influence the designs, but until Finland bought the boat Crichton-Vulcan owned it.[50]

One day before the contract between the Finnish ministry of defense and Crichton-Vulcan was signed, another secret contract, the content of which was, however, known to the Finnish government, was signed between Crichton-Vulcan and IvS. According to this contract, IvS was the one who actually had placed the order for the boat and who thereby was its legal owner until it was sold to Finland or any other potential customer. IvS would finance all the costs of planning and construction, but as with *E1*, the money needed came from the German Navy. Although no contract between IvS and the German Navy has been found, such a contract most likely existed, stating in its turn that the German Navy was the real owner of *CV-707*.[51] The German Navy also sent Bartenbach's and Blum's old friend Papenberg to supervise planning and construction at the Crichton-Vulcan shipyard, thus showing the same interest as they had in *E1*.[52]

Papenberg had since 1928, or at least 1929, worked for the dummy firm Igewit GmbH, which as successor of Mentor Bilanz GmbH was responsible for all contacts between the German Navy and IvS.[53] Within Igewit, which was led by Oberleutnant zur See a.D. Hans Schottky,[54] the German Navy's own submarine design office also had put up its new premises under the aegis of Bartenbach's colleague from Argentina, Friedrich Schürer. The German Navy thus made its own general designs for *E1* and *CV-707*, designs that later were finalized by IvS and improved during the construction and subsequent testing trials by the representatives of the German Navy at the respective shipyards.

German submarine components contractors manufactured all of the important parts for *E1* and *CV-707*. In the case of *E1* the whole hull was built in segments at the Fijenoord shipyard, leaving only the assembly of the segments to be done in Cadiz.[55] But it should be noted that the submarines ordered by Turkey and Finland to a large degree already consisted of German components. This was actually a wish of the Marineleitung, and the German naval advisors in other countries were asked to try to convince their employers to choose German components as often as possible. The reason for the Marineleitung's interest lay in the fact that it wanted to develop a functioning German submarine component industry to which orders could be given immediately if Germany suddenly decided to build a submarine arm of its own.[56]

After the launching in October 1930 of *E1* and of *Liliput*, or *CV-707*, in May 1933, the German Navy secretly owned two submarines, one in Spain and another in Finland. During the test trials the former German submarine officers Robert Bräutigam and Werner Fürbringer acted as commanders of *E1* and *CV-707*, and Papenberg as chief engineer. Papenberg had earlier acquainted himself with both the Turkish and Finnish submarines,[57] and thus fulfilled a very important role in collecting information about their weak points for the German Navy. Part of the idea was to use *E1* and *CV-707* for training young officers as submarine commanders and chief engineers for a new German submarine arm. Of special importance in this respect was *CV-707*, on which the first new, young German submarine commanders and chief engineers were schooled during the summers of 1933 and 1934.[58]

The German Navy in 1933–34 considered the possibility of taking *E1* and *CV-707* home to Germany, but apparently such a move would have caused too great of a diplomatic upheaval. Instead, *E1* was sold to Turkey in 1934 and *CV-707* to Finland early in 1936.[59]

IVS RECEIVES NEW CUSTOMERS: SWEDEN AND THE USSR

Even though IvS had sent out offers for submarines to a large number of countries since 1922, mostly small neutral states,[60] there quite clearly existed a certain hesitation among most countries to cooperate with the Germans in constructing submarines in a way that would violate the Treaty of Versailles. Thus, for nearly ten years IvS seemed to be only able to win projects in countries that had German naval advisors or projects that were totally or partly financed by the German Navy itself. The fact that Finland had dared to commission IvS to build submarines—and gotten away with it without being punished by the former Allies in any way, along with receiving submarines of very high quality—attracted two new customers to IvS in the early 1930s: Sweden and the USSR—both neighbors of Finland, and both well aware of the Finnish projects.

Sweden was the first one of the new customers to come to an agreement with IvS. Sweden had authorized construction of two (later three) mine-laying submarines in 1927, and a Swedish commission was sent to France, Italy, and Holland in order to get acquainted with different bidders. After much wavering Sweden decided in favor of IvS, and in November 1931 IvS signed a contract with the Swedish Navy to supply the required designs and another contract with the Swedish shipyard Kockums Mekaniska Verkstad for design and construction supervision. Additionally, IvS received permission to take part in the test trials of the boats.[61] The project definitely was of great financial importance for IvS, although it clearly was of less interest for the Marineleitung, as the boats had to be built according to Swedish and not German specifications. The Swedish submarines, finally weighing 540 tons, were, however, still closely related to the Finnish mine-laying submarines, which had been of such great interest to the Marineleitung.[62]

The USSR, which had already demonstrated an interest in IvS in 1926, possibly in order to stop Finnish-German cooperation, returned to IvS's office in The Hague early in 1932. The Germans identified them by using the codename "the Flensburgers."[63] IvS first tried to sell the Spanish *E1* to the Russians, because Spain, after the fall of the monarchy, had decided not to use its first buyer's option on the boat. The Russians were even allowed to take part in the test trials of *E1*, which they, however, finally decided not to buy. Instead, they signed a contract with IvS for a slightly changed and enlarged submarine of 828 tons (type E II). According to the contract IvS had to supply all the designs and a group of engineers to supervise the construction in the Ordžonikidze shipyard in Leningrad. The construction of three submarines of this type in the USSR, called the S-class, started in December 1934. Later in the 1930s, the USSR produced another 46 submarines of the S-class however, totally on their own and without any help from IvS.[64] This class proved to be the best Russian submarines during the Second World War.[65]

THE GERMAN NAVY WITHDRAWS FROM IVS

In Germany a political decision to start rebuilding a submarine arm was made in November 1932 in the so-called *Umbau-program.*[66] As Germany was still bound by the regulations of the Treaty of Versailles, the Germans decided in 1933 that the German Navy should collect all components needed for six submarines of the *CV-707* type and two of the *E1* type in guarded sheds in German shipyards.[67] When the former Entente powers would free Germany from the restrictions posed by the Treaty of Versailles, something that the Germans believed would happen soon, then the collected components could be easily put together within a short time. In order not to arouse any suspicion, all these components, as well as the designs, were ordered from IvS in Holland. Furthermore, IvS was told to spread a rumor that the components were meant for further submarine orders made by Finland.[68]

By July 1934, all the components needed for the six *CV-707* and two *E1* submarines had been collected, but Germany still had not managed to convince the former Entente powers to give it the right to have submarines. As Hitler did not yet want to break with them, above all Great Britain, it was decided to not yet assemble the components. Instead, components for yet another six submarines of a slightly changed variant of the CV-707 class were to be collected. However, now the design work was for the first time not given to IvS, but to a new design office at the German Navy shipyard, Deutsche Werke, in Kiel.[69] With this action the German Navy began its withdrawal from IvS.

In the autumn of 1934 Hitler decided to start assembling the submarines for which components had been collected. The first German submarine slid into water only eleven days after the Anglo-German Naval Treaty, which allowed Germany to have submarines once again, was signed in June 1935. By autumn of the same year Germany already had a total of twelve submarines. In order to lead and supervise the construction of the boats and the organization of the new arm, a new submarine department, BU, was founded in the Marinekommandoamt. Bartenbach, who had returned from Finland, became the chief of this department, in which in addition to the former Flandern Flotilla commander, Schottky, Schürer and Papenberg were also employed.[70]

Late in 1934, IvS founded a subsidiary, Schiffbaukontor, at the Deschimag shipyard in Bremen. Here the designs for a new 550-ton submarine were drawn up, a boat that later became the most-produced German submarine of the Second World War.[71] A couple of months later Bartenbach headed the negotiations leading to the German Navy's final withdrawal from IvS, the shares of which were henceforth divided only between two German shipyards.[72] IvS continued its activity as an independent naval design office after the withdrawal of the German Navy and in 1936 opened another subsidiary, Ingenieurkontor für Schiffbau (IfS) in Lübeck, with the help of which it designed and produced submarines for Romania, Turkey, and China.[73] But this activity was no longer illegal and therefore IvS managed to survive the Second World War and continued its activities until 1957, mainly working for the Dutch Navy.[74]

Why then did the German Navy withdraw from its nearly decade long collaboration with and partial ownership in IvS? The final reason, and a very obvious one, was of course the fact that Germany could once again, after the penning of the Anglo-German Naval Treaty, design, construct, and own submarines. There was no longer any reason why part of the design and construction work should be done in another country where it was much more difficult for the German Navy to supervise the work.

Another reason was the fact that IvS did not manage to keep its activities secret, something that the Germans were afraid would have negative political repercussions. Although the Allied powers in the early 1930s took a much more lenient attitude toward German attempts to circumvent the Treaty of Versailles, the risk of such complaints did not disappear until June 1935. In September 1934, the Electric Boat Company had, for example, exposed for the Nye Committee in Washington, D.C., which was investigating armaments industries, a very compromising letter of Techel's that revealed that IvS had delivered submarine material to Germany. The story was blown up by the Dutch press, which required the Dutch government to intervene, and IvS only managed to escape unscathed after both Techel and Blum strongly denied the accusations.[75]

It should be noted that IvS posed a threat not only to Germany's relations with the former Allies but also to the German government in regard to domestic politics. In 1927–28, information about the German Navy's secret funds leaked to the press, and the so-called Lohmann scandal became the topic for a heated and prolonged debate in the Reichstag.[76] In vain, the Reich's Cabinet did its utmost to prevent all details about the secret funds, especially those dealing with the secret rearmament projects, from reaching the Reichstag. Late in 1927, the German newspaper *Die Weltbühne* revealed Canaris's Spanish project to the public in the form of a fairytale with the title "Das

Märchen von den Canarischen Inseln."[77] And in March 1928, a young communist member of the Reichstag managed to get hold of a secret Reich's cabinet report detailing all activities, including the fact that Germany was directly involved in the construction of a submarine in Spain, and read the report aloud for the Reichstag.[78]

Although the German Navy and Cabinet did its best to deny the allegations, the Lohmann scandal still hit all those involved hard. The minister of defense, Gessler, and the chief of the Marineleitung, Admiral Zenker, had to resign from their positions, followed by several lower officers that had worked on the submarine projects. Canaris, who had masterminded the Spanish project, was sent to sea, ending his involvement in the further development of the German submarine arm.[79] The German secret submarine plans were, however, not scrapped, although the organization and financing of them were changed. Thus, from then on the contacts between the German Navy and IvS went through a new dummy firm, Igewit GmbH, that replaced the old Mentor Bilanz GmbH. The new chief of the Marineleitung, Admiral Erich Raeder, managed to transfer whatever remained of the secret funds to the navy's own Budget Department, where they became part of the B-Budget, with the help of which the activity could be financed in the future without publicity.[80]

Yet another reason for the German Navy to withdraw from IvS must have been the risk that the designs and know-how concerning the submarine types chosen for the German mobilization plans through IvS could easily reach the enemies of Germany. The former Entente powers did their utmost in order to be able to put their hands on copies of the designs. As an example, in early 1932 the Russians already had access to the full designs of the Finnish large mine-laying submarines, copies of which they had bought from France! The USSR tried at the same time, apparently without success, to buy the designs of the small Finnish submarine from IvS,[81] but, as we discussed previously, in 1933 they were allowed to buy improved designs of *E1*. They were also assisted in the construction of these boats, which at that time was one of the two secret German submarine prototypes. And Paul Koster, a representative of the Electric Boat Company, tried several times under strange pretexts to buy *CV-707* or at least its designs. This was, however, unsuccessful because Koster first declined to tell whose agent he was and later maintained that he worked for China, which he could not prove.[82] Events like these could of course be avoided if the German Navy withdrew from IvS.

CONCLUSION

The story of IvS and its secret activity is by no means any new chapter in the history of the naval arms trade. However, recent research has broadened our understanding of the secret German submarine exports channeled through the dummy firm in Holland. It is now obvious how IvS from the very beginning, immediately after the ratification of the Treaty of Versailles, was conceived by the Marineleitung as a means of circumventing the treaty's provisions and maintaining German knowledge of submarine design and construction. Spearheading this work was one man, Karl Bartenbach, who dedicated his life to the German submarine arm from its inception in the early days of the twentieth century. After a slow start, German secret activity gained impetus in the mid-1920s, concurrent with a general naval rearmament in the world, a rearmament mainly directed toward submarines. Moreover, IvS's projects were a political issue of such importance that concerns regarding their activities even reached the table of the Conference of Ambassadors of the League of Nations. IvS's activities seem to have been far from as secret as previously believed, and this could actually have been one of the factors in why so few neutral powers along the way finally agreed to cooperate with this German dummy firm.

NOTES

1. Bartenbach served as commander of *U1* from 16 July–4 August 1907 and 5 March 1908–April 1910, Blum as second officer (*Wachoffizier*) from 23 April 1908–30 March 1909, and Papenberg as chief engineer from 12 February 1908–30 March 1909. See B. Forsén and A. Forsén, *Tysklands och Finlands hemliga ubåtssamarbete* (Borgå, 1999), 24–26. This work is also available in Finnish: B. Forsén and A. Forsén, *Saksan ja Suomen salainen sukellusveneyhteistyö* (Keuru, 1999).

2. For Bartenbach's early career, see the yearly *Rangliste der Kaiserlichen Deutschen Marine, 1910–1914*; *Ehrenrangliste der Kaiserlichen Deutschen Marine, 1914–1918*, bearbeitet von Konteradmiral a. D. Stoetzel (Berlin, 1930); and H. Hildebrand and E. Henriot, *Deutschlands Admirale 1849–1945. Die militärische Werdegänge der See-, Ingenieurs-, Sanitäts, Waffen- und Verwaltungsoffiziere im Admiralsrang* (Osnabrück, 1988), 57–58.

3. For the proposal of 1915, see A. Spindler, *Der Handelskrieg mit U-Booten* II (Berlin, 1933), 167–71; Forsén and Forsén, *Tysklands och Finlands hemliga ubåtssamarbete*, 25. According to von Tirpitz, letter of von Tirpitz to von Schoultz, 13 May 1924, Bartenbach's efforts during the First World War could have been decisive for the whole outcome of the war, if only the politicians had given him a free hand! See Forsén and Forsén, *Tysklands och Finlands hemliga ubåtssamarbete*, 70.

4. A. von Tirpitz, *Erinnerungen* (Leipzig, 1919), 522, calls Bartenbach "unser erster Ubootssachverständiger." See also A. W. Saville, "The Development of the German U-Boat Arm, 1919–1935," (Ph.D. diss., University of Washington, 1963), 59.

5. J. H. Ten Cate, "Das U-Boot als geistige Exportware: Das Ingeniuerskantoor voor Scheepvaart N.V. (1919–1957)," in *Deutschland und Europa in der Neuzeit. Festschrift für Karl Otmar Freiherr von Aretin zum 65. Geburtstag* II, ed. R. Melville, C. Scharf, M. Vogt, and U. Wengenroth. Veröffentlichungen des Instituts für Europäische Geschichte Mainz. Abt. Universalgesch.134.2 (Stuttgart, 1988), 912–13. Blum's letter is dated 26 July 1919.

6. Forsén and Forsén, *Tysklands och Finlands hemliga ubåtssamarbete*, 26. See also

Ehrenrangliste . . . 1914–1918. Blum retired on 22 November 1919 and Bartenbach on 26 January 1920.

7. See Saville, "Development of the German U-Boat Arm," 17–28, 38–40.

8. Forsén and Forsén, *Tysklands och Finlands hemliga ubåtssamarbete,* 26.

9. Saville, "Development of the German U-Boat Arm," 38–40; Forsén and Forsén, *Tysklands och Finlands hemliga ubåtssamarbete,* 27. The three German engineers were Heise, Vogel, and Strehlow. From 1915 until the end of the war Bräutigam worked in the German U-Boots-Abnahmekommission. Thus, he was accustomed to testing new submarines and was therefore probably the best officer Germany could offer for this task.

10. Interview with Gisela Bartenbach, 1999. In 1999, Gisela Bartenbach still owned some photographs of Bartenbach, in civilian dress, showing him with his wife and daughter in Costa Rica in 1920.

11. Saville, "Development of the German U-Boat Arm," 59; Forsén and Forsén, *Tysklands och Finlands hemliga ubåtssamarbete,* 27. At the end of the First World War Schürer was in charge of the submarine design section of the Inspektion des Unterseebootswesens, which was responsible for all of the German Navy's submarine design work.

12. For Bartenbach's journey to Europe together with the Argentine officers Ferrer and Ceballos, see Forsén and Forsén, *Tysklands och Finlands hemliga ubåtssamarbete,* 26.

13. See Ten Cate, "Das U-Boot als geistige Exportware," 914; letter from Bartenbach to Blum, 29 December 1921.

14. Saville, "Development of the German U-Boat Arm," 56–58; Ten Cate, "Das U-Boot als geistige Exportware," 914; E. Rössler, "Die deutschen U-Boot-Konstruktionsbüros," *Deutsches Schiffahrtsarchiv* 20 (1997), 305.

15. C. Schüssler, "Der Kampf der Marine gegen Versailles 1919–1935, hrsg. vom Oberkommando der Kriegsmarine, Berlin 1937," in *Trial of Major War Criminals before the International Military Tribunal Nuremberg 14 Nov. 1945–1 Oct. 1946* (Nuremberg, 1949), 34, 39. The document states: "ein leistungsfähiges deutsches U-Boots-Konstruktionsbüro zusammenzuhalten und durch praktische Arbeit für ausländische Marinen in ständiger Übung und auf der Höhe der technischen Entwicklung zu halten."

16. Argentina, Italy, and Sweden are mentioned in a letter of 18 March 1922. See Saville, "Development of the German U-Boat Arm," 56–58. However, in the Krupp planning memo for the founding of IvS of 12 April 1922 Argentina, Spain, and Finland are mentioned. Finnish documents show that the Finnish shipyard Vulcan (which later became Crichton-Vulcan) made the first contact with German submarine experts some time between 13 March and 30 May 1922, thus possibly explaining the appearance of Finland in the Krupp memo of 12 April 1922. For more on this, see Forsén and Forsén, *Tysklands och Finlands hemliga ubåtssamarbete,* 44–47.

17. The best-known case is that of the airplane constructor Fokker, who had already moved to Holland in 1919 and successfully sold airplanes to Holland and the United States. Other examples are Carl Zeiss Optical Works of Jena, which started producing optical instruments in Holland under the name of *Nederlandsche Instrumenten Compagnie Nedinsco N.V.,* and Siemens, which produced fire control equipment under the name of *F. Hazemeyer's Fabriek von Electrische Signal-Apparaten N.V.* After the First World War Holland generally had a very friendly attitude toward Germany and even granted asylum to Wilhelm II.

18. Ten Cate, "Das U-Boot als geistige Exportware," 918; Rössler, "Die deutschen U-Boot-Konstruktionsbüros," 305. The final move took place in October 1925.

19. For Bartenbach's arrival and his first years in Finland, see Forsén and Forsén, *Tysklands och Finlands hemliga ubåtssamarbete*, 66–82.

20. Vice Admiral von Gagern took over the post in Turkey on 31 January 1925. Saville, "Development of the German U-Boat Arm," 161. Blum came to Istanbul for his negotiations early in February 1925. Ibid., 125.

21. According to Ten Cate, "Das U-Boot als geistige Exportware," 917, the Electric Boat Company paid the Turkish minister a total of $12,500, without, however, in the end getting the order. Schüssler, "Der Kampf der Marine gegen Versailles 1919–1935," 39, also mentions French and Italian competitors.

22. For the deal between IvS and the German Navy, cf. Schüssler, "Der Kampf der Marine gegen Versailles 1919–1935," 39; Saville, "Development of the German U-Boat Arm," 126–29; Rahn, *Verteidigungskonzeption und Reichsmarine in der Weimarer Republik*, 217–18; Rössler, "Die deutschen U-Boot-Konstruktionsbüros," 306. For the secret funds of the German Navy, see also Saville, "Development of the German U-Boat Arm," 80–81.

23. Saville, "Development of the German U-Boat Arm," 135–36; Rössler, "Die deutschen U-Boot-Konstruktionsbüros," 306. A similar secret navy fund, the Schwartzefond, also financed another dummy firm, Tebeg GmbH, working on planning the material mobilization of the armament industry, especially concerning submarines.

24. Saville, "Development of the German U-Boat Arm," 126–28, dates the acquisition of Fijenoord to "sometime prior to 1925." Among the former German submarine designers and engineers working for Fijenoord were, for example, Buhr, Rehagen, and Gemberg.

25. Saville, "Development of the German U-Boat Arm," 172–76; Rössler, "Die deutschen U-Boot-Konstruktionsbüros," 305.

26. For the Finnish mine-laying submarines, cf. Forsén and Forsén, *Tysklands och Finlands hemliga ubåtssamarbete*, 89–100.

27. The design and construction work at Crichton-Vulcan was from IvS's side led by Wilhelm Etzbach, Hugo Peine, and Edgar Rickmeier, who for shorter periods were assisted by additional Germans. The German workforce reached its peak late in 1928 with a total of five engineers, three supervisors of work, and eleven workmen. For a detailed description of the German workforce and their tasks, cf. Forsén and Forsén, *Tysklands och Finlands hemliga ubåtssamarbete*, 115–16, 119–22.

28. For the French projects in Poland and Latvia, see Donald J. Stoker Jr., "Undermining the Cordon Sanitaire: Naval Arms Sales, Naval Building, and Anglo-French Competition in the Baltic, 1918–1940—Poland—Finland—The Baltic States" (Ph.D. diss., Florida State University, 1997), 130, 140. It should be mentioned that IvS in Finland hardly was a new, unknown competitor to the French, as IvS already in 1924 had competed for submarine orders to Latvia and Estonia.

29. Forsén and Forsén, *Tysklands och Finlands hemliga ubåtssamarbete*, 89–90.

30. Stoker, "Undermining the Cordon Sanitaire," 202–3, is the first one to refer to the appeal to the Conference of Ambassadors.

31. J. Heideking, *Areopag der Diplomaten. Die Pariser Botschafterkonferenz der alliierten Hauptmächte und die Probleme der europäischen Politik 1920–1931* (Husum, 1979), 305. It should be noted that the conference literally drowned in other complaints with

regard to other possible encroachments of the Treaty of Versailles. For these, see ibid., passim.

32. See Stoker, "Undermining the Cordon Sanitaire," 207–8.

33. For Finland's and Germany's view of the British attempt of getting Finland to employ a British naval advisor, see Forsén and Forsén, *Tysklands och Finlands hemliga ubåtssamarbete*, 126–30. According to Stoker, "Undermining the Cordon Sanitaire," 219–28, Great Britain and France had, since the beginning of the 1920s, each tried to persuade Finland to employ a naval advisor from their respective nations. France had given up at an early stage, but Great Britain clearly stepped up its efforts after the first Finnish submarines were commissioned by Crichton-Vulcan and IvS.

34. The contact with Germany was initiated by the Russians during a visit of the retired chief of the Marineleitung, Admiral Behncke, to the USSR early in 1926. The new chief of the Marineleitung, Admiral Zenker, had a much more cautious attitude toward the USSR. See W. Rahn, "Verteidigungskonzeption und Reichsmarine in der Weimarer Republik. Planung und Führung in der Ära Behncke und Zenker (1920–1928)" (Ph.D. diss, Hamburg, 1976), 176–78.

35. For Russian-German contacts in 1926 and the rumor in Helsinki, see Forsén and Forsén, *Tysklands och Finlands hemliga ubåtssamarbete*, 91–92.

36. Forsén and Forsén, *Tysklands och Finlands hemliga ubåtssamarbete*, 117–19. The strike was broken by mediation in the conflict by the Finnish government. Apparently, the USSR would have liked the strike to continue and was even prepared to continue financing it!

37. For the small 99-ton submarine, see Forsén and Forsén, *Tysklands och Finlands hemliga ubåtssamarbete*, 92–96, 135–38. Bartenbach pleaded especially hard against the Electric Boat Company's designs for the 99-ton submarine, which according to him neither looked like a modern submarine nor like a submarine from 1914! According to the British the order of the small submarine finally went to Kone ja Siltarakennus Oy because of Bartenbach. See Stoker, "Undermining the Cordon Sanitaire," 209.

38. For the Finnish armored ships *Väinämöinen* and *Ilmarinen* cf. the new monograph of T. Niklander, *Meidän panssarilaivamme* (Jyväskylä, 1996).

39. Saville, "Development of the German U-Boat Arm," 77–79; E. Rössler, *Geschichte des deutschen U-Bootbaus* I, 2nd ed. (Bonn, 1996), 131–32, mentions six submarines.

40. For details of the development of the Spanish project in 1924–25, see Saville, "Development of the German U-Boat Arm," 100–124.

41. Rössler, *Geschichte des deutschen U-Bootbaus*, 140, 144–45; id., *Vom Original zum Modell: Uboottyp II—Die "Einbäume"* (München, 1999), 5–8.

42. Saville, "Development of the German U-Boat Arm," 195–207.

43. Schüssler, *Trial of Major War Criminals*, 41, 43.

44. See Saville, "Development of the German U-Boat Arm," 291–99.

45. Rössler, *Die deutschen U-Boote und ihre Werften*, 75–78; id., *Geschichte des deutschen U-Bootbaus*, 137–39.

46. See Schüssler in *Trial of Major War Criminals*, 41–42, according to whom *E1* was "der erste U-Bootsbau der deutschen Marine nach dem Krieg" and "Als Unternehmer des U-Bootsbaus galt nach außen hin Echevarrieta"; that is, in reality someone else was the true enterpriser.

47. Rössler, *Geschichte des deutschen U-Bootbaus*, 139. The navy's representation at the construction site was headed by the submarine designers Schotte and Hey.

48. For the German interest in the 250-ton submarine cf. Rössler, *Geschichte des deutschen U-Bootbaus*, 140–41, 146–47. Rössler, *Vom Original zum Modell: Uboottyp II—Die "Einbäume,"* 7–12.

49. For the early history of the project and the knowledge of the German and Finnish governments, see Forsén and Forsén, *Tysklands och Finlands hemliga ubåtssamarbete*, 202–12.

50. The contract of 7 March 1930 between the Finnish ministry of defense and Crichton-Vulcan was first published in its entirety by K. Kijanen, *Sukellushälytys. Suomalaiset sukellusveneet sodan ja rauhan aikana* (Lahti, 1977), 37–38.

51. For the first reference to the contract of 6 March 1930 between IvS and Crichton-Vulcan and its implications, see Forsén and Forsén, *Tysklands och Finlands hemliga ubåtssamarbete*, 214–17. Rössler, *Vom Original zum Modell: Uboottyp II-Die "Einbäume,"* 9, reaches the same conclusion without knowing the contents of the contract: "Praktisch war jedoch, wie schon im Fall von E1, die deutsche Marineleitung Auftraggeber, der den Bau durch das IvS organisieren und durch 'Igewit' übernehmen liess."

52. The German Navy was represented at the Crichton-Vulcan shipyard by Papenberg, who saw that the work was done in accordance with the designs and suggested improvements to them, as well as Heinrich Kluge, who led the daily work on the submarine. However, the IvS engineers Etzbach, Peine, and Rickmeyer and the construction supervisors Andersen, Niemeier, and Schröder, as well as a handful of German workmen, continued to work for Crichton-Vulcan. See Forsén and Forsén *Tysklands och Finlands hemliga ubåtssamarbete*, 220–21.

53. Forsén and Forsén, *Tysklands och Finlands hemliga ubåtssamarbete*, 162–63. In May–June 1928, Papenberg took part in the delivery of the two Turkish submarines from Holland to Turkey. There are a large number of expert discourses on technical submarine questions written by Papenberg in the German Navy's archive, dating from the beginning of 1929, thus apparently indicating that Papenberg worked for Igewit.

54. During the First World War Schottky had served as second officer on several submarines of the Flandern flotilla, and toward the end of the war he acted as a teacher at the German Navy's submarine school. See Rössler, *Vom Original zum Modell: Uboottyp II-Die "Einbäume,"* 8.

55. For *E1*, see Saville, "Development of the German U-Boat Arm," 296, 302; for *CV-707*, see Forsén and Forsén, *Tysklands och Finlands hemliga ubåtssamarbete*, 218.

56. This concern is mentioned for the first time in a memo of 14 September 1928 but probably had existed for some time before that. Bartenbach had, for instance, been instructed to try to convince the Finns to choose as many German components for the Finnish mine-laying submarines and the small 99-ton submarine. See Forsén and Forsén, *Tysklands och Finlands hemliga ubåtssamarbete*, 85–88 and 124–26.

57. Papenberg did not take part in the actual test trials of the Turkish submarines but acted as chief engineer on one of the boats during their delivery from Holland to Turkey. He was also chief engineer on all the Finnish submarines when they were tested. It is worthwhile noting that four young officers of the German Navy took part in the Finnish test trials in 1930. One of these four young men, Hans Rösing, later became one of the most influential submarine officers during the Second World War and commanded as Führer der U-Boote West all German submarines operating in the Atlantic.

58. The importance of the education given on *CV-707* to the new German submarine arm is well evidenced by the fact that in the autumn of 1935 nine of the twelve of the initial batch of new German submarines had commanders who had taken part in the test trials in Finland. Moreover, three had chief engineers with similar experience. Among those taking part in the trials were also Christopher Aschmoneit and Gustav Diestelmeier, who toward the end of the Second World War would both become leading submarine designers, and Erich Zürn, who in 1934 was only an ordinary enlisted machinist and later became an officer and chief engineer on *U48*, perhaps Germany's most famous submarine during the Second World War. For information on the Germans taking part in the test trials of *CV-707* in 1933–34, see Forsén and Forsén, *Tysklands och Finlands hemliga ubåtssamarbete*, 233–56, 289–92.

59. Rössler, *Die deutschen U-Boote und ihre Werften*, 78; Forsén and Forsén, *Tysklands och Finlands hemliga ubåtssamarbete*, 261–263. *CV-707*, which in the Finnish Navy was named *Vesikko*, is a submarine memorial outside of Helsinki in the Suomenlinna (Sveaborg) fortress.

60. According to Rössler, *Die deutschen U-Boote und ihre Werften*, 75, IvS bid on submarine orders that did not result in a contract to the following states: Argentina, Brazil, Bulgaria, Chile, China, Estonia, Holland, Italy, Japan, Norway, Portugal, Uruguay, and Yugoslavia. According to Stoker, "Undermining the Cordon Sanitaire," 230, IvS also showed an interest in Latvia in 1924. Saville, "Development of the German U-Boat Arm," 158, 163, 364, adds several other countries, some of which, however, could have been offered only surface ships: Colombia, Greece, Lithuania, Mexico, and the United States.

61. This was done, for instance, by the young German officer Hans Rösing in the summer of 1932. See Saville, "Development of the German U-Boat Arm," 426.

62. For the Swedish submarines *Delfinen*, *Nordkaparen*, and *Springaren*, see, for example, Saville, "Development of the German U-Boat Arm," 382–84; Rössler, *Die deutschen U-Boote und ihre Werften*, 92. The IvS supervisors at Kockums were Seligmann, and later Peine; see Forsén and Forsén, *Tysklands och Finlands hemliga ubåtssamarbete*, 284–85.

63. R. Lakowski, *Deutsche U-Boote geheim 1935–1945* (München, 1991), 18; Forsén and Forsén, *Tysklands och Finlands hemliga ubåtssamarbete*, 134–35.

64. For the Russian S-class, cf. Rössler, *Die deutschen U-Boote und ihre Werften*, 80. A submarine of the Russian S-class serves as a submarine memorial in Vladivostok.

65. During the Second World War one of the Finnish mine-laying submarines constructed by IvS, ironically, met and sunk a submarine of the S-class, *S-7*, likewise an IvS-built boat. See G. C. Stevenson, "Submarines of the Finnish Navy", *Warship International* 1 (1986): 39; P.-O. Ekman, *Havsvargar. Ubåtar och ubåtskrig i Östersjön*, 2nd ed. (Helsingfors, 1999), 271–72.

66. Rössler, *Geschichte des deutschen U-Bootbaus*, 146–48; Rössler, *Vom Original zum Modell: Uboottyp II-Die "Einbäume,"* 19.

67. Rössler, Geschicte des deutschen U-Bootbaus, 148; Rössler, *Vom Original zum Modell: Uboottyp II-Die "Einbäume,"* 19–20.

68. Forsén and Forsén, *Tysklands och Finlands hemliga ubåtssamarbete*, 271.

69. Saville, "Development of the German U-Boat Arm," 568–70; Rössler, *Geschichte des deutschen U-Bootbaus*, 148; Rössler, *Vom Original zum Modell: Uboottyp II-Die "Einbäume,"* 20–21.

70. Rössler, *Geschichte des deutschen U-Bootbaus,* 149, 156; Rössler, *Vom Original zum Modell: Uboottyp II-Die "Einbäume,"* 21–22; Forsén and Forsén, *Tysklands och Finlands hemliga ubåtssamarbete,* 277–78.

71. Saville, "Development of the German U-Boat Arm," 578–79; Ten Cate, "Das U-Boot als geistige Exportware," 924; Rössler, *Geschichte des deutschen U-Bootbaus,* 149, 154; Forsén and Forsén, *Tysklands och Finlands hemliga ubåtssamarbete,* 278.

72. Saville, "Development of the German U-Boat Arm," 574–75. Henceforth Deschimag in Bremen (the former Weser shipyard) owned two-thirds and Germaniawerft one-third of IvS's shares. Bartenbach's collaboration with IvS did not come to an end here. At a later stage, when he had fallen out of favor in the eyes of the new rising star of Hitler's submarine arm, Kapitän zur See Karl Dönitz, and retired from active duty in the German Navy, he worked for a couple of years as an advisor to IvS when shortly before the war it built submarines for China and a cruiser for Holland. See Forsén and Forsén, *Tysklands och Finlands hemliga ubåtssamarbete,* 280.

73. According to Rössler, "Die deutschen U-Boot-Konstruktionsbüros," 311–12, IfS was a successor of *Schiffbaukontor.* It is clear that the two different subsidiaries existed parallel to each other at least for some time. See Forsén and Forsén, *Tysklands och Finlands hemliga ubåtssamarbete,* 288. For the Romanian and Turkish submarines, see Rössler, *Die deutschen U-Boote und ihre Werften,* 95–96; for the Chinese submarines, see Forsén and Forsén, *Tysklands och Finlands hemliga ubåtssamarbete,* 280.

74. Ten Cate, "Das U-Boot als geistige Exportware," 926–28. In 1954, when West Germany once again was allowed to construct submarines, a successor to IvS's old subsidiary IfS was reopened in Lübeck under the name Ingenieur-Kontor Lübeck (IKL). IKL still exists today.

75. Saville, "Development of the German U-Boat Arm," 573; Ten Cate, "Das U-Boot als geistige Exportware," 924–25.

76. The whole scandal was revealed because in 1927 a reporter from the *Berliner Tageblatt* found out that Kapitän zur See Lohmann used a secret fund for financing a bankrupt film company named Phoebus, which produced highly nationalistic films glorifying the military achievements of Germany. Starting from this the whole story about Lohmann's financial actions came out. The press, in a masterly way, shaped opinion against the shady operations by writing about Lohmann's Russian liaison, with Mrs. Ektimov, a widow of a Russian general, who occupied a suite of apartments in Lohmann's headquarters and received a monthly stipend of 1,000 reichsmarks from the secret funds of the navy! For the development of the Lohmann scandal, see Saville, "Development of the German U-Boat Arm," 249–59; Rahn, *Verteidigungskonzeption und Reichsmarine in der Weimarer Republik,* 223–28.

77. *Die Weltbühne,* 22 November 1927. See also Ten Cate, "Das U-Boot als geistige Exportware," 918–19. Although the project was presented as a fairytale, the description included all the main details about who was responsible for what. For example, "Der Canarische . . . versprach ihm viel von dem Geld, das er von seinem Volk erhalten hatte, wenn die Esche auch ihm . . . Schiffe bauen würde. . . . die gleich den Fischen unter Wasser schwimmen konnten." The "Esche" in the fairytale naturally refers to Echevarrieta and "die Canarische Inseln" to Canaris.

78. The member of the Reichstag was Ernst Schneller. See Saville, "Development of the German U-Boat Arm," 258–59.

79. Saville, "Development of the German U-Boat Arm," 255, 261–63. Canaris was, however, not sent to sea until June 1928.

80. Ibid., 272–73, 321–22.

81. Lakowski, *Deutsche U-Boote geheim 1935–1945*, 18. See also in detail Forsén and Forsén, *Tysklands och Finlands hemliga ubåtssamarbete*, 131–35.

82. For the Koster story, see Forsén and Forsén, *Tysklands och Finlands hemliga ubåts-samarbete*, 223–26.

CHAPTER 7

The Politics of Arms Not Given: Japan, Ethiopia, and Italy in the 1930s

J. Calvitt Clarke III

Independent states enter into the international arms trade and engage in military exchanges for many reasons. At one level, the motives of receiver states are straightforward: they wish to acquire the material resources and training to beat an enemy on the battlefield, or at least to withstand his onslaught, or to intimidate him to the point of avoiding conflict in the first place. Donor states also have sundry reasons for wishing to deliver arms and training to another state. From a commercial perspective, they might wish merely to improve their international balance of trade statistics. On the other hand, diplomats often use arms deliveries and military exchanges to wrench political influence within a target state. At the same time, such activities become powerful, public statements of patron-client relationships jealously sought, defended, and resisted in the Darwinist struggle for survival of the fittest among nations. Here, the motives of the receiver states become more complex as they seek to maintain their sovereignty by using military exchanges to balance the designs of more powerful and predatory nations.

The relationships among Italy, Ethiopia, and Japan in the early 1930s amply demonstrate the profound political impact of actual—and even rumored—military connections in international affairs.

ITALY'S PROBLEM: REAL AND IMAGINED

Ethiopia, France, Great Britain, and Italy signed the Paris Arms Treaty on August 21, 1930. It provided for publishing information regarding arms and ammunition passing into Ethiopia through the respective colonial territories of the three European powers and for storage warehouses in cities along Ethiopia's border to control the arms traffic. By virtue of this treaty plus the Italo-Ethiopian Treaty of Friendship of 1928, Italy's Duce, Benito Mussolini, believed that he had the right to regulate armaments imports into Ethiopia and to act as Ethiopia's military patron.[1] Spurning Italy's exclusive patronage, however, the Ethiopians looked elsewhere, most importantly engaging a small Belgian military mission to train and organize their army.[2]

At the same time and halfway around the world, Japan's ultranationalists outside of government were emotionally wedded to leading an alliance of the "colored peoples" of the world. Ethiopia, they thought, was to play a crucial role in that alliance.[3] Their machinations sparked concern everywhere. Thus Japan's penetration of Ethiopia, done in the midst of Emperor Haile Selassie's efforts to modernize his army, particularly galled Italy.[4] Italian newspapers—with newspapers and officials the world over chiming in—excitedly and falsely reported that numerous Japanese officers had been retained to replace the Belgians in instructing and reorganizing Ethiopia's troops.[5]

BLATTENGETA HERUY WELDE SELASSE'S MISSION TO JAPAN: THE POSSIBILITIES

Following the signing of a Treaty of Friendship and Commerce between Japan and Ethiopia on November 15, 1930,[6] Foreign Minister Heruy Welde Sellase's mission to Japan especially dramatized the potentialities—including military—of Ethio-Japanese cooperation.[7]

Traveling as a special envoy of Ethiopia's emperor,[8] Heruy and his party left Addis Ababa on September 30, 1931.[9] Officially, they were visiting to salute Japan's emperor and to repay Japan for its representation at the coronation of Ethiopia's emperor the year before. In cultivating mutual relations and commerce, Heruy also wanted to see if Ethiopia's plan for modernizing along Japanese lines could be carried out.[10] As portents for the future, one of the party, Araya Abeba, would create an international stir when he tried to marry Kuroda Masako, a Japanese—for many, the very personification of Ethio-Japanese ties;[11] another, Daba Birrou, would revisit Japan in 1935 searching for support during the Italo-Ethiopian conflict.[12]

Everywhere in Japan, Heruy received an enthusiastic reception.[13] In an audience with Emperor Hirohito, he confirmed Japan as Ethiopia's model for modernization:

Our Ethiopian Emperor is deeply impressed with the Japanese Empire's remarkable and great progress of the last sixty years, and is moved with surprise that the Japanese Empire accomplished such a great deed in such a short time, and he is determined to advocate to his whole nation to take the Great Japanese Empire as the best model.[14]

Heruy and his party met officials and businessmen, visited shrines and tourist attractions, tarried at chambers of commerce and geisha houses, and reveled at banquets and hunting parties. Many of the manufacturing concerns he visited held obvious military implications, including the Mitsubishi Aircraft Manufacturing Plant and the Osaka Arsenal.[15] On November 15, Heruy observed a mock battle in Tochigi Prefecture between the Imperial Bodyguard Division and the Utsunomiya 14th Division. The battle was part of three-day, interdivisional maneuvers.[16]

Admiring Japan's well-disciplined soldiers, Heruy apparently decided to begin Japanizing Ethiopia's troops by adopting Japanese-style military uniforms. After studying samples obtained from the Osaka branch of the Army Clothing Depot and elsewhere, he informally contracted the Toyo and Kanegafuchi spinning companies to supply cloth for uniforms. To make the uniforms in Ethiopia, Heruy wanted to bring home a number of experienced Japanese tailors. He approached Kuroki Tokitaro, but as a government official, Kuroki could not help in selecting tailors. Kuroki, nonetheless, was excited at the possibilities for military cooperation:

The system and the strict discipline of the Japanese Army seem to have impressed the Envoy very much and I think the introduction of the Japanese military system into Ethiopia will be materialized in the future.[17]

The president of the Toyo Spinning Company admitted, however, that a formal contract had not yet been completed. He optimistically believed that the order would come after Heruy returned home.[18]

Heruy's visit, which lasted until December 1931, held important consequences. For Japan, it visibly raised Ethio-Japanese relations to their zenith and encouraged widespread public support for Ethiopia as that country girded for war a few years later. Japan's pan-Asianists began to see Ethiopia as a country where they could put their ideals into practice. These included not just expanding Japan's economic influence but also bringing Ethiopia within its "civilizing" influence.[19] On the Ethiopian side, Heruy's journey spurred hopes that Japan's support might balance Italy's increasing weight in their country. Finally, Heruy's admiration for Japan as a model for modernization alarmed the Western powers, which had no desire for a second Japan—this one in Africa.[20]

Heruy himself always insisted that the trip had but benign purposes:

We had no ulterior motive. . . . It meant a great deal to us to open up diplomatic connections with Japan, and that was the primary reason for my journey.

The second reason was purely economic. Our people are poor, and our export trade has shrunk during the last few years owing to the depression. We had to find a source for cheap everyday goods, and Japan is famous the world over as the country that sells the cheapest goods, especially cotton, which our country now imports in great quantities.[21]

It would seem, however, that the crucial additional reason for Heruy's journey was to request arms and munitions from the Japanese government. But at that time, Japan was dealing with the aftermath of the Manchurian Incident and had worries other than supplying arms and munitions to Ethiopia.[22] The visit, nonetheless, drove to the fore international concern regarding Ethiopia's military development and raised particular antipathy toward Japanese aegis— especially in Italy.

Rome had grounds to be concerned. Before the First World War, Bejirond Tekle Hawaryat had studied artillery at St. Petersburg Military School and had attained the rank of colonel.[23] Drawing upon this training, in 1932 Tekle Hawaryat submitted to the council of ministers a series of recommendations regarding Ethiopia's military reorganization. Rejecting his country's traditional warriors in favor of a modern, regular army, he argued that military victory requires a quantitative and qualitative superiority in arms and manpower, a coordinated defensive and offensive strategy, eternal preparedness, a conscious policy of minimizing financial and human costs, high morale, and an improved supply system. He proposed creating a modern army with seven divisions—infantry, cavalry, artillery, navy, engineering corps, machine gun and tank corps, and aviation engineers. Tekle Hawaryat advocated introducing military service of three to five years by recruiting youths. He simultaneously wanted to retire old soldiers and resettle them as farmers. He worried about moving too quickly, and he cautioned against haste and forcible imposition of the new structures.[24]

As if to emphasize the possibility of a Japanese stamp on Ethiopia's modernization process, on June 7, 1934, the Japanese gunboats *Iwate* and *Asama* sailed into Djibouti, the best maritime door to Ethiopia.[25] En route to Japan, these training vessels had several hundred cadets on board under Commander Vice Admiral General Matsushita Hajime. Emperor Haile Selassie's eagerness in dispatching an official delegation to greet the ships and offer imperial salutations amused the local foreign colony. His three envoys, apparently toting gifts, included Araya Abeba and the governor of Harrar Province. The captain of the *Asama*, Ota Taiji, hosted a party for Araya. The United States representative in Addis Ababa, Addison Southard, did not believe that anything of official importance was discussed. He saw the event, however, as further illustrating the energetic and persistent wooing by the Japanese since Heruy's visit to Japan.[26]

The naval visit presaged Tsuchida Yutaka's tour to Ethiopia that same month of June.

TSUCHIDA YUTAK'S INSPECTION TOUR TO ETHIOPIA, JUNE 1934: MORE POSSIBILITIES

Emboldened by the commercial agreement of 1930 and Heruy's visit, several shady Japanese had visited Ethiopia pushing their sundry schemes.[27] Concerned with the negative foreign reaction to Japan's inroads into Ethiopia and with these unofficial visitors, Tokyo sent Tsuchida Yutaka on an inspection tour of Ethiopia in 1934. He was a secretary at the foreign ministry and an expert on Ethiopia. His Report of Investigation in Ethiopia (*'Echiopia' Koku Shisatsu Hokoku*) summarized his conclusions.[28]

Wanting to protect Ethiopia's independence from the imperialist predations of Britain, France, and Italy, Tsuchida in this report added a political nuance to his economic analysis:

Make Japanese policy aid Ethiopia economically, developmentally, and culturally. . . . At the same time, from a great power from a point-of-view, the hope is to take a pragmatic position protecting Ethiopian independence and thereby protecting established Japanese interests there.[29]

Tsuchida confessed that England, France, and Italy would oppose such a policy. Yet, he was optimistic:

At this moment when the issue of penetration of Japanese goods into world markets is becoming a global matter, [Ethiopia is] the only independent sovereign country on the African continent [that] welcomes Japanese advances. . . . It is certain that we need to pay serious consideration to the fact that we could use Ethiopia's inviting atmosphere as a foothold, and we are capable of developing in this region.[30]

Tsuchida felt that Japan, far from Ethiopia, could not support its imperial ambitions there. He believed, however, that opening a Japanese legation at Addis Ababa would be the first step toward expanding in Ethiopia.[31]

For their part, the Ethiopians had more than general economic development in mind. Haile Selassie apparently asked for price quotes on Japanese munitions and cheap motor cars,[32] and Heruy officially placed with Tsuchida an order for 7,000 infantry rifles, 3,000 cavalry rifles, 350 light machine guns, and 48 heavy machine guns. Heruy also proposed that Ethiopia send ten pilots to Japan for training and that Japan establish a munitions factory in Ethiopia.[33]

An Ethiopian Greek and head of the Industrial Department, B. Diamandaras, had earlier unofficially proposed the latter project to Tsuchida. Haile Selassie had commissioned Diamandaras to find people able to build and operate a cartridge manufacturing company. Diamandaras had first approached another Greek. Haile Selassie, in the meanwhile, had read an article in the *Wall Street Journal* that described an agreement by which Japan would establish a munitions manufacturing company in Romania. Encouraged, the emperor wanted a similar contract, and Diamandaras had sounded out Tsuchida.[34] The rumors reverberated in Rome.[35]

The tangible results of Tsuchida's visit and report are unclear. The Japanese never set up a munitions manufacturing company in Ethiopia, and Tsuchida returned to his duties in Geneva in July 1934.[36]

RUMOR AND REALITY: JAPANESE ARMS TO ETHIOPIA AND AMBASSADOR SUGIMURA YOTARO

On December 5, 1934, the WelWel (Wal Wal) incident broke into the world's headlines. WelWel was an important watering hole sixty miles inside Ethiopia's border, where Italian and Ethiopian troops fired on one another. Mussolini chose to make the WelWel affair a *causus belli* by demanding unacceptable reparations.[37] Moreover, as part of this campaign, Italy's Duce cited the Yellow Peril and merged his wrath toward Ethiopia with his suspicions toward Japan.

In his meeting on December 23, 1934, with Japan's newly appointed ambassador to Rome, Sugimura Yotaro, Mussolini complained that Japan was actively supplying weapons and ammunition to Ethiopia.[38] As instructed, Sugimura assured the Duce that Japan's plans to open a legation in Ethiopia were meant merely to normalize diplomatic and commercial relations between the two countries. Sugimura clearly told the Duce that Japan had no political ambitions in Ethiopia.[39] This meeting marked the beginning of Sugimura's assiduous efforts to placate Italy regarding Ethiopia as well as to dampen his own country's ultranationalists.

The next day, on December 24, Afewerq Gebre Iyesus,[40] Ethiopia's chargé d'affaires at Rome, visited the Japanese ambassador to request military assistance. Again following his instructions, Sugimura explained he had no authority to commit Japan to providing weapons to Ethiopia. He threw a sop—Japan remained interested in expanding its economic interests there.[41] Japan's policy seemed set.

In the face of Italy's military buildup in early 1935, Ethiopia swore its peaceful intentions toward Italy. A spokesman specifically denied rumors of superseding the Belgian military instructors with a Japanese military mission.[42] Additional denials in March, however, did little to quell the international excitement.[43] The Italian and Soviet presses in July falsely accused Japan of long supplying arms to Ethiopia, and they complained that Japanese rifles and bullets had been discovered at Makalia several months earlier. Further, they wrote, the Japanese had opened an official trading agency at Aden, Arabia, which was selling not only textiles but munitions as well.[44]

Not everyone—America's black press, for example—took alarm at Japanese activities. Probably recalling the naval visit to Djibouti the year before, the *Chicago Defender* claimed that the Japanese navy had been conducting deep-sea maneuvers in the Red Sea within easy reach of Italy's port at Massawa. The paper predicted that within a week's notice scores of these "swift relentless cruisers from the third largest navy in the world can dump tons of explosives under Mussolini's very nose in Africa."[45]

Amid this diplomatic and publicity swirl, the so-called Sugimura Affair began innocently enough. On July 10, 1935, foreign ministry spokesman Amau

Eiji denied that Emperor Hirohito was contemplating any move in Ethiopia's favor or even that Japan had diplomatic contacts in Ethiopia. He specifically rejected rumors that Japan was shipping munitions to East Africa.[46] While trying not to sound provocative, Japan was leaving open the possibility that it might interfere at some point to protect its interests. After all, the government was reacting to domestic politics and could not appear too soft: while risking infuriating the Italians, the pro-Ethiopian Japanese nationalists within and without government found little to criticize in this pragmatic policy.[47]

Following the foreign ministry's line, Ambassador Sugimura visited Mussolini on July 16. He again reassured the Duce that Japan, despite its commercial interests, held no political ambitions in Ethiopia and would remain neutral in Italy's coming war. The Italians publicized this statement as a communiqué, and Italy's press put the matter plainly: "This solemn statement is the more important as it puts an end to all rumors which have circulated lately."[48]

Although what Sugimura had said was not much different from what foreign ministry spokesmen had long been saying, to Japan's patriots he seemed too placating. A popular storm engulfed Japan. Inspired newspaper articles accused Sugimura of having exceeded his instructions. Some of the foreign ministry's younger officials demanded his immediate recall.[49]

Making Sugimura's job significantly more difficult, the Italo-Ethiopian conflict was breaking into international headlines just when tensions between the Control Faction (Tosei-ha) and the Imperial Way Faction (Kodo-ha) in the Japanese army were boiling over. The pragmatists who composed the Control Faction advocated a cautious foreign policy and wary concern for the Great Powers. The ultranationalists of the Imperial Way Faction, on the other hand, called for a more assertive, independent, and pan-Asiatic foreign policy. For the pragmatists, the question was not whether to join the colonialists or the colonized but with which of the colonial powers to align. The patriots, for their part, eagerly cultivated relations with non-European powers and wished to join with the oppressed masses to overcome the white man's domination.[50]

For his part, Ambassador Sugimura criticized Japanese attitudes—especially those of the Imperial Way Faction—toward Italy. He clearly thrust realpolitik to the fore:

Based especially on its racial concerns, Japanese public opinion naturally sympathizes with a weak country and tries to help Ethiopia. However, as Japanese military and political power is not as strong in far-away Africa as in East Asia, it is unwise to stiffen Japan's attitude toward Italy by reserving its right to speak out in the future and by asserting its right to supply weapons and ammunition. Moreover, it sounds fine, but it is not wise to attempt to extend our commercial rights based on the racial argument, which directly puts us into a confrontation with England, France, and Italy.[51]

Italy's ambassador at Tokyo, Giacinto Auriti, spoke on July 20 with Vice Foreign Minister Shigemitsu Mamoru, who denied any knowledge of Japan's sending arms to Ethiopia. Ignoring Sugimura's advice, Shigemitsu pointedly added that Japan had a right to send weapons to Ethiopia just as Italy was sending weapons to China—a particularly sore point with the Japanese.[52]

In early August, Italy again inserted the racial argument into the armaments discussion, claiming that certain European states were betraying white civilization by supplying arms to Ethiopia.[53]

Such hyperventilated worries, however, over weapons, military advisers, and volunteers being sent to Ethiopia from Japan had no basis in reality. Despite the emotional uplift of roundtables sponsored by private citizens and organizations, Italian intransigence, circumspection in official Japanese quarters, and the hard truth of Sugimura's understanding of the situation decreed that Haile Selassie's hopes for Japanese arms were doomed.

Acting on a letter from Emperor Haile Selassie, on August 2, 1935, Afewerq visited Sugimura for an hour and spoke about Italy's military strength, Ethiopia's military disorder, the League of Nation's powerlessness, and British duplicity. After this sad litany, he asked for assistance, although he conceded the difficulty of importing weapons from Japan. For a month, the French-run Addis Ababa Railroad had refused to transport weapons from Djibouti, although Ethiopia was importing some weapons by camel from Kenya and the Sudan. Revealing his desperation, Afewerq suggested that Japan send submarines to sink Italian ships supporting Mussolini's military buildup in East Africa! He tearfully pleaded that if this aid was not feasible, Japan should, for the sake of justice, officially support Ethiopia. Sugimura responded that for the moment he could not give any assurances on such important and delicate matters.[54]

Putting an exclamation point to Sugimura's judicious response to Afewerq, a high Japanese official publicly asserted on August 6 that Japan's own army program made it unthinkable that munitions stocks would be diverted to Ethiopia. This was especially true, he continued, because the arms industry was government controlled and because Japan was devoting its energies to the mission of maintaining peace and order in East Asia.[55]

That same day, Ethiopia's foreign ministry formally denied rumors that a Japanese military mission would visit Addis Ababa and that Japan was furnishing arms to Ethiopia. Haile Selassie himself publicly declared that Ethiopia had not received any assurance of Japanese support. An official communiqué described such reports as purely imaginary, and it added that Ethiopia's relations with Japan were being kept on a normal and quite correct basis. Ever paranoid, Rome feared that this statement did not reject an arms deal in the future.[56]

In truth, Haile Selassie was desperately combing the world for credits and equipment. By August 8, newspapers were reporting the growing belief that he was turning to the Orient for the desperately needed munitions the rest of the world had refused him. Specifically, Haile Selassie was seeking credits and military supplies from Japan.[57]

The Ethiopians found some limited success in their search. In August from Addis Ababa, Shoji Yunosuke,[58] a correspondent for the *Osaka Mainichi*, reported that Ethiopia's imports of arms and ammunition had increased from nine tons in 1931 to thirty tons in 1934. The greatest exporter was France, followed by Germany, Belgium, and England.[59] Rumors about Japanese weapons exports to Ethiopia continued, however, to dog Tokyo.[60]

On August 8, Japanese officials—again—denied reports of Japanese assistance to Ethiopia. Amau stated that Japan had heard nothing of the reported Ethiopian arms-purchasing mission coming to Japan. He added that no visas had been asked for or issued. No communication of any kind had taken place between the Japanese government and Ethiopia, and no proposals regarding munitions had been received from Italy or Ethiopia.[61] That same day, Ethiopia's minister in London visited Japan's chargé d'affaires and asked about newspaper reports that Japan had exported a large number of weapons to Ethiopia. The chargé told him that it seemed to be false information. The disappointed minister nonetheless expressed gratitude for the sympathy the Japanese people had shown Ethiopia.[62]

Ever willing to provoke animosity toward Japan—and with no real evidence—on August 26 the Soviet press asserted that Ethiopia's army was partly armed with modern military equipment of Japanese manufacture and that Japanese military deliveries had increased during the last six months. The Japanese were supposedly paying particular attention to Ethiopia's aviation and were assisting in its organization. In the likely event of an Italo-Ethiopian war, Japan would supply Ethiopia with additional arms and ammunition. The paper predicted that this would give rise to differences between Italy and Japan and between Britain and Japan.[63]

Even in the face of such verbiage, Italo-Japanese rapprochement was in the wind—official Rome was beginning to pay more attention to Japanese government spokesmen than to wild rumors. In late August, Italy's press vigorously pointed out that Japan's newspapers had favorably changed their attitude toward Italy. The semiofficial *Giornale d'Italia*, for example, had written:

The position which the Japanese press is now taking on the Italo-Abyssinian dispute shows that a clash between Italy and Japan is not possible in the historical events now developing, and that both nations can be only in one camp. . . . More than ever before Italy and Japan should recognize that their fates are identical, just as the means they consider necessary for realizing their aims are the same.[64]

The Italian paper assured its readers at home and abroad that Italy's claims on Ethiopia in no way encroached on Japanese interests; Italy was not striving for a monopoly or a closed door in Ethiopia. Such statements drew alarm in Moscow; Sugimura rejoiced in them. The practical rapprochement for which Japan's ambassador had worked so assiduously was beginning to take hold—although its grasp was still weak and the final outcome not as yet clear.[65]

Ethiopia's foreign ministry's denial in the last week of August that Addis Ababa had reached an agreement with Japan on military advisers and arms transfers could not quash the rumors that Japan was sending arms and munitions as well as advisers to Ethiopia. The *New York Times*, as one example, reported from Addis Ababa that arms shipments sufficient to meet Ethiopia's needs for six months had been arranged with the Japanese. These arms included rifles, machine guns, revolvers, and ammunition. Japanese were also said to be enlisting for Ethiopia. Ethiopians believed that Italy desired to use its uneasiness regarding Japanese aims, real or imagined, to justify its aggressive policy toward Ethiopia.[66] The Japanese concluded that all this was propaganda by the British, French, and others designed to help Italy protect a white stronghold.[67]

On August 29, Tokyo officially denied once more that Ethiopia had ordered any munitions from Japan and added that no such order was expected. Japan had not and would not send arms or ammunition to Ethiopia. Because munitions exports from Japan were under government control, it was impossible for private firms to conduct sales without official knowledge. Only one Japanese, a newspaper correspondent, was then in Ethiopia. Japan had never negotiated with Italy regarding Ethiopia. Japan would continue its policy of watchful waiting.[68]

ETHIOPIA'S LAST GASP: DABA BIRROU'S VISIT TO JAPAN, 1935

To secure the credits and arms he wanted, in late summer Haile Selassie sent the secretary of Ethiopia's foreign ministry, Daba Birrou, on a secret mission to Japan. Daba Birrou, also director of the Wollata Military School—the national military academy—left Addis Ababa at the beginning of the second week of August. Given the many rumors swirling around the trip, officials tried to keep Daba Birrou's departure as secret as possible. Many pro-Japanese governmental officials and journalists, nonetheless, went to the station in Addis Ababa to see the party off.[69]

Daba Birrou assured Japanese authorities that Ethiopia was ready to pay cash or offer products such as coffee, hides, beeswax, and honey in exchange for arms. He requested from Tokyo military officers, whose salaries would be fixed before their departure, engineers, 24 heavy machine guns, 200 light machine guns, 12 cannons, 1,000 cartridges, antiaircraft weapons, 5,000 rifles, sound locators, army tents, and medical equipment.[70]

To Ethiopia's disappointed envoy, on September 13 Amau clearly repeated his government's official position on the Ethiopian question: that of a spectator watching a fight from a high window. Official Tokyo's attitude remained one of watchful waiting and protection of Japan's commercial interests—interests not terribly large in any case.[71]

In contrast to the official reticence, Daba Birrou's visit sparked as much public excitement in Japan as had Heruy's four years earlier.[72] Even before his arrival, Ethiopia's honorary consulate in Osaka began receiving applications from Japanese who wanted to volunteer to fight for Ethiopia. Japanese youths were contributing small amounts of money.[73] On September 19 about 2,000 members of diverse patriotic, ultranationalistic, and pan-Asiatic organizations welcomed Daba Birrou at the Tokyo station. They carried banners screaming Down With Italy! and Rescue Ethiopia! The Ethiopian representative allowed that he intended to stay in Japan for a year.[74]

A discrete Daba Birrou publicly declared that he was merely seeking expanded commercial ties and political support.[75] Others believed that he wished to negotiate arms purchases based on a grant of credits amounting to at least 50 percent of the value of the orders. Given satisfactory financial arrangements, purchases probably would be considerable.[76] Some speculated that the Osaka munitions makers were especially interested in Daba Birrou. He called on Lieutenant General Prince Higashikuni at Osaka and on Inabata Katsutaro, a prominent industrialist. He received numerous invitations to events from ultranationalist organizations, for example, the Abyssinian Rescue Society (Kyuen Doshi Kai). These groups wished to express Japanese sympathy for Ethiopia in its troubles.[77]

On September 21, the Ethiopian Problems Society (Echiopia Mondai Kondan Kai) held a welcoming party for Daba Birrou. The 251 patriotic guests included Toyama Mitsuru, a founder of the Dark Ocean Society (Genyou sha) and the Black Dragon Society (Kokuryu Kai),[78] both ultranationalist groups. Through Daba Birrou, Ethiopia's emperor deeply thanked them for their passionate sympathy.[79] Western newspapers snidely pointed out that Daba Birrou, "young, coal-black, and English-speaking," appeared dazed by the amount of hand shaking by elderly patriots; he had not realized that no Japanese of importance was present.[80] Inspired, the Ethiopian Problems Society on the night of October 5 pretentiously cabled the foreign minister at Addis Ababa:

The Japanese nation indignantly condemns Italian aggression. God bless righteous Ethiopia. In a war air raids are not the deciding factor. Never lose courage. Transmit this message to your commanders.[81]

Doubtless, such effusive expressions of Japanese public opinion fed suspicions among the Western powers. Government policy was more hardheaded.

After Italy launched its attack on Ethiopia, Japanese officials at Geneva complained that a large element of Japanese public opinion not only sympathized with Ethiopia but was also anti-Italian. Hence, the government faced the dilemma of taking action that would arouse accusations of supporting the league that had opposed Japan in Manchuria or of inaction that would inflict charges of assisting Italy. The government, these Japanese officials continued, had considered action similar to that taken by the United States, that is, an arms embargo against both belligerents. Tokyo regretted not having had the foresight to place itself in the position that the United States occupied. Japanese officials at Geneva openly endeavored to prevent any hint of cooperating in the sanctions the league was then imposing.[82]

In reality, both the foreign ministry and Imperial Army had rejected giving any military aid. Fearing larger diplomatic repercussions and Ethiopia's inability to pay, Japan sent Ethiopia neither arms, munitions, nor a mission. The Japanese limited their aid to sending the Ethiopian Red Cross enough plasters for 10,000 people, 138 boxes of medical supplies, and some tents. Along with most of the rest of the world, Japan protested Italy's use of poison gas and its bombing of Red Cross units.[83]

CONCLUSION

Despite the fervent adulation from patriotic Japanese and tepid assistance to Ethiopia's Red Cross, in the end Ethiopians got none of the tangible and significant aid they had hoped to get from Japan.[84] Ethiopia's army was neither sufficiently armed, trained, nor led to effectively resist for long Italy's invasion. Italian troops entered Addis Ababa in May 1936.

At the crucial moment during the Italo-Ethiopian War, in February 1936 young Imperial Way Faction army officers attempted a coup by occupying the Diet Building and the war ministry in Tokyo and by assassinating traitorous high officials. The coup's failure strengthened the Control Faction, which clamped down on those ultranationalist groups that had also tended most vociferously to support Ethiopia.[85]

One consequence of the pragmatists' victory was that Tokyo ultimately accommodated itself to Italy's conquest of the Ethiopian Empire. The exchange of recognitions on December 2, 1936—Japan's conquest of Manchukuo for Italy's conquest of Ethiopia[86]—paved the way for the reconciliation between Tokyo and Rome. Even someone like Foreign Minister Hirota Koki, who had so sorely vexed Sugimura during the Sugimura Affair and whom so many have taken to be an ultranationalist, in the end proved to be just another pragmatist.[87]

Surely, this volte-face in Rome and Tokyo could not have been accomplished so quickly if the Italians had not been brought to believe Japanese protestations of innocence regarding the arms transfers and training that Ethiopia had so desperately needed. Perhaps they never truly had. But whether they had or not, they had effectively used the rumors of significant Japanese inroads into Ethiopia to disarm potential international opposition to Italy's coming adventure, especially in London, Paris, and Moscow.

After the war, the remnants of the right-wing, patriotic, pro-Ethiopian groups in Japan eventually came to strongly support the Axis alliance that fought together during the Second World War. This wartime coalition ultimately led to mutual devastation and defeat for Italy and Japan. Ethiopia, on the other hand, in 1941 became the first Axis-occupied country to be liberated.

NOTES

1. William M. Steen, "Ethiopia in Danger as Mussolini Begins Expansion Program," September 1934, Papers of the NAACP, Part 11: Special Subject Files, 1912–1939, Series A: Africa through Garvey, Marcus, August Meier and John H. Bracey Jr., eds. (Bethesda, Md.: University Publications of America, 1990), microfilm frames 634–43; *Times* (London), 22 August 1930. In the National Archives (College Park, Md.), Record Group 59, Decimal File (hereafter cited as NA), see Ethiopia (Southard), 1/3/32: 884.242/3.

2. Ethiopia (Southard), 1/14/30: NA 884.20/6; Moffat, 1/16/35: NA 560.ZL/8; Moffat, 1/16/35: NA 765.84/150; Ethiopia (Southard), 1/23/32: NA 884.01A/880; Ethiopia (Southard), 1/16/35: NA 884.242/4. Also see *Times* (London), 16 January 1930. For Mussolini's clear explanation of his motives, see *Times* (London), 1 August 1935.

3. See J. Calvitt Clarke III, "Modernizing Ideologies: Japan and Ethiopia Before the Italo-Ethiopian War, 1935–36," paper presented to the annual meeting of the Florida Conference of Historians, Orlando, Fla., April 2000. For an overview of the Sugimura Affair, see J. Calvitt Clarke III, "Japan and Italy Squabble Over Ethiopia: The Sugimura Affair of July 1935," *Selected Annual Proceedings of the Florida Conference of Historians* 6/7 (December 1999): 105-16.

4. To Ethiopia, 11/21/33: NA 784.94/1A. Teferi Mekonnen was born on 23 July 1892 and served as regent under Empress Zewditu Menilek, who reigned from 1916 to 1930. His policies included international recognition, expanded education, abolition of slavery, and elimination of opposition. Upon Zewditu's death, Teferi was crowned as Emperor Haile Selassie I; he reigned from 1930 through 1974. Italy's invasion of October 1935 interrupted his efforts at promoting centralization of administration, financial regulation, army training, and education. Chris Prouty and Eugene Rosenfeld, *Historical Dictionary of Ethiopia* (Metuchen, N.J.: Scarecrow Press, 1981), 91–93.

5. In NA, see To Ethiopia, 1/28/35: 884.20/433; War Department, 10/5/33: 784.94/1; To Ethiopia, 10/12/33: 784.94/1; To Ethiopia, 11/21/33: 784.94/1a; To Ethiopia, 11/21/33: 784.94/1b; Ethiopia (Southard), 12/26/33: 784.94/5; Ethiopia (Southard), 10/22/34: 784.94/13; and Ethiopia (Southard), 10/22/34: 765.84/62. Also see *New York Times*, 27 December 1934.

Especially interesting was the Soviet role in this hue and cry. Not until late August or early September of 1935 did the USSR come down firmly on the anti-imperialist side against Italy. A major part of the explanation was that Moscow hoped to include Rome in an anti-Japanese coalition. See, for example, in Ministero degli Affari Esteri, Direzione Generale degli Affari Politici, URSS [Ministry of Foreign Affairs, Department of Political Affairs, USSR (Rome)] Berardis, 10/31/33: b(usta)11 (1933) f(oglio)1; Attolico, 1/16/34: b15 f2; Moscow, 12/20/34: b15 (1934) f2. For more explanation why Moscow supported Rome through the first nine months of 1935, see J. Calvitt Clarke III, *Russia and Italy Against Germany: The Bolshevik Fascist Rapprochement of the 1930s* (Westport, Conn.: Greenwood Press, 1991) and "Periphery and Crossroads: Ethiopia and World Diplomacy, 1934–36," in *Ethiopia in Broader Perspective: Papers of the 13th International Conference of Ethiopian Studies*, 3 vols., ed. K. E. Fukui and M. Shigeta

(Kyoto: Shokado Book Sellers, 1997), 1:699–712. A slightly longer version of the latter article, entitled "Japan, Collective Security, and the Italo-Ethiopian War of 1935–36," was presented to the Third Pan-European International Relations Conference and Joint Meeting with the International Studies Association, Vienna, Austria, September 1998.

For more on connections between Japan and Ethiopia, see in *Ethiopia in Broader Perspective*, vol. 1: Messay Kebede, "Japan and Ethiopia: An Appraisal of Similarities and Divergent Courses," 639–51; Donald N. Levine, "Ethiopia and Japan in Comparative Civilizational Perspective," 652–75; Merid W. Aregay, "Japanese and Ethiopian Reactions to Jesuit Missionary Activities in the Sixteenth and Seventeenth Centuries," 676–98; and Aoki Sumio and Kurimoto Eisei, "Japanese Interest in Ethiopia (1868–1940): Chronology and Bibliography," 713–28.

6. Ethiopia (Southard), 12/17/32: NA 784.94/1.

7. Japan (Military Attaché), 1/17/34: NA 784.942/6; *Osaka Mainichi & Tokyo Nichi Nichi* (hereafter cited as OM&TNN), 1 November 1931.

Heruy, born in 1878, authored and published some twenty-eight works. One of Emperor Haile Selassie's trusted advisors, he acted as a diplomat to Paris, Geneva, Japan, and the United States. He went into exile with Haile Selassie in 1936 and died in England in 1939. His honorific, Blattengeta, means "Master of the Pages." Prouty and Rosenfeld, *Historical Dictionary*, 94.

Transliteration from Amharic is confusing. This paper uses the spellings found in Prouty and Rosenfeld. Additionally, Ethiopians normally do not use family names and commonly go only by their first names; when necessary, they will also use their father's first name. This paper will cite Ethiopian names according to Ethiopian practice, that is, first name, then father's first name. Japanese, on the other hand, use their family name first. Again, this paper will conform to Japanese practice, as do the Japanese works included in the bibliography, that is, family name, then first name.

8. Taura Masanori, "Nihon-Echiopia kankei ni miru 1930 nen tsusho gaiko no iso" (A phase of the 1930 commercial diplomacy in the Japanese-Ethiopian relations], *Seifu to Minkan* (Government and civilians), *Nenpo Kindai Nihon Kenkyu* (Annual report, study of modern Japan) 17 (1995): 148–49. I would like to thank Mariko Clarke for translating the pertinent Japanese materials. See as well Adrien Zervos, *L'Empire d'Ethiopie: Le Miroir de l'Ethiopie Moderne 1906–1935* (Alexandria, Egypt: Impr. de l'Ecole professionnelle des freres, 1936), 482; Furukawa Tetsushi, "Japan's Political Relations with Ethiopia, 1920s–1960s: A Historical Overview," unpublished paper presented to the 35th Annual Meeting of the African Studies Association, Seattle, Wash., 20–23 November 1992, 7–8; Furukawa Tetsushi, "Japanese-Ethiopian Relations in the 1920–30s: The Rise and Fall of 'Sentimental' Relations," paper presented at the 34th Annual Meeting of the African Studies Association, St. Louis, Mo., November 1991, 7; and Heruy Welde Sellase, *Dai Nihon* (Great Japan), foreword by Baron Shidehara Kijuro, trans. Oreste Vaccari and Enko Vaccari (Tokyo: Eibunpo Tsuron Hakkojo, 1934), pt. 1. Originally published in Amharic, *Mahidere Birhan: Hagre Japan* (The document of Japan) (Addis Ababa, 1934). Shidehara was foreign minister between 1924–27 and 1929–31; he served as prime minister in 1945–46.

9. Furukawa, "Japan's Political Relations," 6. For Heruy's schedule and his experience in Japan, see his *Dai Nippon*, preface and OM&TNN, 13 August 1935.

10. Furukawa, "Japan's Political Relations," 6; Furukawa, "Japanese-Ethiopian Re-

lations," 6; Richard Albert Bradshaw, "Japan and European Colonialism in Africa, 1800–1937," (Ph.D. diss., Ohio University, 1992), 310–11.

11. J. Calvitt Clarke III, "Marriage Alliance: The Union of Two Imperiums, Japan and Ethiopia?" *Selected Annual Proceedings of the Florida Conference of Historians* 6/7 (December 1999): 9–19. Araya's father was a cousin of Haile Selassie and counted among his relatives some of the most important of Ethiopia's nobility. Hideko Ishihara, "First Contacts Between Ethiopia and Japan," paper presented to the XIIIth International Conference of Ethiopian Studies, Kyoto, December 1997, 11 n. 21. Kuroda Masako was the twenty-three-year-old, second daughter of Viscount Kuroda Hiroyuki of the forestry bureau of the Imperial Household.

12. A protégé of the foreign minister, Daba Birrou came from Gara. He studied at the Swedish mission school in Addis Ababa. After his return from Japan where he acted as a translator, he became an attaché to the ministry of foreign affairs. Later, he was appointed inspector general at Wallagga. In 1934, he obtained the post of director of the Wollata Military School. In 1935, he was appointed secretary to the honorary Ethiopian consulate at Osaka. Zervos, *L'Empire d'Ethiopie*, 120.

13. OM&TNN, 6, 7, 25 November 1931; Taura, "Nihon-Echiopia," 149; Heruy, *Dai Nippon*, 16–19; Bradshaw, "Japan," 308.

14. Shoji Yunosuke, *Echiopia Kekkon Mondai wa Donaru, Kaisho ka Ina: Kekkon Mondai o Shudai to shite Echiopia no Shinso o Katari Kokumin no Saikakunin o Yobo su* (What will happen to the Ethiopian marriage issue, cancellation? or not!!!: I request the re-recognition of the Japanese nation by narrating the truth of Ethiopia with the marriage issue as the central theme) (Tokyo: Seikyo Sha, 1934), 3; OM&TNN, 7 November 1931; Furukawa, "Japan's Political Relations," 6–7; Furukawa, "Japanese-Ethiopian Relations," 6–7; Heruy, *Dai Nippon*, 21–23.

Addison Southard, America's representative in Addis Ababa, noted that Haile Selassie believed that Japan's influential world position had grown out of foreign assistance. He hoped that Ethiopia might accomplish similarly marvelous results by using foreign support. Southard added that Haile Selassie was "unaware, of course, of the vast differences between the two countries and peoples, and their qualifications and resources which place Japan far ahead of what Ethiopia is or ever could hope to be." Southard had spent many years in the Far East before entering the State Department and knew Japan well—but he never thought it "discreet to attempt the probably impossible, and genuinely delicate, task of convincing His Imperial Majesty of the great difference between the two countries and their peoples." Southard did informally and tactfully suggest to Heruy some ways in which he could make practical comparisons during his visit to Japan. Ethiopia (Southard), 10/5/31: NA 033.8411/81.

15. Okakura Takashi and Kitagawa Katsuhiko, *Nihon-Afurika Koryu-shi: Meiji-ki kara Dainiji Sekai Taisen-ki made* (History of Japanese-African relations: From the Meiji period to the Second World War period) (Tokyo: Dobun-kan, 1993), 32–33; OM&TNN, 8, 10, 12, 19, 20, 24, 25, 27, 28 November, and 3, 4 December 1931; Bradshaw, "Japan," 309–10.

16. OM&TNN, 11, 15 November 1931.

17. OM&TNN, 29 November 1931. Kuroki Tokitaro was Japan's longtime vice consul at Port Said, Egypt. By virtue of that position, from 1923 through 1935 Kuroki played a crucial role in structuring the political and commercial relationship between Japan and Ethiopia. Kuroki accompanied Heruy to Japan.

18. OM&TNN, 1 December 1931.

19. Bradshaw, "Japan," 315.

20. Furukawa, "Japan's Political Relations," 7–8; Ishihara, "First Contacts," 3–4.

21. Ladislas Farago, *Abyssinia on the Eve* (New York: G. P. Putnam's Sons, 1935), 127–28.

22. Ishihara, "First Contacts," 7.

23. A close associate of Haile Selassie's, Tekle Hawaryat became minister of finance in 1930. He drafted Ethiopia's constitution of 1931, which he modeled on Japan's Meiji Constitution of 1889. He studied military science and agriculture in tsarist Russia from 1896 through 1902. He went into exile in 1935 and did not return until 1955. His title, Bejirond, means "treasurer and chief of stores." Bahru Zewde, *A History of Modern Ethiopia, 1855–1974* (London: James Currey, 1991), 106; Prouty and Rosenfeld, *Historical Dictionary*, 169.

24. Bahru Zewde, "The Ethiopian Intelligentsia and the Italo-Ethiopian War, 1935–1941," *International Journal of African Historical Studies* 26 (1993): 274–75.

25. Djibouti, an excellent port in French Somaliland on the Gulf of Aden, spent 115 years under French control. The French and Ethiopians agreed on building the railroad connecting Djibouti with Addis Ababa that gave Ethiopia an outlet to the sea and France revenue and trade advantages. Prouty and Rosenfeld, *Historical Dictionary*, 52.

26. Ethiopia (Southard), 6/21/34: NA 784.94/10; Ethiopia (Engert), 8/24/35: NA 784.94/23; Shoji, *Echiopia Kekkon Mondai wa Donaru*, 6.

27. After Heruy's visit, Ethiopia established an honorary consulate in Osaka. Between 1932 and 1934, a few Japanese businessmen traveled to Ethiopia, and some tried to establish a total of six trading companies in Addis Ababa. None had any notable success, however, and few of these businessmen remained in Addis Ababa when war broke out in 1935. Bradshaw, "Japan," 311–15.

28. Taura, "Nihon-Echiopia," 154–58; Ishihara, "First Contacts," 6–7; Ethiopia (Southard), 7/19/34: NA 784.94/11.

29. Taura, "Nihon-Echiopia," 156.

30. Ibid., 156–57.

31. Ishihara, "First Contacts," 8.

32. Ethiopia (Southard), 7/19/34: NA 784.94/11.

33. Ishihara, "First Contacts," 7.

34. Ishihara, "First Contacts," 7; Zervos, *L'Empire d'Ethiopie*, 126.

35. Ministero degli Affari Esteri, Commissione per la Pubblicazione dei Documenti Diplomatici (Ministry of foreign affairs, Commission for the Publication of Diplomatic Documents), *I documenti diplomatici italiani* (Italian diplomatic documents; hereafter cited as DDI), 8th ser.: 1935–1939, vol. 2, no. 2 (Rome: La Libreria dello Stato, 1952).

36. Taura, "Nihon-Echiopia," 158; Ishihara, "First Contacts," 8.

37. Prouty and Rosenfeld, *Historical Dictionary*, 182.

38. Okakura and Kitagawa, *Nihon-Afurika Koryu-shi*, 39. Dr. Sugimura Yotaro was representing his government at Geneva when Japan withdrew from the League of Nations. Named as ambassador to Italy in late 1934, he admired Mussolini, and his daughter converted to Catholicism while in Italy. A pragmatist, he considered Japan's relations with Rome to be of far greater importance than were its relations with Addis Ababa. His efforts to mollify Italian opinion ultimately bore fruit in 1937 when Italy signed the Anti-Comintern Pact. Bradshaw, "Japan," 330–31.

39. Taura, "Nihon-Echiopia," 158–61; Bradshaw, "Japan," 330; OM&TNN, 20 July 1935.

40. Born in 1868, Afewerq studied in Switzerland. He defected to Italy during the Italo-Ethiopian War of 1895–96. He married an Italian in 1904 and was attached to the Orientale Institue in Naples. He wrote two Amharic grammars, the first Amharic novel, a guidebook with many of his political ideas, and a biography of Menilek II. He returned to Ethiopia when Zewditu became empress. From 1931 to 1935, he was Ethiopia's minister to Italy and was pro-Mussolini. A collaborator from 1936 through 1941, after Ethiopia's liberation he was exiled to Jimma where he died in 1947. Prouty and Rosenfeld, *Historical Dictionary*, 6–7.

41. Bradshaw, "Japan," 330–31; Sunday Olu Agbi, *Japanese Relations with Africa* (Ibadan, Nigeria: Ibadan University Press, 1992), 52; Furukawa, "Japan's Political Relations," 11–12; Ishihara, "First Contacts," 7.

42. *Times* (London), 28 February 1935.

43. Ethiopia (George), 3/22/35: NA 884.20/29.

44. *Moscow Daily News*, 28 July 1935; *Corriere della Sera*, 26 July 1935.

45. *Chicago Defender*, 13 July 1935.

46. OM&TNN, 11 July 1935; *Chicago Daily News*, 10 July 1935: Japan, Gaimusho Gaiko Shiryo Kan (Record Office, Ministry of Foreign Affairs, hereafter cited as Gaiko Shiryo Kan) (Tokyo) A461 ET/I1–2, vol. 1; *New York Times*, 11 July 1935; *Japan Times*, 11 July 1935. Iranian papers printed these denials. Okamoto to Hirota, 8/26/35: Gaiko Shiryo Kan A461 ET/I1, vol. 2.

47. Bradshaw, "Japan," 332.

48. *Moscow Daily News*, 21 July 1935; OM&TNN, 18 July 1935; *Japan Times*, 18, 21 July 1935; *New York Times*, 13, 17 July 1935; Taura Masanori, "I. E. Funso to Nihon gawa Taio: Showa 10 nen Sugimura Seimei Jiken wo Chushin ni," (Italo-Ethiopian conflict and the Japanese response), *Nihon Rekishi* (Japanese history) 526 (March 1992): 79–80; Taura Masanori, "Nichii Kankei to sono Yotai (1935–36): Echiopia Senso wo meguru Nihon gawa Taio kara" [Italo-Japanese relations and their conditions (1935–36): From the Japanese response to the Ethiopian war] in *Nihon Kindai-shi no Sai Kochiku*, ed. Ito Takashi (Reexamination of modern Japanese history) (Tokyo: P. Yamakawa Shuppan-sha, 1993), 305; Taura, "Nihon-Echiopia," 163.

49. OM&TNN, 20 July 1935; *New York Times*, 19, 20 July 1935; *Times* (London), 20 July 1935; *Japan Times*, 20, 21 July 1935; *Moscow Daily News*, 21 July 1935; Taura, "I. E. Funso to Nihon gawa Taio," 80–83; DDI, 8th, 1, nos. 555, 569, 570, 571, 587.

50. Bradshaw, "Japan," 320, 361.

51. Taura, "Nichii Kankei," 305.

52. Taura, "I. E. Funso to Nihon gawa Taio," 83. For a general description of Italy's machinations in China and their role in provoking declaration of the Amau Doctrine— Japan's assertion that Japan would be responsible for maintaining peace and order in East Asia—see Bradshaw, "Japan," 324–29. For more on the Sugimura Affair see Italy (Pillow), 7/25/35: NA 765.84/938 and Japan (Neville), 7/26/35: NA 765.84/798.

53. For the months leading to Italy's attack on Ethiopia in October, as a small sample of Italian paranoia regarding military supplies going to Ethiopia from sources as diverse as Germany, Great Britain, France, the United States, Denmark, Spain, Belgium, Switzerland, Yugoslavia, Poland, Greece, the Netherlands, and Czechoslovakia, see DDI, 8th, 1, nos. 61, 82, 98, 124, 128, 170, 174, 177, 195, 205, 217, 220, 223, 277, 280, 304, 363, 436, 461, 476, 477, 528, 552, 601, 607, 625, 628, 641, 701, 713, and

715. Presumed Japanese assistance, however, provoked the greatest emotional response in Rome.

54. Sugimura to Hirota, 8/3–4/35: Gaiko Shiryo Kan A461 ET/I1–7, vol. 1.

55. *New York Times*, 7 August 1935.

56. *New York Times*, 9, 13 August 1935; *Times* (London), 7, 9, 10 August 1935; *Japan Times*, 8, 9, 10, 11 August 1935.

57. OM&TNN, 10 August 1935; *Times* (London), 9 August 1935; Japan (Neville), 9/18/35: NA 894.00/93.

58. Shoji, a pan-Asiatic, outspoken supporter of Ethiopia, was only twenty-six years old when Heruy asked him to accompany Daba Birrou to Japan. He and his newspapers, the *Osaka Mainichi* and the *Osaka Mainichi & Tokyo Nichi Nichi*, played crucial roles in fanning public support in Japan for Ethiopia. Bradshaw, "Japan," 317, 342–45.

59. OM&TNN, 17 August 1935.

60. Sugimura to Hirota, 8/19/35: Gaiko Shiryo Kan A461 ET/I1, vol. 2.

61. *New York Times*, 9, 13 August 1935; *Times* (London), 9, 10 August 1935; *Japan Times*, 10, 11 August 1935. In NA see Italy (Kirk), 8/8/35: 765.84/897 and Italy (Kirk), 8/7/35: 765.84/755.

62. Fujii to Hirota, 8–9 August 1935: Gaiko Shiryo Kan A461 ET/I1–7, vol. 1.

63. *Moscow Daily News*, 26 August 1935. Iranian papers in late August had a better grasp of the situation. Okamoto to Hirota, 8/26/35: Gaiko Shiryo Kan A461 ET/I1, vol. 2.

64. *Moscow Daily News*, 27 August 1935.

65. Sugimura to Hirota, 8/16/35; 8/31/35: Gaiko Shiryo Kan A461 ET/I1, vol. 2; *Japan Times*, 9 August 1935.

66. *New York Times*, 29 August 1935; in NA, see Ethiopia (Engert), 8/24/35: 884.20/44; Ethiopia (Engert), 8/24/35: 884.24/73; and Ethiopia (Engert), 8/24/35: 784.94/23.

67. Chief of the General Staff (September 1935): Gaiko Shiryo Kan A461 ET/I1 I, vol. 1.

68. *New York Times*, 30 August 1935; *Japan Times*, 30 August 1935.

69. OM&TNN, 13 August 1935. See Bradshaw, "Japan," 348–58.

70. Agbi, *Japanese Relations*, 52–53. Agbi claims that the Japanese were tempted, thinking they could sell arms to Ethiopia. As one foreign ministry official asserted, "all we need is British verbal declaration allowing transit." Agbi goes on to say that there is no evidence suggesting that the foreign ministry ever consulted Britain on the issue. He believes that the *Genoa Maru*, which had set sail for East Africa in late August 1935, carried military equipment and volunteers. This seems doubtful.

71. *New York Times*, 14 September 1935.

72. OM&TNN, 14, 15, 16, 17, 18, 20 August 1935; *Japan Times*, 12, 14 September 1935; *New York Times*, 19 September 1935.

73. OM&TNN, 14 September 1935.

74. *New York Times*, 20 September 1935; *Times* (London), 20 September 1935; *Moscow Daily News*, 20 September 1935; Furukawa, "Japan's Political Relations," 10; Japan (Neville), 10/3/35: NA 765.84/2012.

75. *New York Times*, 20 September 1935; *Times* (London), 20 September 1935.

76. *New York Times*, 9, 13, 15 August 1935; *Times* (London), 10 August 1935; *Japan Times*, 10, 11, 13 August 1935; *Moscow Daily News*, 11 August 1935; Ishihara, "First Contacts," 11; Ethiopia (Engert), 8/24/35: NA 784.94/23.

77. *New York Times*, 19 September 1935.

78. A better but less common translation would be "Amur River Society" after the Amur River.

79. Oguri to Goto Mitsuru and Hirota, 9/23/35: Gaiko Shiryo Kan A461 ET/I1–2, vol. 1.

80. *New York Times*, 22 September 1935; *Times* (London), 23 September 1935.

81. *New York Times*, 6 October 1935.

82. Geneva (Gilbert), 10/14/35: NA 765.84.

83. Furukawa, "Japan's Political Relations," 11–12; Agbi, *Japanese Relations*, 57.

84. See the documents in Gaiko Shiryo Kan ET/I1–6, "Sekijuji Kankei (Echiopia Seifu e Eiseizairyo Kizo Kankei wo Fukumu)" (Red Cross including the dispatch of medical supplies to the Ethiopian government): "Activité de la Croix-Rouge en Ethiopie," Geneva, 2/10/36; Brown to Suzuki, nd; Aide Memoire, Addis Ababa, 3/20/36; Heruy to Tokugawa, 10/2/36; "Liste Des Dons Recus De L'Etranger pala Croix Rouge Ethiopienne," nd; and Suzuki to Hirota, 3/27–28/36. For private offers of medical assistance, see Oguri to Goto and Hirota, 7/20/35: Gaiko Shiryo Kan A461 ET/I1–2–1.

85. Bradshaw, "Japan," 358–61.

86. Sugimura to Arita, 10/29/36: Gaiko Shiryo Kan A461 ET/I1, vol. 8; Sugimura to Arita, 87–1, 5/12–13/36; Mushanokoji (Berlin) to Arita, 107, 5/15–16/36; Sugimura to Arita, 87–2, 5/12–13/36: Gaiko Shiryo Kan A461 ET/I1–7, vol. 7; Okakura and Kitagawa, *Nihon-Afurika Koryu-shi*, 45; Bradshaw, "Japan," 358–61. America's representatives followed these events closely. See the many documents in NA 765.94.

87. Bradshaw, "Japan," 321–22.

CHAPTER 8

The Most Unlikely of Allies: Hitler and Haile Selassie and the Defense of Ethiopia, 1935–36

Ed Westermann

The Italo-Ethiopian War of 1935–36, widely recognized as a study in contrasts, incorporated a paradox previously unremarked by history. When Haile Selassie I led his nation to war, Nazi Germany provided the emperor with his greatest source of aid with which to resist Italian aggression. This chapter of German diplomatic history has heretofore remained largely ignored. The bulk of scholarship concerning German diplomatic relations prior to the Second World War focused primarily on Germany's diplomatic relations with the other European powers. In particular, a great deal of attention centered on Italo-German ties, minimizing diplomatic relations between Germany and Ethiopia.[1] The official German diplomatic position in relation to the governments of Ethiopia and Italy, prior to the Italian invasion of October 3, 1935, was strict neutrality. However, the records of the German foreign ministry, the National Socialist Party chancellery, and the personal memoirs of the German diplomat, Curt M. Prüfer, former minister to Ethiopia and deputy director for Anglo-American and Oriental affairs in the foreign ministry, provide evidence of direct German government involvement in the supply of arms to Ethiopia as late as 1936. The discovery of previously unpublished material sheds new light on the roles played by the foreign ministry, members of the National Socialist Party chancellery, and, ultimately, Reich Chancellor

The author would like to thank the Red Sea Press for allowing him to use material from a previously published manuscript. In addition, the author would like to express his gratitude to Gerhard Weinberg, Don McKale, Alan Steinweis, and Peter Garretson for their comments and suggestions on an earlier version of this work.

Adolf Hitler himself in sustaining the resistance of the black African Emperor Haile Selassie I to fascist aggression.

The German decision to supply arms to Ethiopia is doubly intriguing based on the historically tenuous relationship between the two countries. The initial establishment of German-Ethiopian diplomatic relations resulted through a convergence of mutual interests. The Ethiopian government, under Menelik II (1889–1913), sought to establish relations with Wilhelmine Germany as a counterweight to the efforts of the Tripartitepowers—Great Britain, France, and above all Italy—to infringe on Ethiopian sovereignty. The Germans for their part viewed Ethiopia as a potentially significant market for overseas exports. A secondary consideration involved the opportunity for Germany to increase her influence in the Horn of Africa at the expense of Great Britain and France.[2]

Between 1905 and 1935, alternating periods of interest and apathy characterized German-Ethiopian relations. German interest in Ethiopia peaked in the years between 1913 and 1916, with a concerted effort by German agents quite literally to seduce the boy emperor, Lij Yassu, through the use of *Wein, Weib und Gesang* (wine, women, and song) toward an open policy of support for the Central Powers.[3] Domestic political intrigues ultimately resulted in Yassu's downfall. His removal from the throne and the subsequent appointment of Ras Tafari (later Haile Selassie) as regent of the realm inaugurated a period of tepid relations, with the period between 1920 and 1930 characterized by German indifference.[4] One incident in 1929 clearly highlighted the limits of German support for Ethiopia. In a scathing letter, the German minister to Ethiopia, Curt M. Prüfer (1928–30), reprimanded a German national for assisting the new Emperor Haile Selassie in the purchase of an aircraft from the Junkers firm:

For all I care, you can sell the Abyssinians sewing machines or bedpans, but if it should again occur to you to deliver aircraft or similar materiel, then you will have not only the Legation but the entire Foreign Ministry against you.[5]

On the one hand, Prüfer's admonition was a natural extension of the Weimar government's detached policy toward Ethiopia. On the other hand, the continuing restrictions imposed on Germany by the Versailles Treaty also shaped the sharp tone of his reaction to the proposed sale of material with potential military applications.

By the summer of 1930, expectations concerning increased German commercial investment resulted in renewed interest in relations with Ethiopia. A report to the German foreign ministry dated July 4, 1930, predicted that "Abyssinia is expected in the coming years to be an important market area for German industrial products."[6] The 1930 projections for substantial German investment proved overly optimistic as several proposed mining ventures and possible German participation in the construction of a Lake Tsana dam never advanced beyond the initial planning stage. By 1935, the extent of German business investment had not nearly approached the levels anticipated in 1930. German exports to Ethiopia totaled only 800,000 reichsmarks in 1928, 500,000 reichsmarks in 1930, 300,000 reichsmarks in 1931–4, and 400,000 reichsmarks in 1935.[7] A report of January 10, 1935, correctly described German economic interests in Abyssinia as "negligible."[8]

Ironically, it was not commercial ties but rather diplomatic considerations that forced the German foreign ministry to devote increasing attention to the Horn of Africa in the early 1930s. The heightened state of antagonism between Italy and Ethiopia proved the catalyst for the shift. After the Wal Wal incident of December 5, 1934, the German foreign ministry began closely monitoring the diplomatic relationship between the two countries.[9] At first glance, it would seem that Germany's sympathies should rest naturally with Mussolini's fascist government based on both ideological affinity and substantial commercial ties. In contrast to the limited trade with Ethiopia, German economic exports to Italy totaled 227,300,000 reichsmarks in 1933, 245,900,000 reichsmarks in 1934, and 278,300,000 reichsmarks for 1935, including the anticipated delivery of over one-half of Italy's coal imports for 1935.[10] The German foreign ministry, however, chose to pursue a policy of "strict neutrality" in the increasingly bitter dispute between the negus and the Duce.

The prevailing political situation in Europe and not commercial considerations offered the explanation for the National Socialist government's seemingly paradoxical stance. The developing dispute between Italy and Ethiopia offered the German foreign ministry a potential wedge with which to break the "Stresa Front" by holding out the promise of German support for Italian aims in Africa in exchange for Italian support of Germany's objectives in Europe.[11] German-Italian antagonism had reached a peak with the assassination of the Austrian chancellor, Englebert Dollfuss, in an Austrian National Socialist-inspired coup attempt in July of 1934.[12] In this respect, Italian opposition to Hitler's aims in Austria continued to remain a major impediment to the führer's plans for acquiring the *Ostmark.*

While the foreign ministry initially pursued a consistent policy of neutrality, such was not the case for private German entrepreneurs as well as other German governmental agencies. Haile Selassie attempted as early as October of 1934 to enlist German support for the purchase and shipment of arms and material to his empire. In a secret cable of October 28, 1934, the German minister in Addis Ababa, Wilhelm Freiherr von Schoen, reported to the foreign ministry that "The Emperor wishes to send a confidential representative to Germany for the purpose of making purchases, . . . of material for military purposes, probably including aircraft." In his report, von Schoen recommended that the foreign ministry should provide "a friendly evasive answer."[13] In a response on October 31 the foreign ministry accepted von Schoen's suggestion and instructed him to proceed along these lines.[14]

While the emperor attempted to establish contacts for the supply of arms and munitions, representatives of the Ethiopian government also pursued ventures designed to improve the military position of the empire. David Hall, an advisor to the emperor and a German expatriate, approached a retired German military officer, a certain Major von Frauenholz, with the offer of a position in the Ethiopian military. After considering Hall's offer, von Frauenholz contacted the foreign ministry to inquire whether the German government would object to his accepting the proffered position. During a meeting at the foreign ministry, Prüfer, now a senior ranking diplomat, explained to Frauenholz the "difficulties" that would "inevitably" be created "for him [von Frauenholz] personally as well as our political position by a German military advisory to the Abyssinian government."[15] Frauenholz agreed to reject the Ethiopian offer, but he did request permission to consider a civil position with the Ethiopian government to which Prüfer promised the "advice and support of the Foreign Ministry."[16]

The Wal Wal incident of December 5, 1934 and the associated clash between Italian and Ethiopian troops intensified the emperor's efforts to secure arms from foreign sources. In the wake of the incident, Haile Selassie presented a personal letter to von Schoen outlining his desire to purchase arms and munitions from Germany in return for Ethiopian goods in a confidential meeting prior to the minister's departure for Germany.[17] On December 24, the emperor received a letter from Adolf Hitler during a private audience with the German chargé d'affaires, Willy Unverfehrt.[18] Hitler's personal letter to the emperor has not been found. However, during the audience the emperor handed the chargé a request for additional assistance. Unverfehrt cabled that the request "contains detailed requirements . . . The main point is the supply of modern arms and material for chemical warfare. If the German reply is favorable, the intention is to send a special representative to Berlin."[19] In response to the emperor's plea, Unverfehrt adroitly deflected the request for arms by promising continued German diplomatic support in Ethiopia's dispute with Italy.

At the foreign ministry in Berlin, Permanent Secretary Hans Heinrich Dieckhoff supported Unverfehrt's position, asserting that "the Reich Government observes the strictest neutrality in the Italian-Ethiopian conflict . . . We intend to remain uninvolved in every respect in this disagreement."[20] The emperor, however, remained stubbornly attached to the idea of German arms deliveries.[21] The explanation for this "stubborn attachment" to the idea of arms shipments coincided with the arrival, in Addis Ababa, of Major a.D. (retired) Hans Steffen, the Ethiopian consul general in Berlin.[22] Steffen played a central role in Ethiopia's subsequent efforts to obtain arms throughout 1935. In fact, Steffen, a German national, acted not only as a representative of the Ethiopian government but also was secretly working for the Außenpolitisches Amt (Foreign Policy Office or APA) of the National Socialist German Workers' Party (NSDAP).[23] According to David Hall, Steffen met with Haile Selassie on January 18, 1935, in order to persuade the emperor to launch a preemptive attack against the Italians. In addition, Steffen promised the emperor a total of 33,000,000 reichsmarks in arms and material loans for the equipping of three Ethiopian armies.[24]

Steffen's startling proposal can best be explained by examining the development of a long-simmering and increasingly bitter rivalry between the foreign ministry and the APA. In 1934, the APA attempted to subvert foreign ministry policy objectives in Iran "by sending agents and propaganda to Iran, . . . to dominate German policy there and include the country in an anti-Soviet bloc of Balkan and Asiatic states."[25] The foreign ministry and the APA also clashed over policy concerning a deepening rift in relations with Afghanistan. In this context, there appears little doubt that Steffen's visit to Ethiopia at the beginning of 1935 and his offer of extensive military assistance occurred at the direction of the APA. As in the earlier cases, the APA sought to conduct an "Ethiopian policy" independent of the German foreign ministry. The role of Steffen, acting as an agent of the APA, explains in large part the later uncertainty of the foreign ministry in responding to Italian allegations of German government complicity in the delivery of arms and material to Ethiopia in early 1935. Indeed, until July 1935, the foreign ministry could honestly deny any involvement while continuing to maintain a posture of strict neutrality in the burgeoning Italo-Ethiopian dispute.

Prior to July 1935, the foreign ministry's stated position of neutrality remained consistent. On February 13, 1935, Prüfer notified the German legation of the need for the Reich government to "maintain its neutrality" in any eventual conflict.[26] In a secret cable of February 26, 1935, Unverfehrt replied that the emperor "appears to have finally reconciled himself with our position of neutrality."[27] The foreign ministry's apparent success in deterring the emperor proved short lived. During March and April 1935, the Italian press published numerous articles detailing alleged German involvement in the shipment of arms and war material to Ethiopia. The initial reference to allegations by the Italian press of German involvement in arms shipments appeared in a diplomatic cable from Permanent Secretary Dieckhoff to the German legation in Addis Ababa dated March 22, 1935. Dieckhoff informed the legation of Italian press charges that Steffen had arranged for arms shipments from Germany during his last visit to Ethiopia. Dieckhoff observed, "Because we place the greatest value on neutrality in the Italo-Abyssinian conflict, it would be desirable to us if the report could be contradicted."[28] The newly appointed German minister to Ethiopia, Dr. Johann Kirchholtes, replied to Dieckhoff's message on March 24, 1935. Kirchholtes assured the permanent secretary that current shipments "in no way deviate from strict neutrality policy." He added that reports from Rome were "incorrect" and "apparently clearly biased."[29]

Kirchholtes continued by pointing out that agents of other governments had not only negotiated for the supply of war materials but also had started delivery. He cited the following examples:[30]

Firm	Country	Item(s)
Schneider-Creuzot	France	Mountain artillery
Brandt	France	Mortars (some already delivered)
Fabrique Nationale	Belgium	280 machine guns with ammunition (first delivery in December 1934)
Sellier Bellot	Czechoslovakia	4,000,000 cartridges
Oerlikon	Switzerland	Antitank and antiaircraft guns (most delivered by start of 1935)
Madsen	Denmark	Machine guns

The Italian accusations, although not entirely accurate, proved to contain seeds of truth. On March 26, 1935, the state secretary of the foreign ministry, Bernhard von Bülow Jr., cabled the German ambassador to Italy, Ulrich von Hassell, and refuted the Italian claims. State Secretary von Bülow admitted that "some German officers submitted offers to enter Abyssinian service." He then noted that the foreign ministry "intervened" to prevent this in order to maintain "the strictest neutrality in the Italo-Abyssinian conflict."[31]

Bülow also cabled the German legation in Addis Ababa on March 26, 1935, to ensure that Kirchholtes remained precisely aware of current developments as well as the foreign ministry's continuing policy of strict neutrality. He amended his original message by adding a paragraph concerning the activities of Steffen in which he requested, "Please indicate to Steffen the guiding principles of our political position and then inform him, that we will not permit the export of war materials from Germany."[32]

On April 3, 1935, Secretary von Bülow recorded the results of a visit from the Italian Ambassador to Berlin, Vittorio Cerruti. Ambassador Cerruti had informed von Bülow that he had received a report concerning the travel of twenty-five engineers and technicians of the Siemens firm planning to move to Ethiopia. Cerruti also alleged that war materials were being shipped from Czechoslovakia to Ethiopia through the port of Hamburg without being inspected by German customs officials. He further intimated that shipments of chemicals and explosives had taken place from Germany to Ethiopia.[33] Bülow documented the Italian charges and sent copies of his report to the German embassy in Rome and to the legation in Addis Ababa.

On the same day, von Bülow instructed Dieckhoff to verify Cerruti's claim concerning the engineers from Siemens. After investigating the matter, Dieckhoff issued a denial concerning the French and Italian press accusations "that 25 engineers of the Siemens firm departed for Abyssinia in order to build aircraft for Abyssinia."[34] He assured Bülow that Siemens denied reports of any participation by its workers.[35] In any event, Ambassador Cerruti temporarily closed the discussion on the engineers when he sent a letter to von Bülow, dated April 4, 1935, in which he apologized for his accusation, an accusation based on a "report that is entirely incorrect."[36]

Dieckhoff, however, was not allowed a respite. Newspapers in Rome reported that a "certain Major Steffen," a representative of the Junkers company and the Ethiopian consul in Berlin, had "made arrangements . . . on the formation of a German-Abyssinian partnership for commercial and agricultural activities and is delivering to the Abyssinian government, . . . war materials on credit."[37] Bülow's exasperation was apparent in a scribbled note addressed to Dieckhoff that read, "What next! Where is Steffen? Who can issue a denial on his behalf?"[38] It was clear at this time that the foreign ministry was reacting to the published Italian reports but did not appear capable of completely discerning all the facts behind the stories emanating from Rome.

On April 6, Minister Kirchholtes responded to Dieckhoff's earlier memorandum concerning the aircraft technicians. Kirchholtes cabled that "a German pilot-engineer, Weber, . . . employed by the Ethiopian government in its aircraft depot, recommended a plan in the framework of a government proposal in reference to the organization of a national aircraft industry, to procure 20 German technicians. . . . Possible, that regarding this plan something has leaked out."[39] Kirchholtes also included a cryptic but ultimately significant remark concerning Weber's plans to organize an Ethiopian national aircraft industry: "In addition, the Reich Federation of the German Aircraft Industry is completely informed on this question by Steffen, whose own plans are certainly not covered by Weber's."[40] The introduction of Ludwig Weber, a German national, and a vague connection to Hans Steffen provided intriguing possibilities of potential "private" German involvement in Ethiopia's preparations for a war that approached with increasing certainty.

Kirchholtes received more details concerning Weber during a visit by a confidential representative of the emperor in the second week of April. The Ethiopian government had in fact acquired an aircraft from the Junkers firm in 1930, but the aircraft suffered significant damage in a crash sometime in 1931. Junkers dispatched Weber to repair the aircraft sometime between 1932 and 1933. The emperor, pleased by the quality of the repairs, offered Weber a position in the Ethiopian government as a pilot engineer.[41] Kirchholtes revealed that Weber approached the emperor with a plan for the "production of a military style air wing (of approximately 20 fighters and 12 reconnaissance aircraft) in which among other things the recruitment of 20 German technicians for the production of the aircraft is to be provided for."[42] Kirchholtes ended his report with a request for the foreign ministry to contact the Reich Federation of the German Aircraft Industry, and then to provide him with further instructions.

On April 14, Kirchholtes addressed a second issue brought to his attention during the visit of the emperor's confidential representative. During Steffen's last stay in Ethiopia (January–March 1935), he proposed a new plan to the emperor involving the recruitment of Germans who were "young, strong persons in the mold of good sergeants."[43] These individuals were to receive land holdings, in Ethiopia, in exchange for providing Ethiopian nationals with paramilitary physical training and chemical warfare protection training. Kirchholtes informed the emperor's representative that "in the face of the current political relations, the necessary neutrality for us, forbade us in general and especially in this case to support or undertake anything which would deviate from this policy."[44]

By this time, it was obvious that the German diplomatic corps was poorly informed concerning the real scope of Steffen's activities. The foreign ministry, however, doggedly adhered to its policy of strict neutrality. The question of the German technicians received renewed attention after Kirchholtes's reports of April 6 and April 14. On May 2, the Reich air ministry sent a letter to both the Reich and Prussian ministers of the interior, Wilhelm Frick and Hermann Göring. The Reich air ministry commented on the effort to enlist technicians from the aircraft industry in the service of the Ethiopian government for the purpose of organizing a "national air[craft] industry." The air ministry warned that the transfer of German technicians to Ethiopia was inadvisable based on the diplomatic position of the foreign ministry as well as the present urgent German need for specialists in the aircraft industry.[45] The air ministry further requested that the approval of its office be obtained before the issue of passports for foreign travel to Ethiopia "so long as it deals with technicians or specialists of the aircraft industry."[46] The concern of the Reich air ministry with preventing the loss of skilled aircraft technicians to a foreign power appeared, on the surface, understandable. However, both Hermann Göring and Rudolf Hess were aware of, and advocated, Steffen's mission to visit the emperor in January of 1935.[47] In connection with this visit, Steffen, as will be seen later, was authorized to offer the most modern German production aircraft to the Ethiopian government. In fact, Göring, as head of the Reich air ministry, was conducting his own game unbeknownst to the foreign ministry.

The foreign ministry eventually located Steffen, and Deputy Director Prüfer spoke with him. According to Prüfer, Steffen admitted that he intended to recruit "experienced, young Germans" for the education of Ethiopian youth and to train them in paramilitary sport activities.[48] Steffen remarked that it was the Ethiopian intention to mask the activities of the Germans by allowing them to pursue farming activities. Prüfer responded that it would be "preferable" if the hiring of these instructors occurred in "complete openness . . . as long as it actually dealt with the education of youth." However, he warned Steffen that "in comparison with the employment of military specialists for Abyssinia, we would of course have fundamental reservations."[49] Prüfer concluded his report by remarking that Steffen promised him that any applications from military personnel would be rejected.[50]

In contrast to personnel, the issue of war materials was another matter. For example, the foreign office learned in May 1935 that the ordnance office (Waffenamt) of the Reichswehr ministry had placed no restrictions on the export of certain war material of "minor interest." The ordnance office confirmed that "more important weapons, such as artillery and machine-guns, . . . have certainly not been supplied to Abyssinia," although "less important war materiel" including hand grenades and equipment may have been supplied.[51] After inquiries at the Reich air ministry, the foreign ministry established that "the Reich Federation of the German Aircraft Industry, to which all aircraft factories belong, has strict instructions not to undertake and execute . . . [aircraft] deliveries [to Ethiopia]."[52] From this information, the foreign ministry concluded that the reports of German engineers and aircraft technicians traveling to Ethiopia to manufacture aircraft were incorrect, but conceded that "the Reich Air Ministry requested the Reich Ministry of the Interior only recently to stop issuing passports to Abyssinia for aircraft engineers and the like."[53]

The admissions made by both the ordnance office and the air ministry clearly established the degree to which the foreign ministry remained unaware of the true extent of the initiatives being pursued within Ethiopia by other government agencies as well as those by private German industry. Apparently, some shipments of war materials occurred prior to May 1935. Obviously, the position of the foreign ministry in regard to the Italo-Ethiopian dispute was not known, or simply ignored, by other key government departments. As late as May 1935, there were significant opportunities for both individual entrepreneurs and big business interests to take advantage of the situation.

Ironically, confirmation and support for the foreign ministry's position came from a seemingly unlikely source. After a meeting with the Duce on May 13, Ambassador von Hassell reported that "Mussolini then discussed in great detail the question of arms deliveries [to Ethiopia]." Ambassador von Hassell protested to the Italian leader that "Germany was always the first country mentioned in this connection, although we were hardly seriously involved, he [Mussolini] replied that I was right."[54] Hassell remarked that Mussolini's "object was to bring about the Danubian Pact, not only for the sake of general peace, but above all to restore relations of mutual trust between Germany and Italy."[55] Mussolini seemed willing to accept the limited involvement of private German interests in the pursuit of his larger foreign policy objectives while subtly communicating the hope that more substantial official German government support, such as aircraft sales, would be blocked.

On May 16, Permanent Secretary Dieckhoff described the charges concerning the delivery of arms, chemicals, and explosives as well as the transfer of aircraft specialists and engineers to Ethiopia as baseless. He also refuted the press intimations of German government complicity in the affairs of Major Steffen.[56] Dieckhoff wrote, "It is known, that foreign officers are employed as instructors in Abyssinia and that foreign firms, especially Belgian and Czechoslovakian, have delivered weapons and ammunition."[57] He ended his letter with a request that any information concerning arms deliveries by other countries be forwarded to the foreign ministry.

On May 20, a new storm of controversy broke over the foreign ministry. The Reichswehr ministry (Reich ministry for national defense) and the Reich propaganda ministry reacted strongly against Prüfer's suggestion that Steffen be allowed to pursue his plans so long as they involved no military personnel. The head of the Reichswehr ministry, General Walther von Reichenau, personally intervened to call for the "greatest caution in the Abyssinian question."[58] In addition, Reichenau argued that the issue of German instructors fell within the area of interest of the *Wehrmacht* (German armed forces). The objections of von Reichenau and the propaganda ministry resulted in the rejection of the plan proposed by Steffen based on potential "political consequences."[59] This incident once again illustrated the lack of prior communication between the foreign ministry and other governmental agencies concerning Ethiopia. Furthermore, this affair effectively highlighted the polycratic nature of the Nazi regime, a system in which the various ministries jealously protected their own "fiefdoms" from the encroachment of "rival" centers of power while pursuing their own initiatives.

In any event, Prüfer spoke with Steffen on May 22 and received his promise to abandon the effort to recruit German "sport instructors" (*Sportlehrer*) for duty in Ethiopia. Prüfer noted that in light of these events it seemed unnecessary to notify the Reichswehr ministry or propaganda ministry of further developments—yet another case that highlighted the lack of interagency communication and coordination present in the National Socialist system.[60] In order to ensure that Steffen kept his word, Prüfer alerted the legation to monitor any activities related to the employment of German sport instructors.

The "Sportlehrer controversy" coincided with the renewed interest of the Reich air ministry concerning Ludwig Weber's plan for the construction of an Ethiopian national aircraft industry. On May 21, the air ministry drafted a letter to the foreign ministry indicating its agreement in the rejection of the Weber plan as well as the prohibition on the issue of foreign passports to aircraft specialists desiring to travel to Ethiopia. The air ministry also judged that Weber did not possess "sufficient professional knowledge" for the construction of fighter and reconnaissance aircraft.[61] Furthermore, the ministry admitted that it had "already for a longer time" possessed "firsthand knowledge" of Weber's plan.[62] This admission of prior knowledge by the Reich air ministry concerning Weber's plan would prove pivotal in substantiating Steffen's later account of events as well as in providing direct evidence of an air ministry initiative pursued without the knowledge of the foreign ministry.

By the end of May, it seemed that the Ethiopian government could expect neither delivery of German aircraft nor realistic national production under Weber's plan. On June 5, Ambassador Cerruti visited von Bülow and expressed his gratitude and satisfaction with the answers the Italians had received in regard to the shipment of war materials to Ethiopia. Cerruti then requested that von Bülow investigate reports concerning an order for armored cars (*Panzerwagen*) by Major Steffen, the delivery to the Ethiopian Army of spotlights, and finally a report of a German steamer purportedly carrying chemical products for delivery to Ethiopia.[63] These accusations most likely emerged in the wake of the search of a German ship in late May or early June bound for Ethiopia, which had been found to be carrying poison gas and tanks.[64] Apparently, the Italian government sought to put the foreign ministry on the spot concerning their repeated claims of strict neutrality.

Cerruti's allegations concerning the shipment of armored cars and spotlights to Ethiopia also were addressed in a formal letter sent by the Italian Embassy in Berlin to the German foreign ministry on June 5, 1935. Two weeks later von Bülow's office requested the Reichswehr ministry to investigate the Italian claims regarding the spotlights. On July 5, the Reichswehr ministry informed the foreign ministry that the largest spotlight-producing firm in Germany, Siemens-Schuckert, reported no deliveries to the Ethiopian Army. The Reichswehr ministry, however, was unable to ascertain if other firms had delivered the spotlights and suggested that the foreign ministry contact either the "Reich Agency for Foreign Trade" or the "Technical Inspection Agency of the German Export Industries."[65]

By July 1935, the activities of various German government agencies may have remained shrouded in mystery, but one trend was evident: the Ethiopian government was encountering increasing difficulties in receiving foreign assistance. Both England and France had enacted a de jure arms prohibition on shipments to Ethiopia.[66] The British action formalized a de facto prohibition undertaken in May of the same year. Additionally, Haile Selassie failed in an attempt to obtain assistance from the United States in early July.[67] The emperor, however, had one last ace to play, and he played this last trump with the dispatch of his secret envoy, David Hall, to Berlin. Hall, on the express orders of the emperor, approached Prüfer on July 17 at his private residence in the German capital and outlined Ethiopia's present state of military preparation. Hall explained the emperor's "absolute determination to fight," and "did not disguise the fact that the equipment of the Emperor's troops leaves much to be desired, . . . [a] disadvantage, [Hall] said, [which] was not so much due to the fact that arms and other equipment could not be procured abroad . . . as to the fact, that the Abyssinian Treasury was almost exhausted by the purchases that had already been made."[68]

Hall attempted to persuade Prüfer that Italy was a common enemy to both Ethiopia and Germany. He also requested 3,000,000 reichsmarks for the purchase of arms. The purchase was "naturally not to be made in Germany," but rather the arms were to be acquired from the German-owned firms Solothurn and Bofors in Switzerland and Sweden, respectively. Prüfer notified his superiors of Hall's unexpected visit and word of Hall's request quickly reached von Bülow. In turn, von Bülow informed von Neurath that "Prüfer's answer to the emissary [Hall] was, provisionally to refuse . . . I felt that I should inform you of it and leave it to your judgment whether you wish to bring the matter to the knowledge of the Führer and Reich Chancellor for his decision."[69] Bülow's decision to forward the report of Hall's visit to the head of the foreign ministry, Konstantin von Neurath, proved momentous for the fortunes of the emperor and resulted in a sea change in the private diplomatic position of the foreign ministry.

Foreign Minister von Neurath's consultation with Hitler culminated with the Reich Chancellor's approval for the payment of 3,000,000 reichsmarks to assist Ethiopian defense efforts from a special account belonging to the foreign ministry.[70] The main condition for the release of the special funds involved an Ethiopian assurance to keep the venture secret.[71] The exact date of Hitler's decision to provide support to Ethiopia is uncertain. However, on August 10, Bülow outlined the new position of the foreign ministry in a confidential letter to State Secretary Walther Funk of the propaganda ministry. Bülow explained to Funk that "the Italian Embassy is constantly complaining here about German supplies to Abyssinia, although these are actually only to begin now." He continued, "since we wish to remain neutral in our conduct in the Italo-Ethiopian conflict, publication in the press of news about supplies being provided to either of the parties is in itself politically inexpedient . . . I should therefore be very much obliged if you could cause our press to refrain in the future from publishing anything which could be interpreted as a departure from complete neutrality."[72]

The payment of the 3,000,000 reichsmarks took place under a special arrangement with the Reich finance ministry. An envoy from the emperor collected three installments, of 1,000,000 reichsmarks each, on August 23, September 4, and September 23, 1935. In an effort to maintain secrecy during these transactions, the payments occurred in Prüfer's office. In addition, von Neurath instructed Prüfer to keep a copy of the payment receipts in his personal files.[73]

Apparently, these three payments were not the only efforts being pursued to support Ethiopian preparations for war in the late summer of 1935. In a cryptic letter from Hitler's Adjutant Captain (ret.) Fritz Wiedemann to Reich Leader Martin Bormann, chief of staff to Deputy Führer Rudolf Hess on September 18, 1935, Wiedemann revealed:

Dear Party Comrade Bormann!
Concerning the proposed question, I have not been able to obtain the decision of the Führer. However, it is quite clear by the passage of the Reichstag's strict neutrality declaration which position must be assumed. There are things, which are most easily settled in a way that the superior authority can be correct in saying, they knew nothing of the matter![74]

In the last sentence of the letter, Wiedemann is discussing what amounts to "plausible deniability" for Hitler in a matter that concerns Ethiopia. There appear to be two possible explanations for the "proposed question" referred to by Wiedemann. First, this remark may refer to the impending payment of the last loan installment that occurred on September 23, 1935. Hitler was, however, already aware of the payments and previously had authorized the transaction. Therefore, it is most likely that this "proposed question" referred to authorization for a subsequent shipment of arms to Ethiopia, which left Germany in late autumn.[75] The decision to allow this shipment seems surprising in light of the fact that, by late September, Hitler's policy toward Ethiopia began to revert to a neutralist position. It is therefore possible that Wiedemann and Bormann initiated the approval for this late shipment with the support of the APA in continuance of its anti-Italian stance. In any event, Wiedemann's letter offers further evidence of the role of the Nazi Party hierarchy attempting to direct Germany's policy toward Ethiopia independently of the foreign ministry.

The Italian Embassy in Berlin remained particularly sensitive to the subterranean activities of the various Reich agencies. On August 28, the embassy, perhaps sensing a change in the German position, submitted an inquiry to the foreign ministry. The Italians claimed to have "information from reliable sources" that a German weapons and munitions firm, Pacoris Magnus, delivered 20,000 chemical warfare masks to Ethiopia.[76] The exasperation of the foreign ministry with the seemingly endless Italian claims found expression in Bülow's handwritten marginal remark, "What next? Has the war already broken out? . . . I consider that we should by no means respond."[77]

The Italian Embassy in Berlin sent another letter to the foreign ministry on August 30, 1935. This letter alleged that David Hall was negotiating with the firm Rheinmetall for the delivery of weapons and war materiel. Bülow again scribbled a note on the report, which stated, "What next? We should not allow ourselves to become involved with the Italians in any discussion regarding this. What right do the Italians have for such presumptuous inquiries?"[78]

It was clear that the Italians suspected German complicity, whether official or private. The allegation concerning the firm of Rheinmetall also illustrated the accuracy of Italian intelligence. In fact, Hall negotiated with the firm of Rheinmetall-Borsig for the delivery of 30 light antitank guns. Furthermore, the order had required Hitler's personal approval based on the previous commitment of these weapons to the Army Ordnance Office (Heereswaffenamt). The Germans "sanitized" the antitank weapons by removing the factory markings and transported them to the port of Stettin for shipment to Ethiopia.[79]

On October 3, 1935, the Italian Army invaded Ethiopia from bases in Eritrea and Italian Somalia. The Italian invasion threatened to make the question of continued German support to Ethiopia a moot point, as a rapid Italian advance from the south could successfully interdict the flow of supplies to Ethiopia through British Somalia. Nevertheless, in November the emperor attempted to reach agreement with Germany on a trade pact between the two countries. Steffen, with the consent of the emperor, apparently offered a group of German investors land and mineral concessions in return for a government pledge for the delivery of German military hardware.[80] However, the Reich government vetoed the venture based on Germany's enactment of a new law concerning the export and import of war material, on November 6, 1935.[81] In a calculated diplomatic gamble, the foreign ministry announced that the law, in final form since August, should be enacted on the outbreak of hostilities with a simultaneous declaration of neutrality and a promise not to provide material to either combatant.[82] In this case, Ethiopia fell victim to the larger aims of Nazi politics, namely, Hitler's desire to openly reject Versailles Treaty restrictions on the road to German rearmament. The Italo-Ethiopian crisis presented the German foreign ministry with a heaven-sent chance not only to publicly announce rearmament plans but to appear as a sober and reasonable supporter of the League of Nations' arms embargo in the Italo-Ethiopian dispute.

Perhaps the most intriguing questions surrounding the events of 1935 concern Steffen's role. In a letter of December 30, 1935, to Prüfer, Steffen provided a detailed and informative account of the events of the previous year. In response to accusations that he (Steffen) attempted to sell outmoded aircraft at excessive prices to the Ethiopian government during his visit to Ethiopia at the beginning of the year, Steffen rebutted, "I offered absolutely no old or outdated material in Addis Ababa—but, rather, only factory new and essentially the most modern material." Steffen continued: "The offers which I took and delivered down there [Addis Ababa], were worked out by the factories themselves, that is under the organization of their established associations. My entire labor took place in a businesslike manner under the protection of the Foreign Trade Association (Aussenhandelsverband)." Steffen then proceeded to drop a bombshell:

Concerning the aircraft, I worked together with the Reich Federation of the German Aircraft Industry. They had provided me, after thorough consultation on the special Ethiopian requirements were reconciled, with the delivery possibilities of the German aircraft industry, offers for the following models: Trainer aircraft "Kadett" from Heinkel; Fighter-Trainer aircraft from Heinkel (He 74E); Trainer aircraft "Jungmann" from Buecker; Trainer aircraft "Stieglitz" from Focke Wulff (Type F.W. 44D/"Stieglitz").[83]

Steffen reiterated that these aircraft were the "most modern" available from the German aircraft industry. He insisted that the selection had occurred "through the Reich Federation of the German Aircraft Industry," and that the Junkers firm declined to participate "on account of the proposed extended payment conditions."[84]

Steffen's letter highlighted the direct participation by the German aircraft industry in negotiations with the Ethiopian government on the sale of aircraft.

Clearly, the foreign ministry had remained ignorant of these negotiations during Steffen's visit to Ethiopia in early 1935. The offer by the German aircraft industry of the most modern German aircraft designs to Ethiopia provided strong circumstantial evidence of Göring's role in the negotiations. Indeed, it is unthinkable that the German aircraft industry would have made these offers without Göring's express approval.

In his letter, Steffen also detailed his relationship to Ludwig Weber, and, thereby, further illuminated the developments of the past year. Steffen recounted his "disagreement" with Weber in the "aircraft question," as "Herr Weber opposed my offer on the grounds that an independent aircraft industry in Ethiopia could deliver the material at 60% of the price."[85] Steffen recounted that prior to his arrival, Weber received an order to build three training aircraft for the Ethiopian government. However, despite the fact that the aircraft were to be ready on June 1, Steffen remarked that the aircraft were still not flight ready by November 1935.[86]

In his letter, Steffen related a conversation with the emperor in which he (Steffen) proposed a program for "the purchase of approximately 80 aircraft of the above mentioned [German] models." After hearing this proposal, Weber countered that "he was in position to build . . . all of these (including the very high quality Fighter-Trainer aircraft) [in Ethiopia]."[87] Based on the cost savings associated with Weber's plan and his belief in Weber's ability, the emperor rejected Steffen's offer from the German aircraft industry and ordered the start of aircraft construction in Ethiopia.

From the above evidence, it is clear that Steffen was not only working on his own behalf but on behalf of the German aircraft industry as well. Steffen's account also strengthens the contention that Göring was aware of and supported Steffen's mission. It is inconceivable that the offer of these aircraft could have occurred without the consent of the Reich Air Minister. The degree to which Göring coordinated or communicated his activities with the APA is not clear. However, it is highly unlikely that Göring, Hitler's self-described "truest paladin," chose to pursue his own "Ethiopian policy" in early 1935 without at least nominal support from the party apparatus. Steffen's letter of December 30 appeared to close the book on German involvement in the supply of war material to Ethiopia. However, extraordinarily, this was not the case, as German aid to Ethiopia did not end with the shipment of arms to Ethiopia in late autumn of 1935.

Four primary-source accounts exist that provide strong evidence of continued German support to Ethiopia in 1936. Journalist George L. Steer provides the first and by far most easily explained account. This account involves his personal observations in 1936 of the training of Ethiopian soldiers in antitank artillery procedures by "Herbert Masser, the young ex-Reichswehrman [sic] who at the beginning of the year had brought thirty-six German antitank guns to Abyssinia."[88] The antitank guns referred to here were part of the special shipment authorized by Hitler in the late summer of 1935. The fact that

Masser and the guns did not arrive in Ethiopia until early 1936 is best explained by the travel time required for the shipment of goods, including the overland transportation time necessary for such a large number of guns between the British port of Berbera and Ethiopia.

The second primary source description of German aid to Ethiopia appeared in an interview with the emperor, Haile Selassie I, conducted by a French journalist for the newspaper *Le Figaro* on March 25 and 26, 1959. In the interview, the emperor maintained that Germany was the "only nation" that provided concrete support by sending clandestine shipments to Ethiopia, which, in turn, enabled the Ethiopians to prolong the war and later "greatly aided" the guerrillas in their partisan campaign after the Italian victory.[89] The emperor did not provide specific dates or mention specific loans or arms shipments; however, his statements served to confirm the primary role of Germany in assisting Ethiopia in her preparations for war.

The third primary source account involves two separate reports in the *Hamburger Fremdenblatt* and the *Berliner Tageblatt*, on January 24 and 25, 1936, respectively, concerning the arrival in Germany of four unnamed Ethiopian pilot trainees.[90] The publication of this event in the German press is extremely significant, especially in light of Bülow's earlier letter to State Secretary Funk of the propaganda ministry. This action almost certainly constituted a public warning to Italy. On January 17, Hitler spoke with von Hassell in regard to past German-Italian antagonism based on the events in 1934. Apparently, Hitler left von Hassell with the impression that "assuming Italy would not rejoin the Stresa front, he [Hitler] was prepared to continue a policy of benevolent neutrality toward Italy in its African adventure."[91] The public announcement of the training of the pilots was most likely designed as a signal to the Italians that German neutrality should not be taken for granted.

A fourth, previously unpublished, source provides evidence of direct German material support to Ethiopia in 1936. The following reference to arms loans appears in the diary of Curt M. Prüfer:

The ambiguity of the German posture came most clearly to light, as in 1936, in Berlin, a secret emissary of the Emperor appeared. He [the Emperor's emissary] requested money for weapons deliveries to Abyssinia. Incredibly, his request, if only on a very modest scale was complied with. This intermediary then actually purchased war materials in bulk from other countries with German funds, and attempted to deliver the material to Abyssinia. I am unaware to what degree he succeeded. In any case, this incident showed that at that time, there could be no talk of an authentic friendship between the two dictators [Hitler and Mussolini].[92]

The release of German funds in 1936, as Prüfer implies, could hardly have taken place without the concurrence of Reich Chancellor Hitler. Hitler's decision to release the funds to Ethiopia most likely stemmed from a desire to keep Italy tied up in Africa and the interest of the press and world diplomatic community focused on the conflict. Prüfer does not provide an exact date for the emissary's visit. It is quite possible, however, that the decision to provide financial support to Ethiopia occurred in conjunction with German plans for the reoccupation of the Rhineland in March 1936. A related explanation involves the Reich government's desire to see her fascist counterpart engaged in a protracted but ultimately successful campaign that would strengthen Germany's position in Europe vis-à-vis Italy. Hitler later repeated this policy of a "limited fascist victory" in his support of Franco's forces in Spain.[93]

The scope of German involvement in Spain in the summer of 1936 offers significant and startling parallels from which to evaluate German policy of the previous year in Ethiopia. Just as in Ethiopia, the foreign ministry initially argued against any active involvement in the developing conflict and favored a "neutral attitude," a position supported by Foreign Minister von Neurath. In addition, Reich Air Minister Göring was extremely active in supporting aid for Franco's forces, a stance well documented in Spain and implicit in the case of Ethiopia.[94] Gerhard Weinberg has argued that "Germany's Spanish adventure" provided clear evidence of the "eclipse of the foreign ministry." Weinberg rightly contends that "For Hitler, that ministry was not the control agency for the management of Germany's foreign affairs—he would perform that role himself . . . The foreign organization of the party, the chief of military intelligence, the air ministry any one of them could serve as an instrument when the occasion suited . . . if Hitler's policy was served."[95] Based on what has been well documented in the case of German policy in regard to Spain, it is very reasonable to assume that the waning of the German foreign ministry's influence began not with the outbreak of the Spanish Civil War but with the onset of the Italo-Ethiopian crisis.

In the final analysis, official and private German involvement in the supply of war materials to Ethiopia prior to and during the conflict enabled the Ethiopian military to conduct a more effective campaign against the Italians than otherwise would have been possible.[96] However, the amount of German aid was by no means sufficient to tip the scales in favor of an Ethiopian victory. The fact that Germany provided arms and assistance to Ethiopia in 1935 and 1936 reflects, in part, the diplomatic skill of Haile Selassie in taking advantage of an available opportunity and a congruence of German and Ethiopian interests. In addition, the German decision to offer support presents another clue in the examination of Hitler's foreign policy-making process, as well as an intriguing glimpse into the developing battle for control of foreign policy between the party and the foreign ministry. The ultimate irony of this entire affair lies in the fact that, when Ethiopia stood alone against Italian aggression, Hitler's Nazi Germany was the only country willing to assist the emperor in the protection of his country's sovereignty.

NOTES

1. Examples include Gerhard L. Weinberg, *The Foreign Policy of Hitler's Germany, Diplomatic Revolution in Europe 1933–36* (Chicago: University of Chicago Press, 1970); and Hans-Adolf Jacobsen, *Nationalsozialistische Außenpolitik 1933–1938* (Frankfurt: Alfred Metzner Verlag, 1968). These are both seminal works and provide an excellent overview of Nazi foreign policy aims prior to World War II.

2. The amount of scholarship concerned primarily with German-Ethiopian relationships is rather limited. See Bairu Tafla, *Ethiopia and Germany: Cultural, Political and Economic Relations, 1871–1936* (Wiesbaden: Franz Steiner Verlag, 1981). Also R. Fechter, "History of German Ethiopian Diplomatic Relations," *Zeitschrift für Kulturaustausch, Sonderausgabe Äthiopien* (1973): 149–56.

3. Asfa Yilma, *Haile Selassie, Emperor of Ethiopia* (London: Sampson Low, Marston & Co., Ltd., 1936), 123, 126.

4. Tafla, *Ethiopia and Germany*, 136.

5. Ibid., 140. The German national was a pharmacist with the last name of Zahn.

6. Aufzeichnung, 4. Juli 1930, T120 (*The German Foreign Ministry Archives 1920–1945*)/Roll 1523/Frame D625422–23, Collection of the National Archives and Record Administration (hereafter cited as NARA).

7. Statistisches Reichsamt, *Statistisches Jahrbuch für das Deutsche Reich* (Berlin: Verlag von Reimar Hobling, 1929), 232. Also 1933 edition, 220 and 1936 edition (Berlin: Verlag für Sozialpolitik, Wirtschaft und Statistik, 1936), 254.

8. Untitled Report from Deputy Director Prüfer, T120/Roll 1523/D625435, NARA. Prüfer was head of the Anglo-American and Oriental Affairs section and had been posted to Addis Ababa as chargé d'affaires and subsequently as minister from 1927 to 1930.

9. The Wal Wal incident was prompted by the Italian occupation of an oasis 80 miles within the recognized borders of Ethiopia.

10. *Statistisches Reichsamt, Statistisches Jahrbuch für das Deutsche Reich* (Berlin: Verlag für Sozialpolitik, Wirtschaft und Statistik, 1936), 254. Coal export estimate from Auswärtiges Amt, Berlin, den 8. Oktober 1935, III O 4594, T120/Roll 3301/E579352, NARA.

11. Dennis Mack Smith, *Mussolini* (New York: Alfred A. Knopf, 1982), 194. Smith states that by the end of May 1935, Mussolini "was ready for a basic reorientation of policy away from the 'Stresa Front' and against the western democracies." Also Weinberg, *Foreign Policy*, 234. Weinberg mentions German diplomatic efforts designed to prevent antagonizing the Italians with regard to the Ethiopian crisis. He mentions that Hitler, in contrast to the German foreign ministry, "regretted the estrangement from the Italian leader, an estrangement that thwarted his basic approach to German-Italian relations."

12. Weinberg, *Foreign Policy*, 102.

13. *Documents on German Foreign Policy* (hereafter cited as DGFP), C ser., vol. 3, no. 280.

14. Ibid. See footnote 1 of translation. Original T120/Roll 8025/E577712, NARA.

15. Untitled report of the foreign ministry, Berlin, den 25. Oktober 1934, T120/Roll 3297/E575969, NARA. Prüfer was the deputy director of Department III in the foreign ministry. The Department Director Hans Dieckhoff also was present at the meeting with von Frauenholz, a clear indication of the importance attached by the foreign ministry to the issue of any overt German military support for Ethiopia.

16. Ibid.

17. Deutsche Gesandtschaft, Adis Abeba, den 24. Dezember 1934, J.Nr.3227/34, T120/Roll 3297/E575999-E576001, NARA.

18. Telegramm (Geh.Ch.V.), Adis Abeba, den 26. Dezember 1934, Nr. 26 vom 25.12, T120/Roll 3297/E575974, NARA.

19. G.D., C ser., vol. 3, no. 402. Original T120/Roll 3297/E575974, NARA.

20. Berlin, den 27. Dezember 1934, zu III O 4846, T120/Roll 3297/E575975, NARA.

21. Deutsche Gesandschaft in Äthiopien, Adis Abeba, den 31. Dezember 1934, No 3283/34, T120/Roll 3297/E575991, NARA.

22. Manfred Funke, *Sanktionen und Kanonen* (Duesseldorf: Droste Verlag, 1970), 37. Funke states that Steffen, after the First World War, served as an advisor to King Feisal and Ibn Saud before earning the trust and employ of Haile Selassie.

23. *Akten der Parteikanzlei der NSDAP*, Teil 1, Band 2, Frames 126 00648–50. Report of 19 December 1935 in which Alfred Rosenberg, the head of the APA, discussed Steffen's role as an agent.

24. Funke, *Sanktionen*, 37.

25. Donald M. McKale, *Curt Prüfer, German Diplomat from the Kaiser to Hitler* (Kent, Ohio: Kent State University Press, 1987), 119.

26. Berlin, den 13. Februar 1935, zu III O 356/35, 476/35, T120/Roll 3297/E576002, NARA.

27. Deutsche Gesandtschaft in Äthiopien, Adis Abeba, den 26. Februar 1935, J.Nr. 381/35, T120/Roll 3296/E575963, NARA.

28. Berlin, den 22. März 1935, e.o.III O 125035, T120/Roll 3299/E577714, NARA.

29. Telegramm (Geh. Ch. V.), Adis Abeba, den 25. Maerz 1935, Nr. 16 vom 24.3, T120/Roll 3299/E577714, NARA.

30. Ibid.

31. DGFP, C ser., vol. 3, no. 557. Original T120/Roll 3299/E577718–19, NARA.

32. Berlin, den 26. März 1935, Adis Abeba, Nr. 13, T120/Roll 3299/E577720–21, NARA.

33. Untitled report, Berlin, den 3. April 1935, T120/Roll 3299/E577722–23, NARA.

34. Untitled note, Berlin, den 4. April 1935, T120/Roll 3299/E577726, NARA.

35. Untitled report signed by Dieckhoff, Berlin, den 4. April 1935, T120/Roll 3299/E577727, NARA.

36. Untitled letter signed by von Bülow, Berlin, den 4. April 1935, T120/Roll 3299/E577732, NARA.

37. T120/Roll 3299/E577713, NARA.

38. Ibid.

39. Telegramm (Geh. Ch. V.), Adis Abeba, den 6. April 1935 18.00 Uhr. Nr. 19 vom 6.4, T120/Roll 3299/E577734, NARA.

40. Ibid.

41. Deutsche Gesandtschaft, Adis Abeba, den 14. April 1935, J. Nr. 800/35, T120/Roll 5036/M007121–22, NARA.

42. Ibid.

43. Deutsche Gesandtschaft, Adis Abeba, den 14. April 1935, J.Nr. 800/35. Ang. 2, T120/Roll 5036/M007112–13, NARA.

44. Ibid.

45. Der Reichsminister der Luftfahrt, Berlin W8, den 2. Mai 1935, Z.A.Nr. 16233/35 (1a), T120/Roll 5036/M007125–27, NARA.

46. Ibid.

47. McKale, *Prüfer,* 124.

48. Untitled report signed by Prüfer, zu III O 1949, Berlin, den 9. Mai 1935, T120/Roll 5036/M007114, NARA.

49. Ibid.

50. Ibid.

51. DGFP, C ser., vol. 4, no. 83. Original T120/Roll 3299/E577736–37, NARA.

52. Ibid.

53. Ibid.

54. DGFP, C ser., vol. 4, no. 87.

55. Ibid. The idea of the Danubian Pact stemmed from talks between the French prime minister, Pierre Laval, and Mussolini and called for a pledge by the major European powers of noninterference in Austrian domestic politics.

56. Auswärtiges Amt, Berlin, den 16. Mai 1935, Nr. III O 2064, T120/Roll 5036/M007131–32, NARA.

57. Ibid.

58. Zu III O 1949, Eilt sehr!, St.S., T120/Roll 5036/M007116–17, NARA.

59. Ibid. One of these potential consequences involved the German government's responsibility for German nationals who entered service with the Ethiopian government, a situation that the foreign ministry feared might force Germany's hand.

60. Vor Abg., Abt.II. z.g.Kts., zu III O 2179, T120/Roll 5036/M007118, NARA.

61. Der Reichsminister der Luftfahrt, Berlin W8, den 21. Mai 1935, Z.A.1a Nr. 16571/35, T120/Roll 5036/M007134, NARA.

62. Ibid.

63. Untitled report signed by von Bülow, Berlin, den 5. Juni 1935, T120/Roll 3299/E577739, NARA.

64. Alberto Sbacchi, "Legacy of Bitterness: Poison Gas and Atrocities in the Italo-Ethiopian War 1935–1936," *Geneve-Afrique* 13 (1974), 36.

65. Der Reichskriegsminister, Berlin W35, den 5. Juli 1935, Nr. 2105/35 Ausl. Ib geh., T120/Roll 3299/E577745, NARA.

66. George W. Baer, *The Coming of the Italian-Ethiopian War* (Cambridge: Harvard University Press, 1967), 231. Although the British imposed a prohibition on arms shipments, they did permit transshipment of arms from other countries through the British-controlled port of Berbera.

67. Ibid., 221.

68. DGFP, C ser., vol. 4, no. 212.

69. Ibid.

70. Funke, *Sanktionen,* 44.

71. McKale, *Prüfer,* 126.

72. DGFP, C ser., vol. 4, no. 261.

73. McKale, *Prüfer,* 126. See also McKale's footnote 43, 227.

74. *Akten der Parteikanzlei der NSDAP,* Teil 1, Band 1, Frame 124 05056.

75. DGFP, C ser., vol. 4, no. 395.

76. R. AMBASOIATA D'ITALIA, BERLINO, T120/Roll 3299/E577752, NARA; see also Sbacchi, "Legacy of Bitterness," 45. Sbacchi contends that "[m]any masks had

been ordered and delivered at Berbera but . . . the Italians found very few masks as bounty of war."

77. Ibid.

78. R. AMBASOIATA D'ITALIA, BERLINO, T120/Roll 3299/E577753, NARA.

79. Funke, *Sanktionen*, 44; see also George L. Steer, *Caesar in Abyssinia* (London: Hodder and Stoughton, 1936), 359–60. The guns arrived in Ethiopia in early 1936.

80. Funke, *Sanktionen*, 68.

81. Ibid., 67.

82. DGFP, C ser., vol. 4, no. 279.

83. Hans Steffen, Generalkonsul, Berlin W15, den 3012. 1935, T120/Roll 5045/ M010999–011001, NARA.

84. Ibid.

85. Ibid.

86. Ibid.

87. Ibid.

88. Steer, *Caesar*, 61, 359–60.

89. *Le Figaro* (Paris), 26 March 1959.

90. Tafla, *Ethiopia and Germany*, 185.

91. Weinberg, *Foreign Policy*, 247.

92. Hoover Institution, *Collection Prüfer, Curt*, Box Number 1, Folder ID: Manuskript zum Buch I, 64.

93. Weinberg, *Foreign Policy*, 290.

94. Ibid., 288–89.

95. Ibid., 299.

96. *Le Figaro* (Paris), 26 March 1959.

CHAPTER 9

Italo-Soviet Military Cooperation in the 1930s

J. Calvitt Clarke III

POLITICAL BACKGROUND

From the time of the formal diplomatic exchange of recognitions in 1924 to the outbreak of war in Russia in 1941, relations between the Soviet Union and Italy were substantive, active, varied, and generally reflected prewar traditions. For the most part, both the Communists and Fascists felt the other's revolutionary militancy to be rather benign. Ideology rationalized rather than initiated policy.

International politics took on new urgency with Hitler's rise to power in Germany in January 1933. Buffeted by the forces the führer had unleashed, both Rome and Moscow sought to contain the resurgent Germany. In economic, political, ideological, and military matters, each turned to the other for support, especially in southeast Europe, where their self-interested cooperation and competition met head on.

The Soviets were pushing between 1933 and 1935, and the Italians for a brief while were not unwilling, to put Germany "in a straitjacket of peace" through a complex and interlocking alliance system, binding Rome, Moscow, Paris, and the capitals of the Little and Balkan ententes "in a chain of agreements designed to girdle Europe."[1] Most importantly, Italy was the one power both willing and geographically able to stop Nazi aggression with its first step

This article has been adapted (enlarged and revised) from my monograph, *Russia and Italy against Hitler: The Bolshevik-Fascist Rapprochement of the 1930s* (Westport, Conn.: Greenwood Press, 1991).

in Austria. Italy's successful defense of that country in the summer of 1934 seemed to vindicate Soviet policy.

Political rapprochement peaked with the Pact of Friendship, Neutrality, and Nonaggression of September 2, 1933. Much of this drawing together took place in the arena of extensive military contacts between the two states. They were important as a public symbol of their diplomatic ties and for the implied possibility of military coordination to back up their political collaboration. The decline of military cooperation in the last half of the 1930s mirrors the decline of amicable political relations.

MILITARY EXCHANGES
Italo-Soviet Military Visits

Overt acts illuminated the incipient Italo-Soviet rapprochement of 1929 and 1930. In September 1929, for example, two Soviet destroyers of the Black Sea fleet visited Naples,[2] and a Soviet naval mission visited Italy a month after the Litvinov-Grandi meeting at Milan in November 1930.[3] The dramatic visit of an Italian air wing to the Soviet Union anticipated these contacts and showed most clearly that something was happening of political importance.

Italo Balbo, Italy's air minister in this golden age of individual flight records, wanted to mold the heroic efforts of individual *dive* into aerial armadas manned by regular military personnel.[4] Between 1928 and 1933, he participated in or led six such mass aerial cruises. Like traditional naval cruises, these served as training missions, showed Italy's flag, publicized fascism, and displayed Italy's technical prowess to prospective customers. In an age before airfields were common, Balbo found the small flying boat to be durable, versatile, and capable of turning most any body of water into a safe haven.[5]

Balbo received permission to take an expedition to Odessa as a courtesy call after the dramatic rescue of Umberto Nobile and the other survivors of the *Italia* airship crash.[6] He himself led the thirty-five seaplanes of Italy's Royal Air Force, which left Taranto at dawn on June 5, 1929. On the eighth, the planes flew to Odessa. At Soviet request, the aircraft kept twenty kilometers from the coast and reduced that distance by half when five kilometers from Odessa, whereupon the Red Navy and three airplanes from Sevastopol greeted the wing.

Contradictions marked the Soviet welcome. On the one hand, many civil and military authorities, accompanied by Ambassador Vittorio Cerruti, met the Italian aviators.[7] Their hosts had spruced up the town and hailed them as heroes. At the same time, however, the Soviets kept the arrival as secret as possible. Guards patrolled the hills above the anchorage to shoo away the curious. Even so, for a day and a half the Italians roamed about as they pleased.

On the morning of June 10, Soviet squadrons cheered the wing's takeoff. The Italian formation circled Odessa three times and turned homeward. The whole cruise, totaling 5,300 kilometers, impressively demonstrated Italy's naval air prowess.[8]

Both Moscow and Rome used the visit to enhance their diplomatic status and to minimize their ideological differences. The latter was not easy. A widely published photograph of Balbo and Red Army officers saluting the Red Flag particularly galled the anti-Fascist press and the Comintern. Balbo, for his part, showed no ideological qualms; he was merely fulfilling his obligations as an official guest. He eagerly sought common ground with his hosts now that the once-hated Bolsheviks had become fellow soldiers and revolutionaries: "They are good-looking soldiers. . . . Whoever professes a political faith strongly respects that of others, most of all when he opposes it." He even pointed out a certain convergence between fascism and bolshevism, remarking on their common antipathy toward the Western democracies, "rotten to the bone, lying and false, with all the wiles of a superior civilization."[9]

Balbo, however, did not minimize the abyss cleaving Italy from Soviet Russia. At an official lunch, an Italian dignitary praised the limited bloodletting of the Fascist Revolution. When challenged about the bloodthirsty Bolshevik Revolution, a Soviet general laconically replied, "we are not vegetarians." Balbo commented, "The reply makes our blood run cold." He wondered at the "perverse mania" that the revolution had for rendering life "uncomfortable, ugly, squalid."[10]

Balbo's flight was only the beginning. In fact, a series of military visits, consultations, technical collaborations, and constructions carried forward the Italo-Soviet political rapprochement of 1933 and 1934. With these, Moscow also reminded Germany's military and industrial leaders of the value of their own Rapallo-era cooperation with the Soviets, now lost.[11] Further, paralleled by Franco-Soviet political exchanges, the military contacts presumably were thought useful in greasing the ways for Franco-Italian cooperation, which with Italo-Soviet and Franco-Soviet collaboration would immobilize Hitler or—better yet—force Germany to return to Rapallo. For Rome, these contacts were economically important. Finally, they slightly improved Italy's ability to force Hitler toward moderation and, specifically, to thwart *Anschluss.*

As a tangible sign of the cordiality developing between Rome and Moscow, and following up the Italo-Soviet economic accord of May 6, 1933, two Italian submarines—the *Tricheco* and *Delfino*—visited the Soviet Black Sea port of Batum later in the month. Italian dignitaries and the submarine captains met the Soviet naval command and were treated to banquets and tours. The Italians reciprocated with a reception of their own and a visit to the submarines. The first foreigners to be so honored, Italy's ambassador and military attaché went aboard the modern cruiser *Krasnyi Kavkaz,* built in the yards at Novorossiisk and the pride of the Red Navy. The submarines put to sea early on the morning of May 27. Reporting on the tour, Italy's military attaché and ambassador praised Soviet hospitality and naval construction.[12]

During August 1933 as final touches were being negotiated for a treaty of

friendship, neutrality, and nonaggression, Marshal K. E. Voroshilov,[13] the Soviet Union's leading military figure, informed Rome of his intention to send
part of the Black Sea Fleet to Italy in September or October to return the
visit made by the Italian submarines. Voroshilov thought that contact between
the officers of the two countries would be useful, and he invited two infantry
and one aviation officer to attend Soviet military maneuvers. Moscow also
intended to invite Italians to its naval exercises and desired a reciprocal invitation to Italian maneuvers.[14]

On September 2, 1933, Moscow and Rome signed a Treaty of Friendship,
Neutrality, and Nonaggression—a significant step forward in Soviet Russia's
designs to contain Germany through a policy of collective security. Describing
differences in ideology as purely internal matters, the Soviet press laid out
the mutual advantages of this and the economic pact of May 6: Italy needed
Soviet oil and coal, and the USSR wanted technical help in the aviation,
automobile, and naval industries.[15]

The Kremlin-controlled press carefully associated the treaty with the visit
of a military mission then in Rome and strongly implied the possibilities for
further military cooperation. A TASS news story of September 5 described a
luncheon marking the departure of a Soviet military mission from Rome. The
Soviet ambassador expressed his "gratitude for the exceptional attention devoted to the Soviet mission by the Italian command and government." An
Italian general replied that "the Italian Army has feelings which go deeper
than the usual professional ones toward the Red Army. These feelings have
been strengthened as a result of the conclusion of the Italo-Soviet Pact." The
chief of the Soviet military mission invited an Italian mission to attend Soviet
maneuvers.[16]

V. P. Potemkin, Moscow's representative to Rome, on August 12 repeated
to Italy's undersecretary of state, Fulvio Suvich, Voroshilov's plea and invitation.[17] Although Balbo, now heading the Italian Air Force, threw cold water
on the initiative, the other services proved more receptive.[18] An Italian mission, which included a brigadier general, arrived in Moscow on September
24, 1933, for a fortnight's fêting and touring.[19]

There were more visits. To repay Italy for the submarine visit to Batum,
three Soviet vessels, the 5,400-ton cruiser *Krasnyi Kavkaz* and the 1,300-ton
destroyers *Petrovskii* and *Shaumian*, left Sebastopol on October 17, 1933.
They arrived in Naples on October 30 for a five-day visit. To dramatize Foreign Commissar Litvinov's forthcoming trip to Rome, the Soviets asked that
the captains be allowed to go to Rome to call upon Mussolini. They did not
go; the Russian ambassador, however, went to Naples for the occasion. In
addition to the ample courtesy visits, celebrations, and dining, the Russian
crews visited shipyards, Mt. Vesuvius, and Pompeii.[20] Potemkin officially
thanked Suvich for the "excellent welcome" given the Soviet ships,[21] and the
Soviet press emphasized that the naval visit demonstrated the friendship between Italian and Soviet military and civilian authorities.[22]

Relations with Turkey added an interesting nuance. A Soviet military mission had arrived in Ankara while the Russian squadron was at Naples. Meanwhile, the Turkish ambassador at Rome had visited the Russian admiral on board, who, in turn privately called upon the ambassador at his hotel. These overt signs of friendly relations among the three states preoccupied Berlin, where it was noted that Moscow was anticipating the visit of yet another Italian military delegation. The Italians duplicitously denied this latter report.[23]

Contrary to Rome's word to Berlin, the military exchanges picked up again. By mid-April 1934, plans were underway for visits by chemical warfare experts. Based on the success of this exchange in July, during which Potemkin presented the Soviet delegation to Mussolini,[24] Attolico called the mutual military contacts a "tradition," and he emphasized their political and military utility. Both he and the Italian minister of war thought that the moment was propitious for improving relations and that new forms of military cooperation ought to be investigated. The ambassador, for example, suggested that the two aviation services cooperate in a stratospheric navigation. This, he thought, would raise the prestige of the Italian Air Force in Soviet eyes.[25]

Putting an exclamation point to the visits, in the summer of 1934 Mussolini mobilized his troops and marched them to the Brenner Pass. There they sufficiently intimated to Adolf Hitler to end a Nazi putsch in Vienna and to keep Austria independent. Italy had slammed the door to any German advance into the Danubian Basin. Here is the one successful example of collective security working fully as Moscow intended. The Soviets had good reason to value Italy and to hope for the future.[26]

Soon thereafter, and to further solidify mutually friendly relations, three Soviet military Tupolev TB-3 (ANT-6) aircraft officially visited Italy as another repayment for Balbo's 1929 flight to Odessa. The planes, which recently had visited Warsaw, left Kiev on August 6 and traveled to Rome via Kharkov, Odessa, Istanbul, and Athens. The planes carried thirty-nine, including six generals plus civilian aviation figures—all met at the Rome airport by many Italian officials. Hoping to present the Soviet delegation to Mussolini, Ambassador Potemkin delayed his vacation. The Duce, "with his usual cordiality," agreed, and on the hot afternoon of August 8, he, an air force general, and Undersecretary of State Suvich received the Soviet mission in the Palazzo Venezia. After the Duce had praised Russian aviation, the Soviets shouted three "hurrahs."[27] The Italians organized visits to military and industrial establishments, for example, FIAT in Turin, to encourage contracts to supply the USSR with military goods.[28] The Soviet fliers traveled to Casserta and toured the city of Naples by automobile. The Soviets were treated to a farewell banquet attended by five Italian generals and members of the foreign ministry. They departed Rome in grand style on August 13, circling the city several times, much as Balbo had circled Odessa five years before. They then flew near the Palazzo Venezia before heading to Vienna whence they turned homeward on the sixteenth.[29] By making the trip in one stage as a long-distance endurance test, Moscow wished to demonstrate the maturity of its air industry, personnel, and navigation, and the Soviet press reproduced Italian articles on the quality of Soviet air activities.[30]

Dramatizing the political importance of the flight, at the same time another Soviet group had flown to Paris by way of Vienna and returned via Prague. The Soviet press for nearly two weeks avidly followed both flights and usually placed the stories emanating separately from Rome and Paris under one large headline. Clearly, they saw the two military visits as one diplomatic event publicly demonstrating the close cooperation developing among Italy, France, Austria, Poland, Czechoslovakia, and the USSR. The press further stressed, in its own flight of hyperbole, that the visits helped consolidate universal peace.[31]

Military Maneuvers in 1934 and 1935

These military contacts of 1934 culminated in the autumn, when Moscow and Rome exchanged observers to their annual military maneuvers. Desiring contracts for supplying military goods, the Italians again organized the program for the Soviet mission to visit military and industrial establishments. In return, an Italian mission observed the maneuvers held around Minsk from September 6 to the tenth. Given "particular attention and honor" by the Soviets, the mission's head told Attolico that the Red Army's enormous progress had impressed him. The ambassador, for his part, again stressed the political importance of the whole series of military contacts.[32]

Even as tensions were building the next summer over Italy's mobilization against Ethiopia,[33] an Italian delegation attended important Soviet military maneuvers to the west of Kiev from September 12 to 16. Given the city's strategic sensitivity and the concurrent attendance of observers from France and Czechoslovakia, countries with which Moscow recently had signed mutual assistance pacts, the Italian chargé in Moscow credited the Soviet invitation as having special political significance. The Kremlin originally had offered the Italians the opportunity to see special maneuvers in the absence of other foreigners. When refused, the Soviets lamented that the reciprocal Italian invitation had invited them to attend regular exercises in the presence of all foreign military attachés. Moscow righteously complained that merely as one of the many, the Italians did not understand the greater value of seeing "true," full maneuvers, as opposed to "special" and "truncated" ones.[34] In any case, the Italians saw heavily motorized units, many planes, and 500 parachutists. After the exercise, they, along with the French and Czechs, attended a reception. Later they visited a factory complex and then went to Moscow where they arrived on the twenty-second to attend a party with the French and Czech representatives.[35]

In return, Soviet military men headed by four generals attended Italian exercises. The Soviets especially wished that the mission be allowed to tour Italy afterward.[36]

Moscow proved quite determined to preserve its military contacts with Rome. Even while wallowing in the mud slung at one another during the Ethiopian Conflict and the first four months of the Spanish Civil War, on November 10, 1936, twenty high Soviet figures, including marshals M. N. Tukhachevsky and S. M. Budnenny, visited the Italian embassy to see films of Ethiopia's conquest. Tukhachevsky was especially impressed and asked if he, Voroshilov, and others could see additional films.[37] Presumably, this request reflected his own professional interests as well as the Kremlin's larger hope to suggest that it held no insuperable grudge because of Italy's colonial aggression.

The showing of these films, however, proved to be the last gasp. As political relations withered, so too did the *raison d'être* of the military exchanges.

NAVAL CONSTRUCTION

Early Italo-Soviet Cooperation

Productive as these exchanges were for their symbolism and practical support for diplomacy, the Soviets wanted more. Despite rapid industrialization of the USSR by virtue of the Five-Year Plans, the Soviets continued to lack the skills and industrial plant necessary to produce the technology of modern naval weaponry. Stalin sought foreign offers for naval machinery, armor plate, heavy guns, and even complete battleships.

Reviving a significant prewar connection in design and technical expertise,[38] in 1925 the Russians sought Italian help for their naval program, a relationship celebrated by the visit of Italian naval units to Odessa in that year. The new submarine construction, begun in 1927 and 1928, was designed by Cantieri Riuniti dell'Adriatico (CRDA) and resulted in the Dekabrist (D)-class, for which the *Fratelli Bandiera*, built by the same yard at about the same time, may have been the prototype. The first six of these ocean-going submarines appeared in 1929.[39]

In April 1929, the Sixteenth Party Congress accepted Stalin's First Five-Year Plan for developing the Soviet economy and creating the factories necessary for rearming the army and navy. Simultaneously, a five-year ship construction program (1928–33) was confirmed. Much wider than the 1926 program, it foresaw the construction of small ships of all classes. In 1932, the Central Committee and government again resolved to create new shipbuilding enterprises.[40]

Moscow turned to Italy for needed foreign assistance. With an outstanding reputation for warship design and its arsenal labor cheaper than France's and Britain's, Italy was getting a higher return for its naval expenditure than was any other major power. While the Depression racked other nations' yards,

Italian yards were keeping their labor in a higher state of efficiency with regular work. Enviably, they were receiving more foreign than domestic orders, and without labor discord they contrasted strikingly with the practically idle French and British yards.[41]

Although Moscow wanted to place more orders in Italian yards, the Italo-Soviet commercial agreement of 1931 limited Soviet naval purchases to $5,000,000, or 25 percent of total Soviet orders. Why? Italy's ship subsidy law, designed to stimulate the growth of a merchant marine serviceable in peace and war, also applied to the construction of foreign ships. These subsidies, limited to 114,000,000 lire a year from 1930 to 1934, were sufficient to allow Italian shipbuilders to compete comfortably with other nations but not without limits.[42]

Despite the artificial limit, this commercial nexus proved attractive to the Soviets, in part because the technical requirements of both navies were remarkably similar.[43] Both operated on closed, relatively shallow, and sheltered seas, close to home ports, air support, and repair and resupply facilities. Neither, therefore, needed ships with long cruising ranges or extreme endurances. This permitted high, fuel-consuming speeds, increased maneuverability, and reduced protective armor. Further, these ships could afford to mount heavy guns requiring more frequent replacement because their heavier shells fired at higher muzzle velocities. In addition, although the Soviet Union had no treaty displacement limitations on its warships, the relatively shallow depths of the Baltic and Black Seas limited permissible drafts just as effectively. Both were cursed with having their crucially important sea communication routes run through an enclosed sea with outlets controlled by others.

With the Second Five-Year Plan, Stalin moved closer to the concept of a large, balanced fleet strategy. The naval staff, however, informed him that Soviet heavy industry could not construct capital ships on its own. Tenders thus were sought abroad for complete battleships as well as machinery, armor plate, and heavy guns for hulls to be built in the USSR.[44]

In April 1932, a Soviet economic delegation negotiating in Italy asked about collaboration on naval warships. The chief of Soviet naval construction attempted to work out an arrangement. The firms of Ansaldo and CRDA, however, refused to talk, pleading that their technical officials were overburdened and lacked authorization from Admiral Giuseppe Sirianni, the naval minister, to conduct such negotiations. Only after the Soviet representatives had left for Berlin did Moscow receive a letter from Sirianni, dated January 26, 1933, satisfactorily resolving the matter.[45]

In late March with the arrival of the new Soviet naval attaché to his post in Rome, the Soviets indicated their intent to order fast, light cruisers of 6,000–7,000 tons, as well as a smaller type of vessel used in the Italian Navy. Toward this end, they proposed that a technical mission visit Italian shipyards. For political reasons, they did not want these ships to be built entirely in foreign yards, and therefore they wished to order the essential parts in Italy and assemble them in the USSR with Italian technical assistance. In Moscow, Attolico unsuccessfully pressed the Soviets for more than the 50 million lire they were offering to spend.[46]

At the beginning of June, a commission arrived in Italy to conclude the negotiations, but after two and one-half months they came to nothing. Ansaldo and CRDA, Potemkin complained, had not presented detailed offers or prices for either the technical collaboration or the material orders. Despite last-minute hints of progress, the Soviet commission returned home, not wishing to tarry in Italy while waiting for all the documents necessary for a contract. Potemkin suggested that to eliminate obstacles, the two firms ought to promptly communicate prices and guarantees regarding technical collaboration and to compile by the end of August all of the materials necessary for contracts. Attolico urged Rome to move quickly.[47]

Admiral Sirianni explained to the foreign ministry that negotiations between the Soviets and the naval yards, begun in 1932, had not been completed because Moscow had requested ships with unrealistic specifications. The problem was the ratio of desired speeds to displacements. For the next phase of negotiations begun in January 1933, Sirianni further explained that he had intervened indirectly to solve the Soviets' technical collaboration request. And the latest talks, begun in June, had failed to work out the details because the yards had no previous experience in translating the Soviet desires into contractual language. Referring to Potemkin's complaints, Sirianni argued that the contract's complexity and newness had caused problems. Italian yards did not want to give full guarantees because, although the designs were Italian, the motors were to be built in the USSR. In any event, the last problem had been resolved; Ansaldo had agreed to give partial guarantees for the construction of its machinery by Soviet firms. CRDA would follow Ansaldo's lead on this matter, and Sirianni believed that the other problems could be solved as well.[48]

Still, the negotiations for collaboration ground on slowly, with the high prices asked by the Italians a major, but not insuperable, obstacle.[49] Then on February 13, 1934, the chief of the Soviet naval general staff attempted to break the logjam by suggesting to Attolico that he approach Marshal Voroshilov and G. K. Ordzhonikidze to get their support for the negotiations already begun by engineer Enrico of Ansaldo.[50] Attolico took the hint and asked the foreign ministry to tell Ansaldo that the Soviets were prepared to reopen negotiations.[51] The problem of price, however, still haunted the negotiations. The Soviet trade representative in Italy insisted that his government would not pay more than 27 million lire, while Ansaldo was asking for 37.76 million lire for the material and the engineers and technicians who were to remain in Soviet Russia for five years.[52]

Within five weeks, Attolico was able to secure a meeting with Voroshilov.[53] The marshal said that although his government was negotiating with French industry for the construction of torpedo boats, he preferred to see a contract concluded for Italian motor torpedo boats. He lamented, however, that it seemed that Ansaldo did not want to come to a deal, an assertion that Attolico denied. The ambassador guessed that Moscow would compromise enough on price so that a deal could be struck for these vessels. Russia's foreign trade commissar confirmed this opinion, telling Attolico that price was less important than were the conditions of payment.[54]

On April 30, 1934, Ansaldo signed a contract for technical consultations and the supply of naval motors to the USSR at a price of 34,000,000 lire. Attolico told the Kremlin that the price reduction conceded by Ansaldo had resulted from the intervention of the royal authorities responding to Voroshilov's appeal. The company and Mussolini praised the ambassador for his assistance.[55] For his part, Voroshilov expressed satisfaction with this and other contracts with other firms, and he suggested that they would help advance Italo-Soviet political relations. In relaying Voroshilov's sentiments to Rome, Attolico added his conviction that Italy ought to work diligently to fulfill its military contracts with the USSR, not only because Voroshilov sincerely appreciated them but also because they were then the only significant commercial opportunities that Italy had to offer the Kremlin.[56]

Additional Italian Contracts with the USSR

In late April 1934, Attolico sent Rome a complete list of Italian military contracts on the account of the Soviet government.[57] Most important were the contracts with Ansaldo of Genoa. The firm was building, along destroyer lines, two coast guard/escort vessels of 776 tons displacement and seventy-six meters in length. Endowed with Tosi motors and costing 18,650,000 lire, the ships were to be consigned about April or May. These were the *PS 8* and *PS 26*, described later. Ansaldo was also building factories for constructing complete motors for cruisers and supplying technical collaboration for cruiser construction. These contracts were worth 34,000,000 lire and had resulted from the negotiations described previously.

Several firms held additional contracts. Odero-Terni-Orlando of La Spezia was building twelve twin-barrel antiaircraft cannons. Società S. Giorgio of Sestri had finished in March the consignment of forty-six range-finding devices of four meters at the base and detachable in three parts. Silurificio Italiano of Naples was in the course of consigning fifty torpedoes of 533 mm x 7.5 and forty-five of 533 mm x 7.27, as well as two three-tube torpedo launchers of 533 mm. Silurificio Whitehead of Fiume was delivering eighty torpedoes of 533 mm of which twenty-five were incomplete, and fifteen torpedoes of 450 mm, none of which had been completed. Ditta Isotta Fraschini of Milan was supplying spare parts for Asso 750 motors for 606,850.72 lire, plus fifty-one marine units of the type Asso 1000 MAD. Ottico Meccanica Italiana of Rome and Aeronautica Macchi of Varese had made offers of aeronautical material, but no concrete orders had yet come to pass.

Officine Galileo of Florence held several contracts. It was in the process of supplying four complete fire control systems including searchlights, range finders, sight mechanisms, and gyrocompasses for four torpedo boat destroyers. Three of these already had been delivered, and the fourth had passed its trials and was ready. Officine Galileo also was supplying fifteen attack periscopes for submarines, of which five already had been sent, four had passed their tests, and the rest were 90 percent completed. The firm was further supplying fourteen range finders of which ten were of six meters and four were of eight meters. Some were undergoing testing and some were being mounted. Finally, Officine Galileo was supplying 100 mirrors for 150 mm searchlights, of which thirty had been sent and the others were being tested or were still under construction.

Ansaldo Delivers Two Esploratore to Vladivostok

One of the Italian firms most active in working on military contracts with the Soviet Union was Ansaldo of Genoa. Among its contracts, the firm built two escorts designed to protect Soviet fishing smacks in the Vladivostok area. As they neared completion, the questions of their transfer to Soviet nationality and their physical move from Genoa to Vladivostok raised some minor legal and political problems.

Fearing that the trip would cause political complications under the Soviet flag, Moscow wanted the ships to be transferred under the Italian mercantile flag with Italian captains and crews. After all, the two ships would have to traverse oceans controlled by the British and Japanese empires. The problem was that according to Italian maritime law, no foreign national could fully own Italian commercial vessels unless he had resided in the kingdom for at least five years. The ships would pass to the ownership of the Soviet government upon their consignment in Genoa. Rome, desiring to accommodate the Soviet request, batted the problem about.

One possible solution was to have an Italian consul at Vladivostok formally transfer the nationality of the ships, but this would relieve the Soviet Union of any financial-insurance responsibilities during the trip. Alternatively, Ansaldo could consign the ships to the commercial representative, who had more than the five years' residency.

To the additional legal problem of a warship flying a commercial flag, the Soviets replied that the ships could go unarmed to Vladivostok, where they would be armed with their weapons and munitions carried as cargo. The enrollment of such vessels in the merchant marine temporarily removed their military character, and Italy previously had adopted this solution when furnishing warships to other foreign states. Small arms, however, would be carried, in accordance with mercantile practice, to guard against pirates in the eastern seas.

The absence of an Italian consular agent in Vladivostok created a second problem. The acts of transferring nationality, flags, and documents would have to be done by the captains of the two ships, who would then have to give the papers to the first Italian consular official they should meet on their way home. Mussolini, himself, ultimately intervened to ensure that the ships were transferred according to Soviet desires.[58]

The two diesel ships, the *PS 8* and *PS 26*, weighted anchor in Genoa on October 27 manned by probably eighty-seven Italians commanded by officers of the Lloyd Triestino Co. and, learning the ropes, eighteen Soviet officers and men. The latter group included Admiral Kukel, who had served as the Soviet representative at Ansaldo. Capable of making twenty knots and armed with twelve rifles, they passed through the Suez Canal less than a week after departing Genoa and reached Colombo, Ceylon, on November 13. Between Singapore and Hong Kong, they survived a violent monsoon. The long trip, in effect a shakedown cruise, was not marred by the few repairs needed along the way, and the Soviets were pleased with their purchases.[59]

The Italian captains, too, were pleased with the cruise and their treatment at Soviet hands. Together they had celebrated on board the Fascist and Bolshevik holidays of October 28 and November 7, respectively. At the transfer ceremonies, the Soviets even shouted "long live" for both the king and Duce, and they saluted the Italian tricolor. Returning home via the Trans-Siberian Railroad, the Italians spent two days in Moscow, where again they were shown every courtesy. The entire entourage left for Warsaw on December 26, the captains carrying a military report for Rome. The two escort vessels were now armed with three 100 mm guns.[60]

Thereafter, the naval design office of Ansaldo maintained a lively business relationship with the USSR. In October 1934, an Ansaldo delegation attached to the construction office "Bolshevik" completed forty guns of various calibers for the Soviet navy. Notwithstanding the obstacles, especially the deficiencies in the Soviet plant, they had done their job brilliantly and cordially, according to the Italian consul in Leningrad. At the same time, the consul reported that another Ansaldo delegation of about forty had been sent to Leningrad and the Marti shipyard to complete various jobs, among them to construct an escort vessel. Ansaldo asked for and, because there was no political objection, received state guaranteed credits.[61]

SOVIET CRUDE AND THE ITALIAN NAVY

The period of the Italo-Ethiopian War of 1935 and 1936 proved to be difficult for Soviet Russia, and for political and economic reasons Moscow tried to support Britain while not antagonizing Italy. A strong indication of the Kremlin's desire not to let increasing tensions over Ethiopia interfere with good relations with Rome was the series of economic negotiations begun in 1934 and concluded in June 1935 after hard bargaining, mutual recrimination, and expired deadlines.[62] And as Italy aggressively mobilized for war in the fall, some forty Greek freighters hauled Soviet wheat, oats, barley, coal, timber, coal tar, and petroleum for Mussolini's war machine building up in Mas'uwa and Mogadishu. In consequence, a grateful Italy only informally protested the activities of the Seventh Comintern Congress of August, which itself clearly played down the onrushing war. Only Palmiro Togliatti raised the Ethiopian issue at any length, and even he carefully gave his less-than-ringing call to battle solely in the name of the Italian Communist Party and not the Comintern itself.[63]

As important as oil exports were to Soviet balance of payments, this oil was crucial to the Italians. In fact, for twenty years Italy's navy had exclusively used Soviet crude oil, and the Italians (and French) had designed their naval boiler installations to use Russian oil—any other would have reduced their efficiency by 25 percent. Without digressing into the complex politics involved in the League of Nations' attempt to impose oil sanctions on Italy, suffice it to say that the Kremlin fully understood the potential stranglehold on Italy's naval operations if it should join any such sanctions. Russia's representatives in Rome maintained that Italy held no large reserve supplies and that its navy would be immobilized within three months if supplies were cut off. The Soviets publicly maintained that they would impose oil sanctions if other states— particularly the United States and Romania—did.[64]

Would Moscow have actually cut off its oil exports to Italy? If all other states had done so, perhaps. But, certainly, Moscow did not want to go down that road—as Italy had good reason to understand. Apparently, Litvinov told Italy's ambassador that:

We are absolutely opposed to the policy of refusing exports of coal and oil to Italy. We were obliged, as members of the League of Nations, to make the gesture of agreeing to stop exports of coal and oil to Italy if the United States and all other nations would forbid such exports. We did this arranging because we were absolutely certain that the United States could not stop such exports to Italy, and that we should thus be able to continue our exports to you while avoiding offense to the British and to the supporters of the League of Nations.[65]

Despite the political animosities that developed during the Italo-Ethiopian War, after direct negotiations the Soviet oil ministry and the Italian Royal Navy struck a deal. And despite the near rupture of relations during the Spanish Civil War, it was not until 1939 that Soviet oil sales to Italy ceased.[66]

GENERAL UMBERTO NOBILE AND THE SOVIET AIRSHIP PROGRAM

In the early 1930s, America's air attaché in Riga advised that the Soviet Union's general air performance was good—the Soviets were comparatively weak only in airship production and use. Responding to this deficiency, Moscow prepared a program for constructing seven airships with the first to be delivered to the army by fall 1931. A lack of technical equipment, engineering specialists, and flying personnel, however, handicapped the program. Moscow therefore decided in 1931 to set up training schools and to limit the program to four ships.[67]

Between 1931 and 1933, the Soviets constructed small dirigibles for training, the *V-1*, *V-2*, *V-3*, and *V-4*. The USSR's first dirigible, the *V-1*, *Pervoe Maia*, was an airship of 2,200 cubic meters (m³). Launched on April 10, 1932, it underwent successful trials three days later in Leningrad.[68] The *V-2*, *Piatiletka v chetyre goda*, was completed on April 26, 1932. A special airport was set up at Dolgoprudnaia, nineteen kilometers from Moscow. The *V-3* of 6,500 m³ was completed on May 5, 1932. The Soviets were then building a flexible ship of 7,500 m³, the *V-4*, the last of the pre-Nobile Soviet construction.[69]

In this context, General Umberto Nobile lent the Soviets crucial support in the construction of dirigibles.[70] Upon his return from an Arctic expedition aboard the *Malyghin*, Nobile had arrived in Moscow at the end of August 1931. While there, he spoke with the head of civil aviation and the head of its subsidiary organization, Dirizhablestroi (Dirigible Construction Institute). The Soviets quickly made it clear to the general that they wished to expand their civil airship program. Effusively interested, Nobile stressed that a dirigible program had to be just that, a program comprehensively incorporating all the technical and managerial skills necessary from blueprints to functioning air routes.

Nobile was preaching to the converted, and the Soviets quickly asked him to head up such a program and promised that there would be enough money to finance it. Nobile prudently made his acceptance of a long-term obligation contingent upon his government's approval and Moscow's promise to provide him with the means to complete his work. Before leaving for Italy, on September 30 Nobile nonetheless stipulated a preliminary accord for scientific cooperation. Nobile's contract called for the construction of dirigibles of 37,000 m³, 7,000 m³, and 1,000 m³, as well as for Arctic exploration by dirigible.[71]

Pressed to return quickly, before leaving Moscow the general wrote his wife asking her to find his designs for the dirigible *N*, which his government had rejected in 1927, and those of the dirigible *Mr* of 1,000 m³. Nobile planned to use this smaller ship to familiarize Soviet engineers with the construction of the Italian type of semirigid dirigibles.[72]

When Nobile started his work, there were almost no Soviet facilities, materials, or personnel for an airship program. America's air attaché wrote that the program for constructing airships was already behind in its work and that the speedy erection of a building yard was especially important.[73]

That year and the next, with Nobile's assistance, the Soviets constructed three dirigibles of the soft type to serve in a pilots' school. In the spring of 1932, again under Nobile's direction, the Soviets began the study and construction of Italian-type dirigibles, and later they began the study and construction of rigid dirigibles. In 1932, Nobile executed a study for a stratospheric dirigible of 100,000 m³, and, spurred by Soviet desires for high-altitude ships, he continued to work on this project into 1935.[74]

At the end of 1932, the Soviets began constructing semirigid airships. Their program provided for seven dirigibles to be built under Nobile's direction. These were to have a metal fin on which the whole airship rested, a reinforced bow, and a projecting stern. As part of the Second Five-Year Plan, the first larger ship of the rigid type was to be completed by the end of 1935. It was to belong to the Lenin Squadron, which was to be comprised of three large airships, *Lenin*, *Stalin*, and *Klim Voroshilov*, plus smaller ones to be completed before the larger ones.[75]

The Soviets' first semirigid dirigible, the *V-5* of 2,150 m³, underwent its trial flight on April 17, 1933. It carried four passengers and some freight. The second semirigid dirigible, the *Klim Voroshilov*, was of the *Italia* type with technical improvements. It was of 18,500 m³ and for use on the Moscow-Magnitogorsk route.[76]

Dirizhablestroi was planning construction of a special high-speed ship of 9,000 m³. It would reduce air resistance by placing passenger accommodations inside the dirigible. The design work was supervised by another Italian, Felice Trojani, and two Soviet engineers in the record time of one month.[77]

The program, however, suffered several unfortunate accidents. One ship the Italians were helping to build with Dirizhablestroi in 1933 was accidentally destroyed.[78] In 1934, another dirigible was built, but it and another, the *V-7* constructed by Felice Trojani, were consumed by fire along with the wooden hangar housing them.[79] A new dirigible, substantially a copy of the Italian airship *Italia*, was then constructed according to Nobile's plans. Appendicitis, hospitalization, and a long vacation in Italy, however, circumscribed his activities.[80]

Despite these setbacks, by 1935 the Soviets had set up a well-furnished site about twenty-five kilometers from Moscow, and they were constructing another facility at Sverdlovsk to provide anchorage pylons. At Dirizhablestroi, there were 100 qualified engineers and many specialized workers who had learned to construct and mount semirigid dirigibles. The Soviets were projecting the construction of such dirigibles of 2,300, 9,500, and 20,000 m³ in the next three years, and there were plans for a semirigid dirigible of 50,000 m³. The construction of a hangar large enough to contain this giant was slated to begin in 1936.[81]

Soviet construction proceeded apace. The maiden flight of the *V-6*, one of the Italian-designed dirigibles, with Nobile aboard left Moscow on the afternoon of April 21, 1935, and arrived in Leningrad that evening. Two days later it returned to Moscow. The second flight, again under Nobile's personal direction, departed Moscow on May 16, flew to Archangel, and returned to the Soviet capital on the eighteenth.[82]

By late July, Soviet engineers with Nobile's and Trojani's help completed the *V-7 bis*. It and the *V-6* were to establish regular air service between Moscow and Sverdlovsk. In one trial, which lasted forty-one hours, the airship reached the White Sea from Moscow despite bad weather. On the night of October 23 to 24, the *V-7 bis* hit an electric line during a forced landing and was destroyed in the ensuing fire. Ambassador Pietro Arone suggested that the poor quality of Soviet engineers and pilots had caused the accident.[83]

The *V-6* had little better luck. After setting a world-record flight for duration in October 1937, in February of the next year it was destroyed during a test flight in the Murmansk region. Thirteen crewmen died. Responding to the tragedy, numerous representatives at Moscow, including the English, French, and German, sent their condolences to the Soviet government. Ambassador Augusto Rosso explained to Rome that he had refused to follow the German lead because it did not seem to him that the catastrophe was sufficient to justify official condolences.[84]

Nobile's contract with Moscow was due to end in February 1936. Eight months before then, the head of Dirizhablestroi tried to convince him to renew it. Nobile made his acceptance contingent on participation in an Arctic expedition. The Soviets agreed and asked him to prepare voyages for 1936 and 1937 in the Arctic region with a dirigible of 20,000 m³. This ship was to be of the *Italia* type with some significant improvements. Soviet engineers completed the *V-8*, which first flew in 1938.[85]

Meanwhile, in a personal letter to Mussolini the general placed himself at the Duce's disposal. By November 1935, he had decided not to stay, and he wrote Italy's ambassador in Moscow, "At this time [during the war with Ethiopia] . . . it seems intolerable that I should serve a foreign government rather than my own."[86] In that same letter, Nobile asked for the ambassador's help in case the Soviets, anxious for his expertise, decided to keep him after his contract had expired. He got out without difficulty.[87]

In his book *Quello che ho visto nella Russia sovietica*, published immediately after the Second World War, Nobile expressed his profound sympathy for the Soviet experiment. This reflected his genuine, not come-lately, anti-fascism as well as his admiration for the Soviet war effort. He maintained that Fascist censorship had muted his true opinions before the war. The "heroic" temper of the 1930s and the self-denying spirit of Soviet youth striving to create a new world had awed him. This, despite the often poorly organized system that adversely affected his work, and despite his having seen things that repulsed him—after all, his Moscow apartment was across from the infamous Liubianka prison. Even his stay in a Soviet hospital did not dim his enthusiasm. Struck with appendicitis, Nobile was operated on in the hospital serving the Kremlin's leadership, and among his caretakers was Maxim Gorky's doctor, who was later shot during the purges. Nobile was much impressed with the quality of his care—despite a postoperative infection that required a second operation and had him hanging between life and death for a week. In all, he was in the hospital for a month and a half. Finally, Nobile's claim that he had never worked on military matters or even set foot in a military office must be taken as at least naive.[88]

LIMPING TO THE END

The Spanish Civil War of 1936 to 1939 began for completely internal reasons. International intervention, however, soon exacerbated the violence and consequences of the war. Perhaps most significantly, under its cover Italy acquiesced to Austria's *Anschluss* and Germany obtained direct access to Danubian and Balkan Europe. Collective security as originally envisaged in the Kremlin was no longer possible. With Moscow's dashed hopes so too was dashed the imperative for the Soviets to cooperate militarily with Rome. The story leading to Italy's declaration of war against the USSR is interesting but beyond the scope of this article.[89]

Briefly, however, violent press attacks disturbed the two governments,[90] and by late 1938, both were lamenting the collapse of negotiations to restore the commercial relations that had been so mutually beneficial in the first half of the decade. Also stalled were the related discussions concerning the supply of marine diesel to the Italian Royal Navy and the sequestering of a naval vessel purchased by the Soviets and built in Italian yards.[91] The purges took their toll with the arrest and detention of Italians working and living in the USSR— many of whom were working on military projects.[92] Italy's representatives found normal diplomatic courtesies strained.[93] "Pirate" Italian submarines were even sinking Russian merchantmen plying the Mediterranean.[94]

The Kremlin always saw military exchanges as part of a larger international political policy. Up to June 22, 1941, the Soviets continued to work to draw Fascist Italy away from Nazi Germany. As these hopes came to naught, so too did the *raison d'être* for military cooperation with Italy.

NOTES

1. Grandi, 9/5/33: Italy, Ministero degli Affari Esteri, Direzione Generale degli Affari Politici, URSS (Ministry of Foreign Affairs, General Office of Political Affairs, USSR) (Rome) (hereafter cited as AP URSS) b(usta) 10 f(oglio) 1.

2. Charles N. Robinson and N. M. Ross, eds., *Brassey's Naval and Shipping Annual, 1930* (London: William Clowes and Sons, Ltd., 1930), 48. Italian naval units had visited Odessa in 1925. Vasilii Ivanovich Achkasov et al., eds., *Voevoi put' sovetskogo voenno-morskogo flota* (The war fighting way of the Soviet Naval Fleet) (Moscow: Voennoe izdatel'stvo ministerstva oborony SSSR, 1974), 135; Eric Morris, *The Russian Navy: Myth and Reality* (New York: Stein and Day, 1977), 27 n. 12. The political importance of military exchanges had a long tradition in Russo-Italian relations. A Russian naval squadron, for example, visited Naples in February 1908 as a prelude to the Racconigi Agreement of the next year. Guido Donnini, *L'accordo italo-russo di Racconigi* (The Italo-Russian accord of Racconigi) (Milan: A. Giuffrè, 1983), 15–22.

3. Maksim Maksimovich Litvinov was foreign commissar from 1930 until his dismissal in 1939. He personified the Soviet policy of collective security in the 1930s. Appointed foreign minister in September 1929, Dino Grandi worked to end French hegemony on the continent and to create a colonial empire in Africa—but without a European war, which Italy could not survive and which would benefit only communism.

4. A pioneering aviator and popular Fascist leader, from 1929 to 1933 Balbo was minister of aviation. For the following story of the flight by the Società Italiana Aeroplani Idrovolanti to Odessa, see *S.I.A.I. ali nella storia* (History of the Italian Society of Flying Boats) (Florence: Edizioni Aeronautiche Italiane S.r.L, 1979), 17–18, 21–24; and Claudio G. Segrè, *Italo Balbo: A Fascist Life* (Berkeley: University of California Press, 1987), 197–214.

5. Segrè, *Italo Balbo*, 193–94, 213.

6. A designer and builder of dirigibles, General Nobile is best known for his airship explorations of the North Pole. In May 1928, he explored the Arctic in the *Italia* airship, which crashed. For six weeks, a series of rescue attempts splashed across international headlines. Saved by the *Krasin*, an Italian inquiry found against Nobile— after all, he had never supported fascism. William Barr, "The Soviet Contribution to the *Italia* Search and Rescue, 1928," *Polar Record* 18 (September 1977): 561–74; Rudolf Lazarevich Samoilovich, *Na spasenie ekspeditsii Nobile: Pokhod "Krasina" letom 1928 goda* (The rescue of the Nobile expedition: Voyage of the "Krasin" in the summer of 1928) (Leningrad: Gidrometeoizdat, 1967).

7. Cerruti represented Italy in Moscow from 1927 to 1930. He was later stationed in Berlin until Hitler demanded his removal in July 1935. As early as March 1933 he had warned Rome about the Nazi threat to Italian interests, especially in Austria.

8. *Izvestia*, 27 July 1933; Attolico, 7/31/33: AP URSS b11 f1.

9. Segrè, *Italo Balbo*, 207.

10. Ibid., 207–8.

11. On 13 January 1934, the Soviets told the German military attaché that they desired to return to military cooperation. Putting an edge to this wish, they intimated that they were considering equipping their submarines with Italian torpedoes. Germany, Auswartiges Amt. *Documents on German Foreign Policy, 1918–1945* (Washington, D.C.: GPO, 1949–83), C ser., vol. 2, no. 191.

12. de Ferrari, 6/6/33; Attolico, 6/6/33: AP URSS, b8 f2; Suvich, 5/31/33: AP URSS b10 f1.

13. Klementtii Efrimovich Voroshilov, after long tenure in diverse posts under Stalin, opposed Nikita Khrushchev in 1957 and in 1961 was forced into obscurity.

14. Suvich, 8/7/33: AP URSS b10 f1.

15. *Izvestia*, 3, 4 September 1933; *Pravda*, 3 September 1933.

16. *Izvestia*, 10 September 1933; Attolico, 9/11/33: AP URSS b10 f1; Cole (Riga), 10/11/33: United States. National Archives Microfilm Publications. *Records of the Department of State Relating to Political Relations Between the Soviet Union and Other States, 1930–1939*, Decimal File 761, Microcopy T1247: Roll 1.

17. Vladimir Petrovich Potemkin (1878–1946) was Soviet ambassador in Italy from 1932 to 1934. Suvich served as Mussolini's undersecretary for foreign affairs after July 1932. He was the principal architect of the Rome Protocols (March 1934) designed to block German penetration into the Balkan and Danubian areas. His opposition to

Anschluss and rapprochement with Germany made him an embarrassment, and he was exiled to Washington as ambassador in 1936.

18. To Attolico, 9/13/33; Suvich, 8/12/33; Sirianni, 8/17/33; Baistrocchi, 8/19/33; Balbo, 8/30/33: AP URSS b10 f1. Balbo was flush with honors from his transatlantic flight to Chicago and back in early July. *Izvestia* congratulated the Italians for their trans-Atlantic flight and said that the Soviets were studying Italian aviation. *Izvestia*, 27 July and 12, 22 August 1933; *Times* (London), 17 July 1933; Attolico, 8/15/33, 8/29/33: AP URSS b10 f1.

19. Berardis, 10/9/33: AP URSS b10 f1. Suggestive of the web of political possibilities inherent in these military exchanges, in November a Polish flight went to Moscow. *Izvestia*, 4 November 1933.

20. To Attolico, 9/13/33: AP URSS b10 f1; Suvich, 8/12/33; Sirianni, 8/17/33; Berardis, 9/26/33, 9/28/33, 10/21/33; Potemkin, 10/14/33; Salerno Mele, 10/22/33; Rossoni, 10/23/33; to Suvich, 10/23/33; Baratono, 10/31/33, 11/1/33, 11/2/33; to Puppini, 1/11/34; Puppini, 12/9/33; Potemkin, 12/19/33: AP URSS b11 f4; Attolico, 11/14/33: AP URSS b11 f1; to Attolico, 11/27/33: AP URSS b11 f2; Long (Rome), 11/1/33: *Records of the Department of State*, Roll 4; *Izvestia*, 10 November 1933.

21. Suvich, n.d.: AP URSS b8 f4.

22. *Pravda*, 1 November 1933; *Izvestia*, 4 November 1933; Attolico, 11/7/33, 11/14/33: AP URSS b11 f1.

23. Long (Rome), 11/1/33: *Records of the Department of State*, Roll 4; Attolico, 2/1/34: AP URSS b15 f10; *Times* (London), 31 October and 3 November 1933.

24. Attolico, 4/19/34; Aloisi, 5/7/34; Baistrocchi, 5/11/34, 7/9/34; to Attolico, 5/15/34; Baratono, 7/9/34, 7/18/34, 7/20/34; Suvich, 7/11/34; to Baistrocchi, 7/11/34: AP URSS b15 f5; Union of Soviet Socialist Republics, Ministerstvo inostrannykh del SSSR, *Dokumenty vneshniaia politika SSSR* (Documents of Russian foreign policy; hereafter cited as DVP) (Moscow: Izdatel'stvo politicheskoi literatury, 1971), 17, no. 248; *Times* (London), 13 July 1934.

25. Attolico, 6/7/34, 6/30/34; Suvich, 6/23/34: AP URSS b14 f1; Attolico, 7/3/34, 7/4/34; Baistrocchi, 8/13/34: AP URSS b15 f5.

26. *Moscow Daily News*, 23, 24, 27, 28, 29, 30 July 1934; *Pravda*, 29, 30 July; 11, 13 August 1934; *Izvestia*, 11, 27 August 1934.

27. DVP, 17, no. 248; Attolico, 7/4/34, 8/2/34, 8/5/34; Valle, 7/9/34; Suvich, 7/9/34; Aloisi, 7/31/34; Potemkin, n.d.: AP URSS b15 f14; Attolico, 8/9/34: AP URSS b14 f8. This four-engined, all metal, heavy bomber was also used to carry freight and parasite fighters as well as to drop parachutists. Some were adapted to carry armored cars and light tanks between the main undercarriage legs. See John W. R. Taylor, ed. and comp., *Combat Aircraft of the World from 1909 to the Present* (New York: G. P. Putnam's Sons, 1969), 613–15. See *Izvestia*, 19 August 1934; *Pravda*, 2 August 1934.

28. *Pravda*, 11 August 1934. The Italians did find success in selling to the Soviets, who purchased, for example, FIAT A-24R and A-6 engines. *Izvestia*, 18 August 1934.

29. *Pravda*, 13, 15, 16, 17 August 1934; *Izvestia*, 16, 18 August 1934.

30. *Pravda*, 9, 10 August 1934.

31. *Izvestia*, 8, 9, 10, 11, 12, 14, 15, 16, 17, 18, 20 August 1934; *Pravda*, 8, 9, 10, 11, 13, 15, 16, 17, 18 August; 28, 29, 30 September; and 2 October 1934; Attolico, 8/16/34, 8/23/34; Berardis, 11/4/34: AP URSS b15, f2; Berardis, 11/4/34: AP URSS b15 f4. For a French flight to Italy in September, see *Izvestia*, 28 September 1934.

32. Attolico, 8/9/34; to Baistrocchi, 8/24/34: AP URSS b15 f6; Attolico, 9/6/34, 9/13/34; Buti, 8/23/34; Aloisi, 8/29/34; to Attolico, 9/2/34: AP URSS b15 f7.

33. For Soviet reticence to condemn Italy's buildup and aggression against Ethiopia, see J. Calvitt Clarke III, "Periphery and Crossroads: Ethiopia and World Diplomacy, 1934–36," in *Ethiopia in Broader Perspective: Papers of the XIIIth International Conference of Ethiopian Studies*, ed. K. E. Fukui and M. Shigeta, 3 vols. (Kyoto: Shokado Book Sellers, 1997), 1:699–712.

34. Attolico, 8/8/35: AP URSS b17 f2.

35. Chargé d'affaires in Moscow, 8/15/35; Arone, 9/26/35: AP URSS b17 f2.

36. Attolico, 8/8/35: AP URSS b17 f2.

37. Rosso, 11/11/36: AP URSS b21 f5. Mikhail Nikolaevich Tukhachevsky, 1893–1937, was a leading strategist of the Red Army. His execution in June 1937 was a crucial event in Stalin's purge of the military. Semen Mikhailovich Budnenny, 1883–1973, had great success with Red cavalry forces during the Civil War and was named a marshal in 1935.

38. Paul W. Martin, "The Russian Navy—Past, Present, and Future," *United States Naval Institute Proceedings* (June 1947): 658; Jurg Meister, *Soviet Warships of the Second World War* (New York: Arco Publishing Co., 1977), 16–17; René Greger, *The Russian Fleet, 1914–1917*, trans. Jill Gearing (London: Ian Allan, 1972), 9–11.

39. Siegfried Breyer, *Guide to the Soviet Navy*, trans. M. W. Henley (Annapolis, Md.: Naval Institute Press, 1970), 21, 28–30, 143. Not surprisingly, the Soviets rarely, if ever, mentioned the role that foreign technology and expertise played in the development of the Soviet fleets in the 1920s and 1930s. See, for example, Vasilii Ivanovich Achkasov and Nikolai Bronislavovich Pavlovich, *Soviet Naval Operations in the Great Patriotic War, 1941–1945*, trans. U.S. Naval Intelligence Command (Annapolis, Md.: Naval Institute Press, 1981), 1–43, and Sergei Georgievich Gorshkov, *Morskaia mosch gosudarstva* (The sea power of the state) (Moscow: Voennoe izdatel'stvo ministerstva oborony SSSR, 1976), 212–29.

40. Achkasov and Pavlovich, *Soviet Naval Operations*, 5.

41. In *United States Naval Institute Proceedings*, see: "Where Italy Leads" (September 1933): 1361; "Italy: Cruiser Performance" (August 1935): 1176–77; "Italy: Brief Notes" (November 1933): 1650; "Italy: Italian Building" (January 1934): 128–29; "Italy: Italy Sees Menace" (March 1934): 427; "Italy: New Battleships for Italy" (September 1934): 1316–17; "Italy: Mussolini Speaks" (August 1934): 1163; "Italy: Various Notes" (December 1934): 1779; "Italy: Various Notes" (February 1935): 279; and "Italy: Current Building Program" (Decembers 1935): 1866.

42. Hubert Renfro Knickerbocker, *Fighting the Red Trade Menace* (New York: Dodd, Mead & Co., 1931), 21–22. Italian law provided for a basic subsidy of 32 lire per gross ton for all metal hulls. This was increased by 30 percent if the vessels could reach 14 knots and was scaled upward to 235 percent for a speed of 27 knots. A drawback of 100 percent was offered on all customs duties for metal materials imported for ship construction. To promote labor-saving devices, there was a premium for fuel efficiency running from 16 lire to 12 lire per 100 kilograms of weight for all auxiliary machinery installed.

43. William H. Garzke Jr. and Robert O. Dulin Jr., *Battleships: Allied Battleships in World War II* (Annapolis, Md.: Naval Institute Press, 1980), 315.

44. Robert Waring Herrick, *Soviet Naval Strategy: Fifty Years of Theory and Practice* (Annapolis, Md.: United States Naval Institute, 1968), 29.

45. Promemorial, 8/14/33: AP URSS b17 f1.

46. Attolico, 3/20/33; Suvich, 3/29/33: AP URSS b8 f1.

47. To Attolico, 10/9/33; Potemkin, 8/14/33; Suvich, 9/13/33: AP URSS b17 f3. For Soviet ship construction figures, see Attolico, 8/9/33: AP URSS b11 f4.

48. Suvich, 9/13/33: AP URSS b11 f4; Sirianni, 9/24/33; Sirianni, 9/29/33: AP URSS b17 f3.

49. Berardis, 10/22/33; to Sirianni, 11/6/33: AP URSS b17 f3.

50. Grigorii Konstantinovich Ordzhonikidze, the people's commissar of heavy industry.

51. Attolico, 2/14/34; to Asquini, 2/18/34: AP URSS b17 f3.

52. To Attolico, 3/3/34: AP URSS b17 f3.

53. Attolico, 3/24/34: AP URSS b17 f3. For a rumor that France would help build super dreadnoughts for the USSR, see Attolico, 9/23/33: AP URSS b17 f3.

54. Attolico, 3/28/34: AP URSS b17 f3. For more on the Ansaldo-Soviet negotiations for the supply of motors and technical consultation, see Suvich, 3/28/34: AP URSS b17 f3.

55. Aloisi, 4/15/34; Attolico, 4/25/34, 5/10/34; Ansaldo, 5/1/34; to Attolico, 5/3/34; to Sirianni, 5/22/34: AP URSS b17 f3.

56. Voroshilov, 5/16/34; Attolico, 5/17/34: AP URSS b17 f3. For a contract between Silurificio Italiano and the USSR, as well as Sirianni's indignant response that Attolico's advice was unnecessary, see Suvich, 5/28/34; Sirianni, 6/4/34: AP URSS b17 f3.

57. Attolico to Mussolini, 4/25/34: AP URSS b15 f4.

58. For the ships, the Soviets owed Ansaldo 18,645,770 lire with payments spread over 51 months from the date of consignment. Italy guaranteed payments to 65 percent. Puppini, 7/13/34; to Sirianni, 7/21/34; to Giannini, 7/31/34; Potemkin, 7/23/34; to Sirianni, n.d.; Campioni, 7/25/34, 8/4/34; Suvich, 7/31/34; Suvich, 8/18/34, 11/3/34; Puppini, 10/25/34; to Attolico, n.d.: AP URSS b17 f3.

59. Port Said, 11/2/34; Puppini, 11/7/34; Campioni, 11/16/34; Colombo, 11/22/34; Bianconi, 1/3/35: AP URSS b17 f3; Attolico, 12/27/34: AP URSS b18 f10; Puppini, 2/2/35: AP URSS b18 f12.

60. Other vessels of the same pattern were possibly built in Soviet yards. Not until 1938 did the Soviets independently develop a class of escorts, three of which were completed during the Second World War. In dimensions and gun armament, they resembled the Italian-built class. Breyer, *Guide*, 100; Meister, *Soviet Warships*, 144; John Cambell, *Naval Weapons of World War Two* (Annapolis, Md.: Naval Institute Press, 1985), 363. The Soviets also inquired for help in building a salvage vessel. Leningrad, 11/6/34; Quaroni, 11/21/34, 12/4/34; Puppini, 11/29/34: AP URSS b15 f4.

61. Leningrad, 10/24/34; DGAE Uff. 1, 9/1/34; Quaroni, 9/8/34: AP URSS b17 f3.

62. Bastianini, 7/4/34; Buti, 3/22/34, 9/24/34, 10/4/34; Suvich, 10/3/34: AP URSS b14 f1; Suvich, 10/3/34, 2/5/35, 3/16/35: AP URSS b16 f1; Aloisi, 6/5/35: AP URSS b16 f7; Aloisi, 1/4/35; Attolico, 3/6/35, 3/14/35, 5/24/35; DGAE Uff. 3, 4/17/35: AP URSS b17 f2; Suvich, 3/29/35: AP URSS b16 f1; Buti, 12/3/35: AP URSS b18 f5; Rotterdam, 3/22/35; Attolico, 4/17/35; Odessa, 6/3/35; Hamburg, 6/25/35: AP URSS b18 f8; Kenneth Bourne and D. Cameron Watt, *British Documents on Foreign Affairs: Reports and Papers from the Foreign Office Confidential Print*, Part II: *From the First to the Second World War, Series A. The Soviet Union, 1917–1939*, ed. D. Cameron Watt, vol. 13: *The Soviet Union, June 1935-Dec. 1936* (Bethesda, Md.: University Publications of America, 1986), nos. 1, 12, 31; *Times* (London), 9 February 1934 and 15, 19 August

1935; *Izvestia,* 2 January and 17 June 1935; DVP, 17, nos. 3, 82, 90, 109; 18, nos. 2, 82, n. 2, n. 44, n. 43; *Journal de Moscou,* 5 January and 6 April 1934.

63. *New York Times,* 27 August and 2, 6, 8, 10 September 1935; *Times* (London), 21 September 1935. Palmiro Togliatti, *Opera* (Works), cd. Ernesto Ragionieri, vol. 3, pt. 2: *1929–1935* (Rome: Editori Riuniti, 1973), 762. See Giuliano Procacci, *Il socialismo internazionale e la guerra d'Etiopia* (Rome: Editori Riuniti, 1978), 30, 34, 98–99; Rotterdam, 3/22/35: AP URSS b18 f8.

64. Italy (Long), 11/25/35: United States, National Archives (College Park, Md.), Record Group 59, Decimal File (hereafter cited as NA) 765.84/2742.

65. USSR (Bullitt), 11/22/35: NA 765.84/2708.

66. Lowell Ray Tillett, "The Soviet Role in League Sanctions against Italy," *American Slavic and East European Review* 15 (1956): 11–16.

67. Latvia (Shipp), 3/31/33: United States, *U.S. Military Intelligence Reports: The Soviet Union, 1919–1941* (Bethesda, Md.: University Publications of America, 1991), microfilm roll 6: frames 0495–0497.

68. Arneman, n.d.: *Military Intelligence,* 6: 0460–62; *Moscow Daily News,* 13 April 1932.

69. Latvia (Shipp), 3/31/33: *Military Intelligence,* 6: 0495–97. For the *V-1, V-2,* and *V-3* and plans for a Moscow-Gorky-Moscow route, see *Izvestia,* 24 March 1933; for a flight to Murmansk, see *Izvestia,* 28 April 1933; see also *Pravda,* 7 April 1933, for comments on foreign, including Italian, dirigible construction. The *V-1* flew from Sebastopol to Moscow on 28 and 29 August 1933. The airship and its four-man crew covered the 1,400 kilometers in twenty-two flying hours, despite unfavorable weather. Latvia (Shipp), 10/31/33: *Military Intelligence,* 6: 0498–99. The dirigible *V-2* left Moscow for Leningrad a few days before Christmas. In the teeth of headwinds, the *V-2* landed at Krasnogvardeisk. On 5 January 1933, it started again for Leningrad but this time ran into motor trouble and crashed. No lives were lost but the dirigible was destroyed. TASS denied reports of the accident. Latvia (Shipp), 1/13/33: *Military Intelligence,* 6: 0466–67.

70. Nobile, 8/11/35: AP URSS b22 f13; "New Dirigibles Constructed," *Economic Review of the Soviet Union* 9 (August–September 1934): 182.

71. Ovidio Ferrante, *Umberto Nobile,* 2 vols. (Rome: Claudio Tatangelo, 1985), 2:159–63.

72. Ibid.

73. Latvia (Shipp), 3/31/33: *Military Intelligence,* 6: 0495–97.

74. USSR (White), 5/12/34: *Military Intelligence,* 7: 0615–18.

75. Latvia (Shipp), 3/31/33: *Military Intelligence,* 6: 0495–97.

76. Latvia (Shipp), 10/31/33: *Military Intelligence,* 6: 0498–99.

77. Ibid.

78. Attolico, 5/21/33, 6/19/33, 8/21/33, 9/25/33: AP URSS b11 f11.

79. Attolico, 2/14/34, 6/19/34, 8/21/34; Balbo, 2/23/34: AP URSS b15 f14.

80. Berardis, 11/13/34: AP URSS b15 f4. For Nobile's health problems, scc AP URSS b15 f9.

81. Nobile, 8/11/35: AP URSS b22 f13.

82. Attolico, 4/25/35, 5/24/35, 7/24/35: AP URSS b18 f14; Nobile, 8/11/35: AP URSS b22 f13.

83. Arone, 10/30/35; Attolico, 4/25/35, 5/24/35, 7/24/35: AP URSS b18 f14; Nobile,

8/11/35: AP URSS b22 f13. For Soviet dirigible construction and the establishment of an airship line between Moscow and Irkutsk, see *Pravda*, 13, 16 August 1934.

84. Rosso, 2/12/38: AP URSS b29 f1.

85. For more on the Kremlin's plans, see Latvia (Shipp), 3/31/33, 4/18/34: *Military Intelligence*, 6: 0495–97.

86. Nobile, 11/27/35: AP URSS b22 f13.

87. Nobile, 8/11/35: AP URSS b22 f13.

88. Umberto Nobile, *Quello che ho visto nella Russia sovietica* (What I saw in Soviet Russia) (Rome: Atlantica, 1945). See 17–25 for his illness.

89. See my articles in the *Selected Annual Proceedings of the Florida Conference of Historians:* "Italy and the Nazi-Soviet Pact of August 23, 1939," 3 (December 1996): 30–39; "Search for Areas of Cooperation: Italian Precursors to the Nazi Soviet Pact of 1939. Preliminary Comments," 5 (December 1997): 8–20; and "Italy and Plan Barbarossa," 2 (September 1994): 81–103; also see "Soviet Appeasement, Collective Security, and the Italo-Ethiopian War of 1935 and 1936," 4 (December 1996): 115–32.

90. Shtein, 12/12/38: AP URSS b29 f19.

91. AG 4, 1/27/39: AP URSS b34 f6. For some of the contentious negotiations, especially on the price of marine diesel for the Royal Navy, see Ciano, 1/3/39, 1/7/39; Rosso, 1/7/39; 1/9/39: AP URSS b34 f15.

92. For a few of the many reports of Italians arrested in the USSR, see Ciano, 5/25/38: AP URSS b29 f13; Vatican Embassy, 11/18/35: AP URSS b17 f8; Scarpa, 11/15/36; Rosso, 11/18/36, 11/20/36, 11/26/36; Scarpa, 12/22/36: AP URSS b21 f5; Rosso, 10/29/38: AP URSS b34 f7.

93. Rosso, 12/12/38, 1/10/39: AP URSS b34 f15.

94. John Foy Coverdale, *Italian Intervention in the Spanish Civil War* (Princeton, N.J.: Princeton University Press, 1975), 179–80.

CHAPTER 10

United States-Soviet Naval Relations in the 1930s: The Soviet Union's Efforts to Purchase Naval Vessels

Thomas R. Maddux

Many observers, including some historians, frequently ignore or minimize the influence of the governmental bureaucracy on the shaping and carrying out of American policy. The president and officials in the State Department do not function in a vacuum free from a wide variety of considerations, particularly the viewpoints and interests of other departments in the executive branch of the government. Washington's response to diplomatic issues may represent not only an effort to obtain specific objectives but also the end result of a struggle within departments and among the departments over clashing ideas, personality conflicts, and bureaucratic considerations with respect to the maintenance and expansion of the bureaucracy's area of influence.[1] Since the State Department and other executive agencies have to implement policy, the carrying out of the president's policy decisions is also very susceptible to manipulation by the bureaucracies.

An excellent example of the bureaucracy's impact on policy appears in the most significant issue in Soviet-American naval relations in the 1930s: the Kremlin's efforts to purchase a battleship and two destroyers from American shipbuilding firms. Except for this episode, United States naval relations with the Soviet Union were minimal and on the periphery of formal relations even after recognition in 1933. The first visit of United States naval vessels to the Soviet Union, for example, did not occur until July 1937 when Admiral Harry

This is a revised and updated version of Thomas R. Maddux, "United States-Soviet Naval Relations in the 1930s: The Soviet Union's Efforts to Purchase Naval Vessels," *Naval War College Review* (Fall 1976): 28–37.

E. Yarnell, commander in chief of the United States Asiatic Fleet, visited Vladivostok aboard the cruiser *Augusta* accompanied by four destroyers. Although Russian officials were enthusiastic about the visit, Admiral Yarnell was not very impressed. "I saw nothing to indicate that they have any better form of government than that which we have in the U.S.A.," Yarnell confided to Nelson T. Johnson, the American ambassador in China. "Vladivostok is a drab, dreary town and the people are the same," concluded the admiral.[2] In 1939 the State Department recommended against another naval visit to Leningrad.

The Department of the Navy, however, played an important role in the American response to the Kremlin's efforts after 1936 to purchase naval vessels. Although President Franklin D. Roosevelt and the State Department approved the Soviet Union's efforts, senior line officers of the navy successfully resisted the combined efforts of all three as well as those of interested American firms. Navy officials, led by Admiral William D. Leahy, chief of naval operations, resorted to a wide variety of tactics to discourage, delay, and obstruct the various Soviet proposals. When the president intervened at several points to remove the obstacles and get the navy moving, Admiral Leahy always agreed with the president. Yet he allowed bureau chiefs and middle-level officials, despite the efforts of the assistant secretary of the navy, Charles Edison, to continue their obstructionist tactics and thus delayed the proposals until the outbreak of World War II, prompting the State Department to finally reject the Kremlin's advance. The Soviet Union's efforts to purchase naval vessels represented only one dimension of an expanded Soviet effort after 1936 to purchase advanced weapons systems and technical assistance. Since the Kremlin considered the United States the most important source of military technology and war materials, Moscow established in July 1936 a special corporation, the Carp Export and Import Corp. of New York City, to manage its acquisitions. Under the direction of Sam Carp, whose sister was married to Vyacheslav Molotov, president of the Council of People's Commissars of the Soviet Union, the Carp firm stepped up the Soviet Union's purchases, especially in aircraft technology. Over twenty American corporations sold aircraft, accessories, and technical assistance to the Soviet Union. The Glenn L. Martin Co., for example, agreed in 1937 to provide Moscow with the world's largest plane, the Martin Ocean Transport, the design of a new bomber, and the training of Soviet engineers. The Soviet Union also purchased specialized tools, engines, and DC-3 aircraft under a technical assistance agreement with the Douglas Aircraft Co. Although European military firms supplied more armaments and technical assistance to Moscow than did American corporations, the Kremlin obtained technical assistance in several industries, most notably in the production of nitrocellulose and cotton linters for explosives manufacture from the Hercules Powder Co.[3]

Joseph Stalin's decision to seek out American naval assistance in November 1936 was part of his general naval strategy to construct a big, balanced navy, primarily for the purposes of deterrence and prestige. Faced with German and Japanese expansion, the Soviet Union could use battleships to discourage invasion by sea. Stalin, moreover, discovered in the Spanish Civil War that the Soviet Union's submarine force, which was both the world's largest and the main striking unit of the Soviet Fleet, could not be used effectively to support Soviet diplomacy. Consequently, Stalin stepped up the improvement of Soviet shipbuilding yards and the construction of capital ships, most notably of heavy cruisers and three large battleships. The Soviet Union's limited shipbuilding facilities and inadequate capacity for equipping capital ships with large-caliber naval guns, armor plate, and fire control equipment, however, prompted the Kremlin to turn to the United States.[4]

The Soviet Union generally received a favorable reaction from the White House and State Department to its proposed purchases because of President Roosevelt's efforts to reorient relations with the Soviet Union toward cooperation in the Far East and Europe in 1937 and 1938. Faced with the Sino-Japanese War and German expansion, Roosevelt realistically wanted to improve relations with Moscow, which had become embittered in 1935 over the failure to settle Moscow's financial debts to the United States and Stalin's violation of an agreement against interference in America's domestic affairs. The president, for example, approved a reorganization of the State Department in 1937 partially to reduce the opposition of Russian experts to any new démarche to Moscow. Roosevelt also sent Joseph E. Davies, a wealthy Democratic supporter, as ambassador to the Soviet Union in 1936–38. After referring to Davies's appointment as a special mission, the president instructed him to find out which side the Kremlin would support in a war between the Western democratic powers and the Fascist powers and to establish friendly relations with Moscow in light of the Sino-Japanese war.

Despite some opposition from the State Department to cooperation with the Soviet Union, Roosevelt secretly attempted to lay the groundwork for military cooperation with Moscow in the Pacific. The president asked Ambassador Davies in December 1937 to propose to the Kremlin a liaison in the Far East to exchange data concerning the "military and naval situations of the United States and the Soviet Union vis-à-vis Japan and the general Far Eastern and Pacific problem." Although Roosevelt ruled out a pact or secret alliance, he believed that an exchange of information "might be of substantial value in the future by reason of similarity of purposes and necessities even though each power were pursuing separate and independent courses."[5] Finally, Roosevelt warned Davies to keep this matter strictly confidential even from the Moscow Embassy and the State Department. Although Stalin made a favorable reply to the White House's proposal in June 1938, the president, faced not only with isolationist sentiment but also with intense press criticism of Soviet totalitarianism as manifested in Stalin's purges, quickly dropped his own suggestion.

The White House's interest in friendly relations with the Soviet Union ensured that the Kremlin would receive some encouragement when it initiated an effort to purchase various components of a battleship in November 1936. Joseph E. Green, chief of the State Department's Office of Arms and Munitions Control, approved the Carp firm's plans, as did Robert F. Kelley, chief of the Division of Eastern European Affairs. "Assuming the evolution of the Soviet Government eventually into a purely national Government," Kelley argued, "the strengthening of the naval forces of the Soviet Union would not run counter to the national interests of the United States."[6] When the State Department was asked to review a proposed contract between Carp and the Bethlehem Shipbuilding Corp. for a disassembled battleship, Secretary of State Cordell Hull approved the contract, except for two provisions. Hull objected to the installation of sixteen-inch guns because of current negotiations with Japan on the maximum caliber of guns. A provision that the United States Navy would inspect and test the guns and armor before delivery to the Soviet Union was also rejected because it violated a long-standing policy against government promotion of the arms trade.

Senior career officers in the Department of the Navy, however, opposed any naval assistance to the Soviet Union. Admiral Leahy, chief of naval operations; Rear Admiral W. R. Furlong, chief of the Bureau of Ordnance; and Rear Admiral Ralston S. Holmes, chief of the Office of Naval Intelligence emerged as the primary sources of navy resistance. These officials thoroughly disliked the idea of the United States providing any aid to a Communist government, and they successfully thwarted several different efforts by American firms to sell naval technology as well as actual vessels to the Soviet Union after 1935. Admiral Leahy, for example, responded very skeptically to any comments about Soviet-American cooperation in the Pacific and in his diary referred to the Soviet Union as a menace to the United States.[7] These officials also based their objections on legal grounds and established policy. Under the Espionage Act of June 15, 1917, the revelation of military secrets of interest to the national defense was prohibited, and the Navy Department had the responsibility to enforce this legislation on the sale of naval vessels and equipment. Consequently, any Soviet contract with an American shipbuilding firm had to be reviewed and approved by the navy. Furthermore, as Admiral Leahy repeatedly pointed out to the State Department, official policy precluded any navy assistance to the private shipbuilders, but these firms could not supply the necessary armor plate and guns without active help from the navy.

When the navy resisted the proposed contract between Carp and the Bethlehem firm, President Roosevelt tried to bring the navy into line on official policy. At a cabinet meeting on April 3, 1937, Roosevelt instructed the secretary of the navy, Claude A. Swanson, to encourage any shipbuilding firm to accept a contract for a Soviet battleship. "It was evident that the President saw no objection to this ship being built in one of our yards, and neither did Hull," remarked Harold Ickes, secretary of the interior. Roosevelt also told

Admiral Leahy that he wanted the Soviet Union to order a battleship because this would be a favorable move from an international viewpoint.[8]

Despite Roosevelt's endorsement, officials in the Navy Department maintained a somewhat oblique but nevertheless effective opposition to the president. Admiral Leahy, who said he agreed with the president's position, indirectly encouraged this resistance by expressing little enthusiasm for the project and by not reprimanding subordinate officers when they maneuvered against it. Two days after Roosevelt's discussion with Admiral Leahy, for example, the press printed accounts of the proposed contract between Carp and Bethlehem. E. R. Leonard, Bethlehem's representative in Washington, and Joseph Green of the State Department blamed the Navy Department for the leak to the press. Leonard, who was a former navy officer, believed that the navy's Office of Naval Intelligence was the source of the leak. According to Leonard, there were in the Navy Department a number of officers who were so prejudiced against commercial transactions of any character—and particularly transactions involving the sale of arms—with the USSR that they might well have instigated this publicity with the idea that it would make the carrying out of any such transaction as was proposed impossible.[9]

Officials in the Navy Department also delayed the proposed Bethlehem contract on the issue of military secrets under the Espionage Act of 1917. The State Department suggested that an agreement on this matter could be worked out for the proposed Soviet battleship along the lines of a March 1937 agreement between the navy and the Electric Boat Co. of Groton, Connecticut, which wanted to build a submarine for the Soviet Union. Admiral Leahy insisted that the Electric Boat Co. not supply any data that the navy considered confidential, exclude Soviet officials from the construction plant, and "abide by such rules and regulations designed for the preservation of military secrets of interest to the National Defense as the Secretary of the Navy may find it necessary to prescribe from time to time to prevent inadvertent disclosure of confidential information." Leahy's demands, however, prompted the Groton firm to put aside the submarine project.[10] Although Bethlehem officials never presented a formal proposal to the Navy Department, they talked about the project with navy officials who suggested regulations on the protection of military secrets that, according to Bethlehem officials, would make any contract impossible.[11]

As negotiations continued into the summer of 1937, a third method of obstruction by navy officials emerged. Subordinate officers, including Rear Admiral W. R. Furlong, chief of the Bureau of Ordnance, and Rear Admiral Ralston S. Holmes, chief of the Office of Naval Intelligence, privately warned shipbuilding firms to reject a contract with Carp because of their aversion to any assistance to a Communist government. All of the interested participants, including American firms, Carp officials, and Joseph Green of the State Department, complained about this activity. Even several firms like Sperry Gyroscope Co. and International General Electric, which were potential contractors for fire control and propulsion equipment, encountered the navy's opposition. As William R. Herod, vice president of International General Electric, confided to Joseph Green, "officers in the Navy Department were strongly opposed to the whole idea of this Government's permitting the Soviet Government to construct vessels of war in the United States." Since the navy was the principal customer of the several shipbuilding firms approached by Carp, these firms feared reprisals on future contracts if they went against the private warnings of navy officers.[12]

President Roosevelt and Secretary Hull responded to the Navy Department's effective resistance by having Joseph Green approach Admiral Leahy. When asked about the comments of subordinate officers, Leahy "said that it was more than possible that some officers of his Department who were strongly opposed to sales of arms to a communistic government might have made indiscreet remarks." Green responded by pointing out that this had created "a highly embarrassing situation." Leahy expressed agreement but according to Green, "he did not, however, appear to be particularly impressed by what seemed to me to be the serious implications of the situation which has arisen as a result of statements made by his subordinates." Leahy, moreover, in his diary revealed considerable reservations about the whole affair. He referred to the directors of Carp, Morris Wolf and Sam Carp, as international villain types and expressed skepticism about Soviet Ambassador Alexander Troyanovsky's comments on the importance of a battleship considering the similarity of Soviet-American interests in the Far East.[13] Leahy also repeated his conclusion that Bethlehem and the New York Shipbuilding Corp. refused to sign contracts because they could not build an acceptable battleship without extensive assistance from the navy, which violated Washington's policy against governmental involvement in the arms trade.

Despite Carp's failure to obtain a contract, the Soviet Union persisted in its efforts to obtain a battleship and related naval technology. Moscow's techniques were quite sophisticated. Carp, for example, employed former officers of the army and navy as well as Scott Ferris, a former representative in Congress from Oklahoma, to facilitate negotiations. Soviet Ambassador Troyanovsky discussed the battleship issue several times, not only with Navy and State Department officials but also with President Roosevelt. In 1939 Moscow sent over a naval mission headed by Vice Admiral Ivan S. Isakov, Assistant People's Commissar for Naval Affairs, to review the plans for the acquisition of two destroyers. Finally, Joseph Stalin brought up the battleship issue with Ambassador Davies during Davies's final call at the Kremlin in June 1938. Stalin, who met with American officials only twice between 1933 and 1941, informed Davies that he "could not understand why the matter could not go forward." When Davies replied that he also did not understand the delay, Stalin suggested that "if the President of the United States wanted it done he felt sure that the Army and Navy technicians could not stop it."[14]

The Soviet Union shifted its primary attention in 1938 to Gibbs and Cox,

Inc., a leading naval architect, in order to obtain plans for a battleship. Moscow also tried to persuade Bethlehem to build one according to these plans. Gibbs and Cox prepared plans for a thirty-five-knot, 60,000-ton battleship (which would be 15,000 tons larger than any battleship in existence) with eighteen-inch guns, since the State Department had withdrawn its earlier objection to sixteen-inch guns after the collapse of negotiations with Japan. Stalin's order for the world's largest battleship may have been partially a propaganda gesture to impress the major powers with his determination to build a great battleship navy, because later he readily accepted Washington's limit of 45,000 tons. Gibbs and Cox encountered opposition from subordinate officers in the Navy Department who still rejected any aid to a Communist government and, consequently, asked the Navy and State Departments to approve the proposed transaction with the Kremlin.

President Roosevelt then intervened and supported the project. When Gibbs and Cox showed the plans to Charles Edison, assistant secretary of the navy, in March 1938, Edison found the plans so interesting that he arranged for Roosevelt to meet with William Gibbs to review them. The president expressed approval for the construction of a battleship for the Soviet Union and indicated that the United States also might want to use the plans for a new battleship. After the luncheon, Edison told Roosevelt that "there was strong opposition to the proposed transaction on the part of several high ranking officers of the Navy Department" and he asked Roosevelt to "make his position in the matter known to those officers." On April 8 Roosevelt met with Edison, Admiral Leahy, and several navy bureau chiefs in an effort, according to Joseph Green, "to dragoon the naval officers in question into a state of at least apparent conformity with the policy of the government." Some of the officers still opposed the battleship, however, and Assistant Secretary Edison informed the president that he would have to take "further action" to bring the Navy Department into line.[15]

Roosevelt also encountered new reservations from within the State Department. Undersecretary Sumner Welles and Norman Davis, Roosevelt's special representative on disarmament issues, objected to a 60,000-ton battleship because it exceeded the London naval treaty of 1936 and might contribute to a new naval race in Europe. At a cabinet meeting on April 29, the secretary of the navy and Roosevelt agreed to set a 45,000-ton limitation on any battleship.[16]

When State Department officials continued to encounter navy objections to an expression of approval on the battleship, they and Assistant Secretary Edison agreed "to urge the President to take definite action." At a White House conference on June 8, Edison and Hull reviewed the impasse and suggested that a Soviet battleship stationed at Vladivostok "might be of positive advantage to" the United States. In response, Roosevelt approved a battleship of 45,000 tons with sixteen-inch guns and recommended that the government "give all help" to interested shipbuilders and naval architects. The president also suggested that a special officer under Edison's supervision handle the navy's involvement with the plans, probably in order to circumvent the entrenched navy opposition to the project. Furthermore, Roosevelt told the participants in the conference to "start clubbing the resisting naval officers over the head."[17]

Although Roosevelt's intervention prompted the Navy and State Departments to approve a 45,000-ton battleship, this issue was soon overshadowed by the Kremlin's desire to purchase two destroyers. After a visit to Moscow in December 1938 to obtain Soviet acceptance of the revised plans for a 45,000-ton battleship, representatives of Gibbs and Cox returned not only with this but also with a Soviet order for plans for two modern destroyers between 1,500 and 2,000 tons.

When William Gibbs submitted the plans for the destroyers to the navy in April 1939, he again encountered resistance. Gibbs first ran into problems on the issue of ordnance for the destroyers. Since the government had monopolized the construction of naval ordnance, Gibbs requested that the navy supply plans and specifications to a private company. When Gibbs raised this issue with naval officers, he "gained the distinct impression that the very strong opposition on the part of some of those officers to the sale of any arms to a communist government would operate" to defeat his request.[18] In its review of Gibbs's proposal in May 1939, the navy approved the design of a torpedo boat destroyer based on the original specifications for the Mahan class of destroyers dated 1933. The navy, however, objected to a number of aspects of Gibbs's plan that contained confidential navy specifications, most notably the boilers, electrical installation, general machinery and equipment, torpedo tubes, the guns, fire control equipment, and the ammunition. Gibbs complained that a number of the items the navy took exception to on the destroyers had been approved earlier on the plans for the battleship.

President Roosevelt again took up the issue at the request of Carp officials and Gibbs and Cox. Roosevelt "said that he wanted this deal for the destroyers to go through" and he requested Rear Admiral W. R. Furlong, chief of the Bureau of Ordnance, to cooperate. Assistant Secretary Edison also strongly criticized the navy's response, particularly what he considered a tendency to classify as military secrets every conceivable feature of naval vessels. The president's wishes "were clear," Edison argued, and he promised to reduce the items classified as military secrets and "prevent delays and petty attempts to make difficulties" by appointing three senior officers to carry out Roosevelt's instructions.[19]

Although Roosevelt and Edison persuaded the Navy Department to modify its original position on several issues, time ran out on the whole project. By August 1939 Edison informed Gibbs and Cox that the navy's own building program was preempting any preparation of quintuple torpedo tubes that Gibbs and Cox had included in their plans. This firm submitted revised plans on September 5, but the outbreak of World War II and Stalin's cooperation with Hitler scuttled the project. When Edison, who worried about over-crowded conditions in the shipyards because of America's naval rearmament, recommended a formal rejection of Gibbs and Cox plans, Joseph Green of the State Department ironically suggested that the navy privately discourage shipbuilders from making any contracts with the Soviet Union. Edison followed Green's suggestion, and Gibbs and Cox canceled the project.[20]

Navy officers, including Admiral Leahy and the bureau chiefs, ended up as the winners even though they appeared to lose each specific round to Roosevelt, the State Department, and Assistant Secretary Edison. In 1937 Roosevelt approved the construction of a battleship but the navy effectively delayed a contract. Although Roosevelt and Edison persuaded the navy to approve plans for a 45,000-ton battleship in 1938, the navy's obstructionist tactics again prevented a final contract. When Roosevelt endorsed Moscow's bid for two destroyers in 1939, navy officers successfully delayed approval of plans that would be acceptable to Soviet officials.

Subordinate naval officers based their opposition on traditional policy and the Espionage Act of 1917. As Admiral Leahy frequently pointed out, official policy precluded governmental assistance and involvement in the construction of war materials for a foreign government. Neither the battleship nor the destroyers could be built without extensive assistance from the navy. Furthermore, naval officers had a legal obligation under the Espionage Act of 1917 to prevent the release of military secrets. Since the Soviet Union wanted to obtain the latest advances in United States naval technology, naval officers were understandably reluctant to declassify and release information.

The weight of the evidence indicates that Admiral Leahy and the bureau chiefs seemed to respond more to their personal aversions against any naval assistance to the Soviet Union because of its Communist regime than to these other considerations. For example, when President Roosevelt changed traditional policy in 1938 and repeatedly ordered the navy to "give all help" to shipbuilders and naval architects, subordinate naval officers continued to resist the battleship and destroyer projects. Their methods of opposition, moreover, indicated the intensity of their prejudice against communism and the Soviet Union. Navy officers privately discouraged shipbuilding firms from entering into contracts with the Soviet Union, and those firms may have feared reprisals on future navy contracts. Admiral Leahy always said he agreed with Roosevelt or with other senior officials, but he never cracked the whip on his subordinates. Some officers may have moved beyond appropriate opposition to the verge of insubordination against the president's policy, but Admiral Leahy apparently did not think so.

President Roosevelt's handling of the battleship and destroyer issues illustrates some of the general problems any executive faces when he tries to get bureaucracies to carry out his decisions. Interference by subordinate officers with implementation of policy is a regular phenomenon in all executive departments that deal with foreign policy. Considering the limits on Roosevelt's time and the limited importance of this issue as a gesture to improve relations with Moscow, the president devoted considerable attention to it in conferences with Navy and State Department officials, as well as with the Soviet ambassador and Carp representatives. Roosevelt, moreover, tried a number of measures to bring navy officers into line and to circumvent their opposition by going around and above them. Perhaps the only step that Roosevelt neglected was to remove some of the opposing officers. If he had done this, the president perhaps speculated that there would be leaks to the press about his support for naval aid to Moscow. Since the president was sensitive to the strong hostility of American opinion toward the Soviet Union as well as isolationist criticism of any governmental involvement in the arms trade with the European powers, he wanted to avoid any step that might attract public attention. Roosevelt, moreover, rejected a suggestion in 1936 that he ask Congress for a special endorsement of the navy's cooperation with shipbuilders on the Soviet battleship.

In the long run, the United States' failure to cooperate with the Soviet Union on naval assistance did not have a significant impact on Soviet-American relations. Roosevelt's inability to bring the navy into line on official policy probably increased Stalin's doubts about the benefits of diplomatic cooperation with the United States. Yet this was of little consequence since Roosevelt could neither deliver on naval aid as part of his effort to improve Soviet-American relations nor follow up on his own proposal of cooperation in the Far East in 1938. Washington's response, moreover, had little effect on the Soviet Union's resistance to Nazi Germany after 1941. Neither a battleship, which would have taken at least five years to construct, nor the two destroyers could have been completed in time for sale to the Soviet Union. Instead, as the State Department frequently pointed out to the Navy Department, the United States could have, and would have in 1939, taken over the vessels for its own fleet. As it turned out, the sale of United States superior naval technology to the Soviet Union was not in the national interest, considering the basic adversarial relationship since 1945.

This little-known episode clearly signals that historians and other observers must consider the influence of the governmental bureaucracy on the shaping and implementation of policy.

NOTES

1. Charles S. Maier suggested this criticism in his cogent essay, "Revisionism and the Interpretation of Cold War Origins," *Perspectives in American History* 4 (1970): 342–45. Maier's critique may have influenced revisionists such as Bruce Kuklick, *American Policy and the Division of Germany: The Clash with Russia over Reparations* (Ithaca, N.Y.: Cornell University Press, 1972) and Thomas G. Patterson, *Soviet-American Confrontation: Postwar Reconstruction and the Origins of the Cold War* (Baltimore, Md.: Johns

Hopkins University Press, 1973) to give some consideration to the influence of the bureaucracy, as Kuklick does in his early chapters on the reparations issue during World War II.

2. Yarnell to Johnson, 9 August, Johnson to Yarnell, 12 August 1937, Box 3, Nelson T. Johnson Papers, Library of Congress, Washington, D.C. See also Loy W. Henderson dispatch to Cordell Hull, 29 July 1937, Department of State File 711.61/621, Department of State MSS, National Archives (hereafter cited as DSF); and Department of State, *Foreign Relations of the United States: The Soviet Union, 1933–1939* (Washington, D.C.: 1952), 388–391 (hereafter cited as *FRUS Soviet Union*).

3. See Anthony C. Sutton, *Western Technology and Soviet Economic Development 1930 to 1945* (Stanford, Calif.: Hoover Institution on War, Revolution and Peace, 1971), 207–48.

4. For Stalin's naval strategy, see Robert W. Herrick, *Soviet Naval Strategy; Fifty Years of Theory and Practice* (Annapolis, Md.: U.S. Naval Institute Press, 1968), 28–46.

5. Joseph F. Davies dispatches to Hull, 9 June 1938, 17 January 1939, FRUS Soviet Union, DSF 800.51 W 89 U.S.S.R./247. For Roosevelt's reorientation, see Thomas R. Maddux, *Years of Estrangement: American Relations with the Soviet Union, 1933–1941* (Tallahassee: University Presses of Florida, 1980), 81–101.

6. Memorandum by Kelley, 24 March 1937, FRUS Soviet Union, 465–66. See also memorandum by Green, 3 December 1936, and Hull to Claude A. Swanson, secretary of the navy, 26 March 1937, *FRUS Soviet Union*, 458–59, 467–69.

7. See Leahy diary, 14 April, 9 December 1937, and 21 July 1938, William D. Leahy Papers, Library of Congress, Washington, D.C.

8. Ickes diary, 3 April 1937, in Harold L. Ickes, *The Secret Diary of Harold L. Ickes*, 3 vols. (New York: Simon and Schuster, 1953–1955), 2:111; Leahy diary, 15 April 1937, Leahy Papers.

9. Memorandum by Green, 17 April 1937, *FRUS Soviet Union*, 469–70. For editorial commentary, see the *Chicago Tribune*, 17 April 1937, 10, and the *Los Angeles Times*, 17 April 1937, 4.

10. Hull to the Electric Boat Co., 9 March 1937, *FRUS Soviet Union*, 463–64.

11. Memoranda by Green, 17 April and 4 May 1937, *FRUS Soviet Union*, 469–72.

12. See memoranda by Green, 22 September 1937, 15 November 1937, and 27 July 1939, *FRUS Soviet Union*, 480–82, 488–89, 893–94. See also Green to Hugh Wilson, Hugh R. Wilson Papers, Herbert Hoover Presidential Library, West Branch, Iowa; and Jay Pierrepont Moffat Papers, Houghton Library, Harvard Library, Harvard University, Cambridge. Moffat was chief of the Division of European Affairs in the State Department.

13. Memorandum by Green, 24 September 1937, *FRUS Soviet Union*, 482–83; Leahy diary, 14 April and 9 December 1937, Leahy Papers.

14. See *FRUS Soviet Union*, 458, 475, 489, 572–73, 872.

15. See *FRUS Soviet Union*, 680–81, 692; Leahy diary, 8 April 1938, Box 9, Leahy Papers; and Green to Hugh Wilson, 5 May 1938, Wilson Papers.

16. See *FRUS Soviet Union*, 683–88; and Green to Wilson, 5 May 1938, Wilson Papers.

17. See *FRUS Soviet Union*, 689–99; Moffat diary, 8 June 1938, vol. XI., Moffat Papers; and Leahy diary, 1 June and 21 July 1938, Box 9, Leahy Papers. Leahy opposed

any official endorsement and in July referred to the Soviet Union as a menace to the United States.

18. Memorandum by Green, 14 April 1939, *FRUS Soviet Union*, 874.

19. Memoranda by Green, 27 May and 21 June 1939, *FRUS Soviet Union*, 882, 884–85.

20. See *FRUS Soviet Union*, 887–903.

Works Cited

PRIMARY SOURCES

Archives and Manuscript Collections

Austria-Hungary

Haus-, Hof- und Staatsarchiv, Vienna

Gesandschaftsberichte F 94. Karton 16.
Gesandschaftsberichte PA XXXXVII 3. Chile: Berichte, Weisungen 1905–8.
Gesandschaftsberichte Santiago 1; Santiago 2.

Österreichisches Staatsarchiv-Kriegsarchiv

Kriegsministerium, 2A/W43–77/15–4, 1913.
Kriegsministerium, 7A10–4.
Kriegsministerium, Berichte des Prinzen Windisch-Graetz Nr 1180.
Kriegsministerium, Export 1911. De 25 Nr 1180.

Chile

Archivo Nacional

Legación de Chile en Francia, vols. 317, 2306.
Oficios dirigidos al Ministro de Guerra y de Marina, Ministerio de Relaciones Este-
    riores, vols. 1376, 1601.

Czech Republic

Skoda Archivo, Plzen

Protokoll uber die Verwaltungsrat-Sitzung.

Egypt

Dar al-Wathaiq, Cairo

Periode Ismail, carton 179.
Periode Mehemet Aly a Said Pacha.
Soudan et Afrique Oriental, carton 20.

France

Schnieder Archive, Le Creusot

Repertoire General des Livres de Marches.

Service Historique de la Marine, Vincennes, Paris

$1BB^7$ 127 Finlande.
$1BB^7$ 128 Lettonie.
$1BB^7$ 129 Lettonie.
$1BB^7$ 132 Pologne.

Ministré des Affaires Etrangères, Paris

Lettonie 22.
Lettonie 23.

Germany

Auswärtiges Amt, Politisches Archiv, Berlin

Lettland Po 14.

Auswärtiges Amt, Politisches Archiv, Bonn

Akten der Parteikanzlei der NSDAP.
Bundesarchiv-Abteilung Potsdam. Lieferungen der Firma Krupp für die Chilenische
    Regierung Nr. 344.
R 3877, Preussen I Nr 3 Nr 3 Prinz Heinrich von Preussen, vol. 13.
R 16650 Chile I (45 vols.).
Regierungen. Waffenlieferungen dt. Firmen an fremde (Amerika).
Ver. Staat. V. Amerika No 5. Militär- und Marineangelegenheiten.

Krupp, Historisches Archiv, Essen-Bredeney, Familienarchiv

Briefe Adolf Lauter an F.A. Krupp 3CII.
Briefwechsel Krupp . . . und Verschiedenen Personalia, 1887–1901.
Erfahrungen im Kriegsmaterialgeschäft mit dem Auslande 10501 NIK 9.9.1937.
Privatbureau Dr. Gustav Krupp v. B. u. H. Chile. Allgemein.
Privatbureau F.A. Krupp. Chile. Vertretung 1892–94.

Krupp, Historisches Archiv, Essen-Bredeney, Werksarchiv

Besuchwesen 48.
Briefwechsel F.A. Krupp—A. Schinzinger 8.3.1883–1.8.1911.
Briefwechsel F.A. Krupp—Major Betzhold 1889–1900.
Kontrakte zwischen Friedr. Krupp, Essen, und der Republik Chile . . . 4/1051.

Great Britain

British Museum, London
Yusef Hekekyan Papers.

Imperial War Museum, London
Colonel R. B. Goodden Papers, PP/73/137/7.

Public Record Office, London
Admiralty 231.
Foreign Office 78.
Foreign Office 105.
Foreign Office 142.
Foreign Office 371.
Foreign Office 407.
War Office 1.
War Office 106.

Tyne and Wear Archive Services, Newcastle
Lord Stuart Rendel Papers 31.

Italy

Direzione Generale degli Affari Politici, URSS.
Ministero degli Affari Esteri, Rome.

Japan

Gaimusho Gaiko Shiryo Kan, Tokyo. [Record Office, Ministry of Foreign Affairs].

United States

Herbert Hoover Presidential Library, West Branch, Iowa
Hugh R. Wilson Papers.

Herkimer Historical Society, Herkimer, N.Y.
Remington Files.
Shepard and Richardson Papers.

Hoover Institution, Stanford University, Palo Alto, Calif.
Curt Prüfer Collection.

Houghton Library, Harvard University Library, Cambridge, Mass.
Jay Pierrepont Moffat Papers.

Ilion, N.Y., Free Public Library, Historical Room, Library of Congress Manuscript Division
Washington Irving Chambers Papers.
William E. Chandler Papers.
Nelson T. Johnson Papers.
William D. Leahy Papers.

National Archives, Washington, D.C., and College Park, Md.

Department of State. Department of State File 711.61/621.
────. Report of Department of State Relative to the Internal Affairs of Chile, 1910–1929.
Department of the Army. Communications Received from Military Attaches and Other Intelligence Officers "Dispatch Lists," 1889–1941.
Record Group 38. Office of Naval Intelligence and Spanish-American War Correspondence.
Record Group 59. General Records of the Department of State.

Southern Historical Collection, University of North Carolina, Chapel Hill

Charles I. Graves Papers.
Samuel Henry Lockett Papers.
Shepard and Richardson Papers.

Springfield Armory Records

Published Documents and Microfilm Collections

Chile. Camara de Diputados, Sesiones Ordinarias and Estraordinarias, 1909, 1911, 1912.
────. Camara de Senado, Sesiones Ordinarias and Estraordinarias, 1904, 1909, 1912, 1914.
Congressional Record, 46th Cong., 1880, through 52nd Cong., 1892.
Documents on German Foreign Policy, 1918–1945. From the archives of the German Foreign Ministry. Washington, D.C.: GPO, 1949–83.
Egypte. Commission a l'Expostion Universelle de Vienne, 1873. *Catalogue Raisonne de l'Exposition Egyptienne*. Vienne: Imprimerie Imperiale et Royale, 1873.
Fitch, Charles. "Report on the Manufacture of Interchangeable Mechanisms." In United States Congress, *Miscellaneous Documents of the House of Representatives*. Washington, D.C.: 4th Cong., 2d sess., 1882.
Great Britain. *British Documents on Foreign Affairs: Reports and Papers from the Foreign Office Confidential Print*. Edited by Kenneth Bourne and D. Cameron Watt. Frederick, Md.: University Publications of America, 1986.
────. Foreign Office. *British Documents on Foreign Affairs*. Edited by David Gillard. Frederick, Md.: University Publications of America, 1984.
────. House of Commons. Sessional Papers, 1840, Vol. 21: *Reports from Commissioners*. London: HMSO, 1840.
Guindi, Georges, and Jacques Tagher, eds. *Ismail d'apres les documents officials*. Cairo, 1945.
Italy. Ministero degli Affari Esteri. Commissione per la Pubblicazione dei Documenti Diplomatici. *I documenti diplomatici italiani*. Rome: La Libreria dello Stato, 1952.
────. Servizio storico e documentazione. *Inventario delle rappresentanze diplomatiche. Francia e Russia (URSS), 1861–1950*. Rome: Archivio storico diplomatico, 1979.
King, J. W. *Report of Chief Engineer J. W. King, United States Navy, on European Ships*

of War and their Armaments, Naval Administration and Economy, Marine Construction, Torpedo-Warfare, Dock-Yards, Etc. Washington, D.C.: GPO, 1878.

National Association for the Advancement of Colored People. Papers of the NAACP, Part 11: Special Subject Files, 1912–1939, Series A: Africa through Garvey, Marcus. Edited by August Meier and John H. Bracey Jr. Bethesda, Md.: University Publications of America, 1990. Microfilm.

Secretary of the Navy. *Annual Reports.* 1881–89 and 1898–1900.

Sherman Papers, Vol. 27, Microfilm Roll 15, Library of Congress, Washington, D.C.

T-120. *The German Foreign Ministry Archives 1920–1945.* Collection of the National Archives and Record Administration. Microfilm.

Trial of Major War Criminals before the International Military Tribunal Nuremberg 14 Nov. 1945–1 Oct. 1946 34. Nuremberg, 1949.

Union of Soviet Socialist Republics. Ministerstvo inostrannykh del SSSR. *Dokumenty vneshniaia politika SSSR.* Moscow: Politicheskoi literatury, 1970–73.

United States. Congress. House. *Report of the Gun Foundry Board.* House Exec. Doc. 97. 48th Cong., 1st sess., 1884.

———. Senate. *Navy Yearbook: A Resume of Naval Appropriations Laws from 1883 to 1919 Inclusive.* Senate Document 418. 65th Cong., 3rd sess., 1919.

United States. Department of State. *Despatches from United States Consuls in Alexandria, 1835–1873.*

———. *Diplomatic Instructions, Egypt.* National Archives, Washington, D.C.

———. *Diplomatic Instructions of the United States, Turkey.*

———. *Foreign Relations of the United States: The Soviet Union, 1933–1939.* Washington, D.C.: 1952.

———. *Instructions to Barbary Powers.*

———. *Records Relating to the Internal Affairs of Latvia, 1910–1944.* Washington, D.C.: 1981. Microfilm.

United States. National Archives Microfilm Publications. *Records of the Department of State Relating to Political Relations Between the Soviet Union and Other States, 1930–1939.* Decimal File 761, Microcopy T1247.

United States. Military Intelligence Division. *Correspondence of the Military Intelligence Division Relating to General Political, Economic, and Military Conditions in Poland and the Baltic States, 1918–1941.* Washington, D.C., 1981. Microfilm.

United States. *U.S. Military Intelligence Reports: The Soviet Union, 1919–1941.* Bethesda, Md.: University Publications of America, 1991. Microfilm.

Memoirs

Bromfield, William Arnold. *Letters from Egypt and Syria.* London: William Pamplin, 1856.

Duff-Gordon, Lady Lucie. *Letters from Egypt.* Edited by Gordon Waterfield. New York: Frederick A. Praeger, Pub., 1969.

Gadsby, John. *My Wanderings, Being Travels in the East in 1846–47, 1850–51, 1852–53.* London: n.p., 1862.

Garston, Edgar. *Greece Revisited and Sketches in Lower Egypt.* Vol. 2. London: Saunders and Otley, 1842.

Glidden, G. R. *A Memoir on the Cotton of Egypt.* London: J. Madden, 1841.

Henniker, Sir Frederick. *Notes During a Visit to Egypt*. London: John Murray, 1824.

Hoskins, G. A. *Travels in Ethiopia*. London: Longman, 1835.

Ickes, Harold L. *The Secret Diary of Harold L. Ickes*. 3 vols. New York: Simon and Schuster, 1953–55.

Jones, George. *Excursions to Cairo, Jerusalem, Damascus and Balbek from the United States Ship Delaware During Her Recent Cruise*. New York: Van Nostrand & Dwight, 1836.

Louca, Anouar, ed. *Lettres d'Egypte, 1879–1882*. Paris: C.N.R.S., 1979.

Rochfort Scott, C. *Rambles in Egypt and Candia*. Vol. 1. London: Henry Colburn, 1837.

Statistisches Reichsamt. *Statistisches Jahrbuch für das Deutsche Reich*. Berlin: Verlag von Reimar Hobling, 1929.

———. *Statistisches Jahrbuch für das Deutsche Reich*. Berlin: Verlag für Sozialpolitik, Wirtschaft und Statistik, 1933.

———. *Statistisches Jahrbuch für das Deutsche Reich*. Berlin: Verlag für Sozialpolitik, Wirtschaft und Statistik, 1936.

Steer, George L. *Caesar in Abyssinia*. London: Hodder and Stoughton, 1936.

Tirpitz, A. von, *Erinnerungen*. Leipzig, 1919.

Warburton, Eliot. *Travels in Egypt and the Holy Land*. Philadelphia: H. C. Peck and Theo. Bliss, 1859.

Wellsted, J. R. *Travels in Arabia*. Vol. 2. 1838. Reprint, Graz: Akademische Druck-u. Verlagsanstalt, 1978.

Wilde, W. R. *Narrative of a Voyage to Madeira, Teneriffe and the Shores of the Mediterranean*. Vol. 1. Dublin: William Curry, 1840.

Newspapers

Chicago Defender.
Chicago Tribune.
Corriere della Sera.
El Diario Ilustrado (Santiago), 1912.
Le Figaro.
Herkimer Democrat.
Izvestia.
Japan Times.
Journal de Moscou.
Los Angeles Times.
La Lei (Santiago), 1910.
La Mañana (Santiago), 2 April 1912.
El Mercurio (Santiago), 1910–12.
El Mercurio (Valparaíso), 1904, 1909–1910, 1912, 1914.
Moscow Daily News.
New York Times.
Osaka Mainichi & Tokyo Nichi Nichi.
Pravda.
La Razón (Santiago), 1912.
Riga Times.
Times (London).

La Unión (Valparaíso), 1912.
Utica Press.
Die Weltbühne, 22 November 1927.

SECONDARY SOURCES

100 Jahre Schichau, 1837–1937. Berlin: VDI-Verlag, 1937.

125 Jahre Waffen aus Steyr. Steyr: Steyr Mannlicher Ges. M.B.H., 1989.

Achkasov, Vasilii Ivanovich, and Nikolai Bronislavovich Pavlovich. *Soviet Naval Operations in the Great Patriotic War, 1941–1945.* Translated by the United States Naval Intelligence Command. Annapolis, Md.: Naval Institute Press, 1981.

Achkasov, Vasilii Ivanovich, et al., eds. *Voevoi put' sovetskogo voenno-morskogo flota.* Moscow: Voennoe izdatel'stvo ministerstva oborony SSSR, 1974.

Agbi, Sunday Olu. *Japanese Relations with Africa.* Ibadan, Nigeria: Ibadan University Press, 1992.

Albion, Robert Greenhalgh. *Makers of Naval Policy 1798–1947.* Annapolis, Md.: Naval Institute Press, 1980.

Alden, John D. *The American Steel Navy.* Annapolis, Md.: Naval Institute Press, 1972.

Angevine, Robert G. "The Rise and Fall of the Office of Naval Intelligence." *Journal of Military History* 62 (April 1998): 291–312.

Anguita, Ricardo. *Leyes Promulgadas en Chile desde 1810 hasta el 1 de Junio de 1913.* 5 vols. Santiago, 1913.

Annuaire Officiel de la Légion D'Honneur. Paris, 1929.

Aoki Sumio and Kurimoto Eisei. *Japanese Interest in Ethiopia (1868–1940): Chronology and Bibliography.* 3 vols. Kyoto: Shokado Book Sellers, 1997.

Auriant. "Ismail Gibraltar, Amiral Egyptien (1810–1826)." In *Revue Politique et Littéraire: Revue bleu* 64 (1926).

Baer, George W. *The Coming of the Italian-Ethiopian War.* Cambridge: Harvard University Press, 1967.

Bahru Zewde. "The Ethiopian Intelligentsia and the Italo-Ethiopian War, 1935–1941." *International Journal of African Historical Studies* 26 (1993): 274–75.

———. *A History of Modern Ethiopia, 1855–1974.* London: James Currey, 1991.

Ball, Robert W. D. *Mauser Military Rifles of the World.* Iola, Wisc.: Krause Publications, 1996.

Baker, Sir Samuel W. *Ismailia.* London: MacMillan & Co., 1907.

Barker, Edward B. B. *Syria and Egypt Under the Last Five Sultans of Turkey.* 1876. Reprint, New York: Arno Press, 1973.

Barr, William. "The Soviet Contribution to the *Italia* Search and Rescue, 1928." *Polar Record* 18 (September 1977): 561–74.

Beaud, Claude. "De L'Expansion Internationale a La Multinationale Schneider En Russie (1896–1914)." *Histoire, Économie et Société* 4 (1985): 575–602.

———. "Les Schneider marchands de Canons 1870–1914." *Histoire, Economie et Société* 14 (1995): 107–31.

Bell, Christopher. *The Royal Navy, Seapower, and Strategy Between the Wars.* Stanford: Stanford University Press, 2000.

Berry, A. G. "The Beginnings of the Office of Naval Intelligence." *U.S. Naval Institute Proceedings* 63 (January 1937): 102.

Beskrovnyi, L. G. *Russkaia armiia i flot v XIX veke.* Moskva: Nauka, 1973.

Bey, Cattaui, ed. "Une Lettre de Mohammed Aly le Grand." *Bulletin de l'Institut d'Egypte* 32 (1951): 22.

Boelcke, Willi. *Krupp und Die Hohenzollern, aus der Korrespondenz der Familie Krupp 1850–1916.* Berlin: Rütten & Loening, 1956.

Bradshaw, Richard Albert. "Japan and European Colonialism in Africa, 1800–1937." Ph.D. diss., Ohio University, 1992.

Brassey's Naval and Shipping Annual. Eds. Charles N. Robinson and N. M Ross. London: William Clowes and Sons, 1930–35.

Breyer, Siegfried. *Guide to the Soviet Navy.* Translated by M. W. Henley. Annapolis, Md.: Naval Institute Press, 1970.

Brooker, Robert E., Jr. *British Military Pistols, 1603–1888.* Dallas: Taylor Publications, 1978.

Buhl, Lance C. "Maintaining an American Navy, 1865–1889." In *In Peace and War: Interpretations of American Naval History 1775–1978,* ed. Kenneth J. Hagan. Westport, Conn.: Greenwood Press, 1978.

Busch, Dr. Moritz. *Hand-Book for Travellers in Egypt.* Trans. by W. C. Wrankmore. Trieste: Austrian Lloyd, 1864.

Butler, Alfred J. *Court Life in Egypt.* London: Chapman & Hall, 1888.

Butler, David F. *United States Firearms. The First Century, 1776–1875.* New York: Winchester Press, 1971.

Campbell, John. *Naval Weapons of World War Two.* Annapolis, Md.: Naval Institute Press, 1985.

Chaille-Long, Charles. "Letter to the Editor." *Bulletin of the American Geographical Society of New York* 39 (1904): 349.

Charles-Roux, Francois. *Le Coton en Égypte.* Paris: Armand Colin, 1908.

Clarke, J. Calvitt, III. "Italy and Plan Barbarossa." *Selected Annual Proceedings of the Florida Conference of Historians* 2 (September 1994): 81–103.

———. "Italy and the Nazi-Soviet Pact of August 23, 1939." *Selected Annual Proceedings of the Florida Conference of Historians* 3 (December 1996): 30–39.

———. "Japan and Italy Squabble over Ethiopia: The Sugimura Affair of July 1935." *Selected Annual Proceedings of the Florida Conference of Historians* 6/7 (December 1999): 105–16.

———. "Japan, Collective Security, and the Italo-Ethiopian War of 1935–36." Paper presented to the Third Pan-European International Relations Conference and Joint Meeting with the International Studies Association, Vienna, Austria, September 1998.

———. "Modernizing Ideologies: Japan and Ethiopia Before the Italo-Ethiopian War, 1935–36." Paper presented to the Annual Meeting of the Florida Conference of Historians, Orlando, April 2000.

———. "Periphery and Crossroads: Ethiopia and World Diplomacy, 1934–36." In *Ethiopia in Broader Perspective: Papers of the 13th International Conference of Ethiopian Studies.* 3 vols. Edited by K. E. Fukui and M. Shigeta. Kyoto: Shokado Book Sellers, 1997, 699–712.

———. *Russia and Italy Against Germany: The Bolshevik Fascist Rapprochement of the 1930s.* Westport, Conn.: Greenwood Press, 1991.

———. "Search for Areas of Cooperation: Italian Precursors to the Nazi Soviet Pact of 1939: Preliminary Comments." *Selected Annual Proceedings of the Florida Conference of Historians* 5 (December 1997): 8–20.

———. "Soviet Appeasement, Collective Security, and the Italo-Ethiopian War of 1935 and 1936." *Selected Annual Proceedings of the Florida Conference of Historians* 4 (December 1996): 115–32.

Clot-Bey, A. B. *Aperçu Général de l'Égypte*. 2 vols. Paris: Fotin Masson, 1840.

Collier, Basil. *Arms and the Men: The Arms Trade and Governments*. London: Hamish Hamilton, 1980.

Colwell, David G. "The Navy and Greely." *U.S. Naval Institute Proceedings* 84 (January 1958), 71–79.

Combe, Etienne, Jacques Bainville, and Eduard Driault. *Precis de l'Histoire d'Egypte*, Vol. 3. Cairo: L'Institut Français, 1935.

Cooling, Benjamin Franklin. *Gray Steel and Blue Water Navy*. Hampden, Conn.: Archon Books, 1979.

Coverdale, John Foy. *Italian Intervention in the Spanish Civil War*. Princeton, N.J.: Princeton University Press, 1975.

Crabites, Pierre. *Ismail: The Maligned Khedive*. London: George Routledge and Sons, Ltd., 1933.

Crouchley, A. E. *The Economic Development of Modern Egypt*. London: Longmans, Green & Co., 1938.

Cuno, Kenneth M. *The Pasha's Peasants: Land Society and Economy in Lower Egypt, 1740–1858*. Cambridge: Cambridge University Press, 1992.

Deyrup, Felicia Johnson. *Arms Making in the Connecticut Valley*. New York: George Shumway Publisher, 1970.

Dicey, Edward. *The Story of the Khedivate*. London: Rivingtons, 1902.

Dodwell, Henry. *The Founder of Modern Egypt*. Cambridge: University Press, 1967.

Donnini, Guido. *L'accordo italo-russo di Racconigi*. Milan: A. Giuffrè, 1983.

Donoso, Armando. "El Jeneral del Canto." *Pacifico Magazine* 9 (1917): 25–54.

———. *Recuerdos de cincuenta años*. Santiago, 1947.

Dorwart, Jeffery M. *The Office of Naval Intelligence: The Birth of America's First Intelligence Agency, 1865–1918*. Annapolis, Md.: Naval Institute Press, 1979.

Douin, Georges. *Histoire du Regne du Khedive Ismail. Tome III. L'Empire Africain. 1er Part (1863–1869)*. Cairo: L'Institute Francaise, 1941.

———. *Histoire du Regne du Khedive Ismail. Tome III. L'Empire Africain. 3e Partie (1874–1876)*. Cairo: L'Institute Francaise, 1941.

———, ed. *L'Egypte de 1828 à 1830*. Roma: Nell'Istituto Poligrafico, 1935.

———, ed. *Une Mission Militaire Francaise aupres de Mohamed Aly*. Cairo: Société Royale de Géographie d'Egypte, 1927.

Dunn, John. "Remington Rolling Blocks in the Horn of Africa." *Bulletin of the American Society of Arms Collectors* 71 (1994): 25–32.

Durand-Viel, Vice Amiral G. *Les Campagnes Naveles de Mohammed Aly et d'Ibrahim*. 2 vols. Paris: Imprimerie Nationale, 1937.

Ehrenrangliste der Kaiserlichen Deutschen Marine, 1914–1918, bearbeitet von Konteradmiral a. D. Stoetzel, Berlin 1930.

Ekman, P.-O. *Havsvargar. Ubåtar och ubåtskrig i Östersjön*. 2nd ed. Helsingfors, 1999.

[Enfantin, Barthelemy Prosper]. *Oeuvres de Saint-Simon—d'Enfantin*. 1865–78. Reprint, Aalen: Otton Zeller, 1964.

Estado, Mayor Jeneral. *Breve información sobre el ejército del Perú*. Santiago, 1911.

"Etat Comparatif des Forces de Terre et de Mer de la Turquie et de l'Egypte." *Le Spectateur Militaire* 21 (Avril 1835): 85.

Fahmy, Moustafa. *La Revolution de l'Industrie en Egypte et ses Consequences Sociles au 19e Siecle.* Leiden: Brill, 1954.

Falessi, Cesare. *Balbo aviatore: Con 33 fotografie, 4 cartine e 7 illustrazioni a colori fuori testo.* Milan: Mondadori, 1983.

Farago, Ladislas. *Abyssinia on the Eve.* New York: G. P. Putnam's Sons, 1935.

Featherstone, Donald. *Weapons and Equipment of the Victorian Soldier.* Poole, Dorset: Blanford Press, 1978.

Fechter, R. "History of German Ethiopian Diplomatic Relations." *Zeitschrift für Kulturaustausch, Sonderausgabe Äthiopien* (1973): 149–56.

Ferrante, Ovidio. *Umberto Nobile.* 2 vols. Rome: Claudio Tatangelo, 1985.

Forsén, B., and A. Forsén. *Saksan ja Suomen salainen sukellusveneyhteistyö.* Keuru, 1999.

———. *Tysklands och Finlands hemliga ubåtssamarbete.* Borgå, 1999.

Funke, Manfred. *Sanktionen und Kanonen.* Duesseldorf: Droste Verlag, 1970.

Furukawa Tetsushi. "Japanese-Ethiopian Relations in the 1920–30s: The Rise and Fall of 'Sentimental' Relations." Paper presented at the 34th Annual Meeting of the African Studies Association, St. Louis, Mo., November 1991.

———. "Japan's Political Relations with Ethiopia, 1920s-1960s: A Historical Overview." Paper presented to the 35th Annual Meeting of the African Studies Association, Seattle, Wash., 20–23 November 1992.

Garzke, William H., Jr., and Robert O. Dulin, Jr. *Battleships: Allied Battleships in World War II.* Annapolis, Md.: Naval Institute Press, 1980.

Gatrell, Peter. "After Tsushima: Economic and Administrative Aspects of Russian Naval Rearmament, 1905–1913." *Economic History Review,* 2nd ser., XLIII, 2 (1990), 255–70.

———. *Government, Industry and Rearmament in Russia, 1900–1914.* Cambridge: Cambridge University Press, 1994.

Geschichte der Mauser-Werke. Berlin: VDI-Verlag, 1938.

Geyer, Dietrich. *Russian Imperialism: The Interaction of Domestic and Foreign Policy, 1860–1914.* New Haven: Yale University Press, 1977.

Glassman, Jon D. *Arms for the Arabs.* Baltimore: John Hopkins University Press, 1975.

Goldstein, Edward R. "Vickers Limited and the Tsarist Regime." *Slavonic and East European Review* 58 (October 1980): 561–71.

Gonzalez, Mario Matus. *Tradición y Adaptación. Vivencia de los Sefaradíes en Chile.* Santiago, 1993.

Gorshkov, Sergei Georgievich. *Morskaia mosch' gosudarstva.* Moscow: Voennoe izdatel'stvo ministerstva oborony SSSR, 1976.

Gran, Peter. *Islamic Roots of Capitalism: Egypt 1760–1840.* Austin: University of Texas Press, 1979.

Greger, René. *The Russian Fleet, 1914–1917.* Translated by Jill Gearing. London: Ian Allan, 1972.

Guemard, Gabriel. *Les Réformes en Egypte d'Ali Bey el Kebir à Muhammad Ali, 1760–1848.* Cairo: Paul Barbey, 1936.

Gutsjahr, Martin. "Rüstungsunternehmen Österreich-Ungarns vor und im Ersten Weltkrieg. Die Entwicklung dargestellt an die Firmen Skoda, Steyr, Austro-Daimler und Lohner." Ph.D. diss., Universität Wien, 1995.

Halpern, Paul G. *The Mediterranean Naval Situation 1908–1914.* Cambridge, Mass.: Harvard University Press, 1971.

Hatch, Alden. *Remington Arms in American History.* New York: Rinehart & Co., Inc., 1956.

Heideking, J. *Areopag der Diplomaten. Die Pariser Botschafterkonferenz der alliierten Hauptmächte und die Probleme der europäischen Politik 1920–1931.* Husum, 1979.

Hell, Jürgen. "Deutschland und Chile von 1871–1918." *Wissenschaftliche Zeitschrift der Universität Rostock* 14 (1965): 87.

Herrick, Robert Waring. *Soviet Naval Strategy: Fifty Years of Theory and Practice.* Annapolis, Md.: Naval Institute Press, 1968.

Herrick, Walter R. *The American Naval Revolution.* Baton Rouge: Louisiana State University Press, 1967.

Herrmann, David G. *The Arming of Europe and the Making of the First World War.* Princeton: Princeton University Press, 1996.

Heruy Welde Sellase. *Dai Nihon* (Great Japan). Foreword by Baron Shidehara Kijuro. Translated by Oreste Vaccari and Enko Vaccari. Tokyo: Eibunpo Tsuron Hakkojo, 1934. Originally published in Amharic, *Mahidere Birhan: Hagre Japan.* Addis Ababa, 1934.

Heywood-Dunne, James. *An Introduction to the History of Modern Education in Egypt.* London: Luzac & Co, 1938.

Hildebrand, H., and E. Henriot. *Deutschlands Admirale 1849–1945. Die militärische Werdegänge der See-, Ingenieurs-, Sanitäts, Waffen- und Verwaltungsoffiziere im Admiralsrang,* Osnabrück, 1988.

Hinkkanen-Lievonen, Merja Liisa. *British Trade and Enterprise in the Baltic States, 1919–1925.* Helsinki, 1984.

Hirsch, Mark D. *William C. Whitney, Modern Warwick.* New York: Dodd Mead, 1948.

Hogg, Ian V. *The Illustrated Encyclopedia of Artillery.* Secaucus, N.J.: Chartwell Books, Inc., 1988.

———. *The Weapons That Changed the World.* New York: Arbor House, 1986.

Hotz, R. "Egypt Plans Modernized Air Arm." *Aviation Week and Space Technology* 102, no. 26 (July 1975): 12–20.

Hovi, Kalervo. *Alliance de Revers. Stabilization of France's Alliance Policies in East Central Europe 1919–1921.* Annales Universitatis Turkuensis, Ser. B, Tom. 163. Turku, 1984.

———. *Cordon Sanitaire or Barriere de l'Est? The Emergence of the New French Eastern European Alliance Policy 1917–1919.* Annales Universitatis Turkuensis, Ser. B, Tom. 135. Turku, 1975.

Hunter, F. Robert. *Egypt Under the Khedives, 1805–1879.* Pittsburgh: University of Pittsburgh Press, 1984.

Ishihara Hideko. "First Contacts Between Ethiopia and Japan." Paper presented to the 13th International Conference of Ethiopian Studies, Kyoto, December 1997.

Jacobsen, Hans-Adolf. *Nationalsozialistische Außenpolitik 1933–1938.* Frankfurt: Alfred Metzner Verlag, 1968.

James, F. L. *The Wild Tribes of the Sudan.* London: John Murray, 1884.

Janzen, Jerry. *Bayonets from Janzen's Notebook.* Tulsa: n.p., 1987.

Jelavich, Barbara. *Russia's Balkan Entanglements, 1806–1914.* Cambridge: Cambridge University Press, 1991.

Jelavich, Charles, and Barbara Jelavich. *The Establishment of the Balkan National States, 1804–1920.* Seattle: University of Washington Press, 1977.

Jindra, Zdenek. *Der Rüstungs-Konzern Fried. Krupp AG., 1914–1918.* Praha: Univerzita Karlova, 1986.

———. "Zur Entwicklung und Stellung der kanonenausfuhr der Firma Friedrich Krupp/Essen 1854–1912." *Vierteljahrschrift für Sozial- und Wirtschafts-geschichte.* Beiheft 120, Stuttgart: Franz Steiner Verlag, 1995, 966–74.

Johnson, Douglas. "The Myth of Ansar Firepower." *Savage and Soldier: Sudan Issue.*

Katz, Samuel M. *Arab Armies of the Middle East Wars* (2). London: Osprey, 1988.

Keys, Dick, and Ken Smith. *Down Elswick Shipways, Armstrong's Ships and People, 1884–1918.* Newcastle: Newcastle City Libraries, 1996.

Kijanen, K. *Sukellushälytys. Suomalaiset sukellusveneet sodan ja rauhan aikana.* Lahti, 1977.

Kipp, Jacob W. "The Russian Navy and Private Enterprise, A Peculiar MIC." In *War, Business and World Military-Industrial Complexes,* ed. Benjamin Franklin Cooling. Port Washington, N.Y.: Kennikat Press, 1981, 84–105.

Kirkland, K. D. *America's Premier Gunmaker: Remington.* New York: Exeter Books, 1988.

Knickerbocker, Hubert Renfro. *Fighting the Red Trade Menace.* New York: Dodd, Mead & Co., 1931.

Krause, Keith. *Arms and the State: Patterns of Military Production and Trade.* Cambridge: Cambridge University Press, 1992.

Krupp 1812–1912. zum 100 jährigen Bestehen der Firma Krupp und der Gustahlfabrik zu Essen-Ruhr. Essen: Friedrich Krupp A.G., 1912.

Kuklick, Bruce. *American Policy and the Division of Germany: The Clash with Russia over Reparations.* Ithaca, N.Y.: Cornell University Press, 1972.

Lakowski, R. *Deutsche U-Boote geheim 1935–1945.* München, 1991.

Landes, David S. *Bankers and Pashas.* Cambridge: Harvard University Press, 1979.

Layman, George T. *The Military Remington Rolling Block—50 Years of Faithful Service.* Prescott, Ariz.: Wolfe Pub. Co., 1992.

Levine, Donald N. "Ethiopia and Japan in Comparative Civilizational Perspective." 3 vols. *Ethiopia in Broader Perspectives,* 1:652–75.

Ludwig Loewe & Co. Actiengesellschaft Berlin 1869–1929. Berlin, 1930.

Madden, R. R. *Egypt and Mohammed Ali.* London: Hamilton & Co., 1841.

Maddux, Thomas R. "United States-Soviet Naval Relations in the 1930s: The Soviet Union's Efforts to Purchase Naval Vessels." *Naval War College Review* (fall 1976): 28–37.

———. *Years of Estrangement: American Relations with the Soviet Union, 1933–1941.* Tallahassee: University Presses of Florida, 1980.

Maier, Charles S. "Revisionism and the Interpretation of Cold War Origins." *Perspectives in American History* 4 (1970): 342–45.

Manchester, William. *The Arms of Krupp, 1587–1968.* Little Brown, Boston, 1964.

———. *The Arms of Krupp, 1587–1968.* Boston: Bantam Books, 1968.

Mares, Leon. *Les Armes de Guerre à l'Exposition Universelle.* Paris: Didot, 1867.

Marlowe, John. *Spoiling the Egyptians.* New York: St. Martin's Press, 1975.

Marsot, Afaf Lufti al-Sayyid. *Egypt in the Reign of Muhammad Ali.* Cambridge: Cambridge University Press, 1984.

―――. "The Porte and Ismail Pasha's Quest for Autonomy." *Journal of the American Research Center in Egypt* 12 (1975): 89–96.

McCoan, J. C. *Egypt*. New York: Peters Fenelon Collier, 1898.

―――. *Egypt Under Ismail*. London: Chapman & Hall, 1889.

McKale, Donald M. *Curt Prüfer, German Diplomat from the Kaiser to Hitler*. Kent, Ohio: Kent State University Press, 1987.

McNeill, William H. *The Pursuit of Power*. Chicago: University of Chicago Press, 1982.

Meister, Jürg. "Den Lettiska flottan 1918–1941." *Tidskrift i sjöväsendet* 136 (June 1974): 300–301.

―――. *The Soviet Navy 1*. Garden City, N.Y.: Doubleday & Co., 1971.

―――. *The Soviet Navy 2*. London: Macdonald, 1972.

―――. *Soviet Warships of the Second World War*. New York: Arco Publishing Co., 1977.

Mengin, Félix. *Histoire de l'Égypte*. Vol. 2. Paris: Chez Arthus Bertrand, 1823.

―――. *Histoire Sommaire de l'Egypte de Mohammed Aly*. Paris: Firmin Didot Freres, 1839.

Menne, Bernhard. *Blood and Steel, The Rise of the House of Krupp*. New York: Lee Furman, Inc., 1938.

―――. *Krupp or The Lords of Essen*. London: Hodge & Co., 1937.

Merid W. Aregay. *Japanese and Ethiopian Reactions to Jesuit Missionary Activities in the Sixteenth and Seventeenth Centuries*. 3 vols. *Ethiopia in Broader Perspective: Papers of the XIIIth International Conference of Ethiopian Studies*. Edited by K. E. Fukui and M. Shigeta. Kyoto: Shokado Book Sellers, 1997.

Merruau, Paul. *L'Egypte Contemporaine de Mehemet-Ali à Said Pacha*. Paris: Didier et Cie., 1864.

Messay Kebede. *Japan and Ethiopia: An Appraisal of Similarities and Divergent Courses*. 3 vols. *Ethiopia in Broader Perspective: Papers of the XIIIth International Conference of Ethiopian Studies*. Edited by K. E. Fukui and M. Shigeta. Kyoto: Shokado Book Sellers, 1997.

Morris, Eric. *The Russian Navy: Myth and Reality*. New York: Stein and Day, 1977.

Mustafa, Ahmed Abdel-Rahim. "The Breakdown of the Monopoly System in Egypt after 1840." In *Political and Social Change in Modern Egypt*, ed. P. M. Holt. London: Oxford University Press, 1968.

Myatt, Major F. *The Illustrated Encyclopedia of Nineteenth-Century Firearms* (New York: Crescent Books, 1994).

New Chapter in an Old Story, A. New York: Remington Arms, 1912.

"New Dirigibles Constructed." *Economic Review of the Soviet Union* 9 (August–September 1934): 182.

Nicole, David. "Nizam—Egypt's Army in the 19th Century, Part I." *Army Quarterly and Defense Journal* 108 (January 1978).

Niklander, T. *Meidän panssarilaivamme*. Jyväskylä, Gummerus, 1996.

Nobile, Umberto. *Quello che ho visto nella Russia sovietica*. Rome: Atlantica, 1945.

North, Anthony. *Islamic Arms*. London: HMSO, 1985.

Norton, Charles B. *American Breech-Loading Small Arms*. New York: F. W. Christern, 1872.

O'Balance, Edgar. "Problems of the Egyptian Phoenix." *Army Quarterly and Defense Journal* 102 (July 1972): 451–57.

O'Brien, Patrick. "Long Term Growth of Agricultural Production in Egypt: 1821–

1962." In *Political and Social Change in Modern Egypt*, ed. P. M. Holt. London: Oxford University Press, 1968.

Okakura Takashi and Kitagawa Katsuhiko. *Nihon-Afurika Koryu-shi: Meiji-ki kara Dainiji Sekai Taisen-ki made* (History of Japanese-African relations: From the Meiji period to the Second World War period). Tokyo: Dobun-kan, 1993.

Okyar, Osman. "Industrialization as an Aspect of Defensive Modernization (Egypt and Turkey Compared, 1800–1850)." *Revue d'Histoire Maghrebine* 12, no. 37/38 (1985): 125.

Owen, Roger. *Cotton and the Egyptian Economy, 1820–1940: A Study in Trade and Development*. Oxford: Clarendon Press, 1969.

Patterson, Thomas G. *Soviet-American Confrontation: Postwar Reconstruction and the Origins of the Cold War*. Baltimore: Johns Hopkins University Press, 1973.

Paullin, Charles G. *History of Naval Administration, 1775–1911: A Collection of Articles from United States Naval Institute Proceedings*. Annapolis, Md.: Naval Institute Press, 1968.

Pearsall, Ronald. "The Military Breechloaders of 1871." *Army Quarterly and Defense Journal* 104 (October 1973): 90–93.

Pergent, J. "L'Aide militaire de l'U.R.S.S. à l'Egypte." *Est & Ouest* 22 (1–15 July 1970): 16–18.

Peterson, Harold L. *The Remington Historical Treasury of American Guns*. Edinburgh: Thomas Nelson, 1966.

Pfaffenwimmer, Michaela. "Die wirtschaftliche und soziale Entwicklung der 'Österreichischen Waffenfabriks-Aktiengesellschaft' unter der Leitung des Generaldirektors Josef Werndl 1869–1889." Ph.D. diss., Universität Wien, 1985.

Planat, Jules. *Histoire de la Regeneration de l'Egypte*. Paris: J. Barbezet, 1830.

Procacci, Giuliano. *Il socialismo internazionale e la guerra d'Etiopia*. Rome: Editori Riuniti, 1978.

Prouty, Chris, and Eugene Rosenfeld. *Historical Dictionary of Ethiopia*. Metuchen, N.J.: Scarecrow Press, 1981.

Pucklar-Muskau, Prince. *Egypt Under Mehemet Ali*. 2 vols. London: Henry Colburn, 1865.

Ragsdale, Hugh. *Imperial Russian Foreign Policy*. Cambridge: Cambridge University Press, 1993.

Rahn, W. "Verteidigungskonzeption und Reichsmarine in der Weimarer Republik. Planung und Führung in der Ära Behncke und Zenker (1920–1928)." Ph.D. diss., Hamburg, 1976.

Ralston, David. *Importing the European Army*. Chicago: University of Chicago Press, 1990.

Rangliste der Kaiserlichen Deutschen Marine 1910–1914.

Reinschedl, Manfried. "Die Rüstung Österreich-Ungarns von 1880 bis zum Ausbruch des Ersten Weltkriegs." Master's thesis, Universität Wien, 1996.

Ripley, Warren. *Artillery and Ammunition of the Civil War*. New York: Van Nostrand Reinhold, 1970.

Rivlin, Helen Anne B. *The Agricultural Policy of Muhammad Ali in Egypt*. Cambridge, Mass.: Harvard University Press, 1961.

Rössler, E. *Die deutschen U-Boote und ihre Werften* I. München, 1979.

———. "Die deutschen U-Boot-Konstruktionsbüros." *Deutsches Schiffahrtsachiv* 20 (1997): 297–340.

————. *Geschichte des deutschen U-Bootbaus* I. 2nd ed. Bonn, 1996.

————. *Vom Original zum Modell: Uboottyp II–Die "Einbäume."* München, 1999.

Russell, M. *View of Ancient and Modern Egypt.* Edinburgh: Oliver and Boyd, [1850?].

Sacre, Amédée, and Louis Outueborn. *L'Égypte et Ismail Pacha.* Paris: J. Hetzel, 1865.

St. John, Bayle. *Village Life in Egypt.* 2 vols. 1852. Reprint, New York: Arno Press, 1973.

St. John, James A. *Egypt and Mohammed Ali.* 2 vols. London: Longman, 1834.

Sammarco, Angelo. *La Marina Egiziana sotto Mohammed Ali. Il Contributo Italiano.* Cairo: Institut Français, 1931.

Samoilovich, Rudolf Lazarevich. *Na spasenie ekspeditsii Nobile: Pokhod "Krasina" letom 1928 goda.* Leningrad: Gidrometeoizdat, 1967.

Sarhank, Ismail Pasha. *Haqaiq al-Akhbar an Duwal al-Bihar* (A precise history of maritime powers). 2 vols. Bulaq: Matbaah al-Amiriyyah, 1314 a.h.

Saville, A. W. "The Development of the German U-Boat Arm, 1919–1935." Ph.D. diss., University of Washington, 1963.

Sbacchi, Alberto. "Legacy of Bitterness: Poison Gas and Atrocities in the Italo-Ethiopian War 1935–1936." *Geneve-Afrique* 13 (1974): 30–53.

Schaefer, Jürgen. *Deutsche Militärhilfe an Südamerika. Militär- und Rüstungsinteressen in Argentinien, Bolovien und Chile vor 1914.* Düsseldorf, 1974.

Schoelcher, Victor M. *L'Égypte en 1845.* Paris: Pagnerre, 1846.

Scholch, Alexander. *Egypt for the Egyptians.* London: Ithaca Press, 1981.

Schreir, Konrad F. *Remington Rolling Block Firearms.* N.p., 1977.

Schulz, Warren E. *Ilion—The Town Remington Made.* Hicksville, N.Y.: Exposition Press, 1977.

Schüssler, C. *Trial of Major War Criminals before the International Military Tribunal Nuremberg 14 Nov. 1945–1 Oct. 1946.* Nuremberg: International Military Tribunal, 1949.

Schweinfurth, G., et. al., eds. *Emin Pasha in Central Africa.* London: Murray, 1888.

Seel, Wolfgang. *Mauser, von der Waffenschmiede zum Weltunternehmen.* Zürich: Verlag Stocker-Schmid AG, 1988.

Segrè, Claudio G. *Italo Balbo: A Fascist Life.* Berkeley: University of California Press, 1987.

Shoji Yunosuke. *Echiopia Kekkon Mondai wa Donaru, Kaisho ka Ina: Kekkon Mondai o Shudai to shite Echiopia no Shinso o Katari Kokumin no Saikakunin o Yobo su* (What will happen to the Ethiopian marriage issue, cancellation or not: I request the re-recognition of the Japanese nation by narrating the truth of Ethiopia with the marriage issue as the central theme). Tokyo: Seikyo Sha, 1934.

S.I.A.I. ali nella storia (History of the Italian Society of Flying Boats). Florence: Edizioni Aeronautiche Italiane S.r.L, 1979.

Smith, Dennis Mack. *Mussolini.* New York: Alfred A. Knopf, 1982.

Spindler, A. *Der Handelskrieg mit U-Booten* II. Berlin, 1933.

Sprout, Harold, and Margaret Sprout. *The Rise of American Naval Power.* 1939. Reprint, Annapolis, Md.: Naval Institute Press, 1990.

Stein, Stephen. "Washington Irving Chambers: Innovation, Professionalization, and the New Navy." Ph.D. diss, Ohio State University, 1999.

Stevenson, David. *Armaments and the Coming of War: Europe, 1904–1914.* Oxford: Clarendon Press, 1996.

Stevenson, G. C. "Submarines of the Finnish Navy." *Warship International* 1 (1986): 31–46.

Stoker, Donald J., Jr. *Britain, France, and the Naval Arms Trade in the Baltic, 1919–39: Grand Strategy and Failure.* London: Frank Cass, 2003, forthcoming.

———. "Undermining the Cordon Sanitaire: Naval Arms Sales, Naval Building, and Anglo-French Competition in the Baltic, 1918–1940—Poland—Finland—The Baltic States." Ph.D. diss., Florida State University, 1997.

———. "Unintended Consequences: The Effects of the Washington Naval Treaties on the Baltic." *Journal of Baltic Studies* 21, no. 1 (spring 2000): 80–94.

Stone, Carlos [Charles P.]. *Assuntos Militares en Egipto.* Habana: Tipografica de'El EcoMilitaire, 1884.

Stone, Charles P. "Military Affairs in Egypt." *Journal of the Military Service Institution* 5 (1884): 173.

Sutton, Anthony C. *Western Technology and Soviet Economic Development 1930 to 1945.* Stanford, Calif.: Hoover Institution on War, Revolution and Peace, 1971.

Swann, Leonard. *John Roach, Maritime Entrepreneur.* Annapolis, Md.: Naval Institute Press, 1965.

Tafla, Bairu. *Ethiopia and Germany: Cultural, Political and Economic Relations, 1871–1936.* Wiesbaden: Franz Steiner Verlag, 1981.

Taylor, John W. R., ed. and comp. *Combat Aircraft of the World from 1909 to the Present.* New York: G. P. Putnam's Sons, 1969.

Taura Masanori. "I. E. Funso to Nihon gawa Taio: Showa 10 nen Sugimura Seimei Jiken wo Chushin ni" (Italo-Ethiopian conflict and the Japanese response). *Nihon Rekishi* (Japanese history) 526 (March 1992): 79–95.

———. *Nichii Kankei to sono Yotai (1935–36): Echiopia Senso wo meguru Nihon gawa Taio kara* (Italo-Japanese relations and their conditions (1935–36): From the Japanese response to the Ethiopian war). In *Nihon Kindai-shi no Sai Kochiku* (Re-examination of modern Japanese history), ed. Ito Takashi. Tokyo: P. Yamakawa Shuppan-sha, 1993, 302–38.

———. "Nihon-Echiopia kankei ni miru 1930 nen tsusho gaiko no iso" (A phase of the 1930 commercial diplomacy in the Japanese-Ethiopian relations). *Seifu to Minkan* (Government and civilians), *Nenpo Kindai Nihon Kenkyu* (Annual report, study of modern Japan) 17 (1995): 141–70.

Ten Cate, J. H. "Das U-Boot als geistige Exportware: Das Ingeniuerskantoo voor Scheepvaart N.V. (1919–1957)." In *Deutschland und Europa in der Neuzeit. Festschrift für Karl Otmar Freiherr von Aretin zum 65. Geburtstag* II, ed. R. Melville, C. Scharf, M. Vogt, and U. Wengenroth. Veröffentlichungen des Instituts für Europäische Geschichte Mainz. Abt. Universalgesch.134.2. (Stuttgart, 1988), 907–29.

Tillett, Lowell Ray. "The Soviet Role in League Sanctions Against Italy." *American Slavic and East European Review* 15 (1956): 11–16.

Togliatti, Palmiro. *Opera.* Edited by Ernesto Ragionieri. Vol. 3, part 2: *1929–1935.* Rome: Editori Riuniti, 1973.

Trask, David. *The War with Spain in 1898.* New York: Free Press, 1981.

Traub, Paul. "Voyage au pays des Bogos." *Bulletin de la societe neuchateloise de Geographie* 4 (1888): 129.

Trebilcock, Clive. *The Vickers Brothers, Armaments and Enterprise 1854–1914.* London: Europa Publications Ltd., 1977.

United States Department of State. *Despatches from United States Consuls in Cairo.* Washington, D.C.

Vayrynen, R., and T. Ohlson. "Egypt: Arms Production in Transitional Context." In *Arms Production in the Third World,* ed. Michael Brzoska and Thomas Ohlson. Philadelphia: Taylor and Francis, 1986, 105–24.

Vego, Milan N. *Austro-Hungarian Naval Policy 1904–1914.* London: Frank Cass, 1996.

Wallach, Jehuda. *Anatomie einer Militärhilfe, Die preussich- deutchen Militärmissionen in der Türkei 1835–1914.* Dusseldorf, 1976.

Weinberg, Gerhard L. *The Foreign Policy of Hitler's Germany, Diplomatic Revolution in Europe 1933–36.* Chicago: University of Chicago Press, 1970.

Westpahl, Eberhard. *Ein Ostdeutscher Industriepionier, Ferdinand Schichau in sienem Leben und Schaffen.* Essen: West Verlag, 1957.

Westwood, J. N. *Russian Naval Construction 1905–1945.* London: Macmillan Press Ltd., 1994.

Weygand, General Maxime. *Histoire Militaire de Muhammed Aly et de Ses Fils.* Paris: Imprimerie Nationale, 1936.

Wilckens, A. *Hundert Jahre Deutscher Handel und Deutsche Kolonie in Valparaiso 1822–1922.* Hamburg, 1922.

Wilkinson, Sir Gardner. *A Handbook for Travellers in Egypt.* London: John Murray, 1867.

———. *Modern Egypt and Thebes.* 2 vols. 1843. Reprint, Weisbaden: Kraus, 1981.

Winckelbauer, Waltraud. *Die Österreichisch-Chilenischen Beziehungen vom Vormärz bis zum Ende der Habsburger-monarchie.* Cologne, 1988.

Wright, L. C. *United States Policy Towards Egypt, 1820–1914.* New York: Exposition Press, 1969.

Yilma, Asfa. *Haile Selassie, Emperor of Ethiopia.* London: Sampson Low, Marston & Co., Ltd., 1936.

Zervos, Adrien. *L'Empire d'Ethiopie: Le Miroir de l'Ethiopie Moderne 1906–1935.* Alexandria, Egypt: Impr. de l'Ecole professionnelle des freres, 1936.

Index

About the Contributors

J. CALVITT CLARKE III received his Ph.D. in Russian and Soviet History from the University of Maryland and has taught at Jacksonville University since 1990. Primarily interested in the diplomacy of the 1930s that led to the world war, he has published a monograph, *Russia and Italy Against Hitler: The Bolshevik-Fascist Rapprochement of the 1930s*. He has also written a number of articles on diplomatic history, mostly in the *Selected Annual Proceedings of the Florida Conference of Historians*. Currently, he is working on several monographs dealing with Russian and Japanese relations with Ethiopia and the diplomacy of the Italo-Ethiopian War of 1935 and 1936.

JOHN PATRICK DUNN completed his M.A. (History) at Florida Atlantic University and Ph.D. at Florida State University. He teaches at Valdosta State University, studies "third world" military forces of the nineteenth century, and is currently preparing a manuscript on the Egyptian Army of Khedive Ismail.

ANNETTE URSULA EDITH FORSÉN is completing her Ph.D. in History at the University of Helsinki, Finland. She studied at the Johann Wolfgang Goethe University in Frankfurt-am-Main, Germany, in 1996 and worked as a research fellow of different Finnish foundations from 1997 to 1999. She is the author of one book and several articles.

BJÖRN JOHAN BERNHARD FORSÉN completed his Ph.D. at the University of Helsinki in 1996. He was a postdoctoral fellow at the Institute of History, University of Helsinki, Finland, 1997–98; an Alexander von Humboldt research fellow at the University of Heidelberg, Germany, 1998–2000; and at the Center for Hellenic Studies at Harvard University, Washington, D.C. in 2000–2001. He is the author of several books and articles.

JONATHAN A. GRANT earned his Ph.D. from the University of Wisconsin-Madison in 1995, and he is now associate professor of modern Russian history at

Florida State University. He is the author of the book *Big Business in Russia: The Putilov Company in Late Imperial Russia, 1868–1917* (1999) and numerous articles including two about Ottoman defense industries. Currently, he is writing a book on the global arms trade in the nineteenth century.

HOLGER H. HERWIG, Director of Graduate Studies and Research at the Centre for Military and Strategic Studies at the University of Calgary, received his B.A. from the University of British Columbia and his doctorate from the State University of New York at Stony Brook. He has written more than a dozen books and about fifty articles dealing with the German military in the period from 1871 to 1945.

THOMAS R. MADDUX received his Ph.D. from the University of Michigan in 1969 under the supervision of Bradford Perkins. Since 1969 he has offered a variety of courses in United States foreign relations at California State University, Northridge, including special courses on the United States and the Indochina Wars, the United States and Latin America since 1898, and graduate courses on the Cold War and the United States in the 1980s. In 1980 he published *Years of Estrangement: American Relations with the Soviet Union, 1933–1941*. His current research focuses on the Reagan administration, both Cold War issues such as the Geneva summit conference of 1985, and domestic topics such as Reagan's Indian policy and immigration reform.

WILLIAM F. SATER, emeritus Professor of History at California State University, Long Beach, received his A.B. from Stanford University and his doctorate from U.C.L.A. A specialist in Latin American history, he has written five books, as well as more than fifty articles, on Chile.

STEPHEN STEIN earned his Ph.D. in history from The Ohio State University. He currently teaches at the University of Memphis and is completing a book on Washington Irving Chambers and the first years of United States naval aviation.

DONALD J. STOKER JR. received his Ph.D. in history from The Florida State University in 1997. He is Associate Professor of Strategy and Policy for the U.S. Naval War College, Monterey Programs Office. His first book, *Britain, France, and the Naval Arms Trade in the Baltic, 1919–1939: Grand Strategy and Failure*, is forthcoming from Frank Cass Publishers, 2003.

EDWARD B. WESTERMANN received his Ph.D. in modern European history at the University of North Carolina, Chapel Hill. He is a former Fulbright fellow, a German Academic Exchange Service (DAAD) research fellow, and a summer fellow of the Center for Advanced Holocaust Studies. He has published articles related to the Holocaust, German history, and military history in the *German Studies Review*, *War in History*, the *Journal of Military History*, the *Annals of the American Academy of Political and Social Science*, and the *Journal of Conflict Studies*. His book on German ground-based air defenses in World War II was published in 2001.